The Democracy Disadvantage

The Democracy Disadvantage

How Populism Impedes Democracies and Galvanizes Authoritarianism in the Face of Disaster

Brian K. Grodsky

ROWMAN & LITTLEFIELD
Lanham • Boulder • New York • London

Published by Rowman & Littlefield
An imprint of The Rowman & Littlefield Publishing Group, Inc.
4501 Forbes Boulevard, Suite 200, Lanham, Maryland 20706
www.rowman.com

86-90 Paul Street, London EC2A 4NE

British Library Cataloguing in Publication Information Available

Library of Congress Cataloging-in-Publication Data

Names: Grodsky, Brian K., 1974– author.
Title: The democracy disadvantage : how populism impedes democracies and galvanizes
    authoritarianism in the face of disaster / Brian K. Grodsky.
Description: Lanham, Maryland : Rowman & Littlefield, [2024] | Includes
    bibliographical references and index.
Identifiers: LCCN 2023050607 (print) | LCCN 2023050608 (ebook) |
    ISBN 9781538192108 (cloth) | ISBN 9781538192115 (paperback)
    | ISBN 9781538192122 (epub)
Subjects: LCSH: Political culture. | Populism. | Authoritarianism. | COVID-19 Pandemic,
    2020– —Political aspects. | China—Politics and government. | Russia—Politics and
    government. | United States—Politics and government.
Classification: LCC JA75.7 .G76 2024 (print) | LCC JA75.7 (ebook) |
    DDC 320.56/62—dc23/eng/20231204
LC record available at https://lccn.loc.gov/2023050607
LC ebook record available at https://lccn.loc.gov/2023050608

Contents

Preface

As many of us retreated into our homes during the COVID-19 pandemic, I made the tough choice to transform an evolving book project on climate change into something even more pressing. My investigation into the role that regime type plays in determining disaster mitigation and response suddenly became much more focused as I wondered with so many others: How is populism feeding into the disaster now impacting all of us?

I approached this project with a degree of trepidation, knowing that any study of an evolving situation is a precarious endeavor. But I also knew the topic was extraordinarily important given the considerable variation in disaster response and the enormous consequences. In the name of full disclosure, this book was also driven a bit by guilt. I have been a volunteer EMT/firefighter, both locally and nationally, since the 1990s. Ironically, it was during the peak of the pandemic, when medical resources were most strapped, that I had to put my volunteering on hold. It was one thing to risk my own health to help my community. It was another to risk the health of my family. This book, delving into a critical intellectual puzzle that may someday prove useful in thinking about corrective mechanisms to the policy process, was at least a tiny contribution I could make in the meantime.

I see this book as a first step toward theorizing and exploring a critical topic that will grow even more important as the impacts of climate change continue to show up. I hope that it will spark curiosity and inspire other researchers to explore how populism—a seemingly inevitable political phenomenon—might someday be turned into a positive force in policy. To eventually get there, we have to start at the basics, which is what this book aims to do.

Acknowledgments

I owe a huge debt to Alison Spock for her unwavering support and endless optimism. I also want to thank Riya Patel and Eli Vogel for their excellent research support. And a heartfelt thank you goes out to my amazing colleagues, including Felipe Filomeno and Carolyn Forestiere, for their very thoughtful comments.

Chapter 1

Power, Populism, and Policy in the Face of Danger

There's a sort of irony in the fact that much of the world's population was governed by populists when the novel coronavirus, COVID-19, began its rapid spread across the globe in 2020. After all, populists tend to gain power by offering quick and easy solutions to perceived, and sometimes altogether manufactured, crises. Any major policy challenge, be it a financial slowdown, a rise in crime, or a change in demographics, provides a ready cause for populists to exaggerate and leverage for political purposes. Suddenly, in a twist of fate, populists in 2020 were tasked not with constructing or capitalizing on crisis but with managing the greatest emergent disaster in the modern era.

But these populists were not all the same. Personalities aside, they faced radically different constraints by virtue of the institutions in which they were housed. This included everything from the powers of the executive and legislature to the strength of civil society. In their aggregate, we refer to these as regimes—those norms and rules that define how power is exercised. When COVID-19 broke out, there were populists in countries of every type, from liberal democracies to harsh dictatorships. It seemed a safe bet that regime type would trump populism and dictate the likelihood of a strong response to an impending disaster. That is, the so-called "democratic advantage" would hold regardless of populist leadership.

In fact, as the world unknowingly teetered on tragedy in 2020, academics had already compiled indices indirectly suggesting democracy was a very good predictor of epidemic preparedness. Perhaps the best known of these was the 2019 Global Health Security (GHS) Index, spearheaded by the Nuclear Threat Initiative and the Johns Hopkins Bloomberg School of Public Health.[1] Even as global democracy was in full-on recession, leaving just over half of all countries democratic, democracies occupied all but two of the top twenty spots in the preparedness ranking.[2]

1

Shockingly, within just a few months of the coronavirus outbreak, the primacy of these democratic states no longer seemed to hold. The index's top two ranked countries, the United States and the United Kingdom, ended up with some of the largest outbreaks in the world. And of the top ten countries rated highly for their expected "rapid response and mitigation of the spread of an epidemic," three (the United Kingdom and the United States, at the top of the list, and Brazil at number nine) experienced immeasurable misery amidst a pandemic spreading seemingly unchecked.

One critical element that these democratic laggards shared was their populist leadership, and media commentators wasted no time in impugning populism for response failures.[3] Their charges were, at least for liberals, intuitive: politicians who promote simple answers to complex problems and base their legitimacy on doing what is popular, even if that flies in the face of expert advice, should be doomed to failure.

But is populism always an impediment to good governance? More generally, in what ways might populism alter a regime's response to a major policy challenge, such as a disaster?

If we look beyond the rhetoric and recriminations, the road from populism to policy failure is not so straightforward. Contrast, for example, the horrific rise in COVID-19 hospitalizations and deaths in the United Kingdom in the spring of 2020 with the relatively low numbers experienced across the world in populist Sri Lanka during that same period. If populism was the culprit, how did the Sri Lankans get off so easily? With a death rate many times higher in the United Kingdom, there are literally millions of Brits who, touched directly by COVID-19, should be asking this question.

POPULISM AND REGIME

The answer, I argue, is that populism may not have an inherently negative impact on how leaders address major policy challenges, disasters included. In fact, it might even be a good thing. More specifically, I argue in this book that populism can lead to role reversal when it comes to dealing with serious challenges. At the very moment populism erodes the ability of democrats to effectively respond, it actually has the potential to increase the will of nondemocrats to act with resolve.

At first glance, this argument is counterintuitive. Few democrats have ever quibbled with Winston Churchill's famous line that "democracy is the worst form of government, except for all those other forms that have been tried from time to time."[4] Over the second half of the twentieth century, Churchill's sentiment, backed by the economic and military power of advanced democratic states primarily in America and Europe, contributed to a world order where democracy was placed on a pedestal. Even the most vicious autocrats felt the need, both at home and abroad, to portray themselves as their states' popularly accepted leaders.

This idolization of democracy was accompanied by a growing literature claiming that Western states and those that joined them in their ideological approach possess a certain "democratic advantage" over all others; they are not only normatively preferable to non-democratic states, but they are also more effective.

From a theoretical standpoint, that argument seems to make sense.[5] The authoritarian leader who relies on relatively few people to maintain power (say, for instance, the heads of the military and intelligence apparatus, plus perhaps a handful of governors) should have very different priorities than the democratic leader who relies on a much larger number (for example, the majority of citizens over eighteen years old). The democrat has an incentive to provide the sorts of public goods that voters expect, such as functional roads and a competent court system.[6] The non-democrat, obliged to that much smaller group of supporters, is instead incentivized to spend state funds on private goods (cash, villas, vacations) targeted directly at those few stakeholders.[7]

In other words, just as it would be ridiculously inefficient for a democratic leader to try to buy off a majority of voters with private goods, it seems wasteful for non-democratic leaders to provide public goods to those whose support they do not need.

The underpinnings of this democratic advantage lie in mechanisms such as competitive elections, rule of law, and an active civil society that ensure state leaders spend more on their citizens than their friends.[8] Non-democrats, lacking competition, transparency, and accountability, can afford to provide for just a few, leaving their states and populations worse off.

PENDING DISASTER

Assuming this commonsense argument is correct and democrats enter the ring with at least some advantage compared to their non-democratic counterparts, nowhere should this be more visible than in the disaster space. It is in the face of disaster that political elites are most directly challenged to make good on the social contract—at the center of which lies the state's obligation to ensure the population's security.

The best and most efficient way to do this is to invest in mitigation measures that decrease the likelihood that one's population will be in harm's way in the first place. Shy of that, the state can also prepare for what is coming. For a variety of reasons described in chapter 2, however, mitigation and preparedness tend to get short shrift under any regime. Instead, leaders have a habit of focusing their efforts on disaster response and recovery—the most visible, just-in-time disaster policies—and the ones for which they are most likely to be rewarded for success or punished for failure.

In theory, the same democratic mechanisms that purportedly help with the provision of other public goods should push policymakers to safeguard their people from disasters as well. With political accountability as the cornerstone, these include civil society and a media that can put pressure on leaders to effectively deal with disaster threats or, especially, aftermaths.[9] Absent such mechanisms, non-democrats should have little motivation to effectively deal with disasters at the expense of their own pocketbooks. Indeed, they are infamous for denying disasters in live time, and can sufficiently control the media, civil society, and coercive apparatus to make this denial politically effective.[10]

Regime type thus provides a decent rule of thumb for how a particular group in power might govern. But it is also a blunt instrument. The reality is that non-democracies vary immensely, from personalistic despots and military juntas to single-party regimes—all of which have different numbers and types of stakeholders and, hence, different motivations.[11] By the same token, democrats also operate under a range of institutional structures, from two-party presidencies to multiparty parliamentary systems, that can influence their positions.[12]

Moreover, everyday politics have a habit of sometimes transcending and transforming regimes. Nearly all political elites pander to particular constituents with an assortment of carrots. They hold large rallies and make speeches in nationally televised addresses. They make grand promises, promoting policies that they say will contribute to a more secure and prosperous country.

And, most important of all, any political regime can end up with populists at the helm. These populists, I argue, can have a profound impact on the policy process in ways that upset the expectations we advance based on regime type alone.

HOW POPULISTS TRANSFORM THE STATE

Any discussion of populism must begin with a disclaimer: despite a dramatic increase in the prevalence of reported populism over the last few decades, the very term remains vague and contentious.[13] In popular discourse, allegations of cheap populism have been leveled at all sorts of opponent parties and movements, prompting some authors to call it the "contemporary political Zeitgeist."[14] Still, whether they represent the left or the right, the inclusionists

or the exclusionists, populists are said to share a handful of important identifying traits.

For one, they present the world as riven between "the people," on the one
hand, and the "elite" or "establishment," on the other.[15] For rising populists
and their followers, ruling elites inadequately represent the interests of the
people.[16] Populists instead stake their own legitimacy on being those people's
true representatives, a claim that becomes central to their incumbency should
they attain power. Populism is, as one analyst comments, the "permanent
shadow of representative democracy."[17]

A second, and related, characteristic of populists is that they differentiate
the masses they claim to represent (labeled the "virtuous") from competing
political elites and their associates, whom populists from both the left and
right portray as universally corrupt, ineffective, and selfish members of the
globalist establishment.[18] This definition strikes at not only political alternatives but also those in line with them. This can include "establishment" actors
throughout the state bureaucracy as well as their purported enablers in the
media, civil society, economy, and other spheres that promote their views
and power.

Finally, and most importantly, populists rise to power promising to remedy
an identifiable crisis with vague, often unachievable resolutions that are none-
theless instrumental in rallying their base and polarizing society.[19] The nature
of crisis, in conjunction with the challenges populists claim to encounter on
the part of recalcitrant establishment actors, requires strong, decisive leadership to overcome.

Looking at this list, it would seem populists are a recipe for (worsening)
disaster. Their anti-elitism and focus on crude solutions can leave populists
skeptical of expert recommendations needed for prudent policy, even when
those experts emanate from their own state institutions. Populists' attacks on
those not towing their own policy line, coupled with their emphasis on strong
leadership, can disrupt existing checks on their rule. Add to this populists'
reliance on image over substance, and they should leave the state weaker,
less equipped, and less interested in dealing effectively with a disaster.
These expectations are consistent with the record populists have of reducing
state capacity, eroding institutional strength, and undermining democratic
accountability.[20]

This would certainly come as dismal news to the billions of people who
were governed by populists in states around the world, from the United
States and Brazil to the Philippines and China, at the start of the COVID-19
pandemic. But it also paints an incomplete picture. Populist political leaders may be critical agents of policy. But, like it or not, they function within
a set institutional framework that can have profound implications for their
policy preferences and modes of implementation. How might the confluence

of populism and regime type, that most basic building block governing the function of states, affect disaster policy?

Regardless of regime type, the current literature suggests populists should be quick to dismiss or downplay major threats for which there are no quick and easy fixes. The poor response that follows when policymakers try to wish away a problem should be at least somewhat rectified by democratic institutions, which shed external light on uncomfortable truths populists would prefer to bury. But the dilemma may actually be magnified by non-democratic institutions, where lower-level officials and civil society are inclined to tell state leaders what they want, not what they need to hear. This leaves both regimes, but especially non-democratic ones, lagging in their early response.

Once a policy challenge grows too large and publicly visible to ignore, populists—who claim to rule on behalf of the people—might be expected to take on the mantle of leadership. But populists must balance their desire to portray themselves as leaders with a second need for scapegoats in cases of response shortcomings. This can be done by creating distance between themselves and the disaster, akin to the different roles taken by a high-ranking general planning out the war and a sergeant on the front lines. Such space creates safe conditions for displaying leadership while reducing the risk of being solely blamed for losses.

The basic similarities, then, include an early downplaying of the threat, followed by a public show of leadership coupled with attacks on scapegoats. But there are two critical regime-based differences that should fundamentally alter the degree to which populists invest their reputation and resources in a major policy challenge: power and time horizons. By power, I mean the ability of a leader to channel effective resources toward a problem. By time horizons, I refer to the timeline according to which leaders must attain visible gains from their policies in order to remain securely in office. Looking at regime type alone, democrats, with various checks and balances and periodic "performance reviews" at the voting booth, generally have somewhat lower levels of power and much shorter time horizons than do their non-democratic counterparts.

In combination, I argue in this book, these variables have the potential to flip regime-based expectations on their heads: they can deteriorate purported democratic advantages while simultaneously reducing—and even potentially reversing—non-democratic deficiencies.

The simple reason for this is that populism essentially acts as a sort of magnifier. On the democratic side, populism compels democratic leaders with already short time horizons and limited power to pursue the quickest, most popular resolutions, no matter how sub-optimal those policies may be in dealing with the root cause of the crisis.

Non-democrats already possess the much longer time horizons, central-ized power structures, and political strength that allow them to act more deliberately and independently than democrats. What they lack is the will to cater to the broader public's needs. In an authoritarian context, populism has the potential to transform the political calculus, intensifying the need to take tough steps to effectively address a problem in the name of bolstering their popular legitimacy.

To better understand this, consider first the dilemma democratic populists face. To start with, they come to power at war with the "establishment," often struggling against critical, non-cooperative civil society and media groups as well as their own bureaucracies. This threatens to pit populists against their own state apparatus and non-state actors who check their power, undermin-ing cooperation and state capacity. To make matters worse, they have only a finite period to push through, in this difficult environment, the proposed policies that got them elected.

Should there emerge a major policy challenge, such as a disaster, populist democrats are left with a new, and potentially very significant, obstacle to achieving their preferred policies, maintaining their legitimacy, and win-ning the next elections. While non-populist democrats might be expected to lean on their own state's disaster experts as they search out the most optimal policy, populists should not. For one, they risk endangering their brand by reconciling with and deferring to the establishment. And second, the recom-mendations of experts are rarely easy, simple, or popular. For populist demo-crats, the path of least resistance means quick and easy policies that avoid rather than grapple with the enormous problems they face.

From the perspective of non-democratic populists, emerging challenges can look quite different. First, unlike democrats, non-democrats have a high degree of power over both state and non-state institutions, giving them the ability to act. Second, non-democratic populists, lacking true accountability structures, have far more security in office. Third, unlike non-populist author-itarians, non-democratic populists have an eye to popular legitimacy, which is staked on their ability to get things done. If "typical" non-democrats have the ability to act but no interest in doing so, populist non-democrats might actually correct for this lack of will.

When disaster strikes during the reign of populist non-democrats, these authoritarian leaders can readily activate establishment resources if they feel the unfolding disaster is a threat to their legitimacy. Unlike non-populist authoritarians, who can censor and frame disasters in ways that maintain the acquiescence of their subjects, populist authoritarians worried about dem-onstrating their strength and legitimacy might be more willing to act once a crisis has moved to a full-blown disaster. And unlike their democratic coun-terparts, populist authoritarians might be willing to pursue more aggressive interventions, knowing that not only can they frame these as necessary, but they also have more time than their democratic counterparts to prove their successes.

Populism thus has the potential to change the calculus of political leaders in critical ways that can reverse regime-based response expectations. Before populism is injected into our regime-based calculations, we expect accountable democrats to address acute policy challenges such as disasters more assertively than unaccountable non-democratic leaders. But once populists are in power, this can change. Relative to non-populists, democratic populists are more likely to skirt around potentially entangling disasters, while non-democratic populists might actually lean into disaster management to strengthen their own legitimacy, if at the cost of those underlings who are blamed for any failures.

AN INTRODUCTION TO THE CASES

The COVID-19 pandemic provides a massive natural experiment for this book. Most countries around the world were, during the first year of the pandemic in 2020, faced with the dramatic choice of how to respond to a pending disaster. Their laundry list of potential measures included everything from business-as-usual to border shutdowns to full-fledged country lockdowns. The costs of these policies were enormous, but so were the perceived costs of the alternatives.

Locked down at home, I chose early on to conduct an in-depth study of how populists in different regimes were responding. To ensure comparability, these countries had to have roughly similar state capacities, population sizes, and geographical profiles. Ultimately, I settled on a democracy (the United States); a non-democracy (China); and a hybrid regime (Russia).

While there are certainly important differences between these countries, one critical similarity is that they all have the resources and institutional capacity needed to react to disasters. They have some of the largest economies in the world—numbers one and two (the United States and China)—and eleven (Russia), as measured by GDP and are classified by the UN's Human Development Index as very highly functioning (the United States and Russia) or highly functioning states (China). Importantly for this study, these three countries all have robust disaster systems and elements of strong health-care systems, but those health-care systems are also characterized by enormous inequities, often and, again, in all cases, linked to geography.[21]

These countries also all have sizable populations to protect over large territories. They rank in the top ten in terms of population (China at number one, the United States at number three, and Russia at number nine) and are among the four largest countries by land mass. In connection with the latter point, they are all countries with significant land, sea, and air connections, meaning that they are difficult to completely isolate in the case of a cross-border threat such as a pandemic.

Finally, all of these countries were led by populists during the COVID-19 pandemic. In the United States, President Donald Trump came to power promising to upend the establishment and "drain the swamp," as he referred to state and political actors in Washington. In both China and Russia, the populist leaders were actually members of the establishment who worked to distinguish themselves with the help of populist tactics. In Russia, President Vladimir Putin used crude and tough speech, in contrast to other more polished politicians, and designated himself the champion of traditional values and a return to Russian power.[22] In China, President Xi Jinping separated himself from the Communist Party flock by similarly dressing down and frequenting local restaurants, as well as by playing on popular demands for an anti-corruption crusader and a warrior against poverty.[23] Both non-democrats had a record of taking down members of their regime to bolster their own image.

What most differentiates these countries, of course, is their regime type. The United States is an advanced democracy, with established constitutional checks and balances and an active, independent political and civil society. China, by contrast, is a highly authoritarian, single-party state where opposition parties are banned, the rule of law is absent, and open dissent can lead to detention and imprisonment. Russia, during the period under review, which preceded a major crackdown on civil liberties launched at the outset of the 2022 Ukraine war, landed somewhere in between these cases.[24] It fell on the more authoritarian edge of competitive authoritarianism, where political opposition exists but faces enormous obstacles to attaining power, particularly at the national level; independent media functions but is dwarfed by the pro-government state media; and civil society endures but faces significant harassment when it mobilizes against the state.

In choosing the cases for this exploratory study, I have opted for breadth over scientific precision, realizing that at this early stage, such precision is difficult to achieve. For instance, an ideal research design could include two cases for each regime type (including one populist version and one non-populist version of a democratic, authoritarian, and hybrid regime). Yet these cases could still face important challenges. Does populism have a different effect on a presidential versus parliamentary democracy, for instance? Single-party versus personalistic non-democracy? How about other potential variables, such as political culture? The goal here is not to definitively test the proposed theory but instead to assess its plausibility and, in the final chapter, consider ways in which other cases add to or challenge the findings here.

These challenges will have to be addressed in future studies that take this research to the next level through an exploration of many additional cases.

The findings from this three-case study with quite different countries suggest that populism can have a transformative impact on regimes. By the one-year anniversary of the WHO's pandemic declaration, these countries were in dramatically different positions. Whether we gauge policy effectiveness by morbidity or mortality, the United States was easily the poorest performer of the bunch, and China was the strongest. In terms of total cases per capita, China ranked 210th in the world with 63 per million;[25] followed by Russia at 72nd place with 29,873 per million;[26] and the United States at 8th place with 89,854 per million.[27] Looking at death rates, we get similar results: China ranked 190th with just 3 per one million;[28] Russia ranked 57th in the world, with 622;[29] and the United States ranked 12th with 1,631 per one million.[30] These indicators are far from perfect, as I discuss in the country chapters. But they do provide insight into the significant discrepancies between these states.

Interestingly, as we'll see in this book, the responses in all three countries bore some important similarities. For instance, all of these leaders initially steered clear of the growing disaster. Chinese president Xi Jinping practically ignored it for the first weeks of the outbreak and then made little mention of it for weeks following. Russian president Vladimir Putin similarly and uncharacteristically disappeared from view, a far cry from the muscular, bare-chested horseback rider image he preferred to show off. U.S. president Donald Trump, unable to simply ignore the popular press coverage, instead downplayed the threat and belittled those who feared the virus.

After viral infections blew up for all to see, the leaders' responses diverged more sharply. Xi shifted from a policy of coverups to the world's most draconian response, aimed at snuffing the virus out altogether. Trump, by contrast, precariously straddled an imaginary line separating a "serious leader" image from his dismissive, conspiracy pedaling rhetoric, forcing state and local leaders to respond with little federal support. And Putin took a more middle-of-the-road approach, using the federal government to make significant investments in hotspots, including both personnel and infrastructure investments, while leaving power largely in local hands.

It was actually the two authoritarian leaders who responded more forcefully to the disaster yet also took a more circumspect approach to leadership. Xi was most notable for his public absence, having delegated responsibility to subordinates to fight the dirty fight for him. Xi's role was to issue general orders from above. Putin, by contrast, took a more direct and visible approach to fighting the pandemic, but through a carefully orchestrated policy of broker: he probed regional leaders, publicly asking what they needed and fielding their queries, while making it clear that they were the responsible parties on the ground.

While both Xi and Putin stayed largely out of the spotlight except to occasionally claim victories or, in Putin's case, make demands that Russian local leaders respond effectively, it was Trump who most forcefully grabbed the bullhorn. The U.S. president spent hours per day at press briefings defending the government's response and attacking that of the states. He alternated between portraying himself as a strong wartime leader and the hapless overseer of a federal government that had only a very limited, backstopping role in disaster response.

In the end, the picture on the ground was immensely different in each of these countries. Chinese citizens were left clinging to a pendulum that swung from denial to a full-fledged lockdown wherever cases appeared. Americans found their fate, and the seriousness with which the pandemic was addressed, could depend more on their state and locality of residence than the actual case rates. And Russians were left to muddle somewhere in between the two extremes, with the federal government officially leaving policy to local and regional administrators but actively intervening in cases of clear failure.

In all of these cases, the populists in charge were quick to claim successes, even when there was little evidence to support these assertions. They were even quicker to search out villains in areas where the response was visibly poor.

Ultimately, the cases described in this book highlight how the frequent contention that populism is a recipe for policy failure is overly simplistic. We cannot evaluate the impact of populism without considering the broader political context and, especially, the regime type in which populists function. It is here that populism shows its full power—both destructive and productive.

I'll spend the remainder of this book exploring this argument in more depth. In the next chapter, I take a deeper dive into the theory and empirical observations behind my argument and explain my approach to this study. Next, I probe how each of the countries under investigation managed the pandemic in the first year, providing a general timeline of events in each case as well as markers of success and failure. Then, in chapters 4–6, I spend a chapter each exploring in depth how populists in non-democratic China, partially democratic Russia, and democratic United States addressed the COVID-19 pandemic during its first year. Finally, in chapter 7, I look to a broader population of cases to make the argument that the stories that unfolded in the previous chapters are the backdrop to a broader pattern, and I suggest additional considerations for future research.

This book is by nature exploratory. The three cases analyzed here are not intended to be a definitive test of the impact of populism and regime type on public policy and disaster response. Instead, they serve as an opportunity to challenge and reevaluate the conventional beliefs we hold about populists and non-democrats. By looking in depth at the behavior of leaders in three disparate populist countries, I hope to prompt readers to take a step back and consider the interaction between populism and regime type in ways that will lead to new lines of inquiry.

Ultimately, the goal of this book is not simply to help readers understand the essential role politics played in shaping our response to the most monumental global crisis in decades. It is to prepare us for the challenges that lie ahead. In a world where populism continues to gain momentum, at a moment when climate-driven disaster risks are on the rise, it is critical to understand how populism can impact our security in the decades to come. The pages that follow represent a first step toward that goal.

NOTES

1. GHS, "Global Health Security Index: Building Collective Action and Accountability," Nuclear Threat Initiative (NTI), October 2019, https://www.ghsindex.org/wp-content/uploads/2020/04/2019-Global-Health-Security-Index.pdf.

2. Ibid. Drew Desilver, "Despite Global Concerns About Democracy, More Than Half of Countries Are Democratic," Pew Research Center, May 14, 2019, https://www.pewresearch.org/fact-tank/2019/05/14/more-than-half-of-countries-are-democratic/.

3. Uri Friedman, "COVID-19 Lays Bare the Price of Populism," *The Atlantic*, May 9, 2021.

4. Society International Churchill, "The Worst Form of Government," International Churchill Society, https://winstonchurchill.org/resources/quotes/the-worst-form-of-government/.

5. Bruce Bueno de Mesquita et al., "Policy Failure and Political Survival: The Contribution of Political Institutions," *Journal of Conflict Resolution* 43, no. 2 (1999): 149.

6. David A. Lake and Matthew A. Baum, "The Invisible Hand of Democracy: Political Control and the Provision of Public Services," *Comparative Political Studies* 34, no. 6 (2001): 590, 98.

7. Pantelis Kammas and Vassilis Sarantides, "Do Dictatorships Redistribute More?," in *Sheffield Economic Research Paper Series*, ed. University of Sheffield (Sheffield 2016), 1, 27; Robert Deacon, "Public Good Provision under Dictatorship and Democracy," *Public Choice* 139 (2013): 242.

8. Dennis P. Quinn and John T. Woolley, "Democracy and National Economic Performance: The Preference for Stability," *American Journal of Political Science* 45, no. 3 (2001): 635; Hristos Doucouliagos and Mehmet Ali Ulubasoglu, "Democracy and Economic Growth: A Meta-Analysis," ibid., 52, no. 1 (2008): 61; Jonathan K. Hanson, "Democracy and State Capacity: Complements or Substitutes?," *Studies in Comparative International Development* 50 (2015): 308; Quinn and Woolley, "Democracy and National Economic Performance: The Preference for Stability," 635.

9. Tove Ahlbom and Marina Povitkina, "'Gimme Shelter': The Role of Democracy and Institutional Quality in Disaster Preparedness," *V-Dem Institute Working Paper* 35 (2016): 11.

10. Ben Wisner and Henry R. Luce, "Disaster Vulnerability: Scale, Power and Daily Life," *GeoJournal* 30, no. 2 (1993): 134.

11. Barbara Geddes, "What Do We Know About Democratization after 20 Years?," *Annual Review of Political Science* 2 (1999).

12. Thomas Häussler et al., "The Climate of Debate: How Institutional Factors Shape Legislative Discourses on Climate Change. A Comparative Framing Perspective," *Studies in Communication Sciences* In Press (2016): 1; Arend Lijphart, *Patterns of Democracy: Government Forms and Performance in Thirty-Six Countries* (New Haven: Yale University Press, 2012).

13. Ernest Laclau, *On Populist Reason* (London: Verso Books, 2002), 3; Jordan Kyle and Limor Gultchin, "Populists in Power around the World," Tony Blair Institute for Global Change,

November 7, 2018, https://www.institute.global/insights/geopolitics-and-security/populists-power-around-world.

14. B. Guy Peters and Jon Pierre, "A Typology of Populism: Understanding the Different Forms of Populism and Their Implications," *Democratization* 27, no. 6 (2020).

15. Benjamin Moffitt, "The Populism/Anti-Populism Divide in Western Europe," *Democratic Theory* 5, no. 2 (2018): 4.

16. Tom Louwerse and Simon Otjes, "How Populists Wage Opposition: Parliamentary Opposition Behaviour and Populism in Netherlands," *Political Studies* 67, no. 2 (2019): 482.

17. Jan-Werner Müller, *What Is Populism?* (Philadelphia: University of Pennsylvania Press, 2016), 101.

18. Henrik Bang and David Marsh, "Populism: A Major Threat to Democracy?," *Policy Studies* 39, no. 3 (2018): 352; Peters and Pierre, "A Typology of Populism: Understanding the Different Forms of Populism and Their Implications"; Cristina Cremonesi and Eugenio Salvati, "Populism and the 2014 European Elections: A Comparative Study of Party Speeches by the Leaders of Movimento Cinque Stelle and United Kingdom Independence Party," *Journal of Comparative Politics* 12, no. 2 (2019): 20.

19. Kyle and Gultchin, "Populists in Power around the World," 6.

20. Michael Bayerlein et al., "Populism and COVID-19: How Populist Governments (Mis) Handle the Pandemic," *V-Dem Institute Working Paper* 121 (2021): 3.

21. Samuel L. Dickman, David U. Himmelstein, and Steffie Woolhandler, "Inequality and the Health-Care System in the USA," *The Lancet* 389, no. 10077 (2017); Natalia Shartova, Vladimir Tikunov, and Olga Chereshnya, "Health Disparities in Russia at the Regional and Global Scales," *International Journal for Equity in Health* 20 (2021); Linzi Zheng et al., "Unmasking Unexpected Health Care Inequalities in China Using Urban Big Data: Service-Rich and Service-Poor Communities," *Plos One* 17, no. 2 (2022).

22. Julia Gurganus, "Putin's Populism Trap," Carnegie Endowment for International Peace, November 21, 2017, https://carnegieendowment.org/2017/11/21/putin-s-populism-trap-pub-74788; Christian Von Soest and Julia Grauvogel, "How Do Non-Democratic Regimes Claim Legitimacy? Comparative Insights from Post-Soviet Countries," *German Institute of Global and Area Studies*, no. 277 (2015).

23. Cheng Li and Diana Liang, "Rule of the Rigid Compromiser," Brookings Institution, Spring 2019, https://www.brookings.edu/articles/rule-of-the-rigid-compromiser/.

24. Russia since the start of the Ukraine war completed its long dissent into authoritarianism and, with civil society highly muzzled and political opposition essentially banned, would no longer classify as competitive authoritarian.

25. WorldOMeter, "Coronavirus Cases," WorldOMeter, https://www.worldometers.info/coronavirus/#countries. Screenshot taken 2021.03.11, 9:41:29.

26. Ibid. Screenshot taken 2021.03.11, 9:40:35.

27. Ibid. Screenshot taken 2021.03.11, 9:40:05.

28. Ibid. Screenshot taken 2021.03.11, 9:43:16.

29. Ibid. Screenshot taken 2021.03.11, 9:42:26.

30. Ibid. Screenshot taken 2021.03.11, 9:41:55.

Chapter 2

The Perils and Promises of Populism

I started this book by suggesting that populists have the potential to fundamentally alter how a regime responds to major challenges—and even flip the script on the democratic advantage. But what exactly is this so-called democratic advantage?

To begin, it is important to highlight that there are considerable differences between and within regimes. While for the purposes of this book I simplify regimes based on the public role in each (with high degrees of representation and public accountability in democracies and low degrees in non-democracies), available forms of representation and methods of accountability can differ significantly even within a regime. Democratic two-party presidential systems, for example, can operate quite differently from multiparty parliamentary ones.[1] Similarly, personalistic non-democrats face very different pressures than, for instance, military or single-party regimes.[2] Finally, hybrid regimes, which mix elements of democracy and non-democracy, can vary considerably from what we might call "illiberal democracy" to "moderate" or "liberal" authoritarianism, depending on the degree to which political competition and citizen political engagement are allowed to function.[3]

Of all these regimes, scholars and policymakers have long argued that democratic ones have the greatest potential. This ostensive democratic advantage stems largely from the political science literature suggesting that democratic states are not only normatively preferable to non-democratic ones, they are also more effective.[4] Many of these studies work off the premise described by Bueno de Mesquita that democrats are fundamentally different from non-democrats based on the size of their selectorate, or those who participate in the selection of political leaders, and their winning coalition, that subset of this selectorate upon which an incumbent leader relies to maintain their position in power.[5] Democracies have much larger winning coalitions (and, typically, selectorates) than do non-democracies.

These numbers become meaningful when it comes to policy choice.[6] A democratic leader, who must maintain a majority or plurality of votes, has an incentive to provide the sorts of public goods voters expect (such as a quality education system and functioning highways). A non-democrat, obliged to a much smaller group of supporters, has an incentive to provide transfers directly to these specific stakeholders in the form of favors (picture overseas boarding schools in lieu of poorly run local ones and powerful cars capable of traversing poorly maintained streets laden with potholes).[7] A democrat who feeds only her friends does so at her peril. The same goes for a non-democrat who feeds the masses by taking from the bank accounts of his cronies.

Those who support the idea of the democratic advantage argue that competitive elections, rule of law, and active civil society (including independent media) ensure state leaders spend on the majority of their population, for the public good.[8] Democracies, with all their transparency, are better at making meaningful commitments as well as gaining and effectively utilizing information crucial to making policy work.[9] This is particularly true of consolidated democracies, those states where the democratic rules of the game are formally institutionalized and accepted by all major actors.[10]

In the post–World War II era, in part because of this democratic advantage, democracies have increasingly become seen as the only legitimate form of state.[11] This, of course, does not mean all states are democratic, merely that they talk the democratic talk. The world is filled with non-democracies in a range of shapes and sizes, from single-party and military regimes to personalist ones.[12] Hybrid regimes straddle the democracy/non-democracy divide, permitting weak democratic mechanisms so long as they do not pose a meaningful threat to those at the center of power.[13]

To what degree, then, does this theoretical democratic advantage play out in practice? Methodological difficulties aside,[14] there is some evidence that the democratic advantage does, in fact, exist. Greater levels of political freedom, for instance, result in higher gross national incomes and better development and welfare outcomes.[15] Importantly, this holds at both the national level and the local one. Even in isolated, rural areas, local democracy can force elites to redistribute in the form of public goods, leading to diminished poverty and inequality.[16]

This democratic advantage appears to have the power to overcome significant institutional challenges. As new democracies consolidate, for instance, core public goods that democracies are thought to spend more on, such as public health, also improve.[17] Some have even found that this democratic advantage partially carries over to hybrid regimes, which have better health and education outcomes than more closed authoritarian states.[18] Even more impressively, introducing limited and localized participatory opportunities into closed, non-democratic states can also have a positive impact in those affected areas.[19]

The idea of the democratic advantage is not without controversy, however. Some, for instance, have charged that electoral competition may produce more visible policy changes but not necessarily the most meaningful ones.[20] As one scholar commented, "democratically elected politicians are not the omniscient and omnipotent social planners who reside in the textbooks of welfare economists."[21] Others point out that wealth can have a more powerful impact than regime type in the delivery of public goods.[22] Perhaps not surprisingly, in the least developed states, democracy does not appear to confer much of an advantage at all, at least in terms of reducing inequality and poverty.[23]

That may be the case. But given the preponderance of evidence in favor of democracies, it seems the average person would likely prefer to reside in a democracy rather than a non-democracy, all else being equal, in the face of a major policy challenge. No challenge is more daunting than what we think of as a disaster.

While it would be ideal to start our disaster discussion with a simple definition, it turns out that defining disasters is no easy matter at all. Disaster is in many ways like an obscenity, about which one twentieth-century U.S. Supreme Court justice famously quipped, "I know it when I see it."[24] The very label ranks up there, along with other charged words including totalitarian, fascist, and, yes, populist, as one of the most overused and poorly defined terms in our political vocabulary.[25] The constructive ambiguity surrounding the term has allowed various actors to alternatively downplay or exaggerate a particular event or hazard for their own ends.[26]

With this in mind, I adhere in this book to the admittedly imprecise definition of disaster employed by the United Nations Office for Disaster Risk Reduction:

> a serious disruption of the functioning of a community or a society at any scale due to hazardous events interacting with conditions of exposure, vulnerability and capacity, leading to one or more of the following: human, material, economic and environmental losses and impacts.[27]

For the UN and most disaster scholars, a disaster begins with a hazard (such as a hurricane) and ends with an impact (lives and property destroyed). But in between the starting point (hazard) and the end point (impact) lies a critical space that the world's governing body describes as "exposure, vulnerability and capacity." These variables have the power to leave a population unable to effectively mitigate a threat before it occurs or have sufficient resilience to respond to and bounce back from one afterwards.[28]

This idea of vulnerability strips off the "act of God" label reigning political elites have used to shed responsibility for so many disasters. The premise that an uncontrollable natural hazard, such as a flood, is the source of a disaster has been replaced with the realization that disasters are actually social phenomena.[29] This is not a novel idea, but a recycled one. As Jean-Jacques Rousseau noted when Lisbon suffered from a massive 1755 earthquake that led to the death of 20 percent of the population:

> nature did not construct twenty thousand houses of six to seven stories there . . . if the inhabitants of this great city had been more equally spread out and more lightly lodged, the damage would have been much less and perhaps of no account.[30]

Disasters, then, happen not because hazards strike but because humans leave themselves or others vulnerable to such hazards. Vulnerable peoples are those whose situations impair their ability to "anticipate, cope with, resist and recover from the impact of a natural hazard."[31] They are vulnerable not as a result of preferences or genetic faults but because of various elements of the political-socio-economic environment, from settlement patterns and developmental level to access to goods and knowledge.[32] Vulnerability is a function of inequality and a lack of agency, factors largely related to how existing political and economic systems govern access to power and resources. [33]

Before addressing how regimes might impact disaster management, it is important to remember that disasters are unique in that, as predictable as they are, they rarely occupy the policy spotlight until it is too late to stop them from happening. Regardless of regime type, most leaders are prone to psychological phenomena that prevent them from thinking much about disaster risks when they still have time to mitigate or prepare for them.[34] Nor do they have strong political incentives to re-allocate state resources away from expected day-to-day goods to disaster prevention measures that may prove only moderately effective or even unnecessary during their tenure.[35] And in most cases, those vulnerable parts of the population who suffer most from disasters lack political efficacy, decreasing political leaders' urgency to act.

INTRODUCING REGIMES

Given this basic understanding of what a disaster is, whom it impacts and how it can be managed, should democracies or non-democracies be better at dealing with a disaster?

Democracy advocates might argue that many of the democratic mechanisms that purportedly help with the provision of other public goods, such as quality schools and functional roads and courts, should push policymakers to safeguard against disasters, as well. With political accountability the cornerstone, these include competing political parties that provide voters with options to replace failing incumbents. They also include civil society organizations and media that capitalize on information transparency to put pressure on leaders to effectively deal with emergent issues in between electoral cycles.[36]

In the disaster context, however, these are not fail-safes. Over-centralization of disaster response or recovery, for instance, can make it difficult for outside information to have any real impact.[37] Media outlets sometimes provide skewed information that leads to resource misallocation, with aid targeted at areas characterized by higher publicity but lower damage.[38] Advocacy organizations might demand policies favorable to specific groups at the expense of the broader population.[39] Well-meaning civil society volunteers, who might in one context bulwark state capabilities, can overwhelm infrastructure and literally get in the way of better trained and equipped state responders.[40]

Democrats can also use disasters to demand sweeping new powers and limits on constitutional protections that negate the electoral accountability, civil society and media advantages they started with.[41] Even where institutional checks remain intact, political leaders can use the power of incumbency to frame the crisis in ways that downplay disasters and defray blame.[42] The combination of open media and electoral accountability can compel democrats to prioritize message over management of disasters, what one scholar called "governing by publicity."[43] Tactics can include transferring responsibility to their predecessors, subordinates or superiors, or even completely blaming the event itself (a return to the old habit of chalking the disaster up to "God's will").[44]

More importantly, the critical mechanism of electoral accountability can actually create perverse incentives. Policymakers face pressures to work in the here and now in order to show results before the next elections.[45] But politicians looking little further than the next election can actually act against the interests of their voters when it comes to long-term or more abstract political goods.[46] Even democracy's greatest advocates commiserate over the tendency for democrats to "perennially produce short-term policies with dismal results."[47]

As glum as this critique sounds, at least democrats face public pressures to invest in welfare policies, including some related to disaster, that their authoritarian counterparts appear to have little reason to care about.[48] If vulnerable communities contending with disaster threats have a small voice in democracies, their voice is practically absent in the typical non-democracy. The end result is that while democrats are typically compelled to engage in at least certain disaster management policies, authoritarians can be much more resistant.[49]

In other words, as far from ideal as democratic disaster management may be, there should still be a "democratic advantage."

The empirical record lends support to this claim; there is at least some evidence that democracy can have a strong effect on reducing disaster deaths, even after controlling for per capita national income.[50] Democracies are particularly more likely to address hazards that occur more regularly and are therefore more visible and a higher priority among constituents.[51] While the same happens in non-democracies, the effect appears to be weaker.[52]

Yet non-democrats do not have to be the miserable performers we so often assume them to be. In fact, they arguably have two important institutional advantages over their democratic counterparts. The first is more centralized power and, hence, greater control over state resources, allowing them to spend on priority issues as they see fit. The second is the security in office afforded by a lack of electoral accountability, resulting in a longer time horizon conducive to long-term disaster investments.

The problem, of course, is that non-democrats' basic lack of accountability leaves them little incentive to open their treasure chests for the purpose of rescuing elements of the population whose support they do not require to remain in office. As a result, regime type seems to provide a pretty good rule of thumb for how a particular group in power might govern. Democrats may not be great at long-term commitments, but they have a strong incentive to respond to immediate, short-term disasters that threaten their credibility. Non-democrats are arguably better positioned to respond to both short- and long-term threats, but with little to gain politically they are unlikely to do so.

THE AGE OF POPULISM

But what if something could radically shift these dynamics? Is there a scenario where democrats would willingly ignore a large swathe of the suffering population while autocrats would set aside their focus on private goods to put more effort into protecting their broader population? The answer, I argue, may well be populism. Populism can have the effect of decreasing the responsiveness of democrats just as it increases that of non-democrats. The effect can be transformative.

To start with a simple definition of a controversial term, populism can be boiled down to the increasingly accepted ideational approach that "not only depicts society as divided between 'the pure people' versus 'the corrupt elite,' but also claims that politics is about respecting popular sovereignty at any cost."[53] Central components of populism are the ability of populist leaders to frame various issues around insecurities and in language that shows they are not only fighting for the everyman but they are the everyman;[54] an inclination on the part of citizens to seek populists' protection;[55] and an ambivalence or antagonism toward the procedural inconveniences of liberal democracy.[56]

Beneath this straightforward definition lie a number of important caveats. First, populism is generally seen as a strategy rather than an ideology. Populism offers no intelligible recipe for the organization of state and society, meaning individual populists may promote any of a range of ideological alternatives, from democracy to fascism.[57] Some populists are bent on incorporating more societal actors and viewpoints into politics, while others are intent on excluding those who deviate from their own preferences or identity.[58] What makes all of these actors populists is how they frame threats, heighten insecurity, and mobilize constituents.[59] Populism is, as one scholar put it, "something political actors do, not something they are."[60]

Second, populists' focus on dangers to "popular sovereignty" may be based on real threats but also perceived ones, anchored in the belief that everyday citizens have lost control over the political institutions ostensibly there to serve them.[61] The crisis often involves economic dislocation, including inequality, that can cause or be magnified by a growing sense of social and cultural insecurity and perceived loss of status.[62] Such economic grievances can fuel identity politics and nationalism, which frequently go hand in hand with populism.[63]

Third, populists are united by their "outsider" approach to politics, in which they set up a clash between two broad societal actors: the virtuous masses, on the one side, and the greedy and corrupt elites together with their associates, on the other.[64] Populists portray themselves as the true representatives of the "silent majority"[65] and can be tied to real grassroots movements that share a similar anti-establishment zeal.[66] Yet even as they position themselves at the pinnacle of democracy, populists express disdain for liberalism, including the various institutional checks and balances and minority rights that have come to be associated with twenty-first-century democracy, but which populists view as antithetical to the will of the majority.[67]

Fourth, the tactics populists use to strengthen their hold on power range from the mundane to the destructive. To differentiate themselves from mainstream players, populists often embrace crass speech and body language, as well as informal dress.[68] But they also attack those associated with the mainstream, from establishment politicians and state functionaries to a host of intermediaries accused of enabling, or profiting from, the status quo. These include economic elites, civil society actors, journalists, and intellectuals.[69]

Such attacks are designed to win over constituents who feel disempowered by the state. Populists play zero-sum politics, promising policies that benefit the good, hard-working majority ("true people") at the expense of greedy mainstream "establishment" enemies.[70] Whether demanding inclusionary or exclusionary forms of redistribution[71] or anti-immigration measures,[72] populists couch their priorities in the context of an ineffective or corrupt state that threatens sovereignty.[73] Their proposed resolutions are often vague or unachievable ones that shine only in their intuitive appeal to the everyday person unfamiliar with the intricacies inherent in policy implementation.[74]

HOW POPULISTS CAN CHANGE REGIMES

This brings us to the fifth and related point, which is that populists tend to show disdain for liberalism and act on that impulse to the degree they can. While there is a recognition that populists can elevate previously under-represented voices[75] and push through tough reforms,[76] populists' emphasis on strong leadership and their hasty disregard for any opposition can lead to a weakening of institutionalized checks and balances.[77]

Opposing political parties may be the primary target populists engage in. But populists also go after those representative and state institutions they claim subvert the will of the collective.[78] Distrust toward bureaucrats and state experts who challenge populist policies prompts populists to flood government bodies with loyalists, transforming policy structures into beds of politicization and patronage as leaders seek more decisive powers for themselves.[79] Populists also move to declaw unfriendly elements of civil society, blamed for maligning or sidelining populist initiatives.[80] The list of "enemies" can be extensive, ranging from business, media, and intellectual elites to whole groups from other ethnic or belief systems.[81]

The broad consensus, therefore, is that populism poses a challenge to liberal democracy, designed to check strong leaders, ensure a diversity of views, and guarantee rights for those who fall outside the realm of "the people" populists embody.[82] The degree to which populists succeed in disrupting the status quo may depend on institutional design and the maturity of a particular democracy. Multiparty consensus systems, for instance, can be resistant to populist agendas.[83] Long-standing democracies may also be more impervious to populist governance than are newly democratizing states.[84]

Not surprisingly, given these dire threats, much of the literature on "non-democratic populism" centers on political leaders using populism to move away from democracy.[85] Less studied is how populism transforms existing non-democratic regimes. But non-democrats do pursue populism, which can bolster their legitimacy by lending to the "myth of popular participation."[86] Establishing legitimacy, defined as "the degree to which those who seek to rule . . . are accepted by the ruled,"[87] can be useful both internationally, where access to security, economic, and diplomatic goods is frequently limited to those acting in line with prevailing norms,[88] and for winning the acquiescence of internal audiences.[89]

The rise and rule of non-democratic populists bear some important similarities to those of democratic populists. Most clearly, both consolidate power
based on promises to stand up for the common person and address the major
policy crises they purportedly face. Other elements of populism observed
in democracies are present but more muted in non-democratic contexts. For
instance, rather than rallying against the establishment (that they dominate)
altogether, non-democrat populists might instead demonstrate themselves to
be a stern check on other establishment actors. Similarly, instead of denigrating opposing political parties (which may be weak or nonexistent), non-democratic populists might wage their battles against the (ostensibly few) "bad
apples" within their own regime who fail to follow the party line.

As dangerous as such measures are in democracies, these changes may
actually spur a greater degree of responsiveness on the part of authoritarians.
In their quest for legitimacy, some non-democratic populists have actually
inched toward more representational politics, creating very limited consultative mechanisms to gauge public sentiment and legitimate the system.[90] Such
"consultative authoritarianism" can give the public very limited influence
over policy in regimes where the public is typically stuck outside the halls of
power.[91] Any mention of such mechanisms must be qualified by the reminder
that non-democratic populists are less interested in changing the relationship
between elites and society than they are in strengthening the power and support for the ruling leader.[92]

But authoritarian leaders can also make their case for legitimacy based not
on elections but on policy promises and output.[93] Populist non-democrats also
have a track record of creating conditions that appeal to a large section of
their population, despite the ability of these leaders to maintain power through
much more coercive means. One infamous example of this was Adolf Hitler,
whose Nazi regime in the 1930s used extraordinary brutality to destroy any
opposition.[94] Despite this coercive capacity, Hitler appealed to many Germans
early on by using massive subsidies and enormous employment programs to
alleviate poverty. Like other populists, he presented these programs in the
most every day, anti-elite way possible: "As regards economic questions,"
Hitler said in 1936, "our theory is very simple. We have no theory at all."[95]

Yet this same example also gives us reason to pause. Undoubtedly, Hitler
was offering simple solutions to very difficult problems, as populists are so
prone to do. But behind the scenes, he was also building an apparatus that
could accomplish enormous feats, from investing in massive public works
projects to launching a formidable rearmament program to reckon with perceived external threats. With no viable political rivals to speak of, Hitler capi-
talized on the crisis to justify personal leadership and demand his peoples'
"unquestioning obedience."[96] Without decisive action, he warned, "we will
face a catastrophe of incalculable size."[97]

POPULISM ON THE DARKEST NIGHT

Hitler, of course, steered his country directly to devastation. But his incredible mobilization of the German people demonstrates the ability of populist non-democrats to push their people to (eventually) accepting policies that entail significant short-term pain in the name of promised long-term achievements.[98] Could populists mobilize people for something far more positive? Could they use populism to actually increase citizens' security?

When it comes to security, disasters offer the ultimate test of success. Disaster response not only requires a rapid and capable state apparatus but also the political will needed to make essential, often very costly, decisions. It is here that the pros and perils of populism should be particularly evident.

From a theoretical standpoint, populist leaders in both democracies and non-democracies should approach newly emerging disaster threats similarly: by denying or downplaying them. An emergent disaster is a powerful and unwelcome disruption to the policies populists have promised and, thus, a potential threat to the legitimacy of the ruling regime. The fact that the most marginalized in society typically bear the greatest brunt of disasters makes it politically easier for leaders to downplay, rather than address, threats as they emerge.

But it is also at this early stage that regime type should trump populism. More specifically, democratic populists may try to play down an emerging disaster, but democratic mechanisms promoting transparency make hiding the threat extremely difficult, forcing democratic populists to at least acknowledge it. Non-democratic populists, by contrast, are better positioned to use their control over information and activism to help cover up an emerging threat, essentially ignoring their populations as any non-democrats might. When it comes to an approaching hurricane, for instance, non-democrats firmly in control of messaging can afford to look the other way. Democrats may feel compelled to at least pre-position a few resources to avoid scathing attacks from the public that can become a political liability.

As the disaster grows in scale, it is just a matter of time in the modern communication era before cracks emerge in any disaster-denial narrative. As a result, both democratic and authoritarian populists are eventually forced to reckon with the growing damage. But how they do so should vary based, in part, on differing levels of power and time horizons. For democratic populists, aggressive disaster response only makes sense where they have the capacity and jurisdiction to respond, and where that response caters to their potential supporters and is broadly popular, something that rarely lasts beyond the initial days or weeks. The focus on short-term gains for their base over the long-term security of the broader population can compel democratic populists to look for the most rapid and popular, though not necessarily effective, remedy.

Non-democratic populists, at least in theory, have the good fortune of time and control. Enjoying strong, centralized power, broad access to resources, and little to no short-term political threats, authoritarian populists have an incentive to put the weight of the state into effectively dealing with the disaster in ways that elevate their own legitimacy. Their policies, such as razing buildings in a flood zone or cordoning off city blocks, may cause public consternation in the short run. But in the long run, authoritarian populists can, partly thanks to their control of the narrative, demonstrate the benefits of their policies. If the legitimacy of democratic populists is measured by the day or week, that of non-democratic populists is calculated by the month or year.

These broad regime characteristics can cast a long shadow on how a response plays out. One area where this is particularly evident is in communications. Facing uncensored public pressures to act, even democratic populists looking for the easy way out should seek to present themselves as the competent face of disaster response. Disasters provide any democratic incumbent with the opportunity to demonstrate leadership, which can in turn be translated into votes.[99] But populist democrats' simplistic solutions, combined with a distrust of their own experts, should compel them, and not their experienced bureaucrats, to take center stage. By contrast, non-democratic populists, facing less overt public pressure and no strong accountability mechanisms that would shorten their time horizons, have less to gain from standing directly in the spotlight during a disaster. Their need to display strength and competence in the long run is more likely to be served by working in conjunction with, not in opposition to, disaster experts from the institutions they control.

Although both sets of populist leaders seek to appear in charge, therefore, regime type has an impact on how this leadership is manifested. Regime type also has an important effect on how populists might seek to balance the appearance of being in charge with the desire to escape blame for response failures. In both cases, I argue, the answer is delegation of authority. But the ways in which they delegate should differ significantly.

While delegation seems incongruous with the argument that populists seek to maintain their image of control, we can divide delegation into two types. The first, which I call devolutionary delegation, involves assigning responsibility for on-the-ground policy to lower-level leaders who are tasked with creating their own response strategy. In this case, the populist leader outsources the response to others but claims to be the ready hero, stepping in to assist in case of lower-level response failures. The second type, referred to here as top-down delegation, also involves assigning responsibility to lower-level leaders, but tasks them with closely following orders from the top rather than creating their own response plan. In this type of delegation, the leader assumes more credit, but also more responsibility, for disaster response.

Regime type should play an important role in how populists delegate. Populist democrats, susceptible to persistent and public challenges, are more likely to rely on devolutionary delegation because it creates greater space between them and potential response shortcomings. By giving lower-level leaders the ability to manage the disaster on their own, the populist leader can limit her role to making rare and popular interventions while eschewing, or even attacking, less popular ones. Populist non-democrats, with greater control over the narrative, might be expected to compromise on top-down delegation, which allows them to maintain an expected strong leadership image but still provides some (albeit more limited) space to deflect charges of response failures.

This preoccupation with response failure should loom large for both types of populists. But just as democratic and non-democratic populists should differ in their approach to delegation, so should they differ in how they shed blame. In the non-democratic context, where political adversaries are rare and relatively harmless, populists can rely on a principal-agent approach to scapegoating. That is, in spheres or regions where policy has failed, they search out lower-level officials to take the fall. Some of these officials may be guilty of failing to follow orders from above, others may be guilty of inadvertently demonstrating that those commands were insufficient to stymie the disaster. In either case, the scapegoating of lower-level officials can be used to diffuse public anger and demonstrate the leader's resolve.

Democratic populists, with less control and far more outspoken political opponents, seem at least as likely to scapegoat those who cross with their message rather than fail at dealing with the disaster. This can include anyone from lower-level officials to non-state critics. Not only is the "crime" different from what we see under authoritarianism, but so is the punishment. Unlike authoritarian populists, democrats lack the means to simply fire these individuals. Instead, they blame, accuse, and malign them in the hope that accountability will be meted out through public opinion and, where applicable, the voting booth.

What we should find, then, is the potential for a role reversal. Democratic populists should seek to strengthen their standing by downplaying disasters, denigrating contradicting policy expertise, and demonizing political opponents. Meanwhile, non-democratic populists, secure in their office over the short term, may instead calculate that their rule can be strengthened by aggressively tackling the disaster, demonstrating a unity with policy experts, and selectively scapegoating where policy failures are most visible.

HYBRID REGIMES

Of course, we don't live in a world of just democrats and dictators. As noted above, there is a third broad group of states known as hybrid regimes that sits in that muddy space between democracy and non-democracy. This means that they lack the institutional constraints that have the best chance of keeping democrats on their toes (including effective political competition and a robust civil society) while also lacking the elements that could make (benevolent) dictators effective in the disaster context: the time and ability to rule with supreme control.

Under normal circumstances, these hybrid regimes tend to be quite weak. Possessing more power than democrats raises societal expectations that they could act if they wanted to, and having a greater degree of political and civil liberties than non-democrats leaves hybrid leaders susceptible to demands from a more easily organized public opposition. Hybrid leaders kneel atop the quintessential dam, with each thumb plugging a hole. The effective "colored revolutions" that swept the world beginning in the late 1990s are testament to the inherent weakness of hybrid regimes.[100]

In the disaster sphere, the same basic variables that have an important influence on the actions of democrats and non-democrats—power and time horizons—should impact hybrid populists' responses as well. While certain hybrid populists may use disaster as an excuse to impose emergency rule that pushes them closer to traditional authoritarianism, those who maintain semi-democratic functions might instead be expected to occupy a middle ground in our spectrum: they should act more resolutely than populist democrats but less so than authoritarian populists.

There are several reasons for this. First, when it comes to power, hybrid populists generally fit between authoritarian populists, with strong centralized power and the ability to act, and democratic populists, whose power is more constrained by existing institutions. Hybrid leaders' hold on power faces greater challenges from political competitors and civil society, including independent media, than in authoritarian states. Indeed, hybrid leaders' spending on highly visible, finite projects timed around elections is evidence that such leaders are keenly aware of the risks that come with even limited political competition.[101]

Compared to populist authoritarians, characterized by stunted political competition and a constrained civil society, hybrid populists might be expected to be more reluctant to pursue policies that could be good for the population in the long term but bad in the short term. But compared to populist democrats, with more abundant and vocal political opponents in the form of parties, media, and various organizations, they should feel more comfortable authorizing at least some tougher measures.

The visible manifestation of these factors is a hybrid leader who, like the populist authoritarian, should be expected to project power but not embrace it with the zeal of the democratic populist. Hybrid populists also share the concerns of democratic populists, a factor that can eventually weaken their resolve for tough measures that might undermine their popular standing in the long term. Their style of delegation should also fit in the middle—weary of issuing direct orders from the top but reticent to give free reign to lower-level officials. Given their narrative of strong leadership, however, they should be less constrained than their democratic counterparts in terms of punishing lower-level authorities who fail to deliver results.

LOOKING FOR EVIDENCE OF POPULISM'S IMPACT

Ultimately, based on the above argument, we can distinguish three broad types of populists based on regime type: democratic, authoritarian, and hybrid. None of these leaders should welcome an impending disaster, meaning all of them should try to initially minimize it. Authoritarians have the luxury of hiding the facts, while democrats, and to a lesser extent hybrid leaders, are forced by the freer flow of information to instead downplay them.

At some point, though, most populist leaders should feel compelled to acknowledge the rising impact of disaster and deal with it head on. In all regimes, the ruling populists should take charge and assure their population they will deliver a way out.

How they do so, however, should be highly dependent on the type of regime. Without a viable opposition or strong checks from civil society, authoritarian populists have the power and security in office needed to pursue aggressive interventions they believe will ensure long-term success. Sensitive to failings that challenge their legitimacy, populist authoritarians can be inclined to project power through top-down delegation, providing them an image of strength and control but also the distance needed to insulate themselves from policy shortcomings. For populist authoritarians, scapegoating lower-level officials is an easy pressure release valve used to demonstrate that any policy failures are a result of poor implementation below, not strategy from above.

Democratic populists, saddled with political adversaries and a vibrant civil society, should find themselves under pressure to rapidly move past the disruption. Highly responsive to public demands for disaster response, democratic populists might structure their policies along the most popular, not necessarily most prudent, route. As Aristotle commented more than two millennia ago, "Before a crowd, the ignorant are more persuasive than the educated."[102] Democratic populists should balance their zeal for the spotlight with a demand for swift resolution as well as a safe distance from response failures. This should lead to shortcuts, threat dismissal, devolutionary delegation and the demonization of political opponents rather than an investment in those costly measures needed to deal effectively with the threat.

Hybrid populists, occupying the middle ground in terms of power and time horizons, should theoretically be expected to push harder than other authoritarians to show control but resist taking center stage in the response, which could leave them unnecessarily open to critics. Indeed, while hybrid populists might delegate and punish subordinates for local failings more in line with authoritarian expectations, their expected lack of will to follow through on tough measures should be more akin to the approach of democratic populists.

In chapter 1, I briefly described why I chose to conduct a preliminary exploration of this phenomenon in three countries: the United States, Russia, and China. They are large both in territory and population, raising similar challenges to coping with a national disaster. They also have broadly similar capabilities, ranking high both in HDI and the size of their economies, factors known to impact disaster outcomes.[103] In addition, they all have an established, and frequently tested, disaster framework that has been used to deal with everything from floods and wildfires to threats from biological pathogens. In short, these three states are broadly comparable in the challenges they faced from COVID and in the level of institutional capacity and resources they have at their disposal to wage an effective response.

The final element that made these cases so alluring for this study was the fact that all of them were, at the time COVID appeared, governed by populists housed in three quite different regimes: a democracy (USA), non-democracy (China) and hybrid regime (Russia). It is important to acknowledge that my use of these broad regime labels has the potential to elicit controversy. While few would argue that the United States was a democracy or China a non-democracy, for instance, they might raise objections that not all democracies (e.g., presidential vs. parliamentary) or non-democracies (e.g., single party vs. personalistic) are the same. Intra-regime differences are beyond the scope of this book but could be a fruitful direction for future research.

The case of the hybrid regime raises another caution. Given the way hybrid regimes are loosely defined, spanning from illiberal to more overtly hegemonic, it can be difficult to demarcate the borders between hybrid regimes and democracies, on the one hand, and non-democracies, on the other. The Russia case exemplifies this dilemma. While some would argue that Russia had by 2020 transitioned from a hybrid regime to a firmly authoritarian one, these arguments discount the fact that there was still at this point a degree of political competition, civil society activism, and independent media activity that clearly separates such a case from an incontrovertible authoritarian state such as China.[104] Surely, if hybrid regimes are indeed a meaningful designation, this should have an impact on policy.

Finally, it is essential to highlight the place of populism in each of these cases. Given the loose definitions of populism that exist both in popular culture and in academia, labeling any particular leader a populist is courting controversy.[105] Interestingly, there seems to be much greater acceptance for applying the populist label to leaders in more democratic states, such as the United States, the United Kingdom, and Italy, than there is in less democratic ones. The reason for this is intuitive: How could authoritarians rail against ruling elites when they are the elites?

Yet the same argument could be applied in a democratic context. Take, for instance, former U.S. president Donald Trump, a billionaire with a history of political activism, or former UK prime minister Boris Johnson, a politician who spent years in positions of power before taking charge of the country. What made these men worthy of the populist title was not their distance from political elites (which one would struggle to identify) but instead their willingness to flaunt political convention as they worked to mobilize the population around perceived, dire threats. For both, the greatest threats stemmed from the perception that incumbent elites in state and political bodies, both inside and outside the country, were undermining the peoples' sovereignty.[106]

Authoritarian leaders can perform these same functions. In this book, I look at two non-democratic populists, Russia's Vladimir Putin and China's Xi Jinping. To begin on the more democratic side of the authoritarian spectrum, some analysts have gone so far as to call populism "an inalienable feature of Putin's rule."[107] Putin rose to power much like Western populists, using electoral victories as an opportunity to enter office and centralize control.[108] Putin's populist tendencies were visible from the start. These included employing crude language and machismo displays "to show he is a man of the people who will protect the nation."[109] Examples range from flying into war-torn Chechnya, where he promised to kill local terrorists even in the "shithouse," to riding horseback bare-chested and taming Siberian tigers.[110] Putin leveraged gender stereotypes, pursuing a "political masculinity" in a "bad boys yet good fathers" framework,[111] which won him points among his more traditional base (especially rural women) prone to see the role of man as protector.[112]

Putin demonstrated other classic populist tactics early on, including publicly dethroning unpopular and powerful economic and regional actors upon taking power.[113] Over time, Putin began making a show of punishing "disloyal" elites as he sought to improve his own popularity among everyday Russians, including by adopting ever more traditionalist and nationalist tendencies.[114] Putin promised to protect Russian sovereignty by championing a unique Russian political system ("sovereign democracy" as opposed to Western liberalism) and restoring Russia to great power status.[115]

As with other populists, Putin's populist agenda was fueled by crises, particularly the rise of political opposition in 2011–2012 following years of economic shortcomings and unfair elections.[116] Putin attacked pro-Western protesters and members of Western-supported nongovernmental organizations as Western stooges bent on keeping Russia weak. Putin thus created his black-and-white, virtuous-versus-evil framework around both internal and external actors.[117] Much as Donald Trump's supporters portrayed their actions in the January 6, 2021, attack on the Capitol as a last stand against a fundamental threat to the good people of the country, Putin marketed the opposition that had coalesced in 2011 as an existential menace to Russia.[118]

As he dug deeper into populism, Putin relied ever more on the image of a defender of Russian values and civilization against his opponents, whom he portrayed as pro-Western and cosmopolitan. To accentuate the difference, Putin closely allied himself with the Russian Orthodox Church[119] and has continually evoked both Tsarist and Soviet legacies, including victory over the Nazis in World War II, to bolster this common identity and increase patriotism.[120]

While populists in more democratic states are typically painted as oppositionists intent on upending the political stage, Putin's rhetoric has largely been in favor of maintaining the status quo, an approach common to "populists-in-government" (think, for example, of Donald Trump's reelection campaign that kicked off with a "Keep America Great" campaign).[121] At the same time, Putin is persistently marketed as distinct from, and above, other elites. Not only does he maintain political independence (despite having an entire party, United Russia, devoted to keeping him in power), but Putin is also hailed in the state press as the benevolent "intercessor of the ordinary people,"[122] fighting against still imperfect institutions and especially a corrupt and slow bureaucracy that hurts everyday people.[123] Indeed, the presidential office is often depicted as standing up for the people against other Russian institutions.[124]

Putin's brand of populism has entailed aligning himself closely with his voters in a "rule for the people" approach that many Western populists aspire to.[125] This includes rituals such as the annual televised "Direct Line with Vladimir Putin" session where citizens directly complain to the president about conditions on the ground (periodically ending in a presidential tongue lashing, or worse, for responsible local officials).[126] It also means making (oft unrealistic) decrees and personally intervening to roll back unpopular state decisions, such as raising the retirement age, and pushing forward vague, popular initiatives, such as anti-corruption campaigns.[127] Finally, Putin has accentuated the good-versus-evil narrative and bolstered his strong image through foreign military interventions, including against the threat of "terror-ists" in Syria and pro-Western "Nazis" in next door Ukraine.[128]

Putin demonstrates how populism can thrive in a less democratic con-text where the leader in charge appears to be a member of the very elite populists are supposed to revile. But he is not unusual and seems to hint at a bounded populism not uncommon among authoritarians. For such actors, an anti-establishment approach is constrained by the very fact that they are part—even leaders—of the establishment. Yet their efforts to attain or main-tain legitimacy amount to challenging actors within their own institutions by relying on populist sentiment. We can identify similar phenomena in China, where the head of China's ruling Communist Party, Xi Jinping, has used classic populist strategies to legitimize and strengthen his hold on power.[129]

Like Putin, one aspect of Xi's populist agenda has entailed bringing him-self closer to the people, rather than fellow party elites, on a discursive level. Xi's early adoption of a more accessible style and alluring narrative, propa-gated by state media, was intended to make him fit in better with the every-man in China.[130] Not only did Xi articulate a much more down-to-earth form of speaking to his people than is traditional among China's communist elites. He also demanded that the entire party state embrace a less formal "commu-nication style" (wenfeng) to bring the Party closer to the people.

Similar to the case of Putin, Xi's rise to power has been accompanied by a focus on the threats in and around China that are popularly believed to be holding the country down. Scholars have placed Xi in a sort of populism that pits the good, represented by the unified will of the people, versus the evil, nefarious elites bent on depriving society of their sovereign rights to prosper-ity, values, or other tangible and intangible goods.[131] Xi's populist agenda is founded on grandiose hopes for his "great people," amounting to a national-ist form of populism.[132] His vision of the China Dream, or his countrymen's restoration of ancient glory, involves both strengthening the state and build-ing public trust.[133] Embodied in the slogan "China's dream is every Chinese person's dream," Xi's platform has amounted to a populist effort to mobilize his countrymen by tying peoples' individual fates with that of the "great Chinese" identity.[134]

One critical method to achieving all of this was Xi's early implementation of a large-scale anti-corruption or "rectification" campaign aimed at purify-ing his own Party by fighting both "tigers" (powerful leaders) and "flies" (bureaucrats).[135] This anti-corruption campaign formed part of an effort to mobilize mass political support.[136] Critically, the anti-corruption campaign and Xi's style also served to draw a thick line between Xi and other Party and state elites, generating the classic populist image of the strong leader fighting against entrenched state interests, even though Xi is clearly a part of that power structure.[137] Xi has similarly used his promise to eradicate extreme poverty as part of an effort to "recast himself from a princeling to a populist leader" aligned "with the people against the powerful."[138]

Taken together, these non-democratic cases demonstrate a form of populism that is quite comparable to what we find in the democratic context. Consistent with the definition I have adopted for this book, Putin and Xi, like Trump, have espoused an anti-pluralist form of rule that they seek to demonstrate is in the best interest of their community (composed of a significant section of the literal or symbolic, in the non-democratic context, electorate). They cater to a group that possesses a profound distrust of elites occupying the public space, from state institutions and political parties to economic actors. This cynicism is typically a product of perceived threats, often economic in nature, that populists and their followers claim stem from internal and/or external sources. The populists in charge harness these grievances to create broad (frequently nationalist) platforms but also a specific persona characterized by everyday, often "politically incorrect" and distinctly non-professional methods of communication. They claim to fight for the everyman by being the everyman.

Undoubtedly, some will reject the characterization of non-democrats as populists given their control over the political stage. Prematurely dismissing the ability of authoritarians to rely on a populist template, however, leaves us blind to the everyday politics that govern intra-elite and elite-mass relations. In all three of the cases explored here, populist leaders have struck out to heighten their legitimacy by acting the common man both in rhetoric and policy, including promises to shake up the system and assure a grandiose future for their people. As one sociologist noted in the China case, "Today's Communist Party leaders are professional politicians, and no one more so than China's Communist-in-chief Xi Jinping . . . to get things done he still has to cater to public opinion."[139]

IN SEARCH OF THE EVIDENCE: METHODOLOGICAL NOTES

The central task in this book is to make the case that all of this matters in the context of disaster policy and, more specifically, COVID response. If this were a quantitative study, my dependent variable would likely be operationalized through morbidity and mortality rates. One reason I chose to conduct a case study approach, however, is that there are significant (sometimes purposeful and other times inadvertent) data reliability issues. I touch on some of these in future chapters, but it is important to highlight from the start that data problems are visible across regime types, from democracy to non-democracy, and that in each case explored here, political leaders sought to adjust or recast figures in ways intended to bolster their appearance of efficacy. In other words, while non-democrats may have been the devils in the game of politicizing COVID numbers, there were no angels.

Despite these concerns, it would be nonsensical to investigate policy successes and failures without trying to contextualize them using available data. As a compromise, my overview of regime performance in chapter 3 blends these morbidity and mortality figures (including outside assessments that are frequently in opposition to official numbers) with detailed reporting on response measures taken in each case. In other words, instead of relying on these questionable figures as the measure of policy success or failure, I use morbidity and fatality rates as the guide rails for my analysis.

The crux of my investigation is centered on actions taken by the leaders in power and, importantly, their own efforts to demonstrate efficacy. To what degree do elites stake their reputations on disaster performance as opposed to turning attention away from the disaster? What sorts of narratives do they create concerning the scope of the disaster and their own response? What types of resources do governing elites redirect in order to deal with the disaster? The answers to these questions can be found in both official statements or state-dominated media, as well as independent reporting, which serves as a check on the official line and is useful in evaluating the actual efficacy of each of these leaders. My analysis in each country chapter blends these sources in an effort to uncover the real situation on the ground.

Any researcher delving into current events runs the risk of chasing their own tail, never being able to get ahead of the story. To avoid this dilemma, I purposely focus this study on a succinct period of time—the first year of the pandemic. The advantage of this approach is that it allows us to make basic comparisons among countries that are all experiencing similar threats and have comparable tools available to them, thus creating space to focus on the role of leadership and regime type. It is also a sufficient period to observe policy change over time and a logical end point. This timeframe closes with the advent and initial distribution of vaccines, marking an altogether new stage in the pandemic response. Finally, one year provides us with more than sufficient time to compare the COVID response to most acute, sudden onset disasters, which typically peak and pass within a much briefer period.

The case studies in the chapters that follow have been carved from thousands of pages of daily news reports, documenting the daily impacts from, and responses to, the COVID outbreak over the first year of the pandemic, 2020. These reports were pulled from a variety of English-language domestic and international reports catalogued in Nexi Universe and Proquest. In each case, I sought to get the official government line as well as accounts from the independent press that could serve as a check on official reporting. To do this, I kept my searches wide (for example, "China coronavirus").

To get the government read, I used China's Xinhua news agency, considered in China to be a source "of record,"[140] and BBC Monitoring, which includes an assortment of domestic news articles. For Russia, I relied on ITAR-TASS as the publication of record, as well as domestic news articles picked up by BBC Monitoring, CIS General Newswire, and the Economist Intelligence Unit. In the United States, I relied on White House news releases and press conferences for the official story. My primary check on government reports in all three of these cases came from the *New York Times, Washington Post,* and *Wall Street Journal,* as well as the *South China Morning Post* for the China case.

After collecting thousands of news accounts, I combed through these daily reports to piece together a timeline of events for each country and an account of the COVID response along several dimensions. My goal was to understand not only what leaders in each of these states did but also how they did these things. At the most basic level, I tracked COVID-reported cases and deaths, identifying particular hot spots and responses in those areas, as well as how they were presented. In the next chapter, I provide an overview of how the COVID pandemic proceeded in each of the three cases, looking at how the response was coordinated, the resources devoted to it, and the place of expertise in leading the way.

In the country case chapters, I narrow the lens, revisiting crucial points from the timeline as well as teasing out lessons from particular events, issues, or approaches. In all of the cases, I probe how leaders manifested control and the ways in which they delegated power. I pay special attention to the ways these leaders sought to frame their response and the outbreak more generally. And I look at the extent to, and methods through, which they pushed blame for policy failures onto other, lower-level officials. Finally, I look at how these three populists framed their fight with COVID in the broader battle for legitimacy. In China and Russia, this involved the long struggle against the international dominance of Western democracy, while in the United States it was about highlighting the strength of the U.S. response relative to the rest of the world.

There are, of course, inherent limitations to this research design. For one, the sheer scope of this study—following daily events in each country for one year—does not lend itself to easy summary. For this reason, I have chosen to present specific episodes and broad trends in each case rather than expand each case into multiple chapters. This invariably means that some issues are glossed over while others get greater attention.

Perhaps a bigger limitation is the reliance on a small number of cases, which is a function of the intensive nature of this study. Given more time and resources, for instance, it would be ideal to study an analogous non-populist version of each regime type as well. To help address this, I briefly discuss in chapter 7 what the COVID responses from a broader population of states can tell us about regime type and disaster response.

Despite these limitations, this book helps shed a new spotlight on populism, a phenomenon that has already left its mark on twenty-first-century politics. Populism is a rising force around the world; the number of populists taking power has increased by five times from 1990 to 2018.[141] If populism can actually alter the basic functioning of a regime, in essence tampering with the political DNA we have largely taken for granted for so long, this would have profound impacts for billions of people globally as the world faces ever more and graver threats. For now, however, I use this study to highlight the great tragedy and slivers of hope presented by populism during the COVID response.

NOTES

1. Sarani Saha, "Democratic Institutions and Provision of a Public Good," University of California, Santa Barbara Departmental Working Papers, 2007, http://escholarship.org/uc/item/55f3c17g; Juan Linz, "The Perils of Presidentialism," *Journal of Democracy* 1, no. 1 (1990); David J. Samuels and Matthew Soberg Shugart, "Presidentialism, Elections and Representation," *Journal of Theoretical Politics* 15, no. 1 (2003).

2. Barbara Geddes, "What Do We Know About Democratization after 20 Years?," *Annual Review of Political Science* 2 (1999); Bruce Magnusson, "Democratization and Domestic Insecurity: Navigating the Transition in Benin," *Comparative Politics* 33, no. 2 (2001); Alexander Baturo and Jakob Tolstrup, "Personalism and Personalist Regimes: Theory and Comparative Perspective," European Consortium for Political Research, 2020, https://ecpr.eu/Events/Event/PanelDetails/7660; Schmitter and Karl, "What Democracy Is ... And Is Not," *Journal of Democracy* 2, no. 3 (1991); Pantelis Kammas and Vassilis Sarantides, "Do Dictatorships Redistribute More?," in *Sheffield Economic Research Paper Series*, ed. University of Sheffield (Sheffield 2016); Rory Truex, "Consultative Authoritarianism and Its Limits," *Comparative Political Studies* 50, no. 3 (2017).

3. Steven Levitsky and Lucan Way, *Competitive Authoritarianism: Hybrid Regimes after the Cold War* (Cambridge: Cambridge University Press, 2010); Larry Jay Diamond, "Thinking About Hybrid Regimes," *Journal of Democracy* 13, no. 2 (2002); Henry E. Hale, "Regime Cycles: Democracy, Autocracy, and Revolution in Post-Soviet Eurasia," *World Politics* 58, no. 1 (2005); Zhengxu Wang and Ern Ser Tan, "The Conundrum of Authoritarian Resiliency: Hybrid and Nondemocratic Regimes in East Asia," *Taiwan Journal of Democracy* 9, no. 1 (2013); Levitsky and Way, *Competitive Authoritarianism: Hybrid Regimes after the Cold War*.

4. Kenneth A. Schultz and Barry R. Weingast, "The Democratic Advantage: Institutional Foundations of Financial Power in International Competition," *International Organization* 57, no. 1 (2003).

5. Bruce Bueno de Mesquita et al., "Policy Failure and Political Survival: The Contribution of Political Institutions," *Journal of Conflict Resolution* 43, no. 2 (1999): 149.

6. David A. Lake and Matthew A. Baum, "The Invisible Hand of Democracy: Political Control and the Provision of Public Services," *Comparative Political Studies* 34, no. 6 (2001): 590, 98.

7. Kammas and Sarantides, "Do Dictatorships Redistribute More?," 1, 27; Robert Deacon, "Public Good Provision under Dictatorship and Democracy," *Public Choice* 139 (2013): 242.

8. Dennis P. Quinn and John T. Woolley, "Democracy and National Economic Performance: The Preference for Stability," *American Journal of Political Science* 45, no. 3 (2001): 635; Hristos Doucouliagos and Mehmet Ali Ulubasoglu, "Democracy and Economic Growth: A Meta-Analysis,"

ibid. 52, no. 1 (2008): 61; Jonathan K. Hanson, "Democracy and State Capacity: Complements or Substitutes?," *Studies in Comparative International Development* 50 (2015): 308.

9. Schultz and Weingast, "The Democratic Advantage: Institutional Foundations of Financial Power in International Competition"; Alexander K. Bollfrass, "The Half-Lives of Others: The Democratic Advantage in Nuclear Intelligence Assessment" (Princeton University, 2017); Josiah Ober, "Thucydides on Athens' Democratic Advantage in the Archidamian War" (Social Science Research Network, 2009).

10. Juan Linz and Alfred C. Stepan, "Toward Consolidated Democracy," *Journal of Democracy* 7, no. 2 (1996): 15.

11. Brian Grodsky, *The Democratization Disconnect: How Recent Democratic Revolutions Threaten the Future of Democracy* (Boulder: Rowman & Littlefield, 2016).

12. Geddes, "What Do We Know About Democratization after 20 Years?."

13. Levitsky and Way, *Competitive Authoritarianism: Hybrid Regimes after the Cold War*, 3, 20.

14. Hanson, "Democracy and State Capacity: Complements or Substitutes?," 305; George Avelino, David S. Brown, and Wendy Hunter, "The Effects of Capital Mobility, Trade Openness, and Democracy on Social Spending Inlatin America, 1980–1999," *American Journal of Political Science* 49, no. 3 (2005): 634, 36; Stephan Haggard and Robert Kaufman, "Revising Social Contracts: Social Spending in Latin America, East Asia, and the Former Socialist Countries, 1980–2000," *Revista de Ciencia Política* 24, no. 1 (2004): 4; Saha, "Democratic Institutions and Provision of a Public Good"; Lake and Baum, "The Invisible Hand of Democracy: Political Control and the Provision of Public Services," 597.

15. Richard Roll and John R. Talbott, "Political Freedom, Economic Liberty, and Prosperity," *Journal of Democracy* 14, no. 3 (2003): 84; Hanson, "Democracy and State Capacity: Complements or Substitutes?," 305; Bruce E. Moon and William J. Dixon, "Politics, the State, and Basic Human Needs: A Cross-National Study," *American Journal of Political Science* 29, no. 4 (1985): 661.

16. Andrew D. Foster and Mark R. Rosenzweig, "Democratization and the Distribution of Local Public Goods in a Poor Rural Economy," Economics (Brown University, 2004), 36–37.

17. Yi-ting Wang, Valeriya Mechkova, and Frida Andersson, "Does Democracy or Good Governance Enhance Health? New Empirical Evidence 1900–2012," in *The Varieties of Democracy Institute*, ed. University of Gothenberg (Gothenberg 2015), 27; Avelino, Brown, and Hunter, "The Effects of Capital Mobility, Trade Openness, and Democracy on Social Spending In Latin America, 1980–1999," 636; Atif Awad and Ishak Yussof, "Democracy and Human Development Nexus: The African Experience," *Journal of Economic Cooperation and Development* 37, no. 2 (2016).

18. Andrea Cassani, "Social Services to Claim Legitimacy: Comparing Autocracies' Performance," *Contemporary Politics* 23, no. 3 (2017).

19. Renfu Luo et al., "Village Elections, Public Goods Investments and Pork Barrel Politics, Chinese-Style," *Journal of Development Studies* 46, no. 4 (2010): 666, 71.

20. Robin Harding and David Stasavage, "What Democracy Does (and Doesn't Do) for Basic Services: School Fees, School Inputs, and African Elections," *Journal of Politics* 76, no. 1 (2004): 229; Deacon, "Public Good Provision under Dictatorship and Democracy," 259.

21. Lake and Baum, "The Invisible Hand of Democracy: Political Control and the Provision of Public Services," 589.

22. Ibid., 616; Casey B. Mulligan, Richard Gil, and Xavier Sala-i-Martin, "Do Democracies Have Different Public Policies Than Nondemocracies?," *Journal of Economic Perspectives* 18, no. 1 (2004): 58, 71; Hanson, "Democracy and State Capacity: Complements or Substitutes?," 311.

23. Peter Lewis, "Growth without Prosperity in Africa," *Journal of Democracy* 19, no. 4 (2008): 99, 101; Mulligan, Gil, and Sala-i-Martin, "Do Democracies Have Different Public Policies Than Nondemocracies?," 58, 71; Isabela Mares and Matthew E. Carnes, "Social Policy in Developing Countries," *Annual Review of Political Science* 12 (2009): 97.

24. Artemus Ward, "Potter Stewart," The Free Speech Center, https://www.mtsu.edu/first -amendment/article/1359/potter-stewart.

25. Ronald W. Perry, "What Is a Disaster?," in *Handbook of Disaster Research*, ed. Rodríguez Havidán, Enrico L. Quarantelli, and Russell R. Dynes (Springer, 2007), 2.

26. Jeroen Warner, "The Politics of 'Catastrophization'," in *Disaster, Conflict and Society in Crises: Everyday Politics of Crisis Response*, ed. Thea Hilhorst (New York: Routledge, 2013), 77.

27. UNDRR, "Disaster," United Nations Office for Disaster Risk Reduction, https://www.undrr.org/terminology/disaster#:~:text=A%20serious%20disruption%20of%20the,and%20environmental%20losses%20and%20impacts.

28. Fernando I. Rivera and Marc R. Settembrino, "Sociological Insights on the Role of Social Capital in Disaster Resilience," *Disaster Resiliency: Interdisciplinary Perspectives* 5, no. 2 (2013): 48.

29. Perry, "What Is a Disaster?," 12.

30. Jean-Jacques Rousseau, "On Philosophy, Morality, and Religion," in *On Philosophy, Morality, and Religion*, ed. Christopher Kelly (University Press of New England, 2007).

31. Ben Wisner et al., *At Risk: Natural Hazards, People's Vulnerability and Disasters* (New York: Routledge, 2004), 11.

32. Ibid., 53; ibid., 5.

33. Matthew E. Kahn, "The Death Toll from Natural Disasters: The Role of Income, Geography, and Institutions," *The Review of Economics and Statistics* 87, no. 2 (2005): 282; P. A. Raschky, "Institutions and the Losses from Natural Disasters," *Natural Hazards Earth Systems Science* 8 (2008): 628; Wisner et al., *At Risk: Natural Hazards, People's Vulnerability and Disasters*, 53; James Lewis, "Corruption: The Hidden Perpetrator of under-Development and Vulnerability to Natural Hazards and Disasters," *JAMBA: Journal of Disaster Risk Studies* 3, no. 2 (2011); Krzysztof Kaniasty and Fran H. Norris, "Mobilization and Deterioration of Social Support Following Natural Disasters," *Current Directions in Psychological Science* 4, no. 3 (1995): 94; Wolfgang Sachs, "Climate Change and Human Rights," *Development* 51 (2008): 335. Wisner et al., *At Risk: Natural Hazards, People's Vulnerability and Disasters*, 53. Bob Bolin, "Race, Class, Ethnicity, and Disaster Vulnerability," in *Handbook of Disaster Research*, ed. Rodríguez Havidán, Enrico L. Quarantelli, and Russell R. Dynes (Springer, 2007), 125. Ben Wisner and Henry R. Luce, "Disaster Vulnerability: Scale, Power and Daily Life," *GeoJournal* 30, no. 2 (1993): 134. Wisner et al., *At Risk: Natural Hazards, People's Vulnerability and Disasters*, 53; ibid., 11; H. Rodriguez et al., "Communicating Risk and Uncertainty: Science, Technology, and Disasters at the Crossroads," in *Handbook of Disaster Research*, ed. Rodríguez Havidán, Enrico L. Quarantelli, and Russell R. Dynes (Springer, 2007), 479; Eric Klinenberg, *Heat Wave: A Social Autopsy of Disaster in Chicago* (Chicago: University of Chicago Press, 2002), 81–83, 115–116; Wisner and Luce, "Disaster Vulnerability: Scale, Power and Daily Life," 132; Bolin, "Race, Class, Ethnicity, and Disaster Vulnerability," Rivera and Settembrino, "Sociological Insights on the Role of Social Capital in Disaster Resilience," 57.

34. Robert J. Meyer, "Why We under-Prepare for Hazards," in *On Risk and Disaster: Lessons from Hurricane Katrina*, ed. Ronald Daniels, Donald F. Kettle, and Howard Kunreuther (Philadelphia: University of Pennsylvania Press, 2006); Amanda Ripley, *The Unthinkable: Who Survives When Disaster Strikes – and Why* (New York: Three Rivers Press, 2008), 25–28, 159.

35. Philip Keefer, Eric Neumayer, and Thomas Plumper, "Earthquake Propensity and the Politics of Mortality Prevention," *World Development* 39, no. 9 (2011): 1532; Martin L. Weitzman, "Fat-Tailed Uncertainty in the Economics of Catastrophic Climate Change," *Review of Environmental Economics and Policy* 5, no. 2 (2011): 275–292; R. Gifford, "The Dragons of Inaction: Psychological Barriers That Limit Climate Change Mitigation and Adaptation," *American Psychologist* 66, no. 4 (2011); Rodriguez et al., "Communicating Risk and Uncertainty: Science, Technology, and Disasters at the Crossroads," 479; Ted Steinberg, *Acts of God: The Unnatural History of Natural Disaster in America* (New York: Oxford University Press, 2006), 152–153; Scott Gabriel Knowles, *The Disaster Experts Mastering Risk in Modern America* (Philadelphia: University of Pennsylvania Press, 2011), 6–7; E. C. McNie, "Reconciling the Supply of Scientific Information with User Demands: An Analysis of the Problem and Review of the Literature," *Environmental Science & Policy* 10 (2007): 17–38.

36. Tove Ahlbom and Marina Povitkina, "'Gimme Shelter': The Role of Democracy and Institutional Quality in Disaster Preparedness," *V-Dem Institute Working Paper* 35 (2016); Thung-hong Lin, "Governing Disaster: Political Institutions, Social Inequality and Human Vulnerability," in *2012 Annual Meeting of Taiwanese Sociological Association* (2012), 8–9; ibid., 7; Mark Pelling and Kathleen Dill, "Disaster Politics: From Social Control to Human Security," in *Environment, Politics and Development Working Paper Series*, ed. King's College Department of Geography (London 2008), 6–7.

37. Raschky, "Institutions and the Losses from Natural Disasters," 630.

38. Rodriguez et al., "Communicating Risk and Uncertainty: Science, Technology, and Disasters at the Crossroads," 482.

39. Daniel P. Aldrich and Kevin Crook, "Strong Civil Society as a Double-Edged Sword," *Political Research Quarterly* 61, no. 3 (2008): 379; Avelino, Brown, and Hunter, "The Effects of Capital Mobility, Trade Openness, and Democracy on Social Spending Inlatin America, 1980–1999," 634.

40. Bin Xu, "Durkheim in Sichuan: The Earthquake, National Solidarity, and the Politics of Small Things," *Social Psychology Quarterly* 72 (2009).

41. Warner, "The Politics of 'Catastrophization'," 78.

42. Ibid., 84.

43. Klinenberg, *Heat Wave: A Social Autopsy of Disaster in Chicago*, 167, 76.

44. Richard Stuart Olson, "Toward a Politics of Disaster: Losses, Values, Agenda, and Blame," *International Journal of Mass Emergencies and Disasters* 18, no. 2 (2000): 278–279.

45. Thomas Birkland, *Lessons of Disaster: Policy Change after Catastrophic Events* (Washington, DC: Georgetown University Press, 2006), 8; Quinn and Woolley, "Democracy and National Economic Performance: The Preference for Stability," 635.

46. Doucouliagos and Ulubasoglu, "Democracy and Economic Growth: A Meta-Analysis," 61; Richard J. Samuels, *3.11: Disaster and Change in Japan* (Ithaca: Cornell University Press, 2013), 28; Scott Ashworth, "Electoral Accountability: Recent Theoretical and Empirical Work," *Annual Review of Political Science* 15 (2012): 184; Quinn and Woolley, "Democracy and National Economic Performance: The Preference for Stability," 635.

47. Fareed Zakaria, *The Future of Freedom: Illiberal Democracy at Home and Abroad*, 1st ed. (New York: W.W. Norton, 2003), 252.

48. Hazem Adam Ghobarah, Paul Huth, and Bruce Russett, "Comparative Public Health: The Political Economy of Human Misery and Well-Being," *International Studies Quarterly* 48 (2004): 78, 91.

49. Wisner and Luce, "Disaster Vulnerability: Scale, Power and Daily Life," 134.

50. Kahn, "The Death Toll from Natural Disasters: The Role of Income, Geography, and Institutions," 281; Lin, "Governing Disaster: Political Institutions, Social Inequality and Human Vulnerability," 1.

51. Keefer, Neumayer, and Plumper, "Earthquake Propensity and the Politics of Mortality Prevention," 1530.

52. Ibid.

53. Cas Mudde and Cristóbal Rovira Kaltwasser, "Studying Populism in Comparative Perspective: Reflections on the Contemporary and Future Research Agenda," *Comparative Political Studies* 51, no. 13 (2018): 1669.

54. Donatella Bonansinga, "'A Threat to Us': The Interplay of Insecurity and Enmity Narratives in Left-Wing Populism," *The British Journal of Politics and International Relations* 24, no. 3 (2022): 514. S. Obradović, S. A. Power, and J. Sheehy-Skeffington, "Understanding the Psychological Appeal of Populism," *Current Opinion in Psychology* 35 (2020): 125–131.

55. Ibid.; Sandra Obradović, Séamus A. Power, and Jennifer Sheehy-Skeffington, "Understanding the Psychological Appeal of Populism," *Current Opinion in Psychology* 35 (2020): 126. C. Mudde and C. Rovira Kaltwasser, "Studying Populism in Comparative Perspective: Reflections on the Contemporary and Future Research Agenda," *Comparative Political Studies* 51, no. 13 (2018): 1667–1693. Ibid., 128.

56. Mudde and Rovira Kaltwasser, "Studying Populism in Comparative Perspective: Reflections on the Contemporary and Future Research Agenda," 1670.

57. Bart Bonikowski et al., "Populism and Nationalism in a Comparative Perspective: A Scholarly Exchange," *Nations and Nationalism* 25, no. 1 (2019): 62.

58. Jean-Paul Gagnon et al., "Editorial: What Is Populism? Who Is the Populist?," *Democratic Theory* 5, no. 2 (2018): vii; B. Guy Peters and Jon Pierre, "A Typology of Populism: Understanding the Different Forms of Populism and Their Implications," *Democratization* 27, no. 6 (2020); Jordan Kyle and Limor Gultchin, "Populists in Power around the World," Tony Blair Institute for Global Change, November 7, 2018, https://www.institute.global/insights/geopolitics-and-security/populists-power-around-world.

59. Daniel Béland, "Right-Wing Populism and the Politics of Insecurity: How President Trump Frames Migrants as Collective Threats," *Political Studies Review* 18, no. 2 (2020): 163.

60. Bonikowski et al., "Populism and Nationalism in a Comparative Perspective: A Scholarly Exchange," 63.

61. Gagnon et al., "Editorial: What Is Populism? Who Is the Populist?," xii; Kyle and Gultchin, "Populists in Power around the World," 5.

62. Bonikowski et al., "Populism and Nationalism in a Comparative Perspective: A Scholarly Exchange," 63; Thomas Carothers, "Stepping Back from Democratic Pessimism," Carnegie Endowment for International Peace, February 25, 2009, http://www.carnegieendowment.org/publications/index.cfm?fa=view&id=22781; Ernest Laclau, *On Populist Reason* (London: Verso Books, 2002), 74. Henrik Bang and David Marsh, "Populism: A Major Threat to Democracy?," *Policy Studies* 39, no. 3 (2018): 156–159.

63. Kyle and Gultchin, "Populists in Power around the World," 4, 56–57; Bang and Marsh, "Populism: A Major Threat to Democracy?," 356–359; Shabnam J. Holliday, "Populism, the International and Methodological Nationalism: Global Order and the Iran–Israel Nexus," *Political Studies* 68, no. 1 (2020): 14–15; Bang and Marsh, "Populism: A Major Threat to Democracy?"; Holliday, "Populism, the International and Methodological Nationalism: Global Order and the Iran–Israel Nexus," 3; Gagnon et al., "Editorial: What Is Populism? Who Is the Populist?," viii–ix; Benjamin Moffitt, "The Populism/Anti-Populism Divide in Western Europe," ibid., 9.

64. Bang and Marsh, "Populism: A Major Threat to Democracy?," 352; Peters and Pierre, "A Typology of Populism: Understanding the Different Forms of Populism and Their Implications"; Cristina Cremonesi and Eugenio Salvati, "Populism and the 2014 European Elections: A Comparative Study of Party Speeches by the Leaders of Movimento Cinque Stelle and United Kingdom Independence Party," *Journal of Comparative Politics* 12, no. 2 (2019): 20; Moffitt, "The Populism/Anti-Populism Divide in Western Europe," 3.

65. Jan-Werner Müller, *What Is Populism?* (Philadelphia: University of Pennsylvania Press, 2016), 102.

66. Donald T. Critchlow, *In Defense of Populism: Protest and American Democracy* (Philadelphia: University of Pennsylvania Press, 2020), 2.

67. Moffitt, "The Populism/Anti-Populism Divide in Western Europe," 9.

68. Ibid., 4; Kyle and Gultchin, "Populists in Power around the World," 13–16.

69. Cremonesi and Salvati, "Populism and the 2014 European Elections: A Comparative Study of Party Speeches by the Leaders of Movimento Cinque Stelle and United Kingdom Independence Party," 20; Bonikowski et al., "Populism and Nationalism in a Comparative Perspective: A Scholarly Exchange," 62; Müller, *What Is Populism?*, 102.

70. Kyle and Gultchin, "Populists in Power around the World," 4.

71. Bang and Marsh, "Populism: A Major Threat to Democracy?," 354; Bonikowski et al., "Populism and Nationalism in a Comparative Perspective: A Scholarly Exchange," 61; Larry Diamond, "Economic Development and Democracy Reconsidered," in *Reexamining Democracy*, ed. Gary Marks and Larry Diamond (Newbury Park: Sage, 1992), 115; Peters and Pierre, "A Typology of Populism: Understanding the Different Forms of Populism and Their Implications."

72. Bonikowski et al., "Populism and Nationalism in a Comparative Perspective: A Scholarly Exchange," 61; Bang and Marsh, "Populism: A Major Threat to Democracy?," 354.

73. Gagnon et al., "Editorial: What Is Populism? Who Is the Populist?," vii.

74. Kyle and Gultchin, "Populists in Power around the World," 6.

75. Christian Bjørnskov, "Populism: Three Approaches to an International Problem," *Economic Affairs* 39 (2019): 275.

76. Bonikowski et al., "Populism and Nationalism in a Comparative Perspective: A Scholarly Exchange," 65; Gagnon et al., "Editorial: What Is Populism? Who Is the Populist?," vi.

77. Bang and Marsh, "Populism: A Major Threat to Democracy?," 353; Bonikowski et al., "Populism and Nationalism in a Comparative Perspective: A Scholarly Exchange," 65.

78. Cremonesi and Salvati, "Populism and the 2014 European Elections: A Comparative Study of Party Speeches by the Leaders of Movimento Cinque Stelle and United Kingdom Independence Party," 20; Peters and Pierre, "A Typology of Populism: Understanding the Different Forms of Populism and Their Implications"; Kyle and Gultchin, "Populists in Power around the World," 16; Bjørnskov, "Populism: Three Approaches to an International Problem," 274–275.

79. Peters and Pierre, "A Typology of Populism: Understanding the Different Forms of Populism and Their Implications"; ibid.

80. Ibid.; Kyle and Gultchin, "Populists in Power around the World," 18.

81. Cremonesi and Salvati, "Populism and the 2014 European Elections: A Comparative Study of Party Speeches by the Leaders of Movimento Cinque Stelle and United Kingdom Independence Party," 20; Müller, *What Is Populism?*, 102; Bjørnskov, "Populism: Three Approaches to an International Problem," 274–275.

82. Daniel W. Drezner, "The Death of the Democratic Advantage?," *International Studies Review* 24, no. 2 (2022).

83. Tom Louwerse and Simon Otjes, "How Populists Wage Opposition: Parliamentary Opposition Behaviour and Populism in Netherlands," *Political Studies* 67, no. 2 (2019): 480, 91–92. Linz, "The Perils of Presidentialism."

84. Bjørnskov, "Populism: Three Approaches to an International Problem," 274–275.

85. Robert S. Jansen, "Populist Mobilization: A New Theoretical Approach to Populism," *Sociological Theory* 29, no. 2 (2011); Steven Levitsky, "Populism and Competitive Authoritarianism" (paper presented at the Memo Prepared for "Global Populisms as a Threat to Democracy" conference, Stanford University, 2017). Thomas O'Brien, "Populism, Protest and Democracy in the Twenty-First Century," *Contemporary Social Science* 10, no. 4 (2015); Pippa Norris and Ronald Inglehart, *Cultural Backlash: Trump, Brexit, and Authoritarian Populism* (Cambridge: Cambridge University Press, 2019).

86. Mehran Kamrava, "Non-Democratic States and Political Liberalisation in the Middle East: A Structural Analysis," *Third World Quarterly* 19, no. 1 (1998): 65.

87. Robert W. Jackman, *Power without Force: The Political Capacity of Nation-States*, Analytical Perspectives on Politics (Ann Arbor: University of Michigan Press, 1993), 95.

88. John T. Jost and Brenda Major, "Emerging Perspectives on the Psychology of Legitimacy," in *The Psychology of Legitimacy: Emerging Perspectives on Ideology, Justice, and Intergroup Relations*, ed. John T. Jost and Brenda Major (New York: Cambridge University Press, 2001), 4.

89. John Kane, *The Politics of Moral Capital*, Contemporary Political Theory (Cambridge; New York: Cambridge University Press, 2001), 10.

90. Peters and Pierre, "A Typology of Populism: Understanding the Different Forms of Populism and Their Implications."

91. Truex, "Consultative Authoritarianism and Its Limits," 331, 52; Leon Aron, "Yeltsin Russia's Rogue Populist," *The Washington Post*, June 3, 1990.

92. B Makarenko, "Populism and Political Institutions: A Comparative Perspective," *Herald of Public Opinion. Data. Analysis. Discussion* 1, no. 124 (2017): 4.

93. Brad R. Roth, *Governmental Illegitimacy in International Law* (Oxford: Clarendon Press; Oxford University Press, 1999).

94. John A. Garraty, "The New Deal, National Socialism, and the Great Depression," *The American Historical Review* 78, no. 4 (1973): 917–918.

95. Ibid., 917.

96. Ibid., 944.

97. Ibid., 925.

98. Konrad H. Jarausch, *Broken Lives: How Ordinary Germans Experienced the 20th Century* (Princeton: Princeton University Press, 2018).

99. Michael M. Bechtel and Jens Hainmueller, "How Lasting Is Voter Gratitude? An Analysis of the Short- and Long-Term Electoral Returns to Beneficial Policy," *American Journal of Political Science* 55, no. 4 (2011); Andrew Healy and Neil Malhotra, "Myopic Voters and Natural Disaster Policy," *American Political Science Review* 103, no. 3 (2009).

100. Grodsky, *The Democratization Disconnect: How Recent Democratic Revolutions Threaten the Future of Democracy.*

101. Annelies Heijmans, "The Everyday Politics of Disaster Risk Reduction in Central Java, Indonesia," in *Disaster, Conflict and Society in Crises: Everyday Politics of Crisis Response*, ed. Thea Hilhorst (New York: Routledge, 2013), 229.

102. Oliver Taplin, *A Dictionary of Classical Greek Quotations* (New York: I.B. Tauris, 2016).

103. Wisner et al., *At Risk: Natural Hazards, People's Vulnerability and Disasters*, 25; Derek K. Kellenberg and Ahmed Mushfiq Mobarak, "Does Rising Income Increase or Decrease Damage Risk from Natural Disasters?," *Journal of Urban Economics* 63 (2008): 789; Keefer, Neumayer, and Plumper, "Earthquake Propensity and the Politics of Mortality Prevention," 1530; Kellenberg and Mobarak, "Does Rising Income Increase or Decrease Damage Risk from Natural Disasters?," 789, 93; Stewart Williams, "Rethinking the Nature of Disaster: From Failed Instruments of Learning to a Post-Social Understanding," *Social Forces* 87, no. 2 (2008); Carl Benedikt Frey, Chinchih Chen, and Giorgio Presidente, "Democracy, Culture, and Contagion: Political Regimes and Countries Responsiveness to Covid-19," in *Covid Economics* (University of Oxford, 2020).

104. Denis Volkov, "Marc Plattner: 'If Russia Had Become Democratic, the World Would Look Very Different Now'," Institute of Modern Russia, April 2, 2015, https://imrussia.org/en/politics/2220-marc-plattner-if-russia-had-become-democratic-the-world-would-look-very-different-now; Catherine Owen and Eleanor Bindman, "Civic Participation in a Hybrid Regime: Limited Pluralism in Policymaking and Delivery in Contemporary Russia," *Government and Opposition* 54, no. 1 (2019); Miklós Sebők, Ágnes M. Balázs, and Csaba Molnár, "Punctuated Equilibrium and Progressive Friction in Socialist Autocracy, Democracy and Hybrid Regimes," *Journal of Public Policy* 42, no. 2 (2022); Justin Clardie, "Protests in Russia's Regions: The Influence of Regional Governance," *Social Science Quarterly* 103, no. 1 (2022).

105. Jon Elster, "Some Notes on 'Populism'," *Philosophy & Social Criticism* 46, no. 5 (2020): 519.

106. Francisco Panizza, "Trump: Once a Populist Always a Populist," London School of Economics and Political Science, November 13, 2020, https://blogs.lse.ac.uk/government/2020/11/13/trump-once-a-populist-always-a-populist/.

107. Irina Busygina, "Are Post-Soviet Leaders Doomed to Be Populist? A Comparative Analysis of Putin and Nazarbayev," in *Multifaceted Nationalism and Illiberal Momentum at Europe's Eastern Margins* (Routledge, 2021), 503.

108. Natalia Mamonova, "Understanding the Silent Majority in Authoritarian Populism: What Can We Learn from Popular Support for Putin in Rural Russia?," *Critical Agrarian Studies* 46, no. 3 (2019): 207.

109. Tina Burrett, "Charting Putin's Shifting Populism in the Russian Media from 2000 to 2020," *Politics and Governance* 8, no. 1 (2020): 196–197.

110. Economist, "And They Call It Peace," February 28, 2008, https://www.economist.com/europe/2008/02/28/and-they-call-it-peace.

111. Betul Eksi and Elizabeth A. Wood, "Right-Wing Populism as Gendered Performance: Janus-Faced Masculinity in the Leadership of Vladimir Putin and Recep T. Erdoğan," *Theory and Society* 48 (2019): 733.

112. Mamonova, "Understanding the Silent Majority in Authoritarian Populism: What Can We Learn from Popular Support for Putin in Rural Russia?," 212.

113. Neil Robinson and Sarah Milne, "Populism and Political Development in Hybrid Regimes: Russia and the Development of Official Populism," *International Political Science Review* 38, no. 4 (2017): 416.

114. Mamonova, "Understanding the Silent Majority in Authoritarian Populism: What Can We Learn from Popular Support for Putin in Rural Russia?," 207.

115. Robinson and Milne, "Populism and Political Development in Hybrid Regimes: Russia and the Development of Official Populism," 417.

116. Ibid., 413.

117. Mamonova, "Understanding the Silent Majority in Authoritarian Populism: What Can We Learn from Popular Support for Putin in Rural Russia?," 208.

118. Busygina, "Are Post-Soviet Leaders Doomed to Be Populist? A Comparative Analysis of Putin and Nazarbayev," 505.

119. Robinson and Milne, "Populism and Political Development in Hybrid Regimes: Russia and the Development of Official Populism," 420. Sultan Tepe and Ajar Chekirova, "Faith in Nations: The Populist Discourse of Erdoğan, Modi, and Putin," *Religions* 13, no. 5 (2022).

120. Mamonova, "Understanding the Silent Majority in Authoritarian Populism: What Can We Learn from Popular Support for Putin in Rural Russia?," 208.

121. Ibid.

122. Ibid., 221.

123. Philipp Casula, "Sovereign Democracy, Populism, and Depoliticization in Russia: Power and Discourse During Putin's First Presidency," *Problems of post-Communism* 60, no. 3 (2013): 7.

124. Ibid., 10.

125. Burrett, "Charting Putin's Shifting Populism in the Russian Media from 2000 to 2020," 196.

126. Russia, "Direct Line with Vladimir Putin," The Russian Government, June 15, 2017, http://www.en.kremlin.ru/events/president/news/54790.

127. Busygina, "Are Post-Soviet Leaders Doomed to Be Populist? A Comparative Analysis of Putin and Nazarbayev," 512.

128. Burrett, "Charting Putin's Shifting Populism in the Russian Media from 2000 to 2020," 193.

129. Ying Miao, "Can China Be Populist? Grassroot Populist Narratives in the Chinese Cyberspace," *Contemporary Politics* 26, no. 3 (2020): 20.

130. Zheng Yongnian and Lance L. P. Gore, *China Entering the Xi Jinping Era* (New York: Routledge, 2014), 2. Xiaoxiao Shen and Jiehan Liu, "Measuring Populism: Evidence from China," in *Social Science Research Network* (Social Science Research Network, 2022); He Li, "Populism in China," in *The Routledge Handbook of Chinese Studies* (Routledge, 2021).

131. Timothy M. Devinney and Christopher A. Hartwell, "Varieties of Populism," *Global Strategy Journal* 10, no. 1 (2020): 35, 37.

132. Joseph Fewsmith, "Xi Jinping's Fast Start," *China Leadership Monitor* 41, no. 3 (2013): 5–6.

133. Yongnian and Gore, *China Entering the Xi Jinping Era*, 303; Elizabeth J. Perry, "The Populist Dream of Chinese Democracy," *The Journal of Asian Studies* 74, no. 4 (2015).

134. Tianru Guan and Yilu Yang, "Rights-Oriented or Responsibility-Oriented? Two Subtypes of Populism in Contemporary China," *International Political Science Review* 42, no. 5 (2021): 685.

135. Yongnian and Gore, *China Entering the Xi Jinping Era*, 3.

136. Wenfang Tang, *Populist Authoritarianism: Chinese Political Culture and Regime Sustainability* (Oxford: Oxford University Press, 2016), 163.

137. H. Christoph Steinhardt, "Loosening Controls in Times of an Impatient Society: Chinese State-Society Relations During Xi Jinping's Honeymoon Period," *International Affairs at LSE* (2013).

138. Ryan Hass, "Assessing China's 'Common Prosperity' Campaign," Brookings Institution, September 9, 2021, https://www.brookings.edu/blog/order-from-chaos/2021/09/09/assessing-chinas-common-prosperity-campaign/.

139. Salvatore Babones, "Xi Jinping: Communist China's First Populist President," *Forbes*, October 20, 2017, https://www.forbes.com/sites/salvatorebabones/2017/10/20/populism-chinese-style-xi-jinping-cements-his-status-as-chinas-first-populist-president/?sh=520241c2152e.

140. Lara Jakes and Myers Steven Lee, "U.S. Designates China's Official Media as Operatives of the Communist State," *New York Times* (Online), February 18, 2020.

141. Kyle and Gultchin, "Populists in Power around the World," 4.

Chapter 3

Populists Face COVID-19

The First Year of the Pandemic in China, Russia, and the United States

We can't begin to understand how regime type and populism combined to influence the COVID response without establishing a timeline of events. In this chapter, I do just that, providing a general overview of how the pandemic played out in China, Russia, and the United States.

In all of these cases, the experts were clear: isolation or quarantine was the only surefire way to stop the rapid spread of a highly transmissible and debilitating respiratory disease for which there was no vaccine. Short of that, the quickly evolving science suggested that, after the spread was at least partially under control, social distancing and wearing masks could slow the pace of infections, limit fatalities, and keep health-care facilities from being overrun. A third, more fringe option with extremely little support among epidemiologists was to let the virus run its course in the hope that populations would ultimately develop "herd immunity."[1]

While the science was quite clear, policy was far less so. The most drastic and effective health intervention, lockdowns, carried enormous economic and social costs, ranging from unemployment and plummeting government budgets to breakdowns in the educational system for millions of children in each of these countries. Leaders had to reckon with how much economic and social disruption they were willing to shoulder in order to save the most vulnerable populations which, in the case of COVID, were especially the elderly and those with certain pre-existing medical conditions.

It takes only a glance at the differing paths COVID took in these three countries to cause one to do a double take. Adopting a regime-based approach, one would expect to see China perform miserably and the United States magnificently. In practice, that should mean an out-of-control outbreak in China, and to a lesser extent in Russia, that brings tens of millions of cases and likely millions of deaths. In the United States, it should portend small, controlled outbreaks that are carefully and efficiently contained.

Instead, these case overviews point in precisely the opposite direction: a dismal showing by the world's wealthiest democracy and a remarkable record on the part of the world's largest non-democracy, at least when measured purely by health outcomes throughout 2020. Among the populists in this book, it was the democrat who blinked first, shunning the scientific consensus in favor of more politically appealing, laxer rules. The United States was followed by Russia, our hybrid regime. By contrast, years after COVID had been discovered in authoritarian China, that country remained one of the only ones on Earth to maintain a zero-COVID policy, where just one case could trigger lockdown for tens of millions of citizens. While critics have made the strong argument that China's policy remained overly rigid to the detriment of society once vaccines were on the market at the end of 2020, during the first year of the pandemic China's aggressive policies likely saved hundreds of thousands, if not millions, of lives.[2]

The purpose of this overview is to highlight just how stark the difference is between what we should expect based on regime theory and what we find in reality. While there are certain hints as to the role populism had in transforming the outcomes, I save the deep dive into populism's impact for the subsequent country chapters.

CHINA

A classic single-party non-democracy ruled for decades by the Communist Party, China was never expected to be a role model for disaster response. Sure, the country has experienced upward of 300 epidemics since the first on record struck in 243 BC.[3] And nearly half of China's population lives under the threat of natural disasters, which strike around 300 million people and knock off up to 6 percent of China's GDP every year.[4] But the country also has a long history of hiding these disasters rather than dealing with them.[5] The closed political system that exists today conjures up visions of a clumsy, lumbering dragon, either unaware or uninterested in the suffering felt by its subjects.

The theory appeared to align neatly with reality in early December 2019, when the first cases of a novel coronavirus were detected in Wuhan, the capital of Hubei Province in east-central China.[6] In the precious three weeks that transpired before word of the new disease reached the broader world, only a small group of local officials and a larger group of muzzled frontline medics and researchers knew about the mysterious pneumonia outbreak.[7] The silence of authoritarianism left the population vulnerable to disaster.

But official censorship, including China's "Great Firewall," could not contain the online chatter, which eventually prompted action by national authorities. On the last day of December 2019, China's National Health Commission (NHC) dispatched a team to Wuhan to investigate reports of disease.[8] The next day, workers in hazmat suits swarmed in to disinfect a heavily guarded outdoor market in Wuhan, said to be the source of the virus.[9] In an air of transparency and forced by concern spreading across the internet, authorities began posting online notices and informed the WHO about a sudden spike in pneumonia patients.[10]

As if following the non-democratic script, the regime continued to withhold critical information, however, including the precise number of cases and when they first appeared. Moreover, they downplayed the threat and ordered doctors to avoid using the incriminating words "viral pneumonia" lest it sound contagious, and forbade hospitals and commercial labs from publicly releasing information.[11] A mid-January NHC report to Chinese medical centers carefully instructed frontline workers how to deal with the new virus, which had already sickened health-care workers, yet explicitly printed that there was "no clear proof in the cases of human-to-human transmission."[12]

In fact, even as political elites continued to bury the ominous truth, Chinese public health officials and medical professionals rapidly concluded they were dealing with a "ferocious" and transmissible virus.[13] With no hint of irony, at the very moment that his city was emerging as ground zero of the worst global pandemic in decades, Wuhan's mayor promised the municipal People's Congress that he would make the city a leader in the medical industry.[14] As the NHC was issuing its internal warning to the country's medical community, the country's leader, Xi Jinping, conspicuously avoided mention of the exploding virus, focusing his public comments instead on day-to-day economic concerns grounded in trade policy.[15]

At least part of the reason for the sluggish Chinese response lies squarely in a classic authoritarian dilemma in which local leaders, weary of drawing the wrath of their seniors, try to hush up policy failures before they reach the top. This, in turn, can blind senior-level officials, who have the greatest power to act, of the information they need to respond to emerging problems.

Indeed, regional leaders in Hubei sought to conceal the outbreak from their own bosses. It wasn't until a third NHC delegation went to Wuhan on January 18 that regional officials grudgingly acknowledged that medical providers had been sickened by the new virus.[16] Worse, ill people had begun moving around the country. It was at that point that the NHC finally declared an outbreak.[17] With the lid blown off, Xi now demanded "resolute efforts" be taken to stop the spread and promised that "people's safety and health" were the Party's top priority.[18] He ordered a lockdown of Wuhan and the entire Hubei

Province to begin on January 23—more than three weeks after Xi's regime had notified the WHO of a real threat.[19]

By that point, panicked residents and doctors in Wuhan complained the hospitals were understaffed and lacked the personal protective equipment (PPE), testing kits, beds, and other medical equipment needed to treat the onslaught of patients.[20] Medical workers in Wuhan described on messaging apps a "grim" situation with hospitals "full to the brim."[21] Local leaders began appealing to the central government for emergency aid, including tens of millions of surgical masks, millions of protective suits, and thousands of infrared thermometers.

China's early response looked like the poster child for authoritarian negligence and cruelty. As quarantined residents struggled with skyrocketing prices for dwindling supplies of food and other basic goods in the shut-off region,[22] authorities conducted house-to-house searches, forcing infected people into quarantine centers with inadequate heat and few medical personnel.[23] Amidst a transportation ban and ambulance shortage, some of the sickest set out for hospitals on foot, sometimes walking for hours.[24] Those who made it found a dearth of diagnostic tools but also bed space.[25] "Only when the patients are close to death can they be admitted to a hospital," one woman lamented.[26]

Such sentiment and policies were not unique to Wuhan. On the eve of the Hubei lockdown, Chinese officials acknowledged 440 confirmed cases in 13 provinces, describing Wuhan as "the main battlefield."[27] The lockdown, specialists said reassuringly, would contain the virus.[28] But even as the military marched into Hubei to enforce the new rules,[29] evidence of the virus's spread necessitated lockdowns throughout the country. Within days, 30 provinces had reported a combined 1,975 cases and declared Level I emergencies, authorizing local governments to mobilize personnel and equipment, block travel into and out of the region, forcibly quarantine suspected infections, institute price controls, and crack down on "rumormongers."[30]

But it was also at this point that China's non-democratic regime deviated from what we might have expected. Recognizing that their acknowledgment of the epidemic had come too late to stop the millions of Chinese traveling for the weeklong Lunar New Year holiday, the government extended the holiday to keep people in place and rolled out a massive public education campaign, devoting tremendous resources to the response.[31] Emerging from the authoritarian darkness, the NHC began holding daily epidemic briefings[32] and authorities panned the country to get the message out about the virus any way they could. This included everything from netizens and door-knocking campaigns to loudspeakers and drones.[33] Local celebrity singers drove through villages singing through bullhorns songs with lyrics such as "No parties and visits, fewer worries to your relatives" (presumably catchier in Chinese).[34]

The state press featured stories of citizens volunteering for the "patriotic health campaign," educating their neighbors, and taking their temperatures.[35]

Despite these measures, soon after the extended holiday ended in early February, there were more than 17,000 reported cases; an independent assessment a week later put the number at closer to 40,000.[36] By that point, and at an enormous economic cost to the regime, 760 million residents of China faced some sort of restrictions, with at least 150 million under home quarantine.[37]

To maintain the country's pulse, many commercial and state functions went online, marking a shift to telemedicine, virtual courts, and online shopping for basic necessities, including groceries.[38] As China hunkered down, the state press, a propaganda arm of China's ruling Communist Party, took on the role of cheerleader. News reports painted pictures of solidarity and heroics, showing state functionaries braving heavy snows to bring word of the dangerous virus to rural dwellers,[39] as well as selfless farmers and truckers working tirelessly and at great personal risk to get food into the epidemic's locked-down epicenter.[40] COVID spurred a nationalist revival: "The Chinese people, fighting united as one, will definitely secure the final victory in the battle," one spokesperson touted.[41]

The propaganda was matched by a massive and highly visible infrastructure undertaking that showed domestic and international observers the seriousness with which Chinese authorities now treated the disaster. State-owned enterprises transformed pre-existing production lines to produce goods necessary for constructing and supplying new medical facilities.[42] When Wuhan's first 1,000-bed makeshift hospital was completed after just ten days, 1,400 military medical staff took charge.[43] Thousands more were subsequently brought into Hubei, where eventually more than seventy new medical facilities were set up.[44] By early February, 68 medical teams of 8,300 staff had flooded into Hubei; less than two weeks later, this climbed to 217 teams composed of 25,633 medical workers, and by early March, authorities had sent 346 medical teams with 42,600 medical staff to Hubei.[45]

The Wuhan hospital construction—and then the swift tackling of the virus—became a symbol of Chinese ingenuity and determination, emblematic of China's ability to accomplish "mission impossible."[46] While many complained about the conditions imposed, few doubted the moves were saving lives.

In the face of these aggressive tactics, COVID numbers plummeted. By mid-February, China's draconian countermeasures had slowed the spread, and by the end of March, COVID was largely under control.[47] In late February, the number of cases being registered in Hubei was still in the low hundreds, but outside the province, cases barely hit the double digits.[48] By the first week of March, as China surpassed 80,000 total cases, the virus had been curbed everywhere, with the country recording its lowest number of cases since January.[49] A week later, case numbers had fallen to the single digits even within Hubei, and the handful of infections found outside the province were largely imported from abroad.[50]

The sharp reduction in cases and the announcement by health officials that most regions were at a low risk of virus spread brought a seismic shift to the country.[51] Cities and provinces across China celebrated as they released their last patients from hospitals and lifted lockdowns.[52] Even at the epicenter, all of Wuhan's temporary hospitals and clinics closed down.[53] The end of lockdowns came with a new set of restrictions, including frequent temperature checks and mandatory health documentation checks.[54] But these "nimble policy adjustments," as the state press called them, were a major step away from pandemic footing.[55] In early April, the Ministry of Transport announced the country had fully resumed ground public transportation as well as urban rail transit,[56] and on April 8, the seventy-six-day lockdown on Wuhan was finally lifted.[57]

From nearly the start of the reopening, the Chinese approach continued to be to restrict movement. At a national level, the state issued a circular reducing the movement of people in medium- and high-risk regions, where only those with a negative COVID test (and green health code) could commute to other regions.[58] The battle had now turned from one against symptomatic infections to one against asymptomatic carriers and potential imports from abroad.[59] This pivot allowed the Chinese government to frame the threat as a foreign one, and the government shifted its response to the country's land and air borders.[60] Medical experts and equipment were moved to border areas,[61] where temporary hospitals were erected.[62] Officials called those evading China's COVID restrictions "morally condemnable"[63] and offered steep rewards of up to $4,500 to those with information about foreigners illegally in the country.[64] The country also increased penalties for airlines transporting positive cases to China.[65]

By this point, the government had turned its focus to testing capabilities, which they now relied on to swiftly catch and crush the virus.[66] In early summer, the country could conduct 3.8 million nucleic acid tests per day, allowing officials to sweep through a town and test the entire population whenever the virus appeared.[67] And they did. For example, just days after detecting COVID in Qingdao, the city completely tested all 11 million residents who were lined up outside as testers performed their jobs.[68] The same pattern repeated itself in other towns and regions, from Ruili (on the Myanmar border),[69] Urumqi,[70] and Dalian,[71] to Beijing, where millions of people in targeted communities were tested.[72] Thousands were mobilized to get these tests done, including both medical providers and security forces.[73]

Over the remainder of 2020, China's leaders grappled with periodic outbreaks, but they addressed practically every one with the same vigor they applied to the countrywide epidemic, including large-scale lockdowns and detaining patients in quarantine facilities. They also sought to blame these outbursts on imported cases carried by passengers and goods entering the country from abroad.

When virus hot spots emerged over the rest of 2020, officials eager to defray blame pointed the finger at frozen food packaging, including meat and seafood from countries ranging from Russia and Brazil (where the outbreaks were particularly bad) to New Zealand (where there were very few cases at all).[74] Authorities claimed to have uncovered dozens of infected samples, which the WHO called "highly unlikely."[75] Still, many of the scattered post-spring 2020 lockdowns were blamed on imported goods,[76] which, in November, China announced it would begin disinfecting.[77] According to numbers released in the fall, the total number of imported cases was put at nearly 3,000.[78]

From the perspective of China's authorities, weeks of severe, localized restrictions were prudent. Over time, many of the draconian restrictions were limited in scope—putting specific streets, neighborhoods, or districts into "wartime mode," for example.[79] One commentary at the end of December claimed that "local authorities have precisely narrowed down risk areas to villages, subdistricts, and residential compounds" in order to keep life moving.[80] But testing regimens and other restrictions were often still pushed on entire populations.[81] As a result of these measures, the NHC noted China had "far fewer COVID-19 cases and deaths than major developed nations in Europe and North America."[82] By the end of the year China had officially counted more than 86,000 total cases, up just 4,000 from late May, when the epidemic had already receded, and less than the U.S. daily toll in the fall.[83]

Given the opacity of China's communist regime, numerous questions have arisen as to the accuracy of the country's case and death counts. There is strong evidence that early case counts were kept artificially low by both a political reticence to acknowledge viral spread as well as limited testing capabilities.[84] Once new diagnostic tools were employed and information was more forthcoming, overall case counts spiked from an estimated 17,200 infections at the start of February[85] to 75,000 just a couple weeks later.[86] State media brandished the numbers to refute claims of deception, pledging "information transparency" and promoting the "courage of truth-seeking."[87] Still, the official count of just over 80,000 in March may have been off by up to 50 percent given test availability and accuracy issues.[88] The tally also missed presumably large numbers of asymptomatic cases,[89] which became a focus only at Premier Li's direction toward the end of that month.[90]

Similar concerns were raised over the fatality count. By the time Wuhan's lockdown ended, emerging evidence—based in part on the long lines to collect ashes of relatives—suggested the number of dead was far higher than the official toll.[91] When these estimates indicated up to 45,000 had died during the outbreak, Wuhan officials increased their own death count from nearly 2,600 to close to 3,850, claiming the new toll included those who died at home as well as cases misdiagnosed early in the outbreak.[92] Subsequent independent analyses, taking into account excess deaths from the period, suggest the true number may have been up to 13,400.[93] Even at that level, however, Wuhan's COVID death rate would have been a fraction of that of New York's.

China's forceful response to COVID went beyond regime expectations, not only in the massive sacrifices the Party made by freezing the economy but also in the considerable investments it made to reduce the impact of the disease on its citizens. To counterbalance harsh lockdowns, which led to plummeting industrial output and fiscal revenues, and the country's first economic shrinkage in four decades, China's Party leaders invested as few other authoritarians would.[94] Apart from spending billions on containing the outbreak, including bolstering the public health infrastructure, they also spread money to employers and employees.[95]

Much of the Chinese pandemic support focused on assisting businesses so they could continue to pay their workers. The central bank, which functions more like an arm of the government than an autonomous body,[96] made tens of billions of dollars available to banks for lending to small and medium-szied enterprises (SMEs) and continued to cut lending rates into the spring.[97] The amount of loans issued during the first half of 2020 hit a record high of $1.73 trillion.[98] The national government cut fees and taxes on businesses, paused social security payments, pressed insurance companies to lower premiums, and lowered prices for energy.[99] Tax and fee cuts during the first half of 2020 were reportedly worth more than $215 billion, climbing past $363 billion by the end of November.[100] Local authorities also targeted certain industries with assistance, selling tens of billions of dollars in local government bonds to pay for them.[101]

At the same time, it is important to note that China's financial interventions paled compared to those of its democratic counterparts, including Japan (which launched a $1 trillion stimulus plan at the start of the pandemic) and the United States (which launched a $2 trillion rescue package at the start).[102] By the end of 2020, China's fiscal stimulus spending was estimated to be valued at approximately 5.4 percent of GDP, versus more than 13 percent in the United States and 20 percent in Japan.[103] One of the reasons may have been a reluctance to incur the high debt China was still dealing with as a result of interventions during and after the 2008 financial crisis, or the belief that once the epidemic was under control, the economy would spring back.[104] An article in the state press explained the choice to make "targeted" interventions rather than a "flood-like" stimulus.[105]

From early in the pandemic, Chinese media also depicted researchers working feverishly to develop a vaccine. The major general leading the

Academy of Military Medical Sciences' Institute of Bioengineering, Chen Wei, said the vaccine quest was an example of China meeting its "responsibilities as a great power and its contribution to humankind."[106]

China's leaders promised to start vaccine production by the end of the year,[107] and by mid-summer, nearly half of the world's nineteen vaccine candidates in clinical trials had been created by Chinese companies.[108] Already at the start of the summer, China had quietly begun its own vaccination campaign under "urgent use authorization," targeting military personnel, medical workers, and employees at certain state-owned enterprises functioning overseas; it was launched weeks before Russia's much flashier inauguration.[109] In August, China issued its first vaccine patent to the Academy of Military Sciences.[110]

Even as China overcame testing hurdles, it faced obstacles to gaining domestic acceptance of a vaccine in a country rocked by a history of pharmaceutical safety scandals, including defective vaccines and economic malfeasance.[111] To increase public faith, prominent public figures began taking the vaccine.[112] By late September, more than 10,000 people in Beijing had been injected with the Sinovac vaccine, and other cities were identifying groups that might qualify for early inoculations, including those working in schools and residing in nursing homes.[113] But just as Chinese citizens paid for the annual flu shot, they were told the COVID vaccine would also be sold, not given.[114] As scalpers began selling the fast-moving shots for as much as $1,500,[115] the government eventually reversed course and promised the vaccine for free.[116]

While around 80 percent of surveyed Chinese said at the time that they were inclined to take the shot, some Chinese medical workers expressed anxiety about being treated as a "lab rat," compelled to take a vaccine before phase 3 data was released.[117] It wasn't until the end of the year that China reported the efficacy of the two leading vaccines, Sinopharm (reportedly 79 percent effective) and Sinovac (86 percent), but even then, it provided no data to back this up.[118] Despite this, by the end of December, Chinese residents in Shanghai, Guangdong, Jiangxi, Shandong, and Wuhan were also lining up to get shots.[119]

In summary, what we saw from China started off on the typical trajectory of burying the disaster. Once it became clear the scale of destruction made hiding it impossible, the regime did a 180-degree turn and steered the entire state apparatus at the threat. This involved enormous sacrifice and considerable expense for the regime, particularly if measured in the opportunity costs that came with shutting down and retooling large sectors of the economy. But China's leaders apparently determined that securing the population's health was in the regime's best (long-term) interest, a diagnosis non-populist non-democrats might be more reluctant to make.

RUSSIA

Like China, Russia is no stranger to disasters. The largest country on Earth, Russia, averages up to 500 natural disasters per year, with floods accounting for more than one-third.[120] The number has been ticking up as the climate has changed, providing Russian authorities with an unenviable abundance of disaster management experience.[121] Political leaders at all levels are tasked with managing these threats. Russia is divided into eighty-three administrative units of various types, but power in the Russian state is highly centralized, with the federal government responsible for decision-making and effectively controlling regional authorities.[122] Under President Vladimir Putin, power has become decidedly personalized, meaning it is based on strong central control and personal loyalty.[123]

While some have classified Russia as highly authoritarian, and it certainly became so after the start of the Ukraine war in 2022, during the period analyzed here, it is best classified as a hybrid regime.[124] This combination of (mostly) authoritarian and (some) democratic rule produced a system in Russia that included the clientelism typical of authoritarians with a degree of accountability through contested elections reminiscent of democracies.[125] The problem for a hybrid regime like Russia is that its restricted but still relatively free media genrateed expectations among everyday Russians concerning how a crisis should be managed, as well as information about government failures. Just like in democracies, Russian leaders feared public distrust could undermine stability and the legitimacy of their leadership, and the Russian public had a track record of pressuring Russian leaders to adjust policy in critical spheres.[126]

In contrast to China, Russia's information space was free enough that there was no way to totally dismiss the threat COVID posed. Instead, Rospotrebnadzor—an abbreviated form of the Federal Service for Surveillance on Consumer Rights Protection and Human Wellbeing—put out a statement in mid-January playing down the COVID threat, saying that "the chances of a widespread outbreak of the virus are estimated as low."[127] Russia's early response focus was on border controls, primarily with China.[128] Russian officials warned citizens not to visit China and closed border crossings for pedestrian and car traffic in five eastern regions adjacent to the country.[129] Russian state television, run by the Kremlin, reported January 28 that hospitals in border regions "received state-of-the-art test systems to diagnose the coronavirus" and "are ready for any eventuality."[130]

This assurance came just after Russia received its first two confirmed cases (both Chinese nationals entering from China) and was accompanied by a promise from Russian leaders that "there is no risk of further spread of the disease at this point."[131] The first statement from the presidential office came on January 31, when press spokesman Dmitry Peskov (and notably not President Putin) assured citizens that the government was taking "special measures" to mitigate the risk.[132] Besides additional restrictions on travel from China,[133] the central government increased the power of authorities to isolate, quarantine, and, where applicable, deport those found sick.[134] Immediately, authorities in the country's east declared a state of emergency and set up isolation facilities where all Chinese residents entering the area would be subject to a fourteen-day quarantine.[135]

Unlike in China, where law is equated with Party will, Russian authorities initially found they were legally limited in their response. In one example, federal officials complained in mid-February that they lacked the power to keep people in quarantine for the required period. As reports surfaced of quarantined patients escaping from the facilities where they were being housed, government officials, with the ease afforded by a hybrid regime, swiftly moved to expand their powers.[136]

By the start of March, when the case count had dropped off in China, Russians were discovering a few new cases every day.[137] Putin, in rare comments, sought to assure his countrymen that the government "is doing everything necessary [to control] this dangerous disease."[138] This still primarily involved preparing quarantine facilities[139] and expanding travel bans beyond just China.[140] By mid-March, the government had banned nearly all foreign nationals from entering the country until May.[141] It also insisted its COVID numbers were just a fraction of those found in wealthy European democracies,[142] drawing public attacks from Russian oppositionists who claimed low testing levels accounted for the discrepancy.[143]

The purpose of the message was clear, however. It was that democracy was once again failing, a message that Putin had been pushing and conditions he was reportedly sewing for years before COVID hit.[144] But in many ways, Russia shared the constraints of its western neighbors more than it enjoyed the powers of its large southeastern one. Weary of taking the reins in a no-win situation, Putin set aside two decades of power centralization and told the regions they must lead the virus fight themselves. Federal authorities handled the public relations side of the emerging pandemic and promised needed equipment and financial support, but regional and local leaders found themselves responsible for making the tough decisions (for example, on constraining citizen movement) that prevention and treatment on the ground required. Putin later explained that pursuing a "common template" in a country as large and varied as Russia would be "not only inefficient, but even sometimes harmful."[145]

Perhaps even more surprising, leaders in the Kremlin went beyond handing off leadership to actually becoming followers. For instance, immediately after local Moscow authorities in mid-March suspended large public gatherings of more than 5,000,[146] Russia's national coronavirus task force announced recommendations for authorities everywhere to implement such limitations.[147] In another example, Russia's Lipetsk Region, located between Moscow and Volgograd, moved to distance learning for an initial two-week period on March 11.[148] A few days later, the Russian Education Ministry recommended the country's entire school system be moved online.[149] With the early COVID outbreak, the national government demonstrated an uncharacteristic level of deference and a lack of leadership.

It was only around the time that the WHO declared a pandemic in mid-March that Putin returned to his customary place in the spotlight and the Russian government created its formal response structures.[150] Officials announced the preparation of tens of thousands of beds in Russia's infectious disease hospitals as well as plans to rapidly build new modular hospitals of the sort the world had watched China erect in Wuhan.[151] They also paid acute attention to the economic fallout of the pandemic, promising to "neutralize" any negative impacts that might appear.[152] Officials promised billions of dollars in government support for vulnerable economic sectors and the population more generally.[153]

Despite increased activity at the center, Russia's COVID policies remained highly decentralized. Only in late March, after local Moscow authorities ordered a two-and-a-half-week quarantine, did the federal government follow suit, urging but not requiring all Russians to do the same.[154] A strong political hierarchy ensured the government's suggestions were heeded. Indeed, while there was no national state of emergency, the country rapidly closed down.[155] At the start of April, a national poll indicated that about three-quarters of all Russians were self-isolating, twice the figure from just less than two weeks earlier.[156] One of the few measures the federal government enforced everywhere was the shutdown of schools. Other restrictions were mere recommendations, though Putin promised full payment of wages for those unable to work through the suggested quarantine period, which was eventually extended to May 11.[157]

By early April, with total cases at around 3,500,[158] authorities reported that most existing patients had contracted the virus locally; COVID was no longer simply a border control issue.[159] But it was, in Putin's mind, largely a regional one. For Putin, the national government's role was to listen to the science,[160] plug any gaping holes in regional responses, and look in charge.

When it came to holes, federal institutions took some hands-on measures, including trying to address shortages of testing systems and PPE.[161] The Emergency Situations Ministry (MChS), primarily involved in natural disaster management, took part in disinfecting buildings and setting up field hospitals in some hard-hit areas.[162] The military was really the federal quarterback, though, engaging in its own disinfecting campaigns but also transferring its hospitals for civilian care, as well as constructing new hospitals and modular patient treatment facilities. Along with the Health Ministry, these institutions fielded medical missions to nearly a dozen regions in need of assistance.[163] In addition, the government cajoled thousands of medical students around the country into the response.[164]

Despite this mobilization, the Russian state experienced drastic shortages of critical goods, and its medical workers, with more political space to organize than those in China, spoke out. One of the most prominent organizations, known as the Doctor's Alliance, raised red flags at an alleged undercount of cases, warning that Russians were "facing the lie of the authorities."[165] Doctors' open complaints were a thorn in the side of the Kremlin, where officials deflected accusations that medical professionals lacked desperately needed equipment. The Kremlin spokesman dismissed this as "some ill-wishers" who were "trying to use this situation for hysteria."[166] Those speaking out were periodically fined, fired, or faced with personal threats.[167] But Russian authorities were grudgingly tolerant compared to those in China.

Amidst these and other public attacks, perhaps the more active role of the federal government was to preserve the appearance of control. Putin once again began regularly appearing on television, speaking directly to viewers and holding massive videoconferences with governors from across the country to check in and ensure they knew to whom they were ultimately accountable.[168] Even if regions could formally make their own rules and spend federal funds in ways they saw fit, Putin warned that "in allowing for this leeway, we will also demand an account."[169] The president's approach was encapsulated in an October address in which, during the fall wave, he again reminded regional heads, "We are following the situation in every territory, we are helping, and we will help. But please, don't forget about your responsibility."[170]

Gaping problems were visible from the start, with some (especially poorer) regional leaders unable to control the virus and, reminiscent of China's early response, often unwilling to acknowledge their failings until it was too late. Across Russia, the health minister acknowledged that facilities in the spring mistakenly turned away COVID patients in the belief only specialized clinics could accept them.[171] Moreover, in a post-mortem address to the Federation Council in mid-June, Russia's prosecutor general described many medical establishments around the country as being in an "unsatisfactory condition," lacking sufficient personnel and equipment.[172] These unflattering pronouncements went much further than the critiques offered in politically closed China. Arguably, they were made possible by regionalization of the response and localized accountability for its failures, but they were made necessary by the semi-democratic nature of the regime.

The COVID numbers themselves were a cause for both concern and confusion. Just as China was widely believed to be underreporting COVID cases and fatalities in the early period of the pandemic, Russia faced its own accounting issues, particularly when it came to the death count. By the end of April, with nearly 94,000 cases total, Russia claimed to rank 50th in the world in per capita morbidity.[173] But its reported fatality rate of less than 1 percent was, according to officials, more than seven times lower than the global average.[174] Putin chalked this up to the health-care system's flexibility, its highly trained medical workers, and the government's ability to rapidly mobilize resources.[175] But others warned it was more likely thanks to the practice of assigning the cause of death to co-morbidities rather than the COVID infection that pushed otherwise manageable patients over the edge. For many authorities weary of drawing attention from higher-up officials, the easy road was to assign patients a non-COVID cause of death if they died of anything but a lung infection.[176]

When cases subsided and the government rolled out its three-stage strategy to end lockdowns in May, federal authorities again pledged that ultimately decisions for how to loosen restrictions would be made locally by each regional governor based on proposals from the lead regional sanitary doctor.[177] Putin, who had resisted terms such as "quarantines," "emergency," or "restrictions," went out of his way to promise reopening would be based only on "the opinions of scientists, specialists."[178] As regions continued opening up into the summer, Putin repeated this message, urging local leaders to make "balanced and cautious decisions, based on recommendations from specialists."[179]

The restriction rollback was much like its implementation: a modified delegation style we might call centralized decentralization. Regional leaders were free to make their own decisions so long as they did not conflict with Putin's. As one Kremlin official described it, "these powers of the head of the regions should be exercised in close coordination with the government headquarters."[180] Putin was more direct: "I doubt someone in our government or somewhere in a region could say: 'We won't do as the government say[s] or as the president says.'"[181]

As the first wave of the pandemic died down in summer, federal officials were engaged in self-praise. "At the start there were some complaints and some mishaps, but today everything is according to a plan," said one senior health official.[182] Putin echoed this sentiment. "Our [healthcare] system has proved to be flexible and ready to be mobilized," he said. "Our country meets the challenges the entire world has faced."[183]

But after a summer of limited outbreaks, Russia was racked by a full-blown second wave in the fall, which by October brought hospitals to 90 percent capacity for COVID patients.[184] The Kremlin spokesperson emphasized the

need for personal responsibility and following the lead of public health officials.[185] The federal government dispatched teams of medics to overburdened
regions.[186] But it refused to recommend additional lockdowns, one leading
public health official saying, "We need to learn to live with it and work with
it."[187] By late November, according to Putin, Russia had spent 4.5 percent of
its GDP to mitigate the impact of COVID.[188] "Our government knows exactly
how to mitigate the negative consequences for all aspects of our lives and
gradually boost development," the Kremlin spokesperson said.[189] This did not
help residents of the capital, where ambulance wait times jumped from just
twenty minutes to twenty-four hours.[190]

At the end of December, the health minister said 1.1 million people in
Russia were actively being treated for COVID-19, accounting for nearly
one-fifth of the total patients treated over the course of the entire year.[191]
Still, Russian officials were outwardly confident in their performance, continuing to frame their fight in relative terms. But if Russia ranked just past
100 in per capita fatalities by country, as leaders liked to tout, in absolute
numbers it was at number eight—or, if excess deaths were considered,
three.[192] As COVID cases and fatalities blew up in the fall, the Kremlin
spokesperson dismissed a western journalist's suggestion that the mortality
figures were flawed: "Have you ever thought about the possibility of Russia's health care system being more effective [than in other countries fighting
coronavirus]?"[193]

Perhaps surprisingly, the Russian government spent considerably less than
China on fiscal stimulus measures in 2020. The largest share of expenditures
was on support for families with young children, followed by unemployment
benefits, bonuses for medical personnel, and support for small- and medium-
sized enterprises.[194] If the total amount spent was around 4.5 percent, it was a
figure that fell far short of necessity estimates from the state Audit Chamber,
which argued the government would need to spend at least 7 percent of GDP
to effectively ameliorate the impact.[195] But according to Russia's finance
minister, it reflected the budgetary reality. "If ours was a currency of reserve
[like the dollar], we could 'throw money out of a helicopter', spend trillions
of rubles," he told a local business publication. Without such a luxury, he
added, the government had to aim its support at those most in need.[196]

If Russian leaders could not compete with other countries on spending,
they could channel state resources into the holy grail of the COVID fight:
vaccine development. As in China, Russian authorities hoped the creation
of a vaccine would demonstrate the prowess of their system, both at home
and abroad. Putin and other government officials already promised speedy
development of a vaccine back in March before the country had a true
understanding of what awaited them.[197] Over the course of the pandemic, the
vaccine race took on greater urgency as the public health system showcased

frailness.[198] Sputnik V, named after the first satellite launched in space by the Soviet Union, was granted emergency use authorization on August 11, making it the world's first cleared vaccine.[199]

But Russia's victory in the vaccine competition proved tentative. Many at home and abroad questioned a vaccine that was rushed through the approval process. Sputnik was released before phase 3 trials could be safely completed and well before efficacy data was finalized. As a result, less than one-quarter of the 3,000 Russian doctors surveyed by the Health Ministry in the summer said they would take it, two-thirds saying they did not trust it was safe and effective.[200] As the head of the Doctor's Alliance commented, "Doctors are not stupid. They understand what an untested medicine can do."[201]

In summary, Putin initially approached COVID as we might expect from his semi-democratic regime: by deferring responsibility. The president, known for taking care of business very publicly, handed authority to others in his government. Only when COVID became the unavoidable subject of the day did Putin retake the reins, and even then he continued to demand his subordinates bear accountability for the actual response. Putin was himself hesitant to push for politically contentious policies, including harsh lockdowns, instead taking a distant, top-down approach. Rather than take every measure to conquer COVID, as Xi seemed bent on, Putin was more interested in moving past it and returning to the regular political and economic business of the country.

UNITED STATES

The United States appeared from a distance to have every advantage going into the pandemic. It was the wealthiest country in the world. It called itself the "beacon of democracy." And it had a medical system which, for all its faults, was renowned for advanced scientific research. In addition, the United States was believed to have a robust disaster machinery, routinely employed to deal with hurricanes, wildfires, damaging storms, and floods. Little wonder that the 2019 Global Health Security Index ranked the United States number one of 195 countries in pandemic preparedness.

In hindsight, criticism of the United States as a "global laggard" in its pandemic response should not have been surprising.[202] In the twenty years before COVID hit, the United States had been bolstering its pandemic response institutions, from the Centers for Disease Control and Prevention (CDC) and Department of Health and Human Services (DHHS) to the Defense Department and Department of Homeland Security (DHS).[203] But by the time COVID arrived, these institutions had major gaps. Top among these was leadership. President Trump's campaign pledge to "drain the swamp" and fight the "deep state" left dozens of senior positions, including 22 percent of key positions at DHHS, unfilled more than three years into his presidency.[204] "I have a gut, and my gut tells me more sometimes than anybody else's brain can ever tell me," he once said, highlighting his disdain for expertise.

In some ways, U.S. institutions did a fair job correcting for Trump's overwhelming reluctance to acknowledge the coming threat, which, just two weeks before COVID was reported on U.S. soil, seemed more about delayed Amazon packages than a deadly disease. Trump was outwardly dismissive when U.S. authorities identified their first case, a middle-aged man who had recently returned from Wuhan:[205] "It's one person coming in from China, and we have it under control," he said in comments reminiscent of early Russian remarks.[206] Under public pressure, his government increased screenings for travelers arriving from Wuhan, and later from China as a whole.[207] Still, by late January, the United States already had more than 110 people in 26 states under observation for possible infection.[208] Declaring a public health emergency, the Trump administration banned entry to any non-U.S. citizens who had recently been to China.[209]

In other ways, America's democratic institutions were no match for a president bent on avoiding costly measures needed to secure the country from a national disaster. Despite dire daily intelligence briefings on the virus threat, Trump initially did little beyond implementing border restrictions, which fit nicely with his anti-immigrant rhetoric.[210] Between political rallies, golf trips, and a Superbowl party, Trump's fleeting references to COVID in February included a confident and breezy "on top of it 24/7!"[211] "The risk of infection for Americans remains low," assured the Health and Human Services secretary.[212] The CDC, meanwhile, bungled the development and rollout of tests, leaving the United States blind to the true extent of viral spread.[213]

In stark contrast to the leaders of China and, to a lesser extent, Russia, who had greater control over the political space, Trump reacted to the COVID threat by framing the COVID outbreak in political, partisan terms from nearly the beginning. Already in February, he claimed some Democrats were "trying to gain political favor by saying a lot about this,"[214] and he attacked mainstream media for embellishing the threat.[215] His message was picked up by conservative media hosts who attacked Democrats for "weaponizing an infectious disease" that they charged was no worse than "the common cold."[216]

Behind the scenes, however, officials were on alert. At the start of February, DHHS officials told Congress it could need to transfer $136 million to agencies dealing with the virus.[217] By the end of the month, the Trump administration had asked Congress for an additional $1.8 billion in emergency spending to cover everything from lab testing and quarantine costs to vaccine research and support for impacted states.[218] A call that would have received hearty praise in the Russian or Chinese legislatures, the Democratic chairwoman of the House Appropriations Committee called it "woefully insufficient to protect Americans."[219]

As he continued closing borders, Trump refrained from providing national direction, leaving navigating the myriad of contentious disaster management policies to state and local jurisdictions.[220] In mid-March, some localities began limiting occupancy in public spaces, closing down bars and restaurants, banning gatherings of more than twenty-five people, and closing schools.[221] By the time Trump declared a national emergency on March 13, three-fifths of U.S. states had already declared their own states of emergency[222] and 32.5 million public school students had seen their schools shuttered.[223]

The president's March 16 initiative, "15 days to stop the spread," came almost eight weeks after the virus had first been detected on U.S. soil.[224] Federal guidelines now urged people to minimize leaving home and avoid social gatherings of more than ten people.[225] But Trump continued to leave state and local leaders to wrestle with the politically fraught issue of whether and how to implement lockdowns.[226] "The governors, locally, are going to be in command," Trump said. "We will be following them, and we hope they can do the job. And I think they will."[227] Within a week, state and local leaders had put one in three Americans under a compulsory stay-at-home order.[228] But the governors assigned to lead the fight were overwhelmed by the piecemeal approach they were forced to deal with. "We're all building the airplane as we fly it right now," said one. "It would be nice to have a national strategy."[229]

With the mid-March shift, the federal government established a coronavirus taskforce headed by the vice president and charged with broadly overseeing the response. Unlike in China and Russia, where the heads of the disease control agencies made regular public appearances, the CDC director was conspicuously missing from U.S. coronavirus taskforce press briefings.[230] Instead, Trump used taskforce briefings as a public forum to opine on the pandemic, sometimes for hours and frequently in contradiction to the message from taskforce experts.

In more practical terms, the federal government did put the Federal Emergency Management Agency (FEMA) at its highest alert level and deployed at least 50 four-person teams around the country to help jurisdictions with procurement and financing for the response.[231] FEMA was also supposed to coordinate assistance from agencies such as the U.S. Army Corps of Engineers, which could rapidly erect medical facilities, as well as the Department of Transportation, which could relieve overburdened supply chains.[232] As Trump approved a slew of disaster declarations coming in from the states, governors gained access to FEMA's $40 billion Disaster Relief Fund.[233]

Compared to China and Russia, the U.S. federal government also poured massive amounts of money into directly and indirectly dealing with the fallout from COVID. The first round was an $8 billion budgetary adjustment, which Trump signed off on March 6.[234] But that was just a drop in what would become a gushing river of funding. Between March and April, the U.S. Congress passed four bipartisan spending bills worth about $3 trillion.[235]

Finally, the federal government also contributed personnel to the fight. By the end of March, it had mobilized DHHS's Disaster Mortuary Operational Response Teams for New York, North Carolina, and Hawaii.[236] The military also dispatched the 1,000-bed USNS Comfort hospital to New York City in order to relieve hospitals of non-COVID patients.[237] Perhaps most consequentially, by August, nearly 4,000 Public Health Service personnel had been deployed to assist in hospitals and nursing homes around the country.[238]

One important sphere where states hoped the national government could assist was basic medical infrastructure. For instance, the government could construct emergency hospitals, as it did in New York.[239] And it could pay for thousands of National Guard troops to help deliver supplies and disinfect public areas under the control of local governors.[240] The federal government could also utilize the U.S. Army Corps of Engineers to assist in building and transforming existing spaces into temporary medical facilities. Many of these efforts were slower than expected, however. By early April, for example, only seven sites in the entire country had actually been approved and contracted for rapid construction.[241]

When it came to providing essential PPE and testing, the government was in even worse shape. At the time the national emergency was declared, almost 90 percent of mayors responding to a national preparedness survey said they faced a shortage of test kits and PPE, with 85 percent saying they had an inadequate number of ventilators.[242] Without federal assistance, governors engaged in bidding wars with one another on the market for scarce medical goods.[243]

States were left begging the federal government to bolster their testing capacity. In mid-March, as the federal government appeared to take the reins, Trump promised to distribute 5 million tests by the end of the month and establish thousands of testing sites.[244] But when his self-imposed deadline arrived, the Republican head of the National Governors Association insisted Trump's claim that tests had become easily accessible was "just not true."[245] By mid-April, in contrast to Trump's boast that the United States had "the most advanced and robust testing system anywhere in the world," the U.S. testing rate was far under that of other advanced economies.[246] Trump complained that demand for more testing was driven by "Radical Left, Do Nothing Democrats," and renewed his stance that the federal role would be limited to "strategic direction and technical assistance," and "supplier of last resort."[247]

The lack of a national testing and contact tracing plan left states, in the words of one governor, "flying blind" through the pandemic.[248] Decentralization meant the emergence of major testing disparities, with states like New York and Utah testing in early April 1,645 and 1,043 of every 100,000 residents, respectively, while Texas and Georgia were at only 297 and 381.[249] One former CDC director commented: "It's mind-boggling, actually, the degree of disorganization."[250]

A lack of uniform national regulations, lax adherence to isolation orders, and weak testing and contact tracing capabilities impeded efforts to halt the spread of the virus around the country.[251] Worries jumped when Trump crossed with medical experts by promising to open the country up by Easter, in early April.[252] "We cannot let the cure be worse than the problem itself," Trump began saying in late March, referring to the economic and social disruptions caused by shutdowns.[253] Pictures of body bags and freezer trucks lining up in New York City eventually compelled Trump to walk back his promise and extend social distancing recommendations through April 30.[254]

In keeping with the spirit of state and local responsibility, the White House's three-phase reopening plan released in April was kept deliberately vague and, notably, included no national testing strategy.[255] "You're going to call your own shots," Trump told governors.[256] In reality, the plan increased pressure on local leaders, who faced off with groups of angry citizens.[257] An "open it up" caucus in the Republican Party took to conservative media, and small but highly visible protests spread to cities across the country, sometimes including gun-carrying, military-clad participants.[258] Partisanship, fanned from the top, eclipsed health policy. Just as Republican states opened faster than Democratic ones, frequently sidelining medical advisors in the process, conflicts arose between Republican governors bent on reopening and Democratic mayors fearful of the health impact.[259]

Trump's position was clear: He cheered on states that moved more quickly despite not achieving White House health benchmarks, and he criticized those not reopening due to a rise in cases.[260] The administration released opinion pieces pressuring state and local leaders to weigh "the health, social and economic costs of keeping Main Streets across the United States closed for business."[261] "REOPEN THE COUNTRY!" Trump tweeted. "TRANSITION TO GREATNESS."[262]

Premature reopenings led to a surge in infections and localized restriction reinstatements almost immediately.[263] At the end of May, the U.S. case count was the highest in the world, with the 1.7 million confirmed cases almost equal to the total from the next six countries, even though the total U.S. population amounted to just over half of theirs.[264] The case tally nearly doubled to 3.3 million in mid-July[265] before climbing to 5 million in August.[266] As cases climbed early in the summer, the White House downplayed the spread. "We're aware that there are embers that need to be put out," the press secretary told the media in a grave understatement.[267]

Rather than encourage a pause or reversal in the reopening process, Trump repeated the message, contrary to his scientific experts, that the virus would "sort of just disappear."[268] Blaming high test rates for the case spike, Trump called for a testing slowdown.[269] Even after Trump announced a resumption of task force briefings,[270] he continued to praise the "great American comeback"[271] and condemned his less sanguine coronavirus experts.[272] Meanwhile, political fighting increased between governors who demanded their state stay open and local mayors who feared their cities would be unable to cope with the swelling patient population.[273]

With the rise in cases came an increase in deaths. It took two months from the first U.S. death at the end of February for the tally to surpass 3,700 deaths.[274] But by April, more than 1,000 people were dying every day, and by the start of the summer surge, the United States had experienced almost 125,000 deaths.[275] The real number was likely higher, with the CDC admitting under-testing and false negatives made the true count difficult to attain.[276] In fact, despite inadequate testing, the CDC reported that until early April, it was only counting COVID deaths after a lab test confirmed coronavirus in the deceased patient.[277] In some states, just like in Russia, even COVID-positive patients who died could be omitted from the official COVID count if they had no respiratory symptoms or died of an acute event such as a stroke or heart attack.[278]

The political struggle to frame the virus hit a fevered pitch in the run-up to the November presidential elections. Just over a month before election day, Trump tested positive for COVID, though apparently he kept his diagnosis a secret during the first presidential debate.[279] When he was afterward hospitalized, the president continued to play down the threat of the disease, also dismissing his son's diagnosis as evidence of how COVID figures were blown out of proportion. "He has sniffles, he was sniffling. One Kleenex, that's all he needed, and he was better. But he's a case," Trump complained.[280]

But as the fall onslaught continued into mid-November, states and cities felt compelled to return to lockdowns or other less drastic restrictions, such as curfews, limits on gathering size, and strict mask mandates.[281] "People are dying. We're seeing a daily uptick. This is literally a matter of life and death," Chicago's mayor explained. In some localities, the rise in cases was marked by the arrival of mobile morgue trailers.[282] Despite the partisan rancor, even governors of more conservative states, such as Utah and North Dakota, felt compelled to implement restrictions. "Our situation has changed, and we must change with it," one explained.[283]

By December, daily sick counts were topping 200,000 and hit an all-time of 252,000 on December 17.[284] Medical providers began to ration health care in some states, meaning certain patients could not receive the treatments they needed simply because there were not enough resources available.[285] These events did not garner the president's attention, however. More upset by his November electoral defeat, Trump grew silent about the pandemic, prompting a recently resigned CDC chief of staff to fault "a lack of leadership" for the unfolding disaster.[286]

While the bungled U.S. COVID response painted an extraordinarily grim picture, Trump clung to the silver lining: an emergent vaccine.[287] Like his more authoritarian populist counterparts, the U.S. president placed high hopes in a vaccine early on, even promising in March, over the objections of scientific advisors, that a vaccine could be ready for distribution "over the next few months."[288] By spring, the administration had launched "Operation Warp Speed"[289] with the goal of producing hundreds of millions of doses by January 2021. But amidst worries of politicization and a rushed rollout, by the time the first vaccine was released in mid-December, 37 percent of Americans said they would not take it.[290] For those who urgently wanted the shot, supply chain issues slashed the projected amount of vaccine doses to be distributed by late December from 300 million to less than 40 million.[291] Despite this, Trump took credit for his "monumental national achievement,"[292] one of his few post-election references to COVID.

In summary, the U.S. battle against COVID started off as in the other cases: a struggle more over messaging (denial) than over action (preparation). This stands in stark contrast to what we would typically expect from a democratic country where information is free and elected leaders are under close scrutiny. The mechanisms of democracy, and perhaps a hope that the virus could be rapidly stymied, did push the president into belated action. But several factors served to hamper the response. One was the delegation of response authority, which forced a national disaster into the domain of state and local governments that lacked the appropriate tools to address the threat. A second was Trump's insistence on downplaying the dangers of COVID even at a time when he was asking Americans to take tough measures to deal with the disease, something that deepened the level of confusion and sometimes pitted local leaders against their citizens. And a third was Trump's overtly political approach to the pandemic and, relatedly, his determination to quell the virus through rhetoric rather than action. In the end, the U.S. response was the sporting equivalent of a massive upset that few would have predicted.

CONCLUSION

It is worth highlighting several important themes that emerge from this brief overview. The most obvious is that the path of COVID took a remarkably different turn from what we might have expected based solely on regime type, particularly when it came to viral spread. On that note, while there was much discussion in the western press about China underreporting COVID, it was not alone. China may have been the most egregious underreporter, apparently followed by Russia, but the United States was also criticized for underestimating the true rates of COVID cases and fatalities. While some of the errors in all of these cases could be chalked up to inexperience and limited technical capabilities, there is evidence that politics also played a role.

Another critical theme that is visible in these case overviews is the role of power delegation in the response. While China's leaders theoretically have a decentralized disaster response system, central authorities were undoubtedly at the lead once the epidemic had spiraled out of local control. By contrast, the Russians and Americans, with much more pressing electoral considerations, were adamant that painful decisions should be made locally, not nationally.

Yet the Russians and Americans were not at all identical in their approach. It was actually the two authoritarian leaders, Xi and Putin, who placed greater emphasis on the opinions of experts in their response. At every turn, they emphasized that the policies they were following, and that they encouraged lower-level leaders to embrace, must be based on emerging science. By contrast, Trump routinely clashed with medical experts and challenged their credibility. For the former two, and especially Xi, science represented a convenient constraint that they could refer to as they followed or encouraged tough policies. For Trump, science was an obstacle to fulfilling the popular will. It was a liability.

Finally, leadership styles increasingly diverged over time. In all three of these cases, the populist leaders in power initially sought to avoid or downplay the emerging threat until they could do so no more. At that point, each took control in a very different way. Xi Jinping delegated power to close party affiliates, tasking them with running ground operations while he remained in command at the center, a place from which he injected enormous resources into afflicted areas. Putin similarly delegated responsibility to regional leaders but made more of an effort to maintain the image of being in charge, promising to ensure accountability for lower-level leaders and serve as a backstop for those who slipped up. Finally, Trump delegated responsibility while also claiming to be in charge. But even in the grimmest days of the pandemic, he showed a much greater willingness than his more authoritarian counterparts to put a bright spin on an out-of-control disaster. Moreover, the U.S. president also went out of his way to demonstrate that he, and the federal government, had little authority and few resources to throw at the problem. That, and the responsibility to ameliorate the disaster, fell to those below.

It was the populist nature of these leaders, working in conjunction with regime type, that I argue set them on such different paths with such varied policy outcomes. Over the next three chapters, I delve into how populism combined with institutional settings shapes responses with a focus on three broad themes: leadership and information control, delegation and scapegoat-ing, and image projection.

On the first theme, leadership and information control, I use official state-ments and state press to create a narrative, investigating how each leader presented himself, with the expectation that the more democratic the popu-list, the more center stage that populist leader would place himself in the pandemic response as he wrestled with issues of electoral accountability and struggled to counter inconvenient information he could not control.

In the area of delegation and scapegoating, we should expect to find the more authoritarian leaders focused on maintaining the image of overall control while effectively outsourcing the response, and particularly the less savory elements of response, to lower levels. The more democratic a populist is, the more he should relinquish control and responsibility alto-gether, since he faces short-term electoral backlash for inevitable response shortcomings. This feeds into the punishment sphere, where our more authoritarian leaders should work to show their will to punish lower-level leaders accused of (and often scapegoated for) poor performance. The more democratic populist, lacking such punitive powers, should instead purse a public relations campaign against political enemies (including those who clash with his message) in the hope voters will pressure or punish lower-level leaders themselves.

Finally, in all of these cases, we should find leaders obsessed with image projection, favorably comparing their performance with others. But in more authoritarian cases with the least domestic opposition, greater emphasis should be on inter-country and inter-regime comparisons (touting the strength of the populist leader and his regime relative to others), while in more demo-cratic cases we should see an emphasis on distinguishing between the leader in power and potential domestic opponents, including within his own state apparatus.

Based on these broad themes, the three cases employed in this book dem-onstrate the potentially significant impact of populism and regime type on policy response. In the case of COVID and future disasters that are likely to unfold, this combination could literally have life or death implications.

NOTES

1. Christie Aschwanden, "The False Promise of Herd Immunity for COVID-19," *Nature* 587, no. 7832 (2020).

2. Solomon Hsiang et al., "The Effect of Large-Scale Anti-Contagion Policies on the COVID-19 Pandemic," ibid.

3. Wee Kek Koon, "China Has Been Plagued, and Shaped, by Epidemics – It Has Also Over-come Them," *South China Morning Post*, December 21, 2020; ibid.

4. Zhang Qiang et al., "The Pattern of Policy Change on Disaster Management in China: A Bibliometric Analysis of Policy Documents, 1949–2016," *International Journal of Disaster Risk Science* 9 (2018): 55; Yi Kang, *Disaster Management in China in a Changing Era*, Springer Briefs in Political Science (Berline: Springer-Verlag Berlin Heiderlberg, 2015), 23; Chen Gang, "Institutionalization in the Politics of China's Disaster Management," *The Copenhagen Journal of Asian Studies* 32, no. 1 (2014): 26.

5. Kang, *Disaster Management in China in a Changing Era*, 25.

6. BBC, "China Experts Identify 'New Coronavirus' in Pneumonia Outbreak," *BBC Monitoring Asia Pacific*, January 9, 2020.

7. Gerry Shih and Lena H. Sun, "Outbreak of Possible New Virus in Central China Raises Alarms across Asia," *The Washington Post*, January 9, 2020, A14; Anna Fifield, "In China, Some Worry the Official Illness Count Is Too Low," Ibid., January 23, A15.

8. Xinhua, "Commentary: Facts Speak Loud for China's Openness, Transparency in COVID-19 Fight," *Xinhua General News Service*, April 6, 2020.

9. Chris Buckley and Myers Steven Lee, "China Kept World in Dark as Outbreak Rippled," *New York Times*, February 2, 2020, A1; Shih and Sun, "Outbreak of Possible New Virus in Central China Raises Alarms across Asia."

10. Xinhua, "Commentary: Facts Speak Loud for China's Openness, Transparency in COVID-19 Fight."

11. Chris Buckley et al., "25 Days That Changed the World: How COVID-19 Slipped China's Grasp," *New York Times* (Online), December 30, 2020; Buckley and Steven Lee, "China Kept World in Dark as Outbreak Rippled"; Buckley et al., "25 Days That Changed the World: How COVID-19 Slipped China's Grasp."

12. "25 Days That Changed the World: How COVID-19 Slipped China's Grasp"; Amy Qin and Javier C. Hernández, "China Reports First Fatality from New Virus," *New York Times*, January 11, 2020; Shih and Sun, "Outbreak of Possible New Virus in Central China Raises Alarms across Asia"; Louise Minchin, "Breakfast – 9:20 Am Gmt," *BBC News 24*, January 18, 2020.

13. Buckley et al., "25 Days That Changed the World: How COVID-19 Slipped China's Grasp."

14. Buckley and Steven Lee, "China Kept World in Dark as Outbreak Rippled."

15. Buckley et al., "25 Days That Changed the World: How COVID-19 Slipped China's Grasp."

16. Xinhua, "Commentary: Facts Speak Loud for China's Openness, Transparency in COVID-19 Fight"; "China's Fight against COVID-19 Stands the Test of Time: Foreign Ministry," *Xinhua General News Service*, June 3, 2020; Lisa Schnirring, "China Releases Genetic Data on New Coronavirus, Now Deadly," University of Minnesota Center for Infectious Disease Research and Policy, https://www.cidrap.umn.edu/covid-19/china-releases-genetic-data-new-coronavirus-now-deadly.

17. Yuan Li, "In China, Virus Spurred Rush of Blame Shifting: [Foreign Desk]," *New York Times*, February 5, 2020, A1.

18. Xinhua, "Xi Orders Resolute Efforts to Curb Virus Spread," *Xinhua Financial News*, January 20, 2020.

19. "Xi Focus: Chronicle of Xi's Leadership in China's War against Coronavirus (1)," *Xinhua General News Service*, September 7, 2020; Editorial, "What Did Xi Jinping Know About the Coronavirus, and When Did He Know It?" *The Washington Post* (Online), February 19, 2020.

20. Chris Buckley and Javier C. Hernández, "As Fears of Pandemic Grow, China Puts 20 Million on Lockdown: [Foreign Desk]," *New York Times*, January 24, 2020, A1.

21. Fifield, "In China, Some Worry the Official Illness Count Is Too Low."

22. BBC, "Chinese Media Criticise Wuhan Handling of Virus Outbreak," *BBC Worldwide Monitoring*, January 23, 2020.

23. Xinhua, "China's Hubei to Comb for Patients with Fever," *Xinhua General News Service*, February 18, 2020; Amy Qin, "China Expands Chaotic Dragnet in Coronavirus Crackdown," *New*

York Times (Online), February 13, 2020. Amy Qin, Myers Steven Lee, and Elaine Yu, "Beijing Imposes Extreme Limits on Ill in Wuhan: [Foreign Desk]," *New York Times*, February 7, 2020, A1.

24. Amy Qin, "A Fever of 104, Hours to Wait, and No Relief," Ibid., February 3.

25. Wee Sui-Lee, "As Deaths Mount, a Race to Screen Ever More Patients to Slow an Epidemic: [Foreign Desk]," Ibid., February 10, A8.

26. Qin, "A Fever of 104, Hours to Wait, and No Relief."

27. Xinhua, "Xinhua Headlines: China Goes All Out to Contain Novel Coronavirus Amid Travel Rush," *Xinhua General News Service*, January 22, 2020.

28. "China Focus: China at 'Crucial Stage' to Control Novel Coronavirus, Experts Say," *Xinhua General News Service*, January 22, 2020.

29. BBC, "Chinese Media Criticise Wuhan Handling of Virus Outbreak"; Buckley and Hernández, "As Fears of Pandemic Grow, China Puts 20 Million on Lockdown: [Foreign Desk]."

30. Anna Fifield, "In Wuhan, a Shortage of Doctors, Hospitals and Beds. But the Stress Is Plentiful," *The Washington Post*, January 25, 2020, A1. *Hindustan Times*, "China Warns Coronavirus Transmission Ability Getting Stronger, Braces for More Cases," *Hindustan Times*, January 26, 2020; Xinhua, "Xinhua Headlines: China Beefs up Action against Novel Coronavirus as Cases Increase," *Xinhua General News Service*, January 26, 2020.

31. Chris Buckley and Myers Steven Lee, "Chinese Officials Race to Contain Public Fury over Virus Management: [Foreign Desk]," *New York Times*, January 28, 2020, A8.

32. Xinhua, "China Focus: China Has Taken Strictest Measures to Curb Epidemic: NHC," *Xinhua General News Service*, February 1, 2020.

33. Ibid.

34. Xinhua, "Across China: Deep in Chinese Mountains, Folk Songs Spread Anti-Virus Messages," *Xinhua General News Service*, February 11, 2020.

35. "Across China: China's Villages, Communities Mobilized in Fight against Epidemic," *Xinhua General News Service*, February 6, 2020.

36. AFP, "China Stutters Back to Work as Virus Deaths Soar," *Agence France Presse - English*, February 10, 2020.

37. NYT, "New Cases in China Appear to Be Slowing," *New York Times*, February 18, 2020, https://www.nytimes.com/2020/02/18/world/asia/china-coronavirus.html; AFP, "China Leadership Admits 'Shortcomings' in Virus Response," *Agence France Presse - English*, February 3, 2020.

38. Xinhua, "China Focus: Free Online Medical Services Help Curb Coronavirus Outbreak," *Xinhua General News Service*, February 2, 2020; "China Focus: Internet Helps in China's Fight against Novel Coronavirus," *Xinhua General News Service*, February 3, 2020; "Across China: Internet Court Handles Cases Despite Coronavirus Epidemic," *Xinhua General News Service*, March 10, 2020; "China Focus: Online Services Lend a Hand to Everyday Life Amid Epidemic," *Xinhua General News Service*, February 25, 2020.

39. "Across China: Epidemic Prevention in Grassland," *Xinhua General News Service*, March 11, 2020.

40. Raymond Zhong, "$9 Cabbages and Emergency Pork: Health Crisis Tests Food Supply Chain: [Foreign Desk]," *New York Times*, February 5, 2020.

41. Xinhua, "Chinese People Show Patriotism in Coronavirus Fight: Spokesperson," *Xinhua General News Service*, February 6, 2020.

42. "China's Central SOEs Mobilize to Fight against Coronavirus," *Xinhua General News Service*, February 18, 2020.

43. "Factbox: China's Fight against Novel Coronavirus Outbreak," *Xinhua General News Service*, April 15, 2020; "Xinhua Headlines: China Mobilizes Medical Teams to Fight New Coronavirus," *Xinhua General News Service*, January 24, 2020.

44. "Xinhua Headlines: China Beefs up Action against Novel Coronavirus as Cases Increase"; "China's Coronavirus-Stricken Province Races to Tackle Shortage of Protective Gear," *Xinhua General News Service*, January 28, 2020; BBC, "China Discouraging Marriage, Funeral Gatherings Amid Outbreak," *BBC Monitoring Asia Pacific - Political Supplied by BBC Worldwide Monitoring*, January 31, 2020.

45. Xinhua, "China Focus: Bring COVID-19 under Control with Joint Efforts," *Xinhua General News Service*, May 18, 2020; "China Sends 25,633 Medics to Battle COVID-19 in Hubei," *Xinhua General News Service*, February 15, 2020; AFP, "China Leadership Admits 'Shortcomings' in Virus Response."

46. Xinhua, "Xinhua Headlines: China Builds New Hospital in 10 Days to Combat Coronavirus," *Xinhua General News Service*, February 2, 2020.

47. Vivian Wang, "Coronavirus Epidemic Keeps Growing, but Spread in China Slows," *New York Times* (Online), February 18, 2020; NYT, "New Cases in China Appear to Be Slowing."

48. Xinhua, "Wuhan Remains China's Main Battlefield against Epidemic: Official," *Xinhua General News Service*, February 25, 2020.

49. "SW China's Chongqing Lowers Coronavirus Response Level," *Xinhua General News Service*, March 11, 2020; AFP, "China Reports 27 New Virus Deaths, Lowest Rise in Cases since January," *Agence France Presse - English*, March 8, 2020.

50. Xinhua, "China Focus: China Says Its COVID-19 Peak Is Over," *Xinhua General News Service*, March 12, 2020.

51. "Most Regions of China at Low-Risk of COVID-19: Official," *Xinhua General News Service*, March 22, 2020.

52. "SW China's Chongqing Lowers Coronavirus Response Level"; "China's Tianjin Discharges Last COVID-19 Patient," *Xinhua General News Service*, March 15, 2020; "East China Province Lifts Lockdown on Residential Communities," *Xinhua General News Service*, March 19, 2020; "China's Guizhou Cleared of COVID-19 Cases," *Xinhua General News Service*, March 16, 2020; AFP, "As World Cowers, China Glimpses Coronavirus Aftermath," *Agence France Presse - English*, March 18, 2020.

53. Xinhua, "Xinhua Headlines: China's Wuhan Closes All 16 Temporary Hospitals," *Xinhua General News Service*, March 10, 2020.

54. "China Focus: Wuhan Buses Hit the Road after Two-Month Lockdown," *Xinhua General News Service*, March 25, 2020.

55. "Economic Watch: A Tale of Two Fronts: Resilient China Cranks up Economy Amid COVID-19 Fight," *Xinhua General News Service*, March 26, 2020.

56. "China's Public Transportation Services Resumed from Epidemic Standstill," *Xinhua General News Service*, April 4, 2020.

57. "China Focus: China Lifts 76-Day Lockdown on Virus-Hit Wuhan," *Xinhua General News Service*, April 8, 2020.

58. "China Strengthens Personnel Movement Control in Medium- and High-Risk Regions," *Xinhua General News Service*, June 25, 2020.

59. "China Intensifies Screening of Asymptomatic COVID-19 Infections," *Xinhua General News Service*, April 9, 2020; "Factbox: China's Fight against Novel Coronavirus Outbreak"; "China Faces Rising Risk of Imported COVID-19 Cases: Official," *Xinhua General News Service*, March 6, 2020; Anna Fifield, "China Watches as Illness Circles Back," *The Washington Post*, March 5, 2020, A14.

60. Xinhua, "China to Strengthen Epidemic Control Along Land Border," *Xinhua General News Service*, April 2, 2020; "China Sets up 'Three Defense Lines' to Prevent Imported Virus Outbreak: Expert," *Xinhua General News Service*, March 24, 2020.

61. "China Deploys Medical Experts, Resources to Border Regions to Battle COVID-19," *Xinhua General News Service*, April 13, 2020; "China Focus: China Scales up Land Border Control in Epidemic Response," *Xinhua General News Service*, April 13, 2020; "Factbox: China's Fight against Novel Coronavirus Outbreak"; AFP, "China Reports Rise in Imported Virus Cases," *Agence France Presse - English*, March 3, 2020.

62. Xinhua, "China's Border Town to Build Temporary Hospital as Imported COVID-19 Cases Rise," *Xinhua General News Service*, April 9, 2020; "Battle-Hardened Medics to Support China's Border City," *Xinhua General News Service*, April 11, 2020.

63. Christian Shepherd and Emma Zhou Beijing, "China Strict Travel Ban Leaves Nationals Stranded Abroad; Second Wave Fears," *Financial Times*, May 9, 2020; Keegan Elmer, "Coronavirus: People Are Forging Tests to Return to China from Russia," *South China Morning Post*, June 23, 2020.

64. Laura Zhou, "Coronavirus: China Offers US $4,500 Reward for Information About Illegal Foreigners," Ibid., October 30.

65. Xinhua, "China Tightens COVID-19 Control Policies for Inbound Flights," *Xinhua General News Service*, December 16, 2020.

66. "China Calls for Higher Capability, Wider Range of COVID-19 Testing," *Xinhua General News Service*, April 22, 2020.

67. "China's Daily Nucleic Acid Testing Capacity Tops 3 Mln: Official," *Xinhua General News Service*, June 24, 2020.

68. "East China's Qingdao Conducts City-Wide COVID-19 Testing after New Cases Emerge," *Xinhua General News Service*, October 12, 2020; "Live COVID-19 Updates: Over 4.2 Mln Undergo COVID-19 Testing in East China City," *Xinhua General News Service*, October 13, 2020; "China's Qingdao Completes City-Wide COVID-19 Sampling," *Xinhua General News Service*, October 16, 2020; "Xinhua Headlines: Qingdao Safeguards China's COVID-19 Control with Swift Response," *Xinhua General News Service*, October 21, 2020.

69. Alice Yan, "Coronavirus: Second Wave over Winter 'Inevitable' in China, Infectious Disease Expert Says," *South China Morning Post*, September 21, 2020.

70. Xinhua, "China's Urumqi Conducts Citywide COVID-19 Tests," *Xinhua General News Service*, July 21, 2020.

71. "NE China City Tests 1.25 Mln in a Day after New COVID-19 Cases Reported," *Xinhua General News Service*, July 27, 2020.

72. Wang Huiyao, "China's Experience Shows Coronavirus Second Wave Need Not Be a Disaster," *South China Morning Post*, July 2, 2020.

73. Javier C. Hernández, "China Locks Down Xinjiang in West to Stop Covid, Angering Residents: [Foreign Desk]," *New York Times*, August 26, 2020, A5; Xinhua, "Xinhua Headlines: China's Dalian Going All Out to Stem New COVID-19 Infections," *Xinhua General News Service*, July 29, 2020.

74. Javier C. Hernández, "China Peddles Falsehoods to Obscure Origin of COVID Pandemic," *New York Times* (Online), December 6, 2020; Phoebe Zhang, "Coronavirus Found in China on Frozen Chicken Wings from Brazil," *South China Morning Post*, August 13, 2020; Xinhua, "Imported Package Sample Tests Positive for COVID-19 in Ne China City," *Xinhua General News Service*, September 20, 2020; Liu Zhen, "Coronavirus: China Reports More Positive Tests on Imported Frozen Food," *South China Morning Post*, November 15, 2020; Reuters, "New Zealand Says No Word from China on Coronavirus in Frozen Meat," Ibid., November 16; Xinhua, "East China City Finds Coronavirus in Imported Pork," *Xinhua General News Service*, December 3, 2020.

75. Keegan Elmer, "China's Coronavirus Testing Rules for Frozen Meats Give Importers a Chill," *South China Morning Post*, December 5, 2020.

76. Zhuang Pinghui, "Coronavirus: Frozen Food Firms as Culprit in Two Outbreaks in China, Sparking Warning over Cold Imports," Ibid., October 28; Xinhua, "Nearly 140,000 Test Negative after New COVID-19 Cases in East China," *Xinhua General News Service*, September 26, 2020; Kinling Lo, "Coronavirus: Living Samples Found on Frozen Food Packaging in East China's Qingdao, CDC Says," *South China Morning Post*, October 18; Xinhua, "China's Tianjin Completes COVID-19 Testing in Two Medium-Risk Areas," *Xinhua General News Service*, November 11, 2020.

77. Kristin Huang, "China to Disinfect Frozen Food Imports to Curb Coronavirus Spread," *South China Morning Post*, November 10, 2020.

78. Xinhua, "Live COVID-19 Updates: China Reports 16 New Imported Cases, Cuba Makes Progress in Vaccine Development," *Xinhua General News Service*, October 4, 2020.

79. Lily Kuo, "China Grapples with New Cases Ahead of the Lunar New Year," *The Washington Post*, December 30, 2020, A9; Xinhua, "China Focus: Nation Tightens Epidemic Control Amid New Local Cases," *Xinhua General News Service*, December 28, 2020; "Streets in N. China City Classified as COVID-19 Medium-Risk Zones," *Xinhua General News Service*, November 22, 2020; "Northeast China's Dalian Adds 4 Medium-Risk COVID-19 Areas," *Xinhua General News Service*, December 30, 2020.

80. "Xinhua Commentary: China Confident in Minimizing Impact of Sporadic COVID-19 Outbreaks," *Xinhua General News Service*, December 29, 2020.

81. "China's Chengdu to Test All Residents in Virus-Hit District," *Xinhua General News Service*, December 11, 2020; "Two Cities in Northeast China Launch Citywide Nucleic Acid Testing," *Xinhua General News Service*, December 11, 2020; "China's Dalian Conducts Citywide COVID-19 Tests," *Xinhua General News Service*, December 22, 2020; "China's Dalian Samples over 4.75 Mln People for COVID-19 Tests," *Xinhua General News Service*, December 25, 2020.

82. "Xi Focus: Chronicle of Xi's Leadership in China's War against Coronavirus (1)."

83. Nadia Lam, "How China Claimed Victory over the Coronavirus," *South China Morning Post*, November 12, https://www.scmp.com/news/china/article/3109393/how-china-claimed-victory -over-coronavirus; Zhuang Pinghui, "China Admits Coronavirus Exposed 'Weak Links' in Health System as Government Promises to Strengthen Disease Response," *South China Morning Post*, May 23, 2020.

84. Xinhua, "China Reports 291 Confirmed Cases of New Coronavirus-Related Pneumonia," *Xinhua General News Service*, January 21, 2020.

85. AFP, "China Leadership Admits 'Shortcomings' in Virus Response."

86. Wang, "Coronavirus Epidemic Keeps Growing, but Spread in China Slows"; Qin, "China Expands Chaotic Dragnet in Coronavirus Crackdown"; NYT, "New Cases in China Appear to Be Slowing."

87. Xinhua, "Commentary: China's Transparency in Epidemic Control Should Not Be Doubted," *Xinhua General News Service*, February 14, 2020.

88. AFP, "How China Turned the Tide on the Coronavirus," *Agence France Presse - English*, March 13, 2020; Xinhua, "Factbox: China's Fight against Novel Coronavirus Outbreak"; Javier C. Hernández, "China Reaches a Containment Milestone with No New Local Infections: [Foreign Desk]," *New York Times*, March 19, 2020, A6.

89. Yuan Yang et al., "China Medics Query 'Zero New Cases' Claim; National Health Commission; Official Figures Suggest Breakthrough but Experts Cast Doubt on Data," *Financial Times*, March 28, 2020.

90. Xinhua, "China to Strengthen Prevention, Control of Asymptomatic COVID-19 Infections," *Xinhua General News Service*, March 30, 2020.

91. Anna Fifield and Lyric Li, "China Curtails Cemetery Rituals," *The Washington Post*, April 4, 2020, A12; Amy Qin and Li Cao, "Survivors Fume as China Insists on Quiet Burials: [Foreign Desk]," *New York Times*, April 4, 2020, A1.

92. Christian Shepherd, "Wuhan Revises up Death Toll Amid Claims of Cover-up; China," *Financial Times*, April 18, 2020.

93. Economist, "Covid-19 Deaths in Wuhan Seem Far Higher Than the Official Count," *The Economist*, May 30, 2021, https://www.economist.com/graphic-detail/2021/05/30/covid-19-deaths-in -wuhan-seem-far-higher-than-the-official-count.

94. Xinhua, "Economic Watch: China Readies Stronger Policies to Revive Economy as Virus Disrupts Activities," *Xinhua General News Service*, March 16, 2020; AFP, "China Exports Plunge on Coronavirus Epidemic," *Agence France Presse - English*, March 7, 2020; Xinhua, "China's Industrial Output Falls 13.5 Pct as Virus Hurts Activities," *Xinhua General News Service*, March 16, 2020; "China's Fiscal Revenue Down 9.9 Pct in First Two Months," *Xinhua General News Service*, March 24, 2020; *Financial Times*, "China Ends Four Decades of Growth; Historic Contraction; GDP Plunges 6.8% in Starkest Economic Signal from Global Pandemic," *Financial Times*, April 18, 2020, 2020; Keith Bradsher, "Slowed by the Coronavirus, China Inc. Struggles to Reopen," *New York Times* (Online), February 17, 2020; Keith Bradsher and Vindu Goel, "China's Economy Shrinks 6.8 Percent, Ending Four Decades of Growth: [Business/Financial Desk]," *New York Times*, April 17, 2020, B6.

95. Xinhua, "Factbox: China's Fight against Novel Coronavirus Outbreak"; "Biz China Weekly: Pmi, Forex Reserves, Foreign Trade, Anti-Epidemic Credit Support," *Xinhua General News Service*, March 7, 2020.

96. CSIS, "Cheap Talk: China's Central Bank Still Struggles to Speak to Markets," Center for Strategic and International Studies, February 8, 2021, https://www.csis.org/analysis/cheap-talk-chinas-central-bank-still-struggles-speak-markets.

97. Xinhua, "China to Step up Financial Support for SMEs," *Xinhua General News Service*, March 31, 2020; "China's Central Bank Further Cuts Rate for Medium-Term Loans," *Xinhua General News Service*, April 15, 2020; AFP, "China Stutters Back to Work as Virus Deaths Soar." Xinhua, "Chinese City Announces Policy Support for Epidemic-Affected Companies," *Xinhua General News Service*, February 3, 2020; "Lending Support for Anti-Virus Fight Reaches over 200 Bln USD in China," *Xinhua General News Service*, March 13, 2020; AFP, "China to Cut Banks' Reserve Requirement to Combat Virus Fallout," *Agence France Presse - English*, March 13, 2020.

98. Frank Tang, "China Warned to Prepare for 'Big Rise' in Bad Loans as Financial System Braces against Coronavirus, Rising Global Tensions," *South China Morning Post*, July 24, 2020.

99. Xinhua, "Factbox: China's Targeted Support for SMEs During Epidemic," *Xinhua General News Service*, March 3, 2020; "China Unveils New Measures to Keep Foreign Trade, Investment Stable," *Xinhua General News Service*, March 11, 2020; "State Council Unveils New Measures to Mitigate Coronavirus Impact on Chinese Economy," *Xinhua General News Service*, February 26, 2020; "China Boosts Employment with Major Cut in Social Insurance Contributions," *Xinhua General News Service*, July 22, 2020; "Factbox: China's Fight against Novel Coronavirus Outbreak"; "China to Take More Steps to Stabilize Economic, Social Development," *Xinhua General News Service*, March 3, 2020.

100. "China's Tax, Fee Cuts Approximate 2.4 Trillion Yuan," *Xinhua General News Service*, January 1, 2021; "Factbox: China's Progress in Economic Resumption," *Xinhua General News Service*, August 10, 2020.

101. "China's Resort-Rich Province Moves to Resume Tourism Sector," *Xinhua General News Service*, March 12, 2020; "Central China Province to Offer 1 Bln Yuan of Loans to Virus-Hit Cultural, Tourism Sectors," *Xinhua General News Service*, March 27, 2020; "China's Local Gov't Bond Issuance Hits 442.9 Bln Yuan in October," *Xinhua General News Service*, November 17, 2020.

102. Keith Bradsher, "The World Is Turning to Bailouts, but China Is Holding Back: [Business/Financial Desk]," *New York Times*, April 10, 2020, B7.

103. World Bank, "From Recovery to Rebalancing," December 2020, https://thedocs.worldbank.org/en/doc/264421608625565168-0070022020/original/ceuDecember2020Final.pdf; CRFB, "The Fiscal Response to COVID-19 Will Be Larger Than the Great Recession Response," Committee for a Responsible Federal Budget, December 22, 2020, https://www.crfb.org/blogs/fiscal-response-covid-19-will-be-larger-great-recession-response; Jo Harper, "High Corporate Debt Dampens Russia's Growth Prospects," Deutsche Welle, January 22, 2021, https://www.dw.com/en/high-corporate-debt-dampens-russias-growth-prospects/a-56312161.

104. Xinhua, "China's Economic Fundamentals Not Affected by COVID-19: Xi," *Xinhua General News Service*, March 10, 2020; "China Sees No Major Movement of Industrial and Supply Chains to Other Countries Due to Epidemic: FM Spokesperson," *Xinhua General News Service*, March 11, 2020.

105. "Xi Focus: Xi Leads China's Search for Safest Path to Growth Amid COVID-19 Control," *Xinhua General News Service*, April 24, 2020.

106. Yuan Li, "In Ousting U.S. Reporters, China Signals New Kind of Self-Confidence: [Foreign Desk]," *New York Times*, March 19, 2020, A19.

107. Xinhua, "China Steps up Inactivated COVID-19 Vaccine Development," *Xinhua General News Service*, June 1, 2020.

108. Jodi Xu Klein, "US Increasingly Excludes China from Coronavirus Research Projects," *South China Morning Post*, July 7, 2020.

109. Eva Dou, "China Skips Trials to Roll out Vaccine," *The Washington Post*, August 25, 2020, A18; Wee Sui-Lee and Mariana Simões, "China Skirts Convention for Vaccines," *New York Times*, July 17, 2020, B1.

110. Xinhua, "China's First Patent Granted for COVID-19 Vaccine," *Xinhua General News Service*, August 17, 2020.

111. Wee Sui-Lee, "China Hustles for Vaccine, Despite Patchy Reputation: [Business/Financial Desk]," *New York Times*, May 5, 2020, B1.

112. Zhuang Pinghui, "Coronavirus: China CDC Chief Becomes Vaccine 'Mouse' in Shot in Arm to Research," *South China Morning Post*, July 31, 2020.

113. Wee Sui-Lee, "China, in Vaccine Wager, Gives Unproven Shots to Thousands: [Foreign Desk]," *New York Times*, September 27, 2020, A1.

114. Zhuang Pinghui, "China's Public Health Insurance Agency Says It Can't Afford to Provide Covid-19 Vaccine for Free," *South China Morning Post*, October 13, 2020; Guo Rui, "China to Make up to 50 Million Flu Vaccine Doses Available Amid Covid-19 Pandemic, Official Says," Ibid., September 5.

115. Josephine Ma, "Can China Become a Leading Producer of Covid-19 Vaccines?" Ibid., October 27; Wee Sui-Lee and Elsie Chen, "China's Rush to Vaccinate Poses Risks," *New York Times*, November 18, 2020.

116. Zhuang Pinghui, "China Approves Sinopharm's Covid-19 Vaccine, Promises the Public Free Jabs," *South China Morning Post*, December 31, 2020.

117. "On China's Coronavirus Front Line, Not Everyone Wants a Vaccine - Just Yet," *South China Morning Post*, December 23, 2020; Simone McCarthy, "Coronavirus: People in China 'the Most Willing among 15 Countries to Take a Vaccine'," Ibid., December 30.

118. Pinghui, "On China's Coronavirus Front Line, Not Everyone Wants a Vaccine - Just Yet"; Wee Sui-Lee, "Chinese Goal: Quick Vaccine for 50 Million," *New York Times*, December 30, 2020, A1; Simone McCarthy and Zhuang Pinghui, "China's Sinopharm Reports Strong Interim Results for Its Covid-19 Vaccine," *South China Morning Post*, December 30, 2020.

119. Xinhua, "China Focus: Emergency Use of COVID-19 Vaccines Expands to Larger Scale," *Xinhua General News Service*, December 30, 2020.

120. Roger Roffey, "Russia's Emercom: Managing Emergencies and Political Credibility," ed. Lars Höstbeck (Stockholm: Swedish Ministry of Defense, 2016), 48; E. M. Goryushina, "Disaster Politics in the South of Russia," in *IOP Conf. Series: Earth and Environmental Science* (2020), 1.

121. "Disaster Politics in the South of Russia," 1; Vladimir Otrachshenko, Olga Popova, and Pavel Solomin, "Misfortunes Never Come Singly: Consecutive Weather Shocks and Mortality in Russia," *Economics and Human Biology* 31 (2018): 25.

122. Eva Bertrand, "Constructing Russian Power by Communicating During Disasters: The Forest Fires of 2010," *Problems of Post-Communism* 59, no. 3 (2012): 36; Valery Akimov and Boris Porfiriev, "The Institutional Framework and Governance Model of Russia's Crisis Policy: Disaster Focus," in *Crises in Russia : Contemporary Management Policy and Practice from a Historical Perspective*, ed. Boris Porfiriev and Greg Simons (Burlington: Ashgate, 2012), 64; Ingvill Moe Elgsaas, "The Arctic in Russia's Emergency Preparedness System," *Arctic Review on Law and Politics* 9 (2018): 292.

123. Bertrand, "Constructing Russian Power by Communicating During Disasters: The Forest Fires of 2010," 34.

124. Denis Volkov, "Marc Plattner: 'If Russia Had Become Democratic, the World Would Look Very Different Now'," Institute of Modern Russia, April 2, 2015, https://imrussia.org/en/politics/2220-marc-plattner-if-russia-had-become-democratic-the-world-would-look-very-different-now; Andrei Kolesnikov, "Putin's War Has Moved Russia from Authoritarianism to Hybrid Totalitarianism," Carnegie Endowment for International Peace, April 29, 2022, https://carnegieendowment.org/2022/04/19/putin-s-war-has-moved-russia-from-authoritarianism-to-hybrid-totalitarianism-pub-86921; Rustamjon Urinboyev, *Migration and Hybrid Political Regimes: Navigating the Legal Landscape in Russia* (Oakland: University of California Press, 2020); Alina Ryabovolova and Julie Hemment, "'Je Suis Satisfaction:' Russian Politics in the Age of Hybrid Media," *East European Politics* 36, no. 1 (2020); Armando Chaguaceda and Claudia González, "Russia: Citizen Demonstrations in an Electoral Autocracy," *V-Dem Institute Working Paper*, no. 30 (2020).

125. Henry E. Hale, "Eurasian Polities as Hybrid Regimes: The Case of Putin's Russia," *Journal of Eurasian Studies* 1, no. 1 (2010): 33.

126. Roffey, "Russia's Emercom: Managing Emergencies and Political Credibility," 69. Akimov and Porfiriev, "The Institutional Framework and Governance Model of Russia's Crisis Policy: Disaster Focus," 67; Damien Sharkov, "Putin Backs Down on Controversial Pension Reform after Huge Popularity Drop," *Newsweek*, August 29, 2018.

127. ITAR-TASS, "Risk of Chinese Coronavirus Spreading to Russia Is Low, Watchdog Assures," January 21, 2020.

128. Newswire, "All Necessary Measures to Fight New Coronavirus in Russia Taken - Popova," *Russia & CIS General Newswire*, January 22, 2020; ITAR-TASS, "Checkpoints at Russia's Border with China in Amur Region to Stay Closed Till February 1," January 26, 2020; "More Than 1.3 Million People Examined for Coronavirus in Russia - Watchdog," January 27, 2020.

129. ITAR-TASS, "Russia's Watchdog Advises Russians against Visiting China Amidst Outbreak," January 24, 2020.

130. BBC, "TV Says Russia 'Ready' for Coronavirus," *Political Supplied by BBC Worldwide Monitoring*, January 28, 2020.

131. ITAR-TASS, "No Risk of Further Spread of Coronavirus in Russia - Rospotrebnadzor," January 31, 2020.

132. Newswire, "Threat of Novel Coronavirus Importation to Russia Exists - Peskov," *Russia & CIS General Newswire*, January 31, 2020.

133. "Russia Restricts Transborder Traffic, Passenger Rail Service with China," *Russia & CIS General Newswire*, January 31, 2020; "Russia Suspends Visa-Free Tourism, Issuance of Business Visas for China," *Russia & CIS General Newswire*, February 1, 2020; "Russia Could Tighten Epidemiological Control on Domestic Flights - Source," *Russia & CIS General Newswire*, January 31, 2020; BBC, "Russia Restricts Flights to China Amid Coronavirus Outbreak," *Political Supplied by BBC Worldwide*, January 31, 2020.

134. ITAR-TASS, "Russia Ranks Coronavirus among Dangerous Diseases Along with HIV and Plague," February 2, 2020.

135. "State of Emergency Declared in Two Districts in Russia's Far East," February 2, 2020; "Russia Opens Quarantine Points in Border Areas with China," February 2, 2020; Newswire, "Emergency Declared in 3rd District in Russia's Primorye Territory to Address Spread of Coronavirus," *Russia & CIS General Newswire*, February 3, 2020.

136. "Rospotrebnadzor to Propose Stricter Liability for Violation of Quarantine Rules in Russia (Part 2)," *Russia & CIS General Newswire*, February 17, 2020.

137. ITAR-TASS, "Four New Coronavirus Cases Confirmed in Russia over Past 24 Hours," March 7, 2020.

138. Newswire, "Russia Doing Everything Necessary to Stop Coronavirus but the Infection Has Negative Impact on Global Economy - Putin (Part 2)," *Russia & CIS General Newswire*, March 1, 2020.

139. "Rospotrebnadzor Chief: 366 Observation Facilities Prepared in Russia for Coronavirus Quarantine," *Russia & CIS General Newswire*, February 29, 2020.

140. "Six Coronavirus Cases Registered in Russia since Mid-Feb - Rospotrebnadzor," *Russia & CIS General Newswire*, March 3, 2020; "Russia Restricting Foreign Arrivals from S. Korea on March 1 (Part 2)," *Russia & CIS General Newswire*, February 28, 2020; "Russia to Restrict Air Traffic with Italy, Germany, France, Spain from March 13 - Coronavirus Hq (Part 2)," *Russia & CIS General Newswire*, March 11, 2020; ITAR-TASS, "Russia Suspends Trains to and from Ukraine, Moldova, Latvia over Coronavirus," March 15, 2020.

141. "Russia Imposes Entry Ban for Foreigners from March 18 to May 1 over Coronavirus Risks," March 16, 2020.

142. BBC, "Kremlin Says Covid-19 Situation Better in Russia Than Other States," *BBC Monitoring Former Soviet Union - Political Supplied by BBC Worldwide Monitoring*, March 10, 2020.

143. "Navalny Questions Official Line on Coronavirus in Russia," *BBC Monitoring Former Soviet Union - Political Supplied by BBC Worldwide Monitoring*, March 13, 2020; Garry Kasparov,

"Russia Claims It Has Covid-19 under Control. The Facade Is Cracking," *The Washington Post* (Online), March 29, 2020.

144. Missy Ryan, "Russia Spent Millions on Secret Global Political Campaign, U.S. Intelligence Finds," *The Washington Post*, September 13, 2022.

145. Presidential Bulletin, "Russia - April 8," *Russia & CIS Presidential Bulletin*, April 8, 2020.

146. BBC, "Coronavirus in Russia: 11 March 2020," *BBC Monitoring Former Soviet Union - Political Supplied by BBC Worldwide Monitoring*, March 11, 2020.

147. ITAR-TASS, "Task Force Requests Restrictions on Public Gatherings in Russia over Coronavirus," March 11, 2020.

148. BBC, "Coronavirus in Russia: 11 March 2020."

149. Newswire, "Schools across Russia Advised to Temporarily Move Classes Online - Education Ministry," *Russia & CIS General Newswire*, March 14, 2020.

150. Russia, "First Meeting of the Government Coordination Council to Control the Incidence of Coronavirus Infection in Russia," The Russian Government, March 16, 2020, http://government.ru/en/news/39164/; ITAR-TASS, "No Reason to Panic Due to Coronavirus in Russia - Deputy PM," March 17, 2020.

151. "Government Ready to Build Field Hospitals across Russia If Necessary, Says Official," March 17, 2020; Newswire, "Russia Mobilizes Its Medical Institutions for Coronavirus Fight - Golikova," *Russia & CIS General Newswire*, March 17, 2020.

152. "Russia Preparing Action Plan to Neutralize Coronavirus Effects on Economy - Econ Ministry," *Russia & CIS General Newswire*, February 18, 2020; "Russia Doing Everything Necessary to Stop Coronavirus but the Infection Has Negative Impact on Global Economy - Putin (Part 2)."

153. ITAR-TASS, "Russia in 'Peculiar' Position Due to Low Oil Prices and Coronavirus - First Deputy PM," March 16, 2020; Newswire, "Russia to Spend up to 300 Bln Rubles to Support Economy, People in Fight against Coronavirus - PM," *Russia & CIS General Newswire*, March 16, 2020.

154. BBC, "Coronavirus in Russia: 23 March 2020," *BBC Monitoring Former Soviet Union - Political Supplied by BBC Worldwide Monitoring*, March 23, 2020; Elena Teslova, "Moscow Mayor Imposes Home Quarantine for People over 65," Andalou Agency, March 23, 2020, https://www.aa.com.tr/en/asia-pacific/moscow-mayor-imposes-home-quarantine-for-people-over-65/1775599.

155. ITAR-TASS, "TASS: Kremlin Not Considering Possibility of Declaring Emergency Situation in Russia Amid Coronavirus Outbreak - Spokesman," April 1, 2020.

156. Newswire, "Number of People in Self-Isolation Due to Coronavirus Situation Almost Doubles in Russia - Poll," *Russia & CIS General Newswire*, April 8, 2020.

157. "Putin Signs Decree on Measures to Ensure Sanitary-Epidemiological Wellbeing of People on Territory of Russia Amid Coronavirus (Part 2)," *Russia & CIS General Newswire*, April 2, 2020; Andrew Higgins, "Putin, Russia's Man of Action, Is Passive, Even Bored, in the Coronavirus Era," *New York Times* (Online), April 30, 2020; BBC, "BBCM Russia Watchlist for 23 March," *BBC Monitoring Former Soviet Union - Political Supplied by BBC Worldwide Monitoring*, March 23, 2020.

158. ITAR-TASS, "Russia's Coronavirus Cases Top 3,500 - Response Center," April 2, 2020.

159. "Most Coronavirus Cases in Russia Local Transmissions - Deputy PM," April 4, 2020.

160. "Public Order, Security in Russia to Be Safeguarded in Pandemic - Putin," April 3, 2020.

161. Newswire, "Quantities of Coronavirus Test Systems Sufficient in Russia, Rospotrebnadzor Set to Provide All Regions with Them - Golikova," *Russia & CIS General Newswire*, March 16, 2020; ITAR-TASS, "Russia Sets up Two-Week Stock of Medicines over Coronavirus," March 16, 2020.

162. Just days later, the ministry announced 3,300 Ministry of Defence staff had tested positive since March, 2,910 of whom were either military personnel or cadets in training. Presidential Bulletin, "Russia - April 8"; ITAR-TASS, "Emergencies Ministry Teams Disinfect About 1,000 Social Facilities across Russia," April 8, 2020; BBC, "Coronavirus in Russia: 14 Apr 2020," *BBC Monitoring Former Soviet Union - Political Supplied by BBC Worldwide Monitoring*, April 14, 2020; Esmerk, "Russia: Ministry Constructing Medical Center for 160 Patients in Novosibirsk," *M-Brain Russia News*, April 10, 2020, LexisNexis; BBC, "Covid-19 Roundup: Russia 24 April 2020," *BBC*

Monitoring Former Soviet Union - Political Supplied by BBC Worldwide Monitoring, April 24, 2020; "Covid-19 Roundup: Russia 30 April 2020," *BBC Monitoring Former Soviet Union - Political Supplied by BBC Worldwide Monitoring*, April 30, 2020.

163. Presidential Bulletin, "Russia - December 28," *Russia & CIS Presidential Bulletin*, December 28, 2020.

164. ITAR-TASS, "More Than 50,000 Medical Students Help Doctors to Fight Pandemic in Russia - Minister," December 1, 2020.

165. Isabelle Khurshudyan, "Russia's Low Count Raises Skepticism, Even with Moscow's Mayor," *The Washington Post*, March 25, 2020, A14.

166. Presidential Bulletin, "Russia - December 28."

167. Thomas Grove and Ann M. Simmons, "Three Doctors in Russia Have Fallen Out of Hospital Windows; the Incidents Occurred as More Medical Professionals Are Speaking out About the Stress of Treating Coronavirus," May 7, 2020, https://www.wsj.com/articles/three-doctors-in-russia -have-fallen-out-of-hospital-windows-11588887817; Robyn Dixon, "Russian Medical Workers Say Coronavirus Is Ravaging Their Ranks. But Hospital Chiefs Are Silent: Medical Personnel Complain That a Lack of Protective Equipment Leaves Them in Peril as the Pandemic Advances across Russia," *The Washington Post* (Online), April 22, 2020; BBC, "Covid-19 Roundup: Russia 11 June 2020," *BBC Monitoring Former Soviet Union - Political Supplied by BBC Worldwide Monitoring*, June 11, 2020.

168. Ann M. Simmons, "In Russia, Putin Wrestles with Economic Impact of Coronavirus; What Was Tipped to Be Marquee Year for Kremlin Leader Has Turned into One of Toughest Challenges of His 20-Year Reign," *Wall Street Journal* (Online), May 5, 2020.

169. Presidential Bulletin, "Russia - April 8."

170. Presidential Bulletin, "Russia - December 28."

171. ITAR-TASS, "All Medical Institutions in Russia Must Be Ready to Treat Coronavirus Patients - Minister," April 15, 2020.

172. BBC, "Covid-19 Roundup: Russia 17 June 2020," *BBC Monitoring Former Soviet Union - Political Supplied by BBC Worldwide Monitoring*, June 17, 2020.

173. ITAR-TASS, "Russia Ranks About 50th in Cases of COVID-19 Per 100,000 Residents - Official," April 28, 2020.

174. Newswire, "Coronavirus Death Rates 7.4 Times Lower in Russia Than in World as a Whole - Deputy PM Golikova," *Russia & CIS General Newswire*, May 11, 2020; ITAR-TASS, "Russia Has One of World's Lowest Coronavirus Mortality Rates - Health Minister," April 22, 2020.

175. Presidential Bulletin, "Russia - December 28."

176. BBC, "Covid-19 Roundup: Russia 13 May 2020," *BBC Monitoring Former Soviet Union - Political Supplied by BBC Worldwide Monitoring*, May 13, 2020; Robyn Dixon, "In Russia's Pandemic Struggles, Even Putin Couldn't Speed Bonuses to Health Workers: The Country Has the Third-Largest Number of Confirmed Covid-19 Cases, but Its Counting System Raises Question About Relatively Low Death Rates," *The Washington Post* (Online), May 27, 2020.

177. ITAR-TASS, "Russia Proposes Three-Stage Lockdown Exit Strategy," May 6, 2020.

178. Presidential Bulletin, "Russia - December 28."

179. Ibid.

180. Ann M. Simmons, "Moscow, Center of Russia's Coronavirus Crisis, Emerges from Lockdown; Infections Remain High as City Authorities Begin Reopening and Putin Prepares for Parade, Referendum," *Wall Street Journal* (Online), June 9, 2020.

181. Newswire, "Putin Says Russia Exiting Coronavirus Situation with Confidence, in Contrast with U.S (Part 2)," *Russia & CIS General Newswire*, June 14, 2020.

182. ITAR-TASS, "Nearly 500 Doctors Die from Coronavirus in Russia - Healthcare Watchdog," June 18, 2020.

183. "Russia's Healthcare System Proved to Be Flexible and Ready to Mobilize - Putin," June 28, 2020.

184. "Bed Fund for COVID-19 Patients in Russia Is Almost 90% Full - Deputy Health Minister," October 13, 2020.

185. BBC, "Covid-19 Roundup: Russia 29 October 2020," *BBC Monitoring Former Soviet Union - Political Supplied by BBC Worldwide Monitoring*, October 29, 2020.

186. "Covid-19 Roundup: Russia 13 November 2020," *BBC Monitoring Former Soviet Union - Political Supplied by BBC Worldwide Monitoring*, November 13, 2020.

187. ITAR-TASS, "Deputy PM Says Russia Did Not Impose New Lockdown Due to Readiness to Fight Pandemic," December 28, 2020.

188. "Russia Allocates 4.5% of GDP to Mitigate Consequences of Pandemic - Putin," November 21, 2020.

189. "'On Solid Ground': Russia's Fortitude Helped Weather COVID Storm of 2020, Kremlin Says," December 23, 2020.

190. Ann M. Simmons, "Russia's Covid Surge Exacts a Heavy Toll on Its Emergency Responders; a Shortage of Paramedics Pushes Wait Times for Ambulances to 24 Hours as the Virus Continues to Reach New Highs," *Wall Street Journal* (Online), November 7, 2020.

191. BBC, "Covid-19 Roundup: Russia 25 December 2020," *BBC Monitoring Former Soviet Union - Political Supplied by BBC Worldwide Monitoring*, December 25, 2020.

192. Newswire, "Russia Ranks 105th in World in Covid-19 Fatality Rate - Rospotrebnadzor," *Russia & CIS General Newswire*, October 19, 2020; Andrew Higgins, "New Data Triples Russia's COVID-19 Death Toll," *New York Times* (Online), December 29, 2020.

193. Newswire, "Effective Healthcare System Allowed Russia to Deal with Coronavirus - Peskov," *Russia & CIS General Newswire*, June 10, 2020.

194. Harper, "High Corporate Debt Dampens Russia's Growth Prospects."

195. Georgi Kantchev, "Russia Cuts Interest Rate to Shore up Faltering Economy; the Central Bank Takes Action as the Country Lurches Towards a Recession," *Wall Street Journal* (Online), April 24, 2020.

196. BBC, "Covid-19 Roundup: Russia 6 May 2020," *BBC Monitoring Former Soviet Union - Political Supplied by BBC Worldwide Monitoring*, May 6, 2020.

197. Newswire, "Russia Has All Necessary Tools to Develop Coronavirus Vaccine in near Future - Putin (Part 2)," *Russia & CIS General Newswire*, March 17, 2020; ITAR-TASS, "Russia's Medical Biological Agency Hopes to Have Anti-Coronavirus Vaccine in 11 Months," March 20, 2020.

198. Georgi Kantchev and Drew Hinshaw, "Hit Hard by Coronavirus, Russia Joins Global Race for a Vaccine; Being First Would Provide Putin More Economic and Political Leverage as 'Vaccine Nationalism' Spreads," *Wall Street Journal* (Online), June 11, 2020.

199. Andrew E. Kramer, "Russia Is Slow to Administer Virus Vaccine Despite Kremlin's Approval," *New York Times* (Online), November 24, 2020.

200. BBC, "Covid-19 Roundup: Russia 14 August 2020," *BBC Monitoring Former Soviet Union - Political Supplied by BBC Worldwide Monitoring*, August 14, 2020.

201. Andrew E. Kramer, "Russia, Expecting Plaudits for Vaccine, Is Miffed by Its Cool Reception," *New York Times* (Online), August 23, 2020.

202. Joe Davidson, "Former CDC Director Freiden Says U.S. Has Become a 'Laggard' in Global Health," *The Washington Post*, May 30, 2020, A8.

203. Lenny Bernstein and Lena H. Sun, "Gaps Remain in U.S. Preparation," Ibid., January 23, A14.

204. Joe Davidson, "Agency Leadership Vacancies Take a Toll on Crisis Response," Ibid., April 16, A8; Ashley Parker, Philip Rucker, and Rucker Ashley Parker and Philip, "The President Turns to the Experts He's Long Maligned," Ibid., February 28, A12.

205. Anna Fifield, Lena H. Sun, and Lenny Bernstein, "China Tries to Contain Virus as First U.S. Case Confirmed," Ibid., January 22, A13.

206. Lori Aratani and Lena H. Sun, "U.S. Screenings for Pathogen Expanded to Atlanta and Chicago Gateways," Ibid., January 23, A14.

207. Ibid.

208. Gerry Shih et al., "U.S. Steps up Efforts to Contain Coronavirus," Ibid., January 28, A1.

209. Erica Werner et al., "Administration Elevates Response to Coronavirus," Ibid., February 1.

210. Greg Miller and Ellen Nakashima, "President's Intelligence Briefing Book Repeatedly Cited Virus Early in Year," Ibid., April 28, A8; Philip Rucker and Robert Costa, "Trump's Crisis Response Short on Consistency, Long on Blame," Ibid., April 3.

211. Ashley Parker, Josh Dawsey, and Yasmeen Abutaleb, "10 Days of Distraction for Trump after Virus Warning," Ibid., September 17, A1.

212. Ibid.

213. David William, "How CDC Stumbled in Race for a Virus Test," Ibid., December 28; ibid.; Carolyn Y. Johnson and Laurie McGinley, "Faulty Test and Community-Transmission Case Highlight Containment Concerns," Ibid., February 28, A13. William Wan et al., "Spreading Coronavirus Kills First U.S. Patient," Ibid., March 1, 2020, A1."

214. Anne Gearan, Seung Min Kim, and Erica Werner, "Trump: Rivals Hype Crisis for Political Gain," Ibid., February 29.

215. Paul Farhi, "Western Journalists Are Pushed out of China," Ibid., September 17, C1.

216. Ibid.

217. Yasmeen Abutaleb and Erica Werner, "HHS Tells Congress It May Need $136 Million More," Ibid., February 4, A15.

218. Erica Werner, Jeff Stein, and Lena H. Sun, "White House Seeks $1.8 Billion in Emergency Funding for Virus Response," Ibid., February 25, A16.

219. Ibid.

220. Siobhán O'Grady et al., "'They've Been through a Lot': More Americans Flee Wuhan," Ibid., February 6, A1. Lena H. Sun et al., "A Scramble to Execute U.S. Order on Travel," Ibid., February 4."Officials rush to house quarantined passengers in effort to contain virus." Emily Woodruff and Staff Writer, "Mardi Gras 2020 Spawned up to 50k Coronavirus Cases, Likely from a Single Source, Study Says," *Nola*, February 9, 2021, https://www.nola.com/news/coronavirus/article_e4095910-6af1-11eb-a3bc-336456794a5b.html.

221. Nick Miroff et al., "States, Cities Close Businesses, Take Strict Measures as Cases Rise," *The Washington Post*, March 16, 2020, A1; Laura Meckler and Moriah Balingit, "Should Schools Shut? Reactions Vary," Ibid., March 12, A20. Faiz Siddiqui and Heather Kelly, "Bay Area's Remote-Work Expansion May Show What's to Come Elsewhere," Ibid., A11.

222. Dungca Nicole, Jenn Abelson, and John Sullivan, "'They Didn't Move Fast Enough'," Ibid., March 30, A1.

223. Toluse Olorunnipa, Seung Min Kim, and Scott Wilson, "Trump Voices New U.S. Containment Guidelines," Ibid., March 17, 2020.

224. Philip Rucker, "Governors Led as President Minimized Pandemic," Ibid., March 17.

225. Yasmeen Abutaleb and Rachel Weiner, "Experts Wary of Early Reopenings as Federal Distancing Rules End," Ibid., May 1, A4.

226. Philip Rucker, "Trump Takes Spotlight but Leaves Key Calls Largely to States, Cities," Ibid., March 25, A11.

227. Robert Costa and Aaron Gregg, "Trump's Lagging Response Widens Rift with City and State Leaders," Ibid., March 23, 2020, A1.

228. Joseph Guzman, "90 Percent of Americans Now Staying Home to Prevent Coronavirus Spread," *The Hill*, March 27, 2020, https://thehill.com/changing-america/well-being/prevention-cures/489813-majority-of-americans-staying-home-as-much-as; Brady Dennis, "As Virus Cases Surge, U.S. Prepares for a Grim Week," *The Washington Post*, March 24, 2020, A4.

229. Costa and Gregg, "Trump's Lagging Response Widens Rift with City and State Leaders."

230. Ashley Parker et al., "Scientists at Trump's Side Have to Toe a Difficult Line," Ibid., April 23; Lenny Bernstein, Josh Dawsey, and Yasmeen Abutaleb, "Friction between White House, CDC

Hobbles Response," Ibid., May 16, A5; Lena H. Sun, "Leading U.S. Public Health Agency - the CDC - Is Sidelined During Pandemic," Ibid., March 20, A9.

231. Toluse Olorunnipa, Nick Miroff, and Dan Lamothe, "Trump Invokes Wartime Powers to Bolster U.S. Response," Ibid., March 19, A6.

232. Nick Miroff, "Fema Struggles with Sprawling Crisis as Season of Natural Disasters Lurks," Ibid., March 25, A17.

233. Ibid.

234. Yasmeen Abutaleb et al., "70 Days of Denial, Delays and Dysfunction," Ibid., April 5, A1.

235. Erica Werner, Jeff Stein, and Rachael Bade, "McConnell Details Stance on Relief Bill," Ibid., July 7, A13.

236. Matt Zapotosky, "Applying Terrorism Statutes Is Explored," Ibid., March 26, 2020, A6.

237. Colby Itkowitz and Marissa J. Lang, "Death Toll Surges Past 2,000 in U.S," Ibid., March 29, A1; Jada Yuan and Ben Guarino, "The Military's Medical 'Relief Valves' Remain Mostly Empty in New York," Ibid., April 12, 2020, A7.

238. Jessie Bur, "On the Front Lines of COVID Response, This Agency Makes Safety Paramount," *Federal Times*, July 17, 2020, https://www.federaltimes.com/management/2020/07/17/on-the-front-lines-of-covid-response-this-agency-makes-safety-paramount/; Cynthia Geppert, "All Hands on Deck: The Federal Health Care Response to the COVID-19 National Emergency," *Federal Practitioner* 37, no. 8 (2020).

239. Shayna Jacobs et al., "Trump Approves Aid to N.Y. As State Braces for Shutdown," *The Washington Post*, March 23, 2020, A12.

240. Ibid.

241. Katie Zezima et al., "One in Five Americans Told to Stay Home as Authorities Brace for More Cases," Ibid., March 21, 2020, A6; ibid.; Ben Guarino and Isaac Stanley-Becker, "New York Scrambles to Prepare for Crisis's Peak," Ibid., April 2, A4.

242. Nick Miroff, "In Survey, U.S. Mayors Cite Need for Supplies," Ibid., March 28, A3.

243. Jacobs et al., "Trump Approves Aid to N.Y. As State Braces for Shutdown."

244. Philip Rucker et al., "As Deaths Mounted, Trump Fixated on Stalled Economy," Ibid., May 3, A1.

245. Matt Zapotosky, Kim Bellware, and Jacqueline Dupree, "U.S. Deaths Pass 3,700; Officials Say Worst Is yet to Come," Ibid., April 1, A4.

246. Philip Rucker, Josh Dawsey, and Yasmeen Abutaleb, "In Trump Plan, Governors Take on Burdens of Testing, Reopening," Ibid., April 17, A1; ibid.

247. Mike DeBonis, Chris Mooney, and Juliet Eilperin, "U.S. Testing 'Blueprint' Keeps Onus on States," Ibid., April 28, 2020; Karen DeYoung, "As Restrictions Begin to Ease, Battle over Testing Deepens," Ibid., April 21, A4; Karen DeYoung, Miriam Berger, and Katie Mettler, "Governors Chart Different Paths as They Consider Reopening States' Activities," Ibid., April 22.

248. Zapotosky, Bellware, and Dupree, "U.S. Deaths Pass 3,700; Officials Say Worst Is Yet to Come."

249. Juliet Eilperin et al., "In the Absence of a National Testing Strategy, States Are Going Their Own Way," Ibid., April 8, A9.

250. Lena H. Sun, William Wan, and Yasmeen Abutaleb, "Plans to Contain Virus Emerge in Bottom-up Effort," Ibid., April 11, A1.

251. Guzman, "90 Percent of Americans Now Staying Home to Prevent Coronavirus Spread"; Dennis, "As Virus Cases Surge, U.S. Prepares for a Grim Week"; Steve Thompson, "In Contact Tracing Race, Few States Reveal Speed," Ibid., July 5, A1; William Wan, Reed Albergotti, and Joel Achenbach, "Amid Restrictions, a Debate Arises: Save Lives or Save the Economy?," Ibid., March 25.

252. Ian Duncan and Felicia Sonmez, "Trump Extends Distancing Guidelines," Ibid., March 30.

253. Philip Rucker et al., "Trump May Ditch Safety Guidelines to Jolt Economy," Ibid., March 24.

254. Philip Rucker, "As Dark Reality Sets in, President Beats a Retreat on Reopening U.S," Ibid., March 30.

255. White House, "President Donald J. Trump Is Beginning the Next Phase in Our Fight against Coronavirus: Guidelines for Opening up America Again," White House Archives, April 16, 2020, https://trumpwhitehouse.archives.gov/briefings-statements/president-donald-j-trump-beginning-next -phase-fight-coronavirus-guidelines-opening-america/; Lena H. Sun and Josh Dawsey, "White House Reviews Expanded Guidance on Reopening Society in Phases," *The Washington Post*, April 8, 2020, A4; Rucker et al., "As Deaths Mounted, Trump Fixated on Stalled Economy."

256. Rucker, Dawsey, and Abutaleb, "In Trump Plan, Governors Take on Burdens of Testing, Reopening."

257. Toluse Olorunnipa, Shawn Boburg, and Arelis R. Hernández, "Rallies against Governors' Stay-at-Home Orders Grow," Ibid., April 18, A4.

258. Craig Timberg, Elizabeth Dwoskin, and Moriah Balingit, "Protests Spread, Fueled by Economic Woes and Internet Subcultures," Ibid., May 3, A1; Anne Gearan, Felicia Sonmez, and Erica Werner, "Administration Describes Dash for a Vaccine Usable by January," Ibid., May 1, A4; Mike DeBonis, "'Open It up' Bloc in Gop Attacks Restrictions as Others in Party Urge Caution," Ibid., April 18.

259. Isaac Stanley-Becker and Rachel Weiner, "In Deciding to Reopen, Some Governors Reject Counsel of Their Medical Experts," Ibid., April 24, A7; Griff Witte et al., "Warily, U.S. Cracks Doors Open," Ibid., April 26, A1; Stanley-Becker and Weiner, "In Deciding to Reopen, Some Governors Reject Counsel of Their Medical Experts"; Matt Zapotosky, Marisa Iati, and Josh Wagner, "With Fewer Restrictions, States Tiptoe toward Reopening," Ibid., May 5, A4.

260. Toluse Olorunnipa, Griff Witte, and Lenny Bernstein, "Trump Applauds States Reopening Ahead of Guidance," Ibid., A1.

261. Alex M. II Azar, "We Have to Reopen - for Health Reasons," Ibid., May 22, A21; Lenny Bernstein et al., "CDC Offers Scant Guidelines for Reopening Safely," Ibid., May 15, A1; Isaac Stanley-Becker, William Wan, and Ben Guarino, "States Reopening Lack Benchmarks for Reimposing Rules," Ibid., May 16, A7.

262. Michael Scherer and Ashley Parker, "As Trump Pushes Reopening, Democrats Embrace Caution," Ibid., May 23, A6.

263. Arelis R. Hernández, Stead S. Frances, and Ben Guarino, "Texas, Florida Walk Back Reopenings," Ibid., June 27, A1; Joel Achenbach et al., "As Hot Spots Erupt, Researchers Warn of 2nd Wave in South," Ibid., May 21; Anne Gearan, Derek Hawkins, and Siobhán O'Grady, "States' Early Reopenings Fueled 50% Rise in Cases in June," Ibid., July 2, A6.

264. Davidson, "Former CDC Director Freiden Says U.S. Has Become a 'Laggard' in Global Health."

265. Toluse Olorunnipa, "Trump Messaging Sows Confusion in Outbreak Response," Ibid., July 14, A5.

266. Derek Hawkins, Marisa Iati, and Jacqueline Dupree, "U.S. Case Count Soars Past 5 Million," Ibid., August 10, A2; Olorunnipa, "Trump Messaging Sows Confusion in Outbreak Response."

267. Anne Gearan, Brittany Shammas, and Lateshia Beachum, "White House Says Virus Is under Control Despite Surges," Ibid., June 30, A8.

268. Ibid.

269. Yasmeen Abutaleb, Taylor Telford, and Josh Dawsey, "Experts Upset by Trump's Virus Testing Comments," Ibid., June 22, A1; Toluse Olorunnipa, Josh Dawsey, and Yasmeen Abutaleb, "Major Surge in Infections Exposes U.S. Failures," Ibid., June 28.

270. Toluse Olorunnipa and Josh Dawsey, "Bad Numbers Push Trump to Bring Back Virus Briefing," Ibid., July 21.

271. Toluse Olorunnipa, "Virus Briefing Returns with New Approach," Ibid., July 22.

272. Derek Hawkins and Marissa Lati, "Birx Warns of 'New Phase' of Pandemic and Calls for Greater Precautions," Ibid., August 3, A9; Ashley Parker, Josh Dawsey, and Yasmeen Abutaleb, "Top

Virus Official Is New Target for Trump," Ibid., August 4, A1; Ashley Parker et al., "Amid Election Fight, Trump Tunes out Spike in Cases," Ibid., November 15.

273. Griff Witte, "Growing Chorus Pushes for Renewed Shutdown Orders," Ibid., July 10.

274. Wan et al., "Spreading Coronavirus Kills First U.S. Patient," "A man in his 50s with an underlying health condition became the first person in the United States to die of coronavirus infection." Zapotosky, Bellware, and Dupree, "U.S. Deaths Pass 3,700; Officials Say Worst Is yet to Come."

275. Gearan, Shammas, and Beachum, "White House Says Virus Is under Control Despite Surges"; Lena H. Sun and Joel Achenbach, "CDC: Coronavirus May Have Infected 24 Million in U.S," Ibid., June 26, A1; Matt Zapotosky, Isaac Stanley-Becker, and John Wagner, "Single-Day Death Toll in U.S. Tops 1,000 as Trump Insists Country Will Recover," Ibid., April 3, A3.

276. Emma Brown, Beth Reinhard, and Aaron C. Davis, "Experts: Americans Are Dying but Aren't Being Included in Count," Ibid., April 6, A1.

277. Emma Brown, Beth Reinhard, and Reis Thebault, "States Vary in Deciding Which Deaths Count toward Virus Toll," Ibid., April 17.

278. Ibid.

279. Ashley Parker et al., "Trump Tested Positive for Coronavirus before First Debate with Biden, Three Former Aides Say," Ibid., December 1, 2021.

280. Joel Achenbach, Brittany Shammas, and Jacqueline Dupree, "As Cases Spike, Death Toll Inches Up," Ibid., October 31, 2020.

281. William Wan and Mark Guarino, "Officials Weigh New Restrictions, but Face Angry Backlash, as Cases Surge," Ibid., November 14, A9.

282. David J. Lynch, "Raging Virus Triggers New Shutdown Orders and Economy Braces for Fresh Wave of Pain," Ibid., November 15, A1.

283. Hannah Knowles, "States Enacting New Virus Measures," Ibid., A3.

284. Moriah Balingit, "School Leaders Face Closures Again as Cases Rise," Ibid., November 22; Brittany Shammas and Reis Thebault, "Fauci Warns of 'Surge Upon a Surge' as Air Travel Hits Highs During Holidays," Ibid., December 29.

285. Brittany Shammas et al., "Mounting Cases Push Hospitals to Brink," *The Washington Post*, December 17, 2020, A1; Griff Witte, "N.M. Activates 'Crisis Care' to Free up Icu Beds," *The Washington Post*, December 11, 2020, A9.

286. Yasmeen Abutaleb et al., "How Trump's Pandemic Missteps Led to a Dark Winter," Ibid., December 20, A1.

287. Ibid.

288. Glenn Kessler, "Tracking the President's False or Misleading Claims About Threat from the Virus," Ibid., March 22, A4; Philip Rucker, Yasmeen Abutaleb, and Ashley Parker, "Messaging Undermines U.S. Efforts on Virus," Ibid., March 4, A1.

289. Gearan, Sonmez, and Werner, "Administration Describes Dash for a Vaccine Usable by January."

290. Christopher Rowland, "Vaccine Politics, Skewed by Trump's Polarizing Approach, Will Complicate Biden's Path to a Unified Pandemic Response," Ibid., December 13, A7.

291. Christopher Rowland et al., "Vaccine Rollout Smaller Than Pledged," Ibid., December 6, A1.

292. David Nakamura, "Competing Events Highlight Trump's, Biden's Different Approaches to Pandemic," Ibid., December 9, A22.

Chapter 4

The Advantages of Populist Authoritarianism?

China's COVID Fight

The Chinese story starts as most observers probably would have expected from an authoritarian regime. When Dr. Li Wenliang sent out warnings about the virus to an online chat group at the end of December 2019, local authorities wary of acknowledging a public threat immediately jumped. Police quickly tracked down Dr. Li and forced him to sign a statement admitting that his actions amounted to "illegal behavior."[1] Of course, this did nothing to stop the spread of the virus. Nor did it spare Dr. Li, who returned to work at the Central Hospital of Wuhan, from more acute dangers. By the beginning of February, as China's COVID response was shifting to high gear, Dr. Li lay dying from COVID in the very place the global pandemic had festered under the cover of authoritarianism.

With Dr. Li's death came a wave of online grief and anger around the country, accompanied by demands for greater transparency.[2] As angry mourners took to the internet, Chinese authorities lost their advantage in the authoritarian information war. Officials rushed to cleanse websites of any information about Dr. Li and remove his name from trending topics pages, but they were overwhelmed.[3] The central government capitulated by sending a team to Wuhan to investigate Dr. Li's death.[4] Weeks later, it issued a report excoriating local authorities for reprimanding him and promising compensation to his family.[5] By August, the Communist Party had gone from punishing whistleblowers like Dr. Li to selectively praising them for their willingness to "tell an inconvenient truth."[6]

The story of Dr. Li is emblematic of China's COVID experience. It started with a large-scale coverup that lasted until a wave of human misery and fury made the disaster simply too large to conceal. China's populist leader, Xi Jinping, then did a complete turnaround, pivoting to a full-scale, resource-intensive response designed to demonstrate the power and legitimacy of his leadership. His message was clear: China's leaders would resort to extreme measures to protect their population and strengthen their rule. The authoritarian state provided Xi with a means to follow through on this promise and a way to ensure the correct message was broadcast.

In the end, China's lockdowns, described in chapter 3, were brutal but effective. Chinese leaders staunched the pandemic in ways that few would have predicted, and even fewer had the power and will to match. But the path Chinese leaders took was not a foregone conclusion. They could easily have chosen to keep their people in the factories, maintain their economic might, and preserve the image of Party strength. This would have inevitably involved increased levels of repression, a far different propaganda message, and the acceptance of perhaps millions more deaths. But few would doubt that leaders of the Party state, who had a history of weathering disasters of their own making, including the Cultural Revolution and the inaptly named Great Leap Forward, could have pulled it off and maintained their tight grip on power.

That China's leaders chose not to follow this route seems to be a testament to the strength of populism.[7] Xi Jinping had amassed power over the preceding several years as a leader looking out for the common man. His attacks on poverty and corruption, in particular, endeared him to a population frustrated with everyday humiliations. According to official statistics, Xi slashed the number of people living in poverty from nearly 99 million when he took over in 2012 to just 5.5 million in 2019.[8] His anti-corruption campaign was equally aggressive, involving the breakup of a reported 40,000 criminal cells and corrupt companies, as well as the punishment of more than 50,000 Communist Party members who enabled them.[9]

The reality that such cheery poverty statistics were of questionable reliability, or that many caught up in the anti-corruption drive may have been guilty of little more than appearing to be a threat to Xi, is not the point. Xi was a populist determined to use public legitimacy to retain his hold on power, including a push to stay beyond the normal two terms.[10] And his policies were tremendously popular.[11]

Once it became clear that COVID represented a real threat to his populist legitimacy, Xi used the mechanisms of authoritarianism to act in ways we would expect other authoritarians to be loath to do. His long, harsh lockdowns were a show of resolve that only a non-democrat could securely implement. His single-party state, composed of millions of loyal party members and powerful institutions, gave him the power to rapidly mobilize. And his control over the country's pocketbook allowed for the quick diversion of state funds to assist people. Xi acted with a zeal many other authoritarians would lack, while pursuing the sorts of stringent policies less politically secure democrats would likely run from.

It was not just what Xi did, but how he did it, that highlights potential advantages of populist authoritarianism in dealing with disaster. Xi carefully created an image of himself as a leader who was simultaneously in charge of highly effective policies yet distanced from the collateral pain those policies caused. He paid special attention to three tasks: controlling the narrative, including highlighting his own importance in policy victories; exposing scapegoats for policy shortcomings; and demonstrating the superiority of the Chinese political system. Authoritarianism gave Xi a way to do this. Populism, it seems, gave him a reason.

INSIDE XI'S RESPONSE: THE (POPULIST) AUTHORITARIAN ADVANTAGE?

Lacking the constraints of more democratic countries, the Chinese government eventually threw the full weight of the state into the COVID response.[12] The primary way China's leaders managed to staunch the infection rate was through a zero-COVID policy that resulted in repeated, large-scale lockdowns. But they also flooded hard-hit regions with medical aid. This was most visible in the city of Wuhan, ground zero of the outbreak, and the broader province of Hubei, in which Wuhan is located. For instance, by the end of the first week in February, Chinese authorities had sent more than 11,000 medical personnel to Wuhan.[13] Just two weeks later, 30,000 medical personnel had been brought into the province, where dozens of new medical facilities had been constructed.[14] By early March, more than 40,000 medical workers had swarmed the region.[15]

Outside reports, based on social media posts, indicate the military played a critical role in the intervention. This included shutting down transportation networks and dispatching patrols to maintain the quarantine.[16] The military also constructed new medical facilities and injected more than 10,000 military medics into Wuhan, where armed forces ran hospitals with thousands of beds.[17] And party leaders tapped into the military's logistical capabilities, using the military to transport thousands of tons of household goods and medical supplies into the region.

The party system also mobilized, with branches of the party assigned tasks such as monitoring the health of residents and enforcing quarantines.[18] The local administration in Wuhan, for example, dispatched tens of thousands of officials and party members into neighborhoods around the city to disinfect, perform temperature checks, and deliver food.[19] Meanwhile, the national government steered raw materials to factories that began producing key medical equipment 24/7.[20] (Worker shortages still forced the Chinese to import significant amounts of equipment from abroad.)[21] The state press praised the 41 million Communist Party members who it claimed had donated a combined $750 million for prevention and control of the virus.[22]

The dark side to this rosy picture was the severe distress experienced by residents in infection zones, including a great many stranded far from home since lockdowns came during a peak holiday travel period.[23] Residents saw food and other basic goods disappearing from local shelves and skyrocketing prices for whatever remained.[24] But despite some local protests, the Chinese Communist Party was secure in its approach. During the summer 2020 lockdown in Xinjiang, a fruit seller complained to a foreign publication that "the controls are too strict," before adding, "It's useless to have opinions . . . People dare not speak."[25]

The lockdowns China relied on to staunch the contagion went well beyond what we saw in most democratic states. One important reason for this is that the Chinese authoritarian government had extraordinarily high levels of both autonomy and capacity. High levels of political autonomy meant the political ability to override the short-term interests of the population in favor of a longer-term approach to the pandemic. This presented in the form of draconian lockdowns—a bitter medicine—during the height of the pandemic. Later, this high degree of autonomy allowed Xi to carefully balance health needs and economic demands during the country's spring reopening. Unlike in the United States, where regional leaders were pressured from above to reopen the economy as quickly as possible, Xi warned economic actors as the pandemic waned to carefully "push forward work resumption while ensuring the safety and health of their workers."[26]

China's high level of capacity was demonstrated by its sheer mobilization power. But it also included the technological ability needed to monitor and enforce strict lockdowns.[27] These same technologies, including tracking citizen movements through their cell phones, also allowed China to swiftly halt new outbreaks once the winter wave had receded. And where it was deemed safe to reopen, Chinese leaders actively utilized state capacity to ameliorate economic disruptions. For instance, as localized quarantines staunched the availability of goods, workers, or transportation networks,[28] the central government began connecting available, healthy workers to needy employers and even employed special trains to transport hundreds of thousands to industrial locations.[29]

Government intervention took other forms throughout the pandemic as well. Amidst shortages and rising prices, the central government provided nearly $1 billion in monthly subsidies to citizens,[30] including $267 million targeted at low-income people[31] and special allowances for other vulnerable groups, such as orphans.[32] The state also released tons of its emergency pork reserves to stabilize quickly rising food prices.[33] To stimulate the economy, the central government supported a plan for extended weekends, and localities distributed vouchers and digital coupons to jumpstart the economy by getting consumers out in force.[34] China's GDP began to grow again, officially by 3.2 percent in the second quarter[35] and 4.9 percent in the third.[36] Although the precarious state of the global economy kept China's economic future uncertain,[37] the Politburo boasted at the end of the year that it was the only G-20 country to post economic growth in 2020.[38]

Critical for Xi was the appearance that his broader populist agenda continued to progress throughout the pandemic. At the top of this list was his promise to eliminate poverty.[39] The 2020 fund for poverty alleviation amounted to $19.7 billion at the end of March.[40] On the last day of the year, state media reported that the last fifty-two counties had been removed from the poverty list, "despite the unprecedented impacts brought about by the COVID-19 epidemic."[41] Reality continued to conflict with this picture (one farmer commented, "Even if you aren't out of poverty, the country will say you're out of poverty.").[42] But China's leaders were bent on demonstrating that even in the face of a disaster, and perhaps especially in the face of one, they were intent on pursuing their populist agenda.

LEADERSHIP: RULING FROM AFAR

On a personal level, Xi Jinping was not shy about taking credit for the state's successes in fighting COVID over the course of 2020.[43] But the state press framed Xi in a very distinct way: distant yet in control, a commander thinking big strategy while his minions capably executed his orders on the ground. One state assessment seeking to quantify Xi's activity during the pandemic in its first year praised Xi for the many high-level meetings he chaired and attended related to the response. The drawn-out list was literally presented as such. It included seventeen "meetings of the Standing Committee of the Political Bureau of the CPC Central Committee, four meetings of the Political Bureau of the CPC Central Committee, and leadership meetings on law-based governance, cyberspace affairs, foreign affairs and the deepening of reform amid the epidemic."[44] As if to emphasize Xi's on-the-ground work, the report also credited him for carrying out nine inspections related to the epidemic and for effectively mobilizing the military.[45]

This busy agenda might surprise those following early events as they unfolded. Apparently uneager to bring attention to the outbreak before he felt he had no better choice, as any populist or authoritarian would be, Xi spent the bulk of January quietly avoiding any discussion of the new virus. In fact, he made no public comments at all about the virus until January 20, three weeks after his government had warned the WHO of COVID's emergence. Only then did Xi reportedly call for "the prompt release of information on the epidemic and enhanced international cooperation."[46] Once Wuhan went into lockdown on January 23, he took on the role of general, promising his people that "we're sure to be able to win in this battle."[47]

Despite his public silence in the early weeks of the pandemic, the state press went to great lengths to show that Xi was actually actively engaged in stemming the new virus from the start. "I have at every moment monitored the spread of the epidemic and progress in efforts to curtail it, constantly issuing oral orders and also instructions," Xi was quoted as saying.[48] But his claims, including one that he had already "issued demands about the efforts to prevent and control" the virus to his Politburo back on January 7, only add evidence that Xi purposely hid the outbreak from his people.[49]

The depiction of Xi's activities in a September state press series called "Chronicle of Xi's leadership" paints him not as a shirker but as a martyr bearing the burdens of his people. By fall, Xi was attesting to his own courage in locking down Hubei, propounding that without his "resolute action ... there would be trouble."[50] The retrospective reporting continues: "Xi did not sleep well on Chinese New Year's Eve as he shouldered the heavy responsibility to fight the epidemic."[51] During a January 25 Politburo Standing Committee meeting, Xi reportedly "took the lead in making a donation to support epidemic control efforts" and made a series of statements about the need to detect, quarantine, treat, and save lives.[52] In the words of his state press chroniclers, "Xi dedicated himself to leading epidemic control efforts and gave instructions every day at the height of the outbreak."[53] The authors praised Xi, who "personally took charge of the response, marshaling national resources to fight the 'invisible enemy.'"[54]

It is important to emphasize that these accounts emerged months after China had made it through the worst of the pandemic. As events were transpiring, Xi appeared less eager to be on the front pages. Instead, he carefully delegated responsibility for the outbreak response in ways that allowed him to maintain the mantle of leadership while simultaneously distancing himself from the negative phenomena associated with the response. Xi's was a classic case of top-down delegation. When it came to everyday operations, Xi passed the baton to Premier Li Keqiang, sold in state media as "entrusted by Xi Jinping" to take the lead in fighting the outbreak.[55] Li was shown visiting hard-hit hospitals in Wuhan, where he spoke with beleaguered medical staff and urged workers to erect new medical facilities.

Xi inserted Beijing's authority in Wuhan by tasking Vice-Premier Sun Chunlan with leading the central government's initiative there.[56] The vice-premier traveled to Hubei at the end of January to push local party leaders to ensure adequate citizen outreach on the virus and sufficient food and other daily necessities for those under lockdown.[57] When Sun personally took charge of Wuhan in early February, she ordered medical workers to check the temperature of every resident in the city and then interview close contacts of anyone infected. "There must be no deserters, or they will be nailed to the pillar of historical shame forever," Sun ominously warned.[58] Under Sun's eye, the local administration in Wuhan dispatched tens of thousands of officials and party members into neighborhoods around the city, disinfecting, checking temperatures, and delivering food.[59] It took just days to complete Sun's order to check Wuhan's 11 million residents for COVID.[60]

While Premier Li and Vice-Premier Sun took the formal lead in the epidemic response, Xi took actions carefully designed to show he remained at the helm, central to the idea of top-down delegation.[61] He issued an instruction to Party organizations to "unite the people in resolutely implementing the decisions and arrangements of the CPC Central Committee"[62] and promised WHO representatives at the end of January that he was personally in charge.[63] State media reported at the start of February that Xi "has called multiple meetings, heard reports and made important instructions on the prevention and control work."[64] This became boilerplate language in the state press. Xi was praised for his "strong leadership," for calling meetings, taking in field accounts, and issuing orders.[65] He was hailed for his "timely strategy" and "political courage."[66]

Xi also played to the people himself, publicly assuring them that they were at the center of these policies. He called on all Party officials "to unite the people" and "[to keep] in mind the people's interest are the highest priority."[67] He later explained that this involved "closer monitoring and assessment of opinion," but also leading the public, "proactively speaking out and giving positive guidance."[68]

This lofty language positioned Xi as the astute and caring commander issuing orders to his eager and able implementers around the country. Unlike in Russia and the United States, where regional leaders were tasked with running operations on the ground themselves, China's central government promised to "exercise overall command" with lower levels assigned to closely "follow the leadership and instructions of the central authorities."[69] There is evidence, this did not consistently work. Local governments sometimes functioned in informational vacuums and took measures they thought most prudent or most politically palatable, resulting in a patchwork of policies that were sometimes upended by higher-level actors.[70] Despite this, the official narrative was that "All jumped into action after Xi, as the leadership core of the CPC Central Committee and the Party, issued his orders."[71]

By delegating tasks to other members of his government, Xi could insulate himself from such breakdowns that otherwise challenged his legitimacy. Delegation also protected Xi from the painful impact of those policies, particularly lockdowns that were implemented just as the central government ordered. For example, on the day that Vice-Premier Sun announced (presumably at Xi's behest) harsh, house-to-house inspections in Wuhan, leading to the forced removal of anyone found sick, Xi avoided any public appearance.[72] Instead, Xi was later shown visiting a treatment center in less hard-hit Beijing and then visiting a residential community nearby.[73] There, state media reported, he "chatted with residents in a street, asking them about the prices of vegetables" and again reassured them that "we can prevail over the epidemic."[74]

Only in the waning days of the outbreak did Xi feel confident enough to stage high-profile victory laps. One of the most important was Xi's unannounced visit to Wuhan around mid-March, officially sold as a work trip or, in the oft-repeated words of the Chinese state press, "an inspection of the epidemic prevention and control work."[75] Unlike Premier Li's and Vice-Premier Sun's visits, which ushered in a period of struggle and uncertainty, Xi's trip was associated with recovery.[76] As Xi strolled between apartment buildings, he yelled out cheers that heralded the impending end of the world's first COVID lockdown. "Let's keep it up! Hold on for a little longer!" Xi exclaimed.[77] Then, speaking at a symposium, Xi pressed local officials to increase the supply of fish, a popular local food source, to residents still under quarantine.[78]

Xi's populism never extended to an attack on science, which Xi instead called "mankind's most powerful weapon against diseases."[79] With the power to make decisions that go essentially unquestioned, China's top authorities operated in tandem with state experts on the National Health Commission (NHC), who were the public face of the pandemic response. These medical experts issued reports, directives, and official plans, all the way from the initial fourteen-day quarantine to the inclusion of asymptomatic cases in official tallies and the later decision to focus on imported cases.[80]

Rather than consistently refer to NHC rules as a constraint or question their wisdom, as witnessed by some more democratic populists, the Chinese leaders functioned in harmony with NHC recommendations. This juxtaposition of expertise and leadership was manifested in Chinese news stories and commentaries showing both domestic and international expert praise for the government's effective and transparent response.[81] The NHC, in turn, credited the "strong leadership" of the Party, "with Comrade Xi Jinping at its core."[82] Not surprisingly, international concerns, including over China's role in the birth of the pandemic, did not make it to print.[83]

Importantly, Xi did not try to present a perfect record or downplay the tragedy that had unfolded, as other authoritarians might have. When a national day of mourning was declared in April, Xi led the process, standing in silence surrounded by other leaders at a compound in Beijing.[84] During the delayed annual "two sessions" meeting, where party leaders traditionally laud their previous year's achievements and plans for the coming year,[85] Premier Li noted that "many weak links have been exposed" in public health emergency management[86] and Xi stressed the need for specific reforms, including better monitoring and early warning, and a revamped legal and regulatory framework for public health emergencies. A white paper put out by China's NHC seconded the need for more investment in public health and some structural changes.[87] This self-reflection came with little risk in such a closed regime. The state press praised the authorities' "courage to identify and fix governance shortcomings" and claimed this and other steps had earned them public trust.[88]

At the same time, Xi was unrepentant, as the next two years of periodic lockdowns would demonstrate. He was clearly playing the long game, using the safety of his political office to take whatever steps would curb the pandemic, as unpleasant and temporarily disruptive as they might be. At an award ceremony in the fall, Xi emphasized that "[we must] always give [protecting] people's life top priority."[89] This theme hit home in November television broadcasts intertwining the "heroic deeds of party members" with Wuhan's "warriors in white coats" and showing Xi issuing instructions to quash the epidemic.[90]

XI'S INFORMATION WAR

Just as it is difficult to imagine other autocrats with the will to take such high cost moves for so long, it is hard to conceive democrats politically able to maintain such tough measures. As demonstrated above, part of the reason this worked was that Xi could carefully write his own role in the disaster. And this, in good part, stemmed from his high level of control over the media landscape.

As a populist authoritarian, Xi, from the start of his rule, tightened his grip on an already highly controlled information space.[91] One particular area of focus was digital information. To reign in cyber news and discussions, Xi created in 2014 the Cyberspace Administration of China (CAC), whose goal was to censor unwanted information and propagate more favorable narratives.[92] By the time the pandemic hit, the government's "internet police" was estimated to number one per 10,000 people in some regions.[93]

As information about the mysterious novel coronavirus began streaming out of Wuhan in early winter, social media pages overflowed with grim snippets of information. After weeks of chasing online communities Chinese authorities in late January presented a sterilized version of events, rejecting "conspiracy theories" about a government coverup and arguing that with social media, "government agencies cannot hide information even if they want to."[94] Once it became abundantly clear the cat was out of the bag and could not be corralled back in, authorities swiveled to an approach that involved openly, but strategically, reporting on unfolding events. Local officials in Hubei, implicated in the most egregious deception campaign, promised to "eliminate any cover-up, delay, or false reporting of infection cases."[95]

But these authorities could not hold back the wave of distrusting citizens taking to the internet to glean and share illicit information. The Party's biggest test arguably came in early February with the death of Dr. Li Wenliang, described above. As angry mourners took to the internet, authorities pressured websites to eliminate information about Dr. Li and remove his name from trending topics pages.[96] The CAC issued a directive to local offices to "Pay particular attention to posts with pictures of candles, people wearing masks, an entirely black image or other efforts to escalate or hype the incident."[97]

Authorities had their work cut out for them. As the virus took hold in Wuhan, blogs and other online spaces were littered with images and descriptions of exhausted medical personnel and desperate patients.[98] Amidst increased tensions and a growing response, authorities worked to control the message in ways democrats could never master. Senior party leaders said that to maintain social harmony, they would have to "strengthen control over online media," turning attention from outstanding problems to "showing the Chinese people's unity."[99] In Xi's words, tighter controls over online discussion were essential to maintaining "positive energy" and social stability.[100] Authorities issued thousands of directives and memos aimed at cracking down on online "rumors" and redirecting the narrative.[101]

With more internet users (854 million) than anywhere else on the planet, Chinese authorities turned to their "Great Firewall" to stifle discussion by censoring, deleting, or suspending social media accounts.[102] What rapidly emerged was an enormous cat-and-mouse game. Between the end of December and mid-February, the government censored on social media sites terms such as "pneumonia," "disease control and prevention," and "virus."[103] Weibo posts were censored, and WeChat suspended hundreds of accounts for spreading false information. In turn, some of those banned shifted to a new topic category on Weibo, where their complaints were viewed millions more times before authorities caught up with them and removed, them.[104]

Those caught expressing defiance or countering the false state narrative faced significant risks. Internet police were tasked with monitoring online posts, but they were also dispatched to the homes of online critics to take them back to the station, where they were forced to sign loyalty pledges and recant what they wrote.[105] As these officers searched out critics, others deleted their posts and those of their followers. After criticizing the Chinese response and demanding Xi's resignation in a blog post, for instance, one outspoken rights activist was arrested and not allowed visitors.[106] Forced quarantine, or applying political sanctions under the guise of counter-epidemic measures, was also a convenient way to hold dissidents in isolation with no contact to their families, amounting to what one foreign human rights researcher called "de facto enforced disappearance."[107]

As the Chinese leadership struggled to dominate messaging, they simultaneously found themselves tussling with foreign states over information control. During the winter COVID peak, Chinese leaders fought back against outside reports that the case rate was actually climbing, even quoting international authorities in their rebuttals,[108] and denied concealing the true extent of cases. "We should discard the differences of ideology and social systems, take full account of the humanitarian spirit, devote our time and energy in fighting against the pandemic and saving lives, so as to defeat the pandemic as soon as possible," said a foreign ministry spokesperson.[109]

Much of the influence campaign involved countering external criticisms or, in the words of one state commentary, Westerners "peddling one wicked theory after another."[110] State media in early April published a "rumor busters" article pressing the case that China's rapid reaction bought the world precious time to prepare, time which, they pointedly noted, many in the West squandered.[111] "China has fulfilled its due international obligations and taken drastic and effective measures to safeguard global health security," ran another commentary.[112]

Amidst the increase in Chinese propaganda, the U.S. State Department notified China in February that five Chinese state news agencies, Xinhua, China Global Television Network (CGTN), China Radio, China Daily, and The People's Daily, would be treated as foreign government agencies rather than independent news outlets.[113] Then, at the start of March, the United States announced it would halve the current number of Chinese journalists allowed to function in the country.[114] China condemned the U.S. move as remnants of "a Cold War mindset and ideological bias"[115] and, pointing to President Trump's acrid relationship with his own domestic press, accused the United States of allowing press freedom only "for deep-pockets, vested interest groups and the powerful."[116]

U.S. restrictions on Chinese state news in America gave Chinese authorities an excuse to further reduce accountability by cracking down on major U.S. news sources in China.[117] They started with the expulsion of three Wall Street Journal reporters (who had published an editorial entitled "China Is the Real Sick Man of Asia")[118] and then followed with the expulsion of New York Times and Washington Post reporters.[119] State media called the expulsions "a reciprocal, necessary, legitimate and justified move"[120] in response to the "escalating oppression of Chinese media" in the United States.[121] This tit-for-tat pattern continued over the year, with the United States limiting work visas for some Chinese journalists in May and then designating Chinese media outlets as foreign missions in October, followed by new Chinese restrictions on American media in the fall.[122]

On the home front, Chinese media spun retrospectives emphasizing sacrifice and unity.[123] Already in late February, as China hit 79,000 cases and 2,700 deaths, Xi flipped the narrative of suffering by promising a book documenting China's experiences so others could learn from them.[124] The hundreds of thousands of "cybersoldiers" monitoring social media were also tasked with posting pro-Party messages.[125] Hundreds of state-sponsored journalists were similarly charged with drafting emotional stories about frontline workers to turn attention from potential state failures to emotive and celebratory human interest pieces.[126]

The result was that the Chinese media was peppered with comments from domestic and foreign medical experts praising the government's effective and transparent response.[127] The Party was depicted as leading the capable response, one documentary highlighting "how Party members and medical workers have braved the virus to make their contributions to the fight."[128] The Publicity Department of the Communist Party of China (CPC) Central Committee released a 6-part documentary highlighting these contributions.[129]

Some of these efforts went beyond hyperbole and into overt deception. In the spring, for example, the foreign ministry posted a video of Italians apparently cheering China as aid arrived, even playing the Chinese national anthem.[130] The video, played heavily on state television, was replete with falsities, apparently splicing disparate scenes unassociated with the Chinese (such as Italians clapping for their own medical workers in other parts of the country) in what one fact-checker called an "artfully created montage."[131]

These efforts did not go unopposed. There were reports of local Chinese reporters pressing for the truth in their writing, challenging the official narrative.[132] One strategy these journalists utilized was to focus their reporting on mistakes made by local, rather than national, officials, or share sources with rival publications in case their own stories were suppressed.[133] Even when censors did take down critical stories, online readers frequently managed to download and recode them in emojis or vague language more difficult for censors to spot when posted elsewhere.[134] And sometimes these words even appeared to compel local authorities to change their approach, demonstrating a surprising degree of regime responsiveness.[135]

Thanks to social media and independent-minded reporters, state leaders could never totally control the COVID story line. For instance, as infections dried up, desperate Hubei residents, concerned about abandoned pets and family members with non-COVID illnesses, adopted the hashtag "When will Hubei be unblocked," read at least 100 million times on Weibo.[136] They spoke of frustration about paying rent for homes they could not return to, expressing worry about pets left alone for weeks and concern for loved ones suffering from non-COVID medical conditions that medical personnel still would not prioritize.[137] In August, the Xinjiang government also faced complaints on Weibo from residents who were stuck at home for more than a month during a summer outbreak there.[138]

These successes did not come without cost. Some bloggers and reporters posting on conditions through social media went missing; others were openly arrested.[139] One who was arrested in May was months later found guilty of "picking quarrels and provoking trouble," and sentenced to four years in prison.[140] Punishment was not limited to the usual suspects. One popular real estate developer with strong connections to Party elites published an essay on social media criticizing the top leadership's handling of COVID, referring to Xi as a power-hungry "clown" and excoriating the Party for silencing whistleblowers. In return, officials expelled him from the Party and launched an investigation into "serious violations of discipline and law," "colluding with his children to accumulate wealth without restraint," and "smearing the party and country's image."[141]

Nor was the Party state the sole agent of rule enforcement. One older Chinese novelist who gained millions of fans by documenting the everyday realities of seventy-six days in lockdown, including noting response failures, eventually had her diary published as an English-language e-book, "Wuhan Diary: Dispatches from a Quarantined City."[142] This time, it was Chinese nationalists, harnessed by the Party, who exacted retribution, attacking the sixty-something on social media for smearing China's name, and labeling her a traitor.[143] Reporters also faced flak from citizens who, influenced by Xi's brand of populist nationalism, accused the wayward press of sullying China's reputation.[144]

The Chinese government was not only interested in influencing domestic opinion. Chinese leaders also used the state apparatus to wage an active disinformation campaign, including the use of fake social media accounts and efforts to manipulate and strengthen pre-existing political divisions.[145] State-owned CGTN, for example, produced a video shown in the Middle East pointing to "some new facts" indicating the coronavirus may have actually originated from American participants visiting Wuhan in October for a military sports competition.[146]

The Chinese also took to Twitter, blocked in China itself, but frequently used by Chinese diplomats and Communist Party members to push content abroad.[147] In June, Twitter announced it had uncovered and deleted 23,750 accounts "highly engaged" in spreading misinformation, "spreading geopolitical narratives favorable to the Communist Party of China,"[148] as well as another 150,000 accounts used to retweet and like the content.[149] Much of this was aimed at influencing readers about weeks of Hong Kong protests, but some focused on the COVID story.

Even as China was accused of spreading misinformation, the Chinese foreign ministry said China was actually the victim of "disinformation, rumors and slanders spread by people with ulterior motives"[150] intent on blaming China for the pandemic. In August, China's Cyberspace Administration released the United Rumor Debunking Platform, an app that could be run on various platforms, including social media, in order to "quickly fact-check online rumors by providing access to relevant articles from official news media."[151]

SCAPEGOATING: ACCOUNTABILITY
AS A SAFETY VALVE

Xi's Party thus used its high degree of information control as a means to strengthen its own power and guarantee it more time to act resolutely. But as the Chinese attacks on both internal and external actors indicates, one important aspect of sculpting China's COVID narrative was to spread blame for the disaster. Relatedly, national authorities could also use disciplinary actions against lower-level officials in order to shed their own blame for policy shortcomings and demonstrate the Party's popular legitimacy. Criticisms, firings, and imprisonments of regional and local functionaries served as a pressure release valve for Xi's government as well as an additional way to ensure the national authorities were the heroes in the COVID story.

The irony, of course, is that some of these local failings resulted precisely from the fact that lower-level officials withheld critical information for fear of retribution from above. One of the central reasons the virus festered so long in Hubei was that local authorities knew reporting negative, destabilizing news to those higher up on the political ladder amounted to a political death sentence.[152] These threats of intimidation spread down the political hierarchy so that even hospital administrators, accountable to local government leaders, preferred to hold their tongues.[153] So long as there was any hope the problem could be contained and handled quietly without provoking the wrath of superiors, better not to poke the dragon.

In Hubei's case, it was only after Beijing officials heard about cases from whistleblowers and leaked local documents that the local government acknowledged an outbreak, and even then a much smaller one than was actually occurring.[154] Despite the fact that Xi claims to have already been in the know by January 7 (a week after the Chinese warned the WHO), a late January editorial in the state-owned press criticized Wuhan officials (not national ones) for their "slow response" and failures in both treatment and stopping the spread, and issued a warning to local governments in other places that may be doing the same.[155]

It was in this context that Wuhan's mayor admitted on state television in late January that he and the city's Communist Party secretary had failed to keep the public informed early on and offered their resignations to "appease public indignation."[156] This did not go far enough for leaders in Beijing. By the time Xi used a Politburo meeting to warn that those shirking their responsibilities would be punished, case counts, death tolls, and firings were already piling up.[157] For instance, the mayor of the hard-hit city of Huang-gang announced the dismissal of six officials and disciplinary measures against another 337 for their poor performance.[158] In another case, two health officials and the vice-mayor of the eastern city of Yueqing were fired for failing to take actions needed to staunch infections.[159] In mid-February, Xi Jinping removed Hubei's top-two Party officials, replacing them with figures close to Xi and, tellingly, with substantial experience in public security.[160]

As the party machinery sought to insulate Xi by laying blame on local leaders, the country experienced a glasnost moment of sorts: the state unof-ficially declared open season on local officials.[161] China's State Council used the popular WeChat messaging app to collect popular complaints about local government missteps in the epidemic response.[162] Social media gripes targeting local government failures went uncensored. Officials claimed by mid-April to have reopened a majority of their local level "reception venues for public complaints."[163] And the Supreme People's Court even protected whistleblowers from local officials, commenting that "It might have been a better way to prevent and control the new coronavirus today if the public had believed the 'rumor' then."[164]

The firings were not just aimed at those hushing up bad news. They were also targeted at those whose (in)actions made the state response appear inef-fective or unjust. In early February, hundreds of officials from different cities in Hubei were fired or otherwise penalized for their "unshirkable responsi-bility for problems" that included insufficient testing personnel, inadequate patient screening, and poor tracking of infected patients.[165] A week later, another round of firings and other disciplinary procedures was launched against Hubei officials, some of whom were guilty of illegally entering or "deserting" the province during lockdown.[166]

As the virus spread beyond Hubei, so did the punishments. Officials asso-ciated with prisons, where the spread was arguably difficult to contain, lost their jobs in droves, accused of delaying reports and "dereliction of duty."[167] City party bosses were issued demerits or fired for their poor response.[168] And those running the health system were pushed out.[169] Outgoing leaders, infamous for their rebuttals that they had acted within the constraints of the system, were mocked online for engaging in a passing-the-buck ("tossing the wok" in Chinese) competition.[170]

National authorities also bolstered their legitimacy by showing they were tough on COVID-related crimes. This included cracking down on price gouging for goods in short supply.[171] It also involved treating those found "permissibly spreading the coronavirus" as guilty of a "crime of endangering public safety by dangerous means."[172] Authorities criminalized the deliberate spread of COVID, profiteering, illegally buying endangered wildlife, as well as abuse of power and "dereliction of duty in anti-epidemic efforts."[173]

As the fight wore on, the range of crimes grew. It soon became criminal to slander medical workers or engage in behaviors that could expose them to infection.[174] It was also illegal to refuse examination, isolation, and treatment or knowingly expose others while concealing one's sickness.[175] By the end of March, authorities had prosecuted 1,919 suspects in 1,561 cases that included transmitting the virus by failing to take preventative measures, price gouging, and the production or sale of fake, substandard medical products.[176] Regular reports in the state press tracked the number of suspects involved in these illicit pandemic-related activities, even as the case count in China dwindled. Between the start of April and July, the number of prosecutions climbed from nearly 2,200 to 6,755.[177]

While the tough-on-COVID approach may have bolstered Xi's image of standing up for the little people, there were clearly limitations on just how much justice the regime would allow. For instance, attempts by citizens to sue local governments were rejected, sometimes punitively, even in Wuhan, suggesting any real accountability had to come from the top.[178] In addition, personnel changes could not account for systemic weaknesses.[179] In other words, there was little reason to suspect replacements for those terminated would act any differently given institutional (dis)incentive structures.

Populism thus compelled Xi to act with a ruthless determination to deal with the disaster but also to look for scapegoats who could be blamed for policy shortcomings. Power and security in office provided Xi with a ready mechanism, but also a reason, to push lower-level leaders out as a sort of pressure release valve, which extended the time he could continue pursuing his aggressive anti-COVID activities.

SYSTEMIC LEGITIMACY: TECHNOLOGY, MOBILIZATION, AND THE BENEFITS OF ANTI-LIBERALISM

Given the unlikelihood that these dismissals would result in institutional change, it is perhaps another piece of irony that senior Chinese leaders confidently used their COVID experience as testimony to the legitimacy of their party system. For a while, China undoubtedly made enormous strides in stopping the virus, but the same system bore considerable responsibility for unleashing it.

Despite this observation, already in late February, Xi declared that his success in reining in COVID "demonstrated the notable advantages of the leadership of the CPC and the system of socialism with Chinese characteristics."[180] "Daring to fight and daring to win is the Chinese Communist Party's distinct political character, and our distinct political advantage," Xi said.[181] "It has been proven that the CPC Central Committee's judgment on the situation of the epidemic is accurate, all work arrangements are timely, and the measures taken are effective," according to Xi. "The results of the prevention and control work have once again demonstrated the notable advantages of the leadership of the CPC and the system of socialism with Chinese characteristics."[182]

Later, as the economy began to rebound despite a global, COVID-driven crash, Xi asserted that "China's socialist system has demonstrated its strengths."[183] These messages were amplified by the publication in state media of selective quotes from leaders around Europe praising the Chinese message of multilateralism.[184]

Chinese authorities made clear that their approach to the virus was bolstered by their high level of state capacity and autonomy, as demonstrated by the country's invasive and enduring use of technology. Having established its reputation as a "surveillance state" well before the pandemic, Chinese authorities used their technological capabilities to attack the virus early on. By the start of February, China Unicom, a telecom company, launched a system to collect data on the movements of people in virus-stricken areas and share with users medical-related updates.[185] China's CDC apparently used data from Unicom and other cellular providers to warn residents traveling to Wuhan to abide by the lockdown.[186] The government also promoted various private tracking apps, including Alipay, WeChat, Tencent, and other commonly used apps, to track potential virus spread.[187]

The Ministry of Industry and Information Technology was apparently at the forefront of this effort.[188] But by mid-February, as workplaces began to open up, more than 100 cities adopted the use of QR codes that could help track cell phone users' movements in order to determine if they had been in virus-hit areas.[189] This data could be used to notify individuals if they had been in proximity of a person found to be infected.[190] Over time, it became an essential fixture of life in many reopening cities and provinces that used the data to rate users as "green," "yellow," or "red" based on the risk level of areas they had visited. This QR code became a sort of passport to enter businesses and other venues.[191]

Authorities did not stop with personal cell phone surveillance. Some local authorities, for example, demanded that building managers closely monitor their residents by installing cameras to track them.[192] Authorities also used drones to conduct patrols in compliance with mask mandates as well as identify illegal border crossings with the potential to bring COVID in from abroad.[193] Chinese neighborhoods also increasingly adopted facial recognition technology, and companies started experimenting with instruments that used infrared heat and iris recognition technology to detect the faces of those wearing PPE such as masks.[194]

While Chinese authorities brandished these technological capabilities as evidence of their regime's prowess, these measures also demonstrated the Chinese government's soft spots. For instance, there were persistent coordination issues between national and regional actors, and different bureaucratic players.[195] In addition, authorities relied on data gathered by private companies, many of which were eager to expand overseas and worried that handing over data could stain their reputation and limit growth abroad.[196] These concerns were not easily assuaged by promises from Chinese authorities that the data utilized was fully protected.[197]

Indeed, while internet regulators issued formal rules designed to keep personal information gathered in the fight against the epidemic from being used for other purposes, there were holes that left that open to interpretation.[198] The Chinese, in turn, took a much broader approach to contact tracing using cell phones than in (democratic) countries, which are more concerned about privacy.[199] And even after the worst of the pandemic had ended in the spring, the government continued collecting location data on millions, with few clear limits.[200] Distrust was substantiated by reports in the state and non-state press about online vendors selling facial data,[201] a violation of rules but one for which no unified legal framework existed and where only minor punishments were offered.[202]

Even where the data were used for their primary purpose, facilitating infection control, there were significant questions related to methodology and transparency. Residents complained that the algorithms used to assess an individual's safety level were unclear and their levels sometimes fluctuated for no apparent reason.[203] The imprecise nature of the location data, pieced together from transmission towers that can only estimate locations with errors of up to 2 kilometers, may have helped account for these changes.[204] But they had major ramifications on the lives of residents, whose automatic status change could result in a fourteen-day quarantine.[205] Additional concerns and a social media backlash were sparked when officials began to discuss a broader "personal health index" that would go beyond location to include more personal information, such as sleep, exercise, drinking, and smoking habits.[206]

Through their ability to heavily influence the public narrative, as described earlier, Chinese leaders pushed past these concerns in the first year of the pandemic. Much of the messaging took on nationalist tones. Commentators recalled "heroic battles by people from across the country, some of them have sacrificed their lives."[207] They showed images of red banners hanging from cities with phrases such as "War of Resistance Against Pneumonia" and "Everyone Must Contribute to the Patriotic Hygiene Campaign."[208] They featured stories about heroic, dehydrated medical workers, fatigued police and market inspectors, and tireless factory managers (creating sterilizers).[209] They especially praised medical personnel, characterized by "high responsibility and perseverance"[210] and "excellent character,"[211] but they also hailed the entire society's "collectivism and patriotism."[212]

In this narrative, Party leaders were the glue that bound the country as one. The Chinese system, commentators wrote, "ensures the whole country works together and stimulates the enthusiasm of all aspects to mobilize resources for major undertakings."[213] This mobilization theme was present in multiple state commentaries. One praised the Chinese system for its "ability to mobilize huge resources and its sheer national strength."[214]

Propagandists took advantage of perceived failings abroad to drive this point home. Criticizing advanced democracies for excessive liberties that ultimately endangered people's health and safety, one commentator disparagingly wrote in early March, before stay-at-home orders (less draconian than Chinese lockdowns) were announced in much of the West, that "It's impossible for European countries to adopt the extreme measures that China has implemented."[215] As the crisis deepened in the West, Chinese diplomats suggested that older residents in nursing homes were being abandoned to die.[216] State media described large-scale outbreaks in the West in terms such as "purgatory" and "apocalypse."[217]

One obvious difficulty Chinese leaders faced as they boasted of their COVID response was the fact that China was actually the birthplace of the pandemic. The Chinese at first deflected such charges, arguing instead that the international community owed China for taking "forceful measures" and bearing a "huge sacrifice" that bought "valuable time for the world to respond."[218] They condemned "arbitrary and unfounded"[219] and "groundless"[220] accusations blaming China for the virus, metaphorically referring to such charges themselves as an "information virus" or "political virus."[221] Eventually, they began floating the possibility that the United States was a critical conduit for the virus's spread and, as noted above, even accused U.S. military labs of being the initial source of the disease.[222] U.S. attacks on China were, they concluded, designed by the United States to "cover up its own opacity, inability and unaccountability in handling the outbreak."[223]

The Chinese made their case that U.S. failings on everything from testing to economic policy were a result of democracy's weakness and, in turn, evidence of their own system's superiority.[224] They pointed to "vicious partisan fighting" and racial injustice as contributors to a disaster where U.S. leaders put "political gains above people's wellbeing."[225] One foreign ministry spokesperson appealed to the United States to "take effective measures to safeguard the life and health of its people, and work with the international community to safeguard global public health security."[226]

This strategy represented a clear role reversal, with the United States having long criticized China and others for causing undue suffering to their own populations. Now Chinese leaders and their commentators brandished themselves as the true guardians of human rights. Commentators argued that the "rights to life and health are among the most fundamental human rights" and that China shined as it "made all-out efforts to safeguard the lives and health of its people."[227] Pointing to the United States, which was grappling with its own racial injustices leading to what Chinese commentators called a "degenerative human rights track record,"[228] one piece said: "The glaring contrast between the two major countries makes people wonder: Who is the better upholder of human rights?"

A subsequent commentary pointed to the obvious answer to this question: "China's prevention and control measures were met with doubt, ridicule, accusations of human rights violations and even racist attacks from certain Western politicians," it read. "Yet rising above these smears, the country has set a noble example by putting people's lives first no matter the cost."[229] The Chinese pushed their case on a global scale with their vaccine rollout, which rapidly became a cornerstone of Chinese diplomacy.[230]

CONCLUSION

Given the slow trickle of information at the start, many have claimed that authoritarianism, and the censorship it breeds, slowed the local and global response to COVID.[231] There is little doubt that China's authoritarian leaders followed that script, to great detriment both at home and abroad. Some health experts have estimated that initiating an aggressive response just one week earlier could have lowered the number of infections by two-thirds.[232]

But the story does not end there. China's leaders demonstrate the power of populism even in a closed regime. Once they were finally compelled to act amidst a groundswell of popular angst, Chinese authorities steered the entire, massive state into the headwinds. Chinese leaders used their overwhelming power to launch the sorts of draconian lockdowns that are much more difficult to strictly implement for extended periods in more democratic states, where leaders are consistently minding the clock on the way to the next elections. They simultaneously plowed resources into stemming the virus and its economic impact, in ways inconsistent with our traditional take on authoritarianism.

Evidence that the Chinese handling of COVID was a function of authoritarian strength joined with populist responsiveness surfaces in the acts and words of China's leadership. Xi carefully positioned himself as a commander setting the strategy but distanced himself from his policy's most excruciating consequences. His tactics involved closely controlling the narrative to disperse indictments and tout accomplishments. But they also involved sacrificing lower-level officials who could take the blame for systemic failures, even as the system was extolled for its superior performance.

Of course, the Chinese response had numerous weaknesses, from the calamitous initial coverup of the pandemic and early undercounts to later accusations that the government was too inflexible with its zero-COVID policy after vaccines became available. Misgivings could be heard at home, as when one small business owner expressed suspicion on WeChat over government loans. "I am not an idiot," he said. "They are for the enterprises to pay the employees to ease social unrest, but we business owners are the ones to bear the consequences."[233] Mistrust also reverberated abroad. When released data showed Chinese vaccines to be less effective than their Western counterparts, for instance, states once grateful for Chinese vaccine offers made a humiliating about-face.[234] "Cambodia is not a dustbin, and not a place for a vaccine trial," declared the Cambodian prime minister in a stinging rebuke of China.[235]

Despite these criticisms, it is hard to argue that the Chinese were not highly effective in saving lives in 2020. Secure in his office, but keen to use his control of information to maintain the domestic legitimacy his populist policies had won him before the pandemic, Xi chose to play the long game that few democrats felt they could afford to play—and that few autocrats would be willing to pay for.

NOTES

1. Chris Buckley and Myers Steven Lee, "China Kept World in Dark as Outbreak Rippled," *New York Times*, February 2, 2020, A1.

2. Amy Qin, Myers Steven Lee, and Elaine Yu, "Beijing Imposes Extreme Limits on Ill in Wuhan: [Foreign Desk]," Ibid., February 7; AFP, "Death of Whistleblower Ignites Calls for Political Reform in China," *Agence France Presse - English*, February 9, 2020; Yuan Li, "Online Revolt in China as a Doctor Is Lionized: [Business/Financial Desk]," *New York Times*, February 8, 2020, B1.

3. Raymond Zhong et al., "'Be Sleek and Silent': How China Censored Bad News About Covid: [Foreign Desk]," Ibid., December 20.

4. Kiki Zhao, "The Coronavirus Story Is Too Big for China to Spin," *New York Times* (Online), February 14, 2020.

5. Xinhua, "1st Ld: China Releases Investigation Report on Issues Concerning Dr. Li Wenliang," *Xinhua General News Service*, March 19, 2020.

6. "Profile: Zhong Nanshan: Outspoken Doctor Awarded China's Top Honor," *Xinhua General News Service*, August 15, 2020.

7. Cheng Li and Diana Liang, "Rule of the Rigid Compromiser," Brookings Institution, Spring 2019, https://www.brookings.edu/articles/rule-of-the-rigid-compromiser/.

8. Xinhua, "Xinhua Headlines: China Determined to Win Battle against Poverty Despite Epidemic," *Xinhua General News Service*, March 18, 2020; "China's Determination to Achieve Goal of Poverty Elimination Unwavering: Official," *Xinhua General News Service*, March 12, 2020; Javier C. Hernández, "'We Couldn't Be Poorer': Pandemic Hinders China's Antipoverty Efforts: [Foreign Desk]," *New York Times*, October 26, 2020, A12.

9. Emily Feng, "How China's Massive Corruption Crackdown Snares Entrepreneurs across the Country," *National Public Radio*, March 4, 2021.

10. Susan L. Shirk, "China in Xi's New Era: The Return to Personalistic Rule," *Journal of Democracy* 29, no. 2 (2018).

11. William Zheng, "Chinese Rate Government 'More Capable Than Ever before', Long-Term Harvard Study Finds," *South China Morning Post*, July 21, 2020.

12. Kai Kupferschmidt and Jon Cohen, "China's Aggressive Measures Have Slowed the Coronavirus. They May Not Work in Other Countries," *Science*, March 2, 2020, https://www.science.org/content/article/china-s-aggressive-measures-have-slowed-coronavirus-they-may-not-work-other-countries?cookieSet=1.

13. Xinhua, "China Sends over 11,000 Medics to Wuhan Amid Epidemic," *Xinhua General News Service*, February 7, 2020.

14. BBC, "China Discouraging Marriage, Funeral Gatherings Amid Outbreak," *BBC Monitoring Asia Pacific - Political Supplied by BBC Worldwide Monitoring*, January 31, 2020; Xinhua, "1st Ld-Writethru: China Sends over 30,000 Medics to Aid in Battle against COVID-19 in Wuhan," *Xinhua General News Service*, February 17, 2020.

15. "China Focus: Bring COVID-19 under Control with Joint Efforts," *Xinhua General News Service*, May 18, 2020; "China Sends 25,633 Medics to Battle COVID-19 in Hubei," *Xinhua General News Service*, February 15, 2020; AFP, "China Leadership Admits 'Shortcomings' in Virus Response," *Agence France Presse - English*, February 3, 2020.

16. BBC, "Chinese Media Criticise Wuhan Handling of Virus Outbreak," *BBC Worldwide Monitoring*, January 23, 2020.

17. Xinhua, "Factbox: China's Fight against Novel Coronavirus Outbreak," *Xinhua General News Service*, March 2, 2020; "Xinhua Headlines: China Beefs up Action against Novel Coronavirus as Cases Increase," *Xinhua General News Service*, January 26, 2020.

18. "Across China: China's Villages, Communities Mobilized in Fight against Epidemic," *Xinhua General News Service*, February 6, 2020; Chris Buckley, Amy Qin, and Wee Sui-Lee, "In China's War on the Coronavirus, a Community Is Besieged," *New York Times* (Online), February 28, 2020.

19. Xinhua, "1st Ld-Writethru: China Focus: Wuhan Sends 34,000 Gov't Workers, Party Members to Fight Coronavirus in Communities," *Xinhua General News Service*, February 11, 2020.

20. "Xinhua Headlines: China Endeavors to Ensure Supply of Masks, Necessities Amid Epidemic," *Xinhua General News Service*, February 3, 2020.

21. AFP, "China Leadership Admits 'Shortcomings' in Virus Response."

22. Xinhua, "China Underscores Allocation of CPC Members' Donation for COVID-19 Fight," *Xinhua General News Service*, March 28, 2020.

23. "Factbox: China's Fight against Novel Coronavirus Outbreak," *Xinhua General News Service*, April 15, 2020; "China Helps Stranded Individuals Tide over Epidemic," *Xinhua General News Service*, March 14, 2020.

24. BBC, "Chinese Media Criticise Wuhan Handling of Virus Outbreak"; Javier C. Hernández, "China Reaches a Containment Milestone with No New Local Infections: [Foreign Desk]," *New York Times*, March 19, 2020, A6.

25. "China Locks Down Xinjiang in West to Stop Covid, Angering Residents: [Foreign Desk]," *New York Times*, August 26, 2020, A5.

26. Xinhua, "Xi Focus: Xi Leads China's Economic Reopening on Sustainable Track," *Xinhua General News Service*, May 15, 2020.

27. "China Focus: China Beefs up Novel Coronavirus Tracking and Prevention with Big Data," *Xinhua General News Service*, February 2, 2020; "Economic Watch: China Accelerates Reform to Empower Private Sector Amid COVID-19," *Xinhua General News Service*, September 9, 2020.

28. Keith Bradsher, "Slowed by the Coronavirus, China Inc. Struggles to Reopen," *New York Times* (Online), February 17, 2020; Xinhua, "1st Ld-Writethru: China Resumes Construction of Major Civil Aviation Projects," *Xinhua General News Service*, March 6, 2020.

29. "China Transports 84,000 Workers by Train for Resumption of Production," *Xinhua General News Service*, February 27, 2020; "China Ferries 332,000 Workers Back to Work with Special Trains," *Xinhua General News Service*, March 16, 2020; "China Launches Large Online Job Vacancy Market," *Xinhua General News Service*, March 20, 2020.

30. "China Issues 6.6 Bln Yuan in Subsidies to Offset Price Hike Amid COVID-19," *Xinhua General News Service*, April 10, 2020.

31. "China Distributes 1.9 Bln Yuan of Price Subsidies Amid COVID-19 Impact," *Xinhua General News Service*, April 10, 2020.

32. "China Offers Allowances to over 400,000 Children in Need Amid Epidemic: Official," *Xinhua General News Service*, April 10, 2020.

33. AFP, "China Inflation Slips but Stays High on Virus, Food Worries," *Agence France Presse - English*, March 10, 2020. Department of Price under the National Development and Reform Commission Xinhua, "China Readies 20,000 Tonnes of Pork for COVID-19-Affected Areas," *Xinhua General News Service*, March 19, 2020.

34. Sidney Leng, "China's Plan for 2.5-Day Weekend to Aid Coronavirus-Hit Economy Met with Mixed Reactions," *South China Morning Post*, July 23, 2020; Xinhua, "East China City Starts Trial of 2.5-Day Weekend," *Xinhua General News Service*, July 13, 2020; "China Issues Measures to Support Hubei Free-Trade Zone," *Xinhua General News Service*, June 4, 2020; "Factbox: China's Progress in Economic Resumption," *Xinhua General News Service*, September 21, 2020; "Economic Watch: Long-Awaited Holiday Ignites Spending Revival in China," *Xinhua General News Service*, May 6, 2020; "S. China Province Raises Tax Rebate Rates to Shore up Foreign Trade Firms Amid Epidemic," *Xinhua General News Service*, March 25, 2020; "China Focus: China Hands out Vouchers to Spur Virus-Hit Consumption," *Xinhua General News Service*, March 19, 2020; "China Focus: Chinese Cities Launch Voucher Campaigns to Boost Epidemic-Hit Consumption," *Xinhua General News Service*, March 25, 2020; "Factbox: China's Fight against Novel Coronavirus Outbreak"; "East China Province Offers Vouchers to Stimulate Consumption," *Xinhua General News Service*, May 19, 2020; "China City Hands out 238-Mln-Usd E-Vouchers to Spur Virus-Hit Consumption," *Xinhua General News Service*, March 26, 2020; "Central China Province Issues E-Coupons to Boost Consumption Amid Epidemic," *Xinhua General News Service*, March 28, 2020.

35. Finbarr Bermingham and Orange Wang, "China's Coronavirus Recovery Plan Falls Back on Old Playbook of Debt and Construction," *South China Morning Post*, June 15, 2020; Amanda Lee, "China Needs to Weigh Economic 'Consequences' of Coronavirus Stimulus, Top Beijing Researcher Says," Ibid., July 27.

36. Finbarr Bermingham and Orange Wang, "China's Economic Rebound Shows Upside to 'Stringent Lockdowns, Testing, Tracking', Analysts Say," Ibid., October 19.

37. He Huifeng and Sidney Leng, "As China's Coronavirus Rebound Gathers Steam, Export-Oriented Manufacturers Struggle to Find Workers," Ibid., December 25.

38. Zhou Xin, "China's Coronavirus Success Boosts Confidence That Its System Is the Best Answer to the Country's Challenges," Ibid., December 28.

39. Xinhua, "China's Determination to Achieve Goal of Poverty Elimination Unwavering: Official"; "Xinhua Headlines: China Determined to Win Battle against Poverty Despite Epidemic."

40. "China's Poverty Relief Fund Tops 139 Bln Yuan in 2020," *Xinhua General News Service*, March 31, 2020.

41. "Xinhua Headlines: In Tough Year, China Makes Decisive Progress in Ending Absolute Poverty," *Xinhua General News Service*, December 31, 2020.

42. Hernández, "'We Couldn't Be Poorer': Pandemic Hinders China's Antipoverty Efforts: [Foreign Desk]."

43. Anna Fifield, "In China, Some Worry the Official Illness Count Is Too Low," *The Washington Post*, January 23, 2020, A15.

44. Xinhua, "Xi Focus: Chronicle of Xi's Leadership in China's War against Coronavirus (1)," *Xinhua General News Service*, September 7, 2020.

45. Ibid.

46. Ibid.

47. Amy Qin, "China's Leader, under Fire, Says He Led Coronavirus Fight Early On," *New York Times* (Online), February 15, 2020.

48. Ibid.

49. Xinhua, "China Informs Public Right after COVID-19 Human-to-Human Spread Determined: White Paper," *Xinhua General News Service*, June 7, 2020; Qin, "China's Leader, under Fire, Says He Led Coronavirus Fight Early On"; Chris Buckley et al., "25 Days That Changed the World: How COVID-19 Slipped China's Grasp," Ibid., December 30.

50. Xinhua, "Xi Focus: Chronicle of Xi's Leadership in China's War against Coronavirus (1)."

51. Ibid.

52. Ibid.

53. Ibid.

54. Ibid.

55. Xinhua, "Chinese Premier in Wuhan, Demands All-out Efforts in Epidemic Prevention, Control," *Xinhua General News Service*, January 27, 2020.

56. "Chinese Vice Premier Stresses Community-Level Prevention in Fight against Epidemic," *Xinhua General News Service*, February 17, 2020.

57. "Chinese Vice Premier Visits Hospital, Communities Amid Coronavirus Outbreak," *Xinhua General News Service*, January 31, 2020.

58. Qin, Steven Lee, and Yu, "Beijing Imposes Extreme Limits on Ill in Wuhan: [Foreign Desk]."

59. Xinhua, "1st Ld-Writethru: China Focus: Wuhan Sends 34,000 Gov't Workers, Party Members to Fight Coronavirus in Communities."

60. Ibid.

61. Chris Buckley and Myers Steven Lee, "Chinese Officials Race to Contain Public Fury over Virus Management: [Foreign Desk]," *New York Times*, January 28, 2020, A8.

62. Xinhua, "Xi: Rely on People to Win Battle against Epidemic," *Xinhua General News Service*, January 27, 2020.

63. BBC, "China Discouraging Marriage, Funeral Gatherings Amid Outbreak."

64. Xinhua, "Xi Focus: Commanding China's Fight against Novel Coronavirus Outbreak," *Xinhua General News Service*, February 2, 2020.

65. "Xinhua Headlines-Xi Focus: How China Fights War against COVID-19 under Xi's Command," *Xinhua General News Service*, February 25, 2020.

66. Ibid.

67. Xinhua, "Xi: Rely on People to Win Battle against Epidemic."

68. Qin, "China's Leader, under Fire, Says He Led Coronavirus Fight Early On."

69. Xinhua, "Xi Takes Charge of China's COVID-19 Response: White Paper," *Xinhua General News Service*, June 7, 2020.

70. Buckley, Qin, and Sui-Lee, "In China's War on the Coronavirus, a Community Is Besieged"; Raymond Zhong and Paul Mozur, "To Tame Coronavirus, Mao-Style Social Control Blankets

China," Ibid., February 15. Zhuang Pinghui, "China Admits Coronavirus Exposed 'Weak Links' in Health System as Government Promises to Strengthen Disease Response," *South China Morning Post .com*, May 23, 2020, https://advance-lexis-com.proxy-bc.researchport.umd.edu/api/document?collection=news&id=urn:contentItem:5YYV-2611-JC8V-154M-00000-00&context=1516831.

71. 吉晓东, "Xi to Attend Meeting Commending Role Models in China's Fight against COVID-19 Epidemic," *Xinhua General News Service*, September 6, 2020 Sunday, https://advance -lexis-com.proxy-bc.researchport.umd.edu/api/document?collection=news&id=urn:contentItem :60SC-TS51-DY91-H2D7-00000-00&context=1516831.

72. Qin, Steven Lee, and Yu, "Beijing Imposes Extreme Limits on Ill in Wuhan: [Foreign Desk]"; Xinhua, "Xi to Attend Meeting Commending Role Models in China's Fight against COVID-19 Epidemic," *Xinhua General News Service*, September 6, 2020.

73. AFP, "China President Makes Rare Visit to Meet Virus Workers, Patients," *Agence France Presse - English*, February 10, 2020.

74. Xinhua, "Xi Focus: Chronicle of Xi's Leadership in China's War against Coronavirus (3)," *Xinhua General News Service*, September 7, 2020.

75. "Factbox: China's Fight against Novel Coronavirus Outbreak"; AFP, "Italy Locks Down as China Signals Major Progress in Own Virus Fight," *Agence France Presse - English*, March 10, 2020.

76. "China's Xi Pays First Visit to Virus Epicentre Wuhan," *Agence France Presse - English*, March 10, 2020.

77. Xinhua, "Xi Focus: Chronicle of Xi's Leadership in China's War against Coronavirus (3)."

78. Ibid.; AFP, "Italy Locks Down as China Signals Major Progress in Own Virus Fight."

79. Xinhua, "Xi Focus-Timeline: Xi Leads China to Fight COVID-19 with Sci-Tech," *Xinhua General News Service*, March 4, 2020.

80. BBC, "Chinese Media Criticise Wuhan Handling of Virus Outbreak"; Xinhua, "China Focus: China Has Taken Strictest Measures to Curb Epidemic: NHC," *Xinhua General News Service*, February 1, 2020; "China Faces Increasing Risks of Imported COVID-19 Cases: NHC," *Xinhua General News Service*, November 13, 2020; Yuan Yang et al., "China Medics Query 'Zero New Cases' Claim; National Health Commission; Official Figures Suggest Breakthrough but Experts Cast Doubt on Data," *Financial Times*, March 28, 2020.

81. Javier C. Hernández, "China Spins Coronavirus Crisis, Hailing Itself as a Global Leader," *New York Times* (Online), March 3, 2020; Xinhua, "1st Ld-Writethru-Xinhua Headlines: China's Unprecedented Measures Effectively Contain Epidemic," *Xinhua General News Service*, January 31, 2020.

82. Fifield, "In China, Some Worry the Official Illness Count Is Too Low."

83. Javier C. Hernández, "China Peddles Falsehoods to Obscure Origin of COVID Pandemic," *New York Times* (Online), December 6, 2020.

84. Xinhua, "Factbox: China's Fight against Novel Coronavirus Outbreak."

85. "Xi Focus: Amid Hardships, Xi Leads China's Sprint to Milestone," *Xinhua General News Service*, May 28, 2020.

86. Zhuang Pinghui, "China Admits Coronavirus Exposed 'Weak Links' in Health System as Government Promises to Strengthen Disease Response," *South China Morning Post*, May 23, 2020.

87. Echo Xie, "China Plans to Overhaul Health System, but Better Communication with Public Is Off the Radar," Ibid., June 8.

88. Xinhua, "Commentary: China Boosts National Pride in Coronavirus Fight, but Not to Export 'Chinese Model'," *Xinhua General News Service*, May 9, 2020.

89. Guo Rui, "President Xi Stands Besides Covid-19 Heroes and Hails China's 'Decisive Action' in Containing Coronavirus," *South China Morning Post*, September 8, 2020.

90. Vivian Wang, "With Propaganda Push in China, Wuhan Emerges as a Star," *New York Times*, November 7, 2020, A7.

91. Yuan Li, "In Ousting U.S. Reporters, China Signals New Kind of Self-Confidence: [Foreign Desk]," Ibid., March 19, A19.

92. Zhong et al., "'Be Sleek and Silent': How China Censored Bad News About Covid: [Foreign Desk]."

93. Paul Mozur, "China's Internet Police Crack Down on Outrage: [Business/Financial Desk]," Ibid., March 18, B6.

94. BBC, "Chinese Media Deny Cover up, Rumours on Coronavirus Outbreak," *BBC Monitoring Asia Pacific - Political Supplied by BBC Worldwide Monitoring*, January 21, 2020.

95. Anna Fifield, "Quickly Spreading Virus Raises Fears across China," *The Washington Post*, January 21, 2020, A1.

96. Zhong et al., "'Be Sleek and Silent': How China Censored Bad News About Covid: [Foreign Desk]."

97. Ibid.

98. Yuan Li, "Coronavirus Weakens China's Powerful Propaganda Machine: The New New World," *New York Times* (Online), February 26, 2020.

99. Raymond Zhong, "Beijing Tightens Its Grip on News Coverage as Cases Continue to Surge: [Foreign Desk]," *New York Times*, February 6, 2020.

100. AFP, "China Censored Virus News for Weeks, Say Researchers," *Agence France Presse - English*, March 3, 2020.

101. Zhong, "Beijing Tightens Its Grip on News Coverage as Cases Continue to Surge: [Foreign Desk]." Zhong et al., "'Be Sleek and Silent': How China Censored Bad News About Covid: [Foreign Desk]."

102. Linda Lew, "Coronavirus Pandemic Shows Global Consequences of China's Local Censorship Rules," *South China Morning Post*, June 7, 2020.

103. AFP, "China Censored Virus News for Weeks, Say Researchers."

104. Lew, "Coronavirus Pandemic Shows Global Consequences of China's Local Censorship Rules."

105. Mozur, "China's Internet Police Crack Down on Outrage: [Business/Financial Desk]."

106. AFP, "China Charges Xi Critic with 'Subversion', Say Activists," *Agence France Presse - English*, March 9, 2020.

107. Wee Sui-Lee, "Activists Say China Uses Quarantines to Stifle Dissent," *New York Times*, July 31, 2020, A12.

108. Xinhua, "Rumor Buster: Facts Prove COVID-19 Cases in China Are Really Going Down," *Xinhua General News Service*, March 17, 2020.

109. "Chinese Embassy Refutes Media Reports About China Concealing COVID-19 Situation," *Xinhua General News Service*, April 4, 2020.

110. "Commentary: China-Bashing Syndrome Makes Coronavirus Pandemic Deadlier," *Xinhua General News Service*, April 6, 2020.

111. "Xinhua Headlines: Rumor Buster: Six Facts About China's Fight against COVID-19," *Xinhua General News Service*, April 9, 2020.

112. "Commentary: Smearing China's Goodwill to Europe Hurts Fight against COVID-19," *Xinhua General News Service*, April 16, 2020.

113. Lara Jakes and Myers Steven Lee, "U.S. Designates China's Official Media as Operatives of the Communist State," *New York Times* (Online), February 18, 2020.

114. AFP, "China Ordered to Slash State Media Staff in US," *Agence France Presse - English*, March 2, 2020.

115. "China Threatens Retaliation over US 'Bullying' of State Media," *Agence France Presse - English*, March 3, 2020.

116. Xinhua, "Commentary: Washington's China Media Cap Exposes Fake Press Freedom," *Xinhua General News Service*, March 5, 2020.

117. Alexandra Stevenson, "China Expels 3 Wall Street Journal Reporters as Media Relations Sour," *New York Times* (Online), 2020; AFP, "China Expels US Journalists in Biggest Crackdown in Years," *Agence France Presse - English*, March 17, 2020; ibid.; Jakes and Steven Lee, "U.S. Designates China's Official Media as Operatives of the Communist State."

118. Stevenson, "China Expels 3 Wall Street Journal Reporters as Media Relations Sour."

119. AFP, "China Expels US Journalists in Biggest Crackdown in Years."

120. Xinhua, "Commentary: China's Countermeasures against U.S. Press Bullying Legitimate," *Xinhua General News Service*, March 18, 2020.

121. Ibid.

122. Vivian Wang, "U.S. Escalates Media War with New Restrictions on Chinese Journalists [with Graphic(S)]," *New York Times*, May 9, 2020; Owen Churchill, "China Imposes Limits on 6 More US-Based News Outlets, Including ABC, LA Times, Newsweek and Bloomberg Industry Group," *South China Morning Post*, October 27, 2020.

123. Li, "Coronavirus Weakens China's Powerful Propaganda Machine: The New New World."

124. Hernández, "China Spins Coronavirus Crisis, Hailing Itself as a Global Leader."

125. Xinhua, "1st Ld-Writethru-Xinhua Headlines: China's Unprecedented Measures Effectively Contain Epidemic."

126. Hernández, "China Spins Coronavirus Crisis, Hailing Itself as a Global Leader."

127. Xinhua, "1st Ld-Writethru-Xinhua Headlines: China's Unprecedented Measures Effectively Contain Epidemic."

128. "China to Air Documentary on COVID-19 Fight," *Xinhua General News Service*, August 31, 2020.

129. Ibid.

130. Miles Johnson, "Italian Applause Videos Fuel Suspicions of China Propaganda; Aid Supplies," *Financial Times*, May 4, 2020.

131. Ibid.

132. Javier C. Hernández, "As China Tries to Stifle Coverage, Defiant Journalists Do Exposés: [Foreign Desk]," *New York Times* (Online), March 16, 2020.

133. Ibid.; Adam Taylor, "Chinese Journalists Offer a Glimpse Behind State's Propaganda on Covid-19," *The Washington Post*, April 10, 2020, A16.

134. Hernández, "As China Tries to Stifle Coverage, Defiant Journalists Do Exposés: [Foreign Desk]."

135. Mimi Lau and Phoebe Zhang, "Coronavirus: Students Protest against China University Lockdowns Citing Lack of Virus Cases, Lack of Consistency," *South China Morning Post*, September 24, 2020.

136. AFP, "People at Centre of China's Virus Outbreak Say Time to End Lockdown," *Agence France Presse - English*, March 8, 2020.

137. Ibid.

138. Lau and Zhang, "Coronavirus: Students Protest against China University Lockdowns Citing Lack of Virus Cases, Lack of Consistency."

139. Gerry Shih, "China Detains a Leading Critic of Xi," *The Washington Post*, July 7, 2020, A11. Mimi Lau, "Coronavirus: China Sets Trial Date for Citizen Journalist Zhang Zhan," *South China Morning Post*, December 18, 2020; Lew, "Coronavirus Pandemic Shows Global Consequences of China's Local Censorship Rules."

140. Vivian Wang, "Chinese Citizen Journalist Receives 4 Years in Prison for Virus Reports: [Foreign Desk]," *New York Times*, December 29, 2020, A9; Guo Rui, "China Jails Citizen Journalist Zhang Zhan for Four Years over Wuhan Coronavirus Reports," *South China Morning Post*, December 28, 2020.

141. Javier C. Hernández, "Chinese Tycoon May Face Prosecution after Expulsion from Communist Party: [Foreign Desk]," *New York Times* (Online), July 24, 2020; "China Eyes Party Gadfly Who Bashed Xi over Virus: [Foreign Desk]," *New York Times*, April 8, 2020, A19.

142. Dwight Garner, "An Angry, Eerie View from inside Quarantine in China: [Review]," Ibid., May 19, C5.

143. Yuan Li, "With Selective Coronavirus Coverage, China Builds a Culture of Hate [with Graphic(S)]," *New York Times* (Online), April 22, 2020; Christian Shepherd, "Wuhan Diary Stirs Tussle for Control of Virus Response Narrative; China," *Financial Times*, May 16, 2020.

144. Taylor, "Chinese Journalists Offer a Glimpse Behind State's Propaganda on Covid-19."

145. Edward Wong, Matthew Rosenberg, and Julian E. Barnes, "Chinese Operatives Helped Sow Panic in U.S., Officials Say," *New York Times*, April 23, 2020, A13.

146. Ibid.

147. Ellen Nakashima, Elizabeth Dwoskin, and Anna Fifield, "Twitter Suspends 23,000 Accounts, Alleges Ties to China's Communist Party," *The Washington Post*, June 12, 2020, A11.

148. Linda Lew, "Twitter Removes 23,750 China-Linked Accounts for Spreading Disinformation," *South China Morning Post*, June 12, 2020.

149. Kate Conger, "Twitter Deletes Accounts Linked to Chinese Misinformation Efforts: [Business/Financial Desk]," *New York Times*, June 12, 2020, B4.

150. Xinhua, "China Calls for Global Crackdown on COVID-19 Disinformation," *Xinhua General News Service*, June 10, 2020.

151. Iris Deng, "China's Internet Watchdog Tightens Online Controls with New App to Squash Rumours," *South China Morning Post*, August 13, 2020.

152. Max Fisher, "An Iron Fist with Flaws a Virus Can Fit Through: [Foreign Desk]," *New York Times* (Online), January 26, 2020; Steven Lee Myers and Chris Buckley, "Novel Virus Tests China's Authoritarian Bargain: [Foreign Desk]," *New York Times*, January 27, 2020, A1; Yuan Li, "In China, Virus Spurred Rush of Blame Shifting: [Foreign Desk]," Ibid., February 5.

153. Steven Lee Myers, "China Had a Fail-Safe Way to Track Contagions. Officials Failed to Use It.: [Foreign Desk]," Ibid., March 30.

154. Ibid.

155. BBC, "Chinese Media Criticise Wuhan Handling of Virus Outbreak."

156. Buckley and Steven Lee, "Chinese Officials Race to Contain Public Fury over Virus Management: [Foreign Desk]"; BBC, "Chinese Media Criticise Wuhan Handling of Virus Outbreak."

157. Xinhua, "2nd Ld Writethru-Xinhua Headlines: China Penalizes Derelict Officials in Coronavirus Fight," *Xinhua General News Service*, February 5, 2020.

158. "Chinese City Sacks 6 Officials over Poor Performance in Anti-Coronavirus Effort," *Xinhua General News Service*, February 2, 2020.

159. "East China City Fires 2 Officials over Dereliction of Duty in Anti-Epidemic Effort," *Xinhua General News Service*, February 3, 2020.

160. Steven Lee Myers, "China Ousts 2 Party Officials Amid Outrage About Coronavirus Response," *New York Times* (Online), February 13, 2020.

161. Gerry Shih, "China Rushes to Limit Political Risk from Health Crisis," *The Washington Post*, January 30, 2020, A15.

162. Xinhua, "China Focus: Internet Helps in China's Fight against Novel Coronavirus," *Xinhua General News Service*, February 3, 2020.

163. "China Reopens Reception Venues for Public Complaints," *Xinhua General News Service*, April 10, 2020.

164. Buckley and Steven Lee, "China Kept World in Dark as Outbreak Rippled."

165. Xinhua, "2nd Ld Writethru-Xinhua Headlines: China Penalizes Derelict Officials in Coronavirus Fight."

166. "China's Hubei Punishes Officials for Misdeeds in Anti-Virus Fight," *Xinhua General News Service*, February 12, 2020.

167. "China Orders Prison Overhaul after COVID-19 Outbreak," *Xinhua General News Service*, March 4, 2020; "1st Ld-Writethru: COVID-19 Cases Confirmed in East China Prison, Concerned Officials Removed," *Xinhua General News Service*, February 21, 2020; "11 under Investigation over Prison Coronavirus Outbreak in East China," *Xinhua General News Service*, March 4, 2020.

168. Christian Shepherd, "Fresh Outbreak in China's North-East Threatens to Stall Coronavirus Recovery," *Financial Times*, April 20, 2020; Alice Yan, "Coronavirus: Two Health Officials in China Removed after Cluster of 12 Cases Found at East Coast Hospital," *South China Morning Post*, October 15, 2020.

169. Xinhua, "1st Ld-Writethru: Health Official Suspended in China's Qingdao after Fresh COVID-19 Cases," *Xinhua General News Service*, October 15, 2020.

170.   Li, "In China, Virus Spurred Rush of Blame Shifting: [Foreign Desk]."

171.   Xinhua, "China Capable of Ensuring Daily Necessities Supply Amid Epidemic, Official," *Xinhua General News Service*, February 1, 2020; Yuan Li, "Emergency Measures Create Hurdles for Farmers and Small Businesses: [Foreign Desk]," *New York Times* (Online), February 1, 2020.

172.   Xinhua, "China Cracks Down on Illegal Acts of Refusing Isolation Treatment, Deliberately Spreading Coronavirus," *Xinhua General News Service*, February 7, 2020.

173.   "China Stresses Harsh Punishment on Epidemic-Related Crimes," *Xinhua General News Service*, February 11, 2020.

174.   "1st Ld-Writethru: China Tightens Crackdown on Violence against Medical Workers," *Xinhua General News Service*, February 21, 2020.

175.   Ibid.

176.   Xinhua, "China Prosecutes 1,144 Suspects Involved in Epidemic-Related Crimes," *Xinhua General News Service*, March 4, 2020; "Over 1,700 Prosecuted for Epidemic-Related Crimes in China," *Xinhua General News Service*, March 20, 2020; "China Prosecutes 1,919 Suspects Involved in Epidemic-Related Crimes," *Xinhua General News Service*, March 27, 2020.

177.   "1st Ld-Writethru: Offenses Concerning Imported COVID-19 Cases in China Made Public," *Xinhua General News Service*, April 3, 2020; "Thousands Prosecuted for Epidemic-Related Crimes in China," *Xinhua General News Service*, August 28, 2020.

178.   AFP, "'I Can Never Be Happy Again': Grieving Wuhan Families Say China Is Blocking Coronavirus Lawsuits," *Agence France Presse - English*, September 17, 2020.

179.   Buckley and Steven Lee, "Chinese Officials Race to Contain Public Fury over Virus Management: [Foreign Desk]"; "China Kept World in Dark as Outbreak Rippled."

180.   Xinhua, "Xi Says Positive Trend of China's Epidemic Control Is Expanding," *Xinhua General News Service*, February 23, 2020.

181.   Vivian Wang, "China, Citing Fewer Cases, Tries to Rewrite Its Role in Crisis," *New York Times*, April 9, 2020, A6.

182.   Xinhua, "Xi Says Positive Trend of China's Epidemic Control Is Expanding."

183.   "Xi Focus: Chronicle of Xi's Leadership in China's War against Coronavirus (5)," *Xinhua General News Service*, September 7, 2020.

184.   "Xinhua Headlines: China, Europe Willing to Promote Multilateralism, Oppose Cold War Rhetoric," *Xinhua General News Service*, September 2, 2020.

185.   "China Focus: China Beefs up Novel Coronavirus Tracking and Prevention with Big Data."

186.   Steven Lee Myers and Giulia Marchi, "Virtual Shutdown Clears out China's Capital: [Foreign Desk]," *New York Times*, February 4, 2020, A7.

187.   Alexandra Stevenson and Li Cao, "China's Coronavirus Back-to-Work Lessons: Masks and Vigilance," Ibid., May 12; Xinhua, "Economic Watch: China Accelerates Reform to Empower Private Sector Amid COVID-19"; ibid.

188.   Xinhua, "China Turns to Tech Tools in Precise Control of Epidemic," *Xinhua General News Service*, February 19, 2020.

189.   "Over 100 Chinese Cities Adopt Qr Codes for Coronavirus Control, Work Resumption," *Xinhua General News Service*, February 20, 2020; ibid.

190.   AFP, "As World Cowers, China Glimpses Coronavirus Aftermath," *Agence France Presse - English*, March 18, 2020; "New Normal in Virus-Hit China: High-Tech Tracking and Fever Checks," *Agence France Presse - English*, March 4, 2020; Xinhua, "China Focus: China Values Privacy by Using Encrypted Data in Battle against Epidemic," *Xinhua General News Service*, March 9, 2020.

191.   AFP, "As World Cowers, China Glimpses Coronavirus Aftermath." "New Normal in Virus-Hit China: High-Tech Tracking and Fever Checks."

192.   "New Normal in Virus-Hit China: High-Tech Tracking and Fever Checks."

193.   Xinhua, "China Focus: Unmanned Aerial Vehicles Assist Fight against Novel Coronavirus," *Xinhua General News Service*, February 10, 2020; "China Focus: Modern Technology Aids Spring Farming Amid Epidemic," *Xinhua General News Service*, March 9, 2020.

194. "Ai Tech Aids Anti-Epidemic Fight," *Xinhua General News Service*, June 28, 2020; Xinmei Shen, "Facial Recognition Data Leaks Are Rampant in China as Covid-19 Pushes Wider Use of the Technology," *South China Morning Post*, October 8, 2020.

195. Yuan Yang Nian et al., "Seizing the Moment for Surveillance; Ft Big Read. China; for All Its Monitoring Powers, China's Efforts to Track Coronavirus Cases Have Often Been Haphazard. Private Companies Have Been Reluctant to Hand over Data but Are Facing Heavy Government Pressure to Comply," *Financial Times*, April 3, 2020.

196. Ibid.

197. Xinhua, "China Focus: China Values Privacy by Using Encrypted Data in Battle against Epidemic."

198. Raymond Zhong, "China's Virus Apps May Outlast the Outbreak, Stirring Privacy Fears," *New York Times*, May 26, 2020.

199. Melissa Zhu, "Inside China Tech: Privacy Vs Urgency in Covid-19 Contact Tracing," *South China Morning Post*, June 6, 2020.

200. Zhong, "China's Virus Apps May Outlast the Outbreak, Stirring Privacy Fears."

201. Shen, "Facial Recognition Data Leaks Are Rampant in China as Covid-19 Pushes Wider Use of the Technology."

202. Ibid.

203. Nian et al., "Seizing the Moment for Surveillance; Ft Big Read. China; for All Its Monitoring Powers, China's Efforts to Track Coronavirus Cases Have Often Been Haphazard. Private Companies Have Been Reluctant to Hand over Data but Are Facing Heavy Government Pressure to Comply."

204. Ibid.

205. AFP, "New Normal in Virus-Hit China: High-Tech Tracking and Fever Checks."

206. Zhong, "China's Virus Apps May Outlast the Outbreak, Stirring Privacy Fears."

207. Xinhua, "Commentary: Blood and Sweat in China's Anti-Virus War to Be Glorified in World Cause," *Xinhua General News Service*, March 10, 2020.

208. AFP, "New Normal in Virus-Hit China: High-Tech Tracking and Fever Checks."

209. Xinhua, "Feature: Faces in China's Anti-Epidemic Fight," *Xinhua General News Service*, February 17, 2020.

210. "Across China: China's Young Medics Show Responsibility, Perseverance in Fighting Epidemic," *Xinhua General News Service*, March 9, 2020.

211. "China Honors Late Female Role Models Battling COVID-19," *Xinhua General News Service*, March 13, 2020.

212. "Commentary: Collectivism Plays Indispensable Role in China's COVID-19 Fight," *Xinhua General News Service*, March 17, 2020.

213. "Commentary: Institutional Strength: China's Key to Beating Novel Coronavirus," *Xinhua General News Service*, March 10, 2020.

214. "Commentary: Collectivism Plays Indispensable Role in China's COVID-19 Fight."

215. AFP, "China Seeks to Recast Itself from Virus Pariah to Helping Hand," *Agence France Presse - English*, March 5, 2020.

216. Steven Erlanger, "China's Missteps and Aggressive Diplomacy Fuel a Global Backlash to Its Ambitions: [Foreign Desk]," *New York Times*, May 4, 2020, A6.

217. Li, "With Selective Coronavirus Coverage, China Builds a Culture of Hate [with Graphic(S)]."

218. Xinhua, "Shifting Blame to China Won't Help U.S. Curb Epidemic: Spokesperson," *Xinhua General News Service*, March 12, 2020.

219. "Commentary: China Acts Responsibly in Global Fight against Coronavirus," *Xinhua General News Service*, March 6, 2020.

220. "China Opposes U.S. Stigmatization by Calling Coronavirus 'Chinese Virus'," *Xinhua General News Service*, March 17, 2020.

221. "Calling Novel Coronavirus 'China Virus' Extremely Irresponsible: FM Spokesperson," *Xinhua General News Service*, March 4, 2020.

222. Bedah Mengo, "Kenya's Most COVID-19 Cases Imported from Outside China: Analysis," Ibid., May 12; Xinhua, "Spotlight: New Research Shows COVID-19 May Have Been in L.A. Before China Announces Its Outbreak," Ibid., September 11; "China Wants U.S. Bio-Labs Open to Media Scrutiny: FM Spokesperson," *Xinhua General News Service*, August 12, 2020.

223. "Commentary: Bashing China over Pandemic Despicable, Futile," *Xinhua General News Service*, April 29, 2020.

224. "COVID-19 Tests Conducted in China Three Times Higher Than in U.S. Since Coronavirus Outbreak: Media," *Xinhua General News Service*, June 29, 2020; "China to Emerge from COVID-19 in Better Shape Than U.S.: Media," *Xinhua General News Service*, June 29, 2020.

225. Javier C. Hernández, "China Revels as Unrest Spreads across U.S.: [Foreign Desk]," *New York Times*, June 3, 2020, A12; Chris Buckley, "China's Nationalists Sneer at U.S. Troubles: [Foreign Desk]," Ibid., December 14, A10; Xinhua, "China Urges U.S. To Stop COVID-19 Stigmatizing," *Xinhua General News Service*, July 6, 2020.

226. "China Urges U.S. To Respond to Concerns of Its People, World on Epidemic," *Xinhua General News Service*, April 27, 2020.

227. "Commentary: In COVID-19 Response, China Deserves Credit in Human Rights Protection," *Xinhua General News Service*, May 26, 2020.

228. "Commentary: China's Human Rights Progress Deserves Applause Instead of Smearing," *Xinhua General News Service*, July 18, 2020.

229. "Commentary: Honoring Anti-Virus Heroes Will Boost China's March Ahead," *Xinhua General News Service*, September 7, 2020.

230. Simone McCarthy, "Coronavirus: China Positions Itself for 'Vaccine Diplomacy' Push to Fight Covid-19," *South China Morning Post*, August 4, 2020.

231. Lew, "Coronavirus Pandemic Shows Global Consequences of China's Local Censorship Rules."

232. Myers, "China Had a Fail-Safe Way to Track Contagions. Officials Failed to Use It.: [Foreign Desk]."

233. Cissy Zhou, "Coronavirus: China's Pandemic Lifeline for Small Firms Draws Lukewarm Response from Business Owners," *South China Morning Post*, May 22, 2020.

234. Eva Dou, "In Vaccine Trials, Mixed Results for China's Sinovac," *The Washington Post*, November 19, 2020, A14.

235. Maria Siow, "Cambodia's Caution over China's Covid-19 Vaccine a Signal to US: Analysts," *South China Morning Post*, December 20, 2020.

Chapter 5

Populists Stuck in the Middle

How Russia Struggled to Control COVID

By the very nature of his hybrid regime, Russian president Vladimir Putin never had the same chance as his Chinese counterpart to bury the outbreak. Rather than facing the equivalent of medical dissidents and online quasi-conspirators as Xi had, Putin found his less fettered civil society was able to voice concerns far more publicly.

This put the authorities in an awkward place vis-à-vis their medical personnel: the individuals and groups speaking out on systemic deficiencies were the same people whom these authorities relied upon to help ameliorate the situation. The result was that throughout the pandemic, Russian officials bounced between publicly praising their medical professionals for their grueling work and harassing them for exposing response failures. Just as Putin commended health-care workers for "holding the line of defense against the advancing epidemic" at the start of the outbreak, for example, the outspoken head of the independent Alliance of Doctors was stopped by police as she attempted to deliver needed medical supplies to a poor rural hospital.[1]

The disparity between words and meaningful action infected the entire medical response. Even while the government talked up promises of (oft undelivered) monetary bonuses for frontline medical staff, for example, it was unable to provide increasingly outspoken personnel with the basic PPE and medical equipment needed to safely treat their patients.[2] As in China, doctors grew sick in hospitals and clinics around the country.[3] And as Russian medics used their limited freedoms to warn of looming disaster, they found themselves under threat from local authorities uneager to broadcast this reality lest they be held politically accountable.[4]

In some cases, frontline workers were taken in for questioning over social media posts in which they complained about deteriorating conditions.[5] In others, outspoken doctors were fired and put under investigation for divulging

117

"medical secrets."[6] Some hospital personnel faced charges of disseminating "fake news," "spreading rumors," and "stirring unrest."[7] More menacingly, a scattering of individual doctors—some known for speaking out against official COVID conditions and policies—mysteriously began falling from high-up hospital windows to their deaths below.[8]

The plight of these frontline workers highlights the double-edged sword of competitive authoritarianism during a disaster. On the one hand, Russians had just enough freedom to publicly expose dangerous deficiencies in their system. On the other hand, the more they spoke out, the more they risked losing those very tenuous liberties.

But these and other voices in the somewhat free media landscape also made it clear to Russia's leaders that they would be unable to hide COVID to the extent that China did in the early period. So instead, Putin chose to bureaucratize it. Knowing that nothing good could come from the approaching storm, he took the extremely uncharacteristic measure of retreating into the shadows while his state apparatus began anxiously patrolling the country's far eastern Chinese border.

Well known for his public micromanagement of high-profile crises, Putin had good reason to keep a surprisingly low profile. Over his two decades of rule, he had steered the state ever deeper into authoritarianism. But he lacked the supreme power of China's Xi. United Russia, Putin's party of power, was the dominant political force, but it was not the only one. Undoubtedly, the other large parties played a submissive role to United Russia, but individual members occasionally showed that meek was not synonymous with subservient. Tens, even hundreds, of thousands of Russians periodically demonstrated their willingness to challenge the state, taking to the streets in episodes that China had not witnessed in decades.

This is the context in which the Russian COVID response template was forged. At the start of February, Prime Minister Mikhail Mishustin, ostensibly the head of government but in reality a political figure who largely took his cues from Putin, assumed the lead. He placed the new coronavirus on a list of especially dangerous diseases, alongside HIV and tuberculosis, giving Russian authorities the power to isolate, quarantine, and, where applicable, deport those found sick.[9] Immediately, authorities in a handful of districts in Russia's far eastern Primorsky Region declared states of emergency and set up isolation facilities where all Chinese residents entering the area would be subject to a 14-day quarantine.[10]

The emergent role of the federal government was to safeguard the borders and assist in the provision of protective equipment and medicine.[11] Before Russians needed two hands to count the number of cases identified at home, the country had designated 366 quarantine facilities with nearly 30,000 available beds.[12] But Russia's more politically vulnerable leaders were reluctant to launch a China-style lockdown, continuing to promise into late March, as the case count hit 400, that "no tough quarantine will be introduced soon."[13]

It was just days later that Moscow's mayor, thousands of miles from the Chinese border, ordered all Muscovites over 65 years old and those with underlying health conditions to quarantine from March 26 until April 14 (later extended into May).[14] Prime Minister Mishustin, in a separate statement, urged all Russians to do the same, though he did not require it.[15] The federal government closed schools through April 12, and severely limited international travel, but left other measures up to local authorities.[16]

Seeing the writing on the wall, most authorities complied with the central government's suggestions. Region after region, from Murmansk[17] and Kaliningrad[18] in the west to Yamalo-Nenets[19] and Primorsky in the east,[20] followed suit. Guided by the central authorities, the vast majority of Russians entered into a period of self-isolation.[21]

Even as Russia's subjects were hunkering down, a tussle ensued between government officials, who insisted growing case numbers just reflected increased testing capabilities,[22] and Kremlin critics, who alleged official case counts were artificially low and accused the authorities of purposely classifying actual COVID patients into other diagnostic categories.[23] The government blinked first. Under international pressure, the Health Ministry in April began treating all pneumonia cases as COVID cases.[24] By the end of the month, with nearly 94,000 cases, Russia claimed to rank fiftieth in the world (per capita).[25] But with its large population, Russia was clocking in more cases in absolute numbers than almost anywhere else.[26]

Sky-high numbers persisted throughout the spring, even amidst ongoing suspicions that the official case and fatality counts were being artificially held down. Certain regions were obviously underreporting; scarce COVID tests were being denied to some symptomatic patients; local reports showed increased levels of crematorium activity in the absence of high official fatality figures; and the government was strategically releasing incomplete data that made the situation appear less dire.[27] Perhaps the most egregious accounting manipulation involved a failure to account for excess fatality numbers which, when discovered in late spring, indicated a major undercount of COVID deaths.[28] The government's reluctance to consider these data was understandable since they flew in the face of the government's silver lining, which was that Russia's fatality rate was many times below the global average.[29]

Even with these various accounting tricks, by mid-April, every Russian region had registered cases of COVID.[30] It became obvious that, with all the infections, local health facilities could not manage. Over the spring, medical professionals complained they had far too little PPE to stay safe, and their ranks were thinned by sickness and death.[31] By the end of April, the government announced residents in much of the country would have to endure at least two more weeks at home to prevent the health system's collapse.[32]

As regional and local governments bore the brunt of the disaster, the federal government, through the military, Health Ministry, and Emergency Situations Ministry (MChS), plugged holes where it could. Military and MChS personnel disinfected health, transportation, and industrial facilities.[33] The military took charge of preparing thousands of hospital beds, building modular medical facilities, and providing medics to short-staffed regions, from Buryatia and Crimea in the south to eastern Siberia's Transbaikal Territory.[34] All told, during the spring surge, the Defense, Health, and Emergency Situations' Ministries fielded at least sixteen missions to eleven regions, opened six new hospitals and converted dozens of existing military hospitals into civilian COVID treatment centers.[35]

Russian leaders tried to follow China's lead by using big tech to slow the spread, including using cell phone geolocation data to track and isolate potential infections.[36] In Moscow, where authorities had been investing in China-style facial recognition cameras before COVID, the technology was used to enforce stay-at-home orders, leading to phone calls, home visits, fines, and arrests.[37] But most Russian regions lacked this technology and going beyond this proved difficult even in Moscow. When some Russian regions began using QR codes to limit time outside of home, for instance, Moscow's mayor was forced to abandon the effort under pressure from the sorts of political opposition and rights groups that have no voice in China.[38] The effectiveness of digital passes authorizing some to leave quarantine was undermined by the emergence of fake permits.[39]

As Russians looked for light at the end of the tunnel, Putin provided it, giving the government a deadline to announce a strategy to end lockdowns. If Putin was shy about forcing regions into quarantine, he reveled in the role of liberating them. But he also pledged that decisions to end restrictions in any area would be heavily based on expert views. According to the three-stage strategy announced on May 6, each region's lead sanitary doctor would submit a proposal, based on factors such as infection growth rate, hospital space, and test availability, to the local governor, who would make the final call on easing restrictions.[40] Each stage would expand the list of public spaces to be reopened.[41]

The official line, with some rare exceptions, was that Russia's spring COVID response had been a great success. State media reported Russia's health-care system, with its Soviet roots, had passed the COVID test with flying colors. It was able to "quickly switch into operating in 'combat' conditions,"[42] one report read, adding the important comment that regional officials credited "effective cooperation with Moscow" for their successful response.[43]

But authorities could not ignore the problems that had emerged. In the midst of the spring wave, the health minister conceded the disease had taken them by surprise and left confusion on the part of some hospital and clinic staff over which providers were required to treat infectious COVID patients.[44] Moreover, the country's prosecutor general in June described the "unsatisfactory condition" of many medical facilities, including a severe deficit in personnel and equipment—and even a lack of running water.[45] Russia's deputy prime minister acknowledged enormous disparities in the health system: while medical facilities in major cities tended to be passable, many hospitals and clinics in outlying districts were in "poor, if not terrible, condition."[46]

At the same time, officials carefully couched these shortcomings as ephemeral, one noting that despite "some complaints and some mishaps" at the start, "today everything is according to a plan."[47] "Our [healthcare] system has proved to be flexible and ready to be mobilized," Putin summarized.[48] The Moscow mayor, heading Putin's coronavirus taskforce, agreed: "The system has coped brilliantly."[49]

Regardless of the system's performance, Putin's decision to reopen the country in May was closely connected to two important political projects. Just as Chinese leaders bent over backward to hold their "two sessions" conference (albeit only once the virus had subsided), Putin was determined to hold his (postponed) May 9 Victory Day parade, commemorating the seventy-fifth anniversary of the Soviet Union's victory over Nazi Germany, on June 24, and a constitutional referendum soon after.[50] Testing regimes and mask mandates could remain, but Putin, eager to move forward, began referring cautiously to a return to "normal" even as COVID cases continued to pile on.[51]

The Victory Day parade was a classic Potemkin display. As Russia neared 600,000 cases, Putin and a crowd of elderly, unmasked veterans (all of whom had reportedly spent two weeks in isolation to attend) watched as more than 14,000 troops and a barrage of land and air military hardware crossed Red Square.[52] But less than two weeks before the Victory Day parade, Moscow's mayor urged residents not to attend.[53] More than a dozen cities, ordered by Putin to hold their own military parades, canceled or delayed plans in response to pandemic conditions.[54] Sticking with his pledge to follow the science, Putin did nothing to intervene.

Just days after the Victory Day celebration, Russians came out to vote on a series of constitutional amendments, a referendum initially scheduled to take place in April.[55] Federal health authorities publicly assured Russians the vote would be safe, with the Kremlin spokesperson (oddly abetted by the local WHO representative)[56] repeating the line that "life is returning to normal."[57] After seven days of voting, 68 percent had reportedly cast their ballot with more than three-quarters supporting the changes, thus giving Putin the pos-sibility of serving as Russia's longest ruling leader since Joseph Stalin.[58]

The same willful denial of reality that facilitated these two events contin-ued throughout the summer and into the early fall as cases climbed.[59] Tourism and COVID went hand in hand, and by mid-September, Russia had climbed to rank fortieth in the world in per capita COVID cases.[60] As in the United States, officials blamed rising cases on the sheer number of tests done and recommended that asymptomatic cases not be counted.[61] They continued to boast of their low mortality rate, which they put at around 100th in the world.[62]

By mid-October, however, national leaders were forced to admit their fall spike was even more severe than what they'd experienced in the spring.[63] But they promised the health-care system was now stronger and there was no need for "harsh, wholesale restrictive measures."[64] In actuality, many of the problems present in the spring remained throughout the autumn. For example, polls showed that many hospitals faced oxygen shortages.[65] They lacked adequate ambulance services.[66] And the beds continued to fill up, despite the fact that many cases were going unreported since large numbers of Russians distrusted local doctors and opted for self-diagnosis and treatment.[67]

With the fall wave, national government officials again insisted regional leaders would be free to decide for themselves whether to implement quaran-tines, effectively disseminating political responsibility.[68] Some did, starting with stay-at-home orders for those over sixty-five or suffering from chronic medical conditions.[69] Even those who one month promised not to impose "extreme measures," including curfews, business closures and, lockdowns, found themselves implementing limits the next month.[70] The same went for masking requirements, which the health minister said fell to regional gover-nors.[71] There would be no new federal interventions, the health minister said, since "restrictive measures" must be based on "the epidemiological situation in a certain region."[72]

Indeed, there was no national lockdown through the remainder of 2020.[73] Putin's reticence to impose a national lockdown was political. Unlike in the United States, where restrictions were challenged in courts, Putin's Consti-tutional Court had a long track record of deference.[74] Unlike in China, where organized opposition was virtually nonexistent, Putin was weary that taking such an unpopular move could feed the loosely organized opposition move-ment. Partly as a result of this decentralized decision-making, there was enormous variation in positivity rates, from 1.8 per 1,000 in Tatarstan to 57.5 in Karelia and, by the end of the year, 70.14 in St. Petersburg.[75,76]

By this point, in December, Russia was reaching record-high daily case counts of around 29,000, and more than 5 million had been treated over the year.[77] National leaders began transitioning in force to a "we need to learn to live with it" approach.[78] Even as they did so, December's daily deaths exceeded 600 for the first time, and Russia's official death count surpassed 50,000.[79] The true death count for the year may have surpassed 186,000, more than three times higher than the official count and higher than in most European countries (though lower than in the United States).[80] The government clung tight to the official numbers, however, saying only that specialists would have to engage in "profound analysis" to understand how COVID has impacted Russia's mortality rate.[81]

Despite these figures, at the end of the year Putin boasted that Russia "has demonstrated its high preparedness for the rapid mobilization of resources."[82] In particular, Putin noted that the government created 270,000 beds and built 40 medical centers, three-quarters of which were constructed by the Defense Ministry.[83] More than 100 federal teams had reportedly been deployed since the start of the pandemic to assist in the regions.[84] Putin especially lauded being "the world's first country" to develop a vaccine.[85] While the much hailed Sputnik vaccine suffered from rollout delays and a trust deficit, an estimated 700,000 Russians had received their jab by the time Putin gave his New Year's speech marking the end of 2020.[86]

LEADERSHIP AND DELEGATION:
A DELICATE BALANCE

From Putin's perspective, it was hard to imagine, as the pandemic infiltrated Russia, that the outcome was going to be enviable. As an increasingly populist, semi-authoritarian leader, Putin must have realized that all eyes were on him. But unlike in China, where dissent was a nuisance largely limited to a few corners of the internet, in Putin's Russia just enough freedom—of assembly, of expression—remained to threaten the president in the streets and potentially, though a stretch, in parliament. While Xi's strict authoritarianism gave him the freedom to sit out tough times, and bask in the good, Putin's more democratic regime created pressures that required him to hold the reins. His monumental task in 2020 was to make a show of force without actually taking on responsibility for the building disaster.

When Russia confirmed its first two cases in late January, government officials quickly grabbed the microphones to play down "the risk of further spread"[87] and affirm "the situation is definitely under control."[88] Oddly, these reassurances did not come from President Putin, who is typically depicted as the country's hands-on manager. In fact, throughout the early development of the coronavirus crisis, Putin was conspicuously absent.[89] Putin's office broke its silence to note that the government was taking "special measures" to mitigate the risk.[90] But it was Putin's press spokesman, Dmitry Peskov, who made the comments, not Putin himself. Nearly a week later, Peskov was back to assure Russians that Putin was being briefed on events "daily or even hourly."[91]

Yet over the following month and a half, Putin remained uncharacteristically quiet, leaving the approaching storm to his political subordinates. It was Prime Minister Mishustin, not Putin, who promised Russians after the WHO declared a pandemic that "despite the difficult situation outside of Russia, the threat of the infection spreading in our country has been minimized."[92] The prime minister also maintained that "the president and the government have the situation in the Russian economy under control,"[93] while Putin's spokesperson continued to push the message that "the president is working at full throttle, as always."[94] Even the leader of Russia's upper house of parliament claimed to be following policies that reflected "the president's position."[95]

In Putin's public absence, Prime Minister Mishustin established a council to coordinate anti-coronavirus measures that would incorporate the already existing anti-coronavirus task force with an economic stability commission, but would also include regional governors and other relevant actors.[96] Putin, in turn, established a lower-key corresponding body at the State Council that was chaired by Moscow's mayor, Sergey Sobyanin, who simultaneously served as bridge and deputy chair to the government council.

It wasn't until nearly a week after the pandemic declaration in March that Putin finally reemerged in the captain's seat, promising Russians that "everything is under control" and retaking his place as a fixture of the news cycle.[97] The president reappeared on state TV, urgently advising Prime Minister Mishustin and his deputy that they should inform people how to protect themselves, as well as directing them to increase testing capacity, boost medical workers' salaries, and crack down on counterfeit medications.[98]

With this staged show of force, Putin was back, chairing meetings in which governmental ministers assured him that their quick measures had managed to contain any potential outbreak.[99] Putin reverted to a long-standing Kremlin template in which the president held televised one-on-ones with regional leaders, asking pointed questions about developments in their jurisdiction and issuing his own series of demands. In one typical example, Putin sat down with the head of the Crimea Republic, who dutifully thanked the president for his "instructions."[100]

A few days later, Putin went back to another staple publicity event mode. Over the past two decades, Putin had done everything from visiting Crimea in a submarine to hang-gliding with cranes in an effort to introduce them to flying in the wild. As he began tackling COVID, Putin donned a full bio-containment suit and held a meet-and-greet at a hospital treating COVID patients.[101] State media positioned him as the heroic and brave leader, entering an area even his aides and bodyguards would not. In one televised report, broadcasters compared Putin's COVID actions to some of his other previously broadcasted feats, including visiting Russian soldiers on the front lines of Syria and flying in a fighter jet. Putin "shows up in person everywhere," the commentator said.[102]

When Putin made his first national address two weeks after the pandemic declaration, he spoke with the vulnerability of a democrat but the resolve of an authoritarian populist. He warned his citizens that while Russian actions at the border had managed to constrain the "wide and rapid spread of the disease," the country could not "fence itself off from the threat."[103] But he assured viewers that Russia had both the "means" and "experience" to deal with the crisis and would implement the "maximum concentration of all resources, the most stringent implementation of doctors' recommendations."[104] Putin expressed hope that within three months the virus would be gone and that Russia would suffer from "minimal losses" if it acted "in an organized and disciplined manner."[105]

But, as noted above, Putin made a conscious choice to not run the show. Instead, he delegated this enormous task to lower-level leaders. Putin explained to his Security Council that regional leaders were in the best position to gauge what they needed to do.

Putin said,

> We have a lot of small communities, towns, and simply villages and townships. The situation is different everywhere. The economy is in a difficult situation as it is, and therefore, it wouldn't be the right thing to do to issue some general directives undermining economic activities.[106]

This strategy meant leaving politically volatile decisions and announcements to subordinates, including Mayor Sobyanin and Prime Minister Mishustin, who in turn called on local leaders to announce their own unpopular stay-at-home orders. Putin himself resisted terms such as "quarantines," "emergency," or "restrictions." As one former Kremlin advisor noted, Putin likely estimated that as the virus ripped through his land, "the best thing to do is stand to the side."[107] The stark contrast between everyday politics, when decision-making was highly centralized, and COVID-era politics, when unpopular policy decisions were delegated all the way down to regional and municipal authorities, was stark.[108]

While government subordinates were stuck with delivering a long stream of bad news and local leaders were responsible for imposing painful lockdowns, Putin cast himself as a sort of fairy godfather, granting goods that could reduce the harm being done.[109] So, for example, at a time when Mishustin was encouraging "tough decisions" at the regional level, including the closure of public spaces, Putin announced a special holiday week during which nonessential workers would continue to receive pay while staying at home.[110]

In true authoritarian populist form, the Kremlin cast Putin as the anti-populist, out to "save lives, to cure those who need treatment and then to revive the economy."[111] But as the pandemic worsened, Putin signed a series of decrees his administration promised would ameliorate the difficult situation, part of the continued strategy of disassociating Putin with the negative COVID policies that were increasingly inevitable.[112] This included the guarantee of full payment of wages for those unable to work through April 30.[113] It also opened the government's reserve fund to "all those areas [of the economy] which will simply not survive without state support."[114] In addition to suggesting tax and insurance payment deferrals for small and medium-sized enterprises, and implementing a six-month moratorium on bankruptcy, Putin extended welfare payments for six months and promised a temporary extra allowance for certain eligible families with young children.[115]

Devolving unpopular lockdown decisions to others led to an uncharacteristic amount of policy variance as regional officials took "diverging interpretations" about what they could and should do to stop the virus.[116] As Moscow and Chechnya tightened the screws, for example, the governor in the Amur region allowed hotels, restaurants, hairdressers, and others to continue to operate; the leader of the Nenets Autonomous Region allowed sports facilities to function; and Tatarstan permitted oil and gas companies to work.[117] Others used their new authority to ban alcohol sales, following a dramatic increase in consumption and a reported spike in related crime.[118]

Not only was there confusion about what could and should be done, there was also encroachment on federal powers in ways that more authoritarian China had never seen. When officials from Chechnya, as well as Chelyabinsk and Sakha, went so far as to close their republics' domestic borders, Prime Minister Mishustin awkwardly reminded regional leaders not to "confuse regional powers with federal ones,"[119] and Putin, again appearing concerned about publicly unpopular policies, warned excessive measures could have "destructive consequences"[120] on the economy.[121] In an apparent attempt to emphasize this point, Putin explicitly limited regional authority on interregional transportation and shielded from closures certain essential services, from medical facilities and grocery stores to "urgent" repair or financial services.[122] "All of our decisions should be commensurate with the threat and proportionate to the situation," Putin said.[123]

Putin's COVID management could be summarized as power without responsibility, his delegation style fitting closer into the devolutionary delegation model but with top-down characteristics. Putin went out of his way to appear in control, reminding lower-level leaders that while they were charged with devising their own plans, he would ensure cooperation "between all levels of power—municipal, regional and federal."[124] This, Putin said, meant that he would be "watching what's going on very closely" and continuing to hold teleconferences with the leaders as a form of accountability.[125] Putin reminded regional heads they "should be prepared to overcome all difficulties that might emerge"[126] and that they were "personally responsible" for defeating COVID on their terrain.[127] He authorized dispersing federal funds to the regions, but with a stiff warning that "we will also demand an account."[128]

But the fact was that even as Putin sought to regain a degree of visibility, he was no longer the face of the state. Fear of COVID prompted Putin to shift away from the in-person meetings he was long known for, which were complicated by the Kremlin's insistence that guests be quarantined, tested, examined, and forced to walk through a disinfecting mist.[129] In his place, other government officials, including the deputy prime minister running the COVID operation and the head of the consumer protection agency, regularly stood at the podium answering reporters' questions. Explaining Putin's decreased visibility, relative to others in the government, his spokesperson said the president was working from his country residence, where he continued his "daily or even hourly involvement in the operation of the entire state machinery."[130] Raising his status to specialist, Putin was said to be using his time to build an "expert level of understanding" of virology.[131]

All of this meant that Putin was sharing the spotlight much more than he had before. In lieu of personal meetings, Putin was regularly shown on television, speaking directly to viewers and then running videoconferences with regional governors.[132] He grazed over aggregate national numbers, such as bed availability, and urged regional leaders to "maximally increase the pace and report back today" with any problems, adding that "monitoring here must be constant."[133]

Many of Putin's orders appear to have been simply designed to make his presence known and often involved stating the obvious. In one of the many such examples, Putin at the end of April instructed his Health Ministry to "carry out nonstop monitoring of the situation nationwide and in every constituent region of our Federation, to constantly update its plans, given that the situation changes practically every day." "I repeat," Putin added for emphasis, "we must continue being pro-active, as we have been until now."[134]

Putin's wise commander role was mixed with one of stern father and a sort of people's representative, demanding the sorts of things from the government that everyday Russians might. For instance, he reprimanded the government's focus on long-term viral spread, demanding instead "a good and professional" daily forecast.[135] He pressed the government to ensure it had whatever surplus equipment it needed to "endure any scenario that might develop in each of our territories."[136] And while any Russia observer knew that over the past two decades the government served at the behest of Putin, he distanced his office from the running of the state. His spokesperson went so far as to insist the Kremlin had not coordinated with the government on "normative and legal acts" related to the pandemic, since "this is the absolute prerogative of the government."[137]

If Putin sought to build an independent profile for himself, he made no effort to hide that he was still in charge of the central government. He outlined that the "sacred duty" of state leaders was to "explain to people—very carefully and tactfully, but patiently and persistently—about the reality of the current situation and offer unburdensome but absolutely necessary measures and means of protection."[138] He later told his Security Council that although the situation was improving, "we certainly need to carefully monitor developments in every region on a regular basis and promptly respond to the changing situation."[139] When Putin decided it was time to end lockdowns, he ordered that there "be no excessive bureaucracy in making these decisions."[140] Later, pointing to price increases during a meeting with the government, Putin said, "I expect not only proposals on the matter from you, but also concrete measures and timelines."[141] Days later, the government introduced popularly supported price caps on various foods.[142]

The vague guidance coming out of the Kremlin on ending the lockdown was reminiscent of the guidance initiating it. The rule of thumb was local autonomy, said a Kremlin spokesperson, who went on to add that "these powers of the head of the regions should be exercised in close coordination with the government headquarters."[143] In Putin's words, local leaders "should continue to have room for maneuver, for flexible, independent decision-making based on the local situation and in consultation with experts."[144]

Unlike in China, Putin's spring victory over COVID was much more tenuous, leaving him little to celebrate. With Russia experiencing about 10,000 new cases per day, some regions began relaxing their lockdowns, while others extended them.[145] There were still regional and local leaders who described their health-care system as "completely paralyzed"[146] and "catastrophic,"[147] and the federal government continued to regularly dispatch medical professionals and equipment to the regions.[148] Despite these troubles, Putin did sneak in his two politically vital events—Victory Day celebrations and the constitutional referendum—during the summer period.

One of the regions that managed to hold a Victory Day parade in June was Dagestan, a southern republic that provides insight into what Putin's hands-on style of devolutionary delegation of the COVID response really meant for regional leaders facing the outbreak.[149] Dagestan, one of the poorest regions in Russia, was also one of the worst hit in the spring wave.[150] While at the start of April officials in Dagestan reported just fifty cases,[151] such reports quickly became suspect. One giveaway was the number of small villages reporting two or three fatalities in a given day, while the number of funerals skyrocketed.[152] As one cleric complained publicly to Putin: "No one is keeping statistics on the people who are dying of illnesses in their homes . . . They die, they are buried according to tradition, and no one counts them."[153]

By late April, a large surge of reported infections in the region prompted the federal Labor Ministry to suggest a lockdown of all assisted-living facilities and psychoneurological care homes, where the outbreak was most widespread.[154] In early May, Russia's health minister publicly said the high infection rate and subpar performance of the local health-care system in Dagestan "seriously worries" him.[155] Just a week later, the region drew scrutiny from Putin, who contrasted the "relative stabilization" of the COVID situation in Russia in general with Dagestan's situation where, in Putin's words, "people are saying they cannot receive the necessary medical assistance always and everywhere in full."[156]

It was only after the Dagestani health minister announced in May the death of at least 657, including tens of medics, that the Kremlin felt compelled to react.[157] Days later, Putin held a video meeting with Dagestani officials that aired on national television. In it, one local official called the situation a "catastrophe" and requested government assistance. Off camera, a Dagestani NGO leader blamed the artificially low regional figures for the center's slow initial response. "It looked like the number was relatively low, and that was why we didn't get enough assistance from the federal center when we really needed it."[158] Putin sought to avoid blaming the regional leaders, however, saying that the "main cause of severe complications in the region's residents is delay in seeking medical assistance and self-treatment at home."[159]

Putin responded to the crisis by ordering the federal Health Ministry to "provide additional assistance," including test systems, medications, equipment, and staff,[160] but he also appealed to Dagestanis:

> Dagestan's ability to overcome the threat of the epidemic as soon as possible depends on our joint steps, on the efforts of all residents of the republic, on your solidarity, your firmness, responsibility, and your strict observance of the recommendations of doctors and specialists.[161]

As part of this campaign, Putin encouraged the majority Muslim population to stay home for the Eid holiday celebrations.[162]

While the deputy health minister claimed half of Dagestan's COVID-designated beds were empty, Putin ordered MChS to immediately send medical specialists and disinfection equipment to the region.[163] After a working group from the Health Ministry visiting Dagestan in late May criticized the local response as "insufficient,"[164] the Defense Ministry deployed to the region two field hospitals, capable of holding a combined 200 patients, and began constructing hospitals there at a cost of $27 million.[165] As external assistance flowed into the region, the head of Dagestan appeared to minimize the seriousness. He said the situation "is not simple, but it is under control and is gradually getting better."[166] He also maintained that one-third of the 9,000 beds designated for COVID and "pneumonia sufferers" continued to remain empty which, if true, would make the national government's moves more for show than practical effect.[167]

By mid-June, Putin was holding the Dagestan case up as a showpiece for central government readiness and control. When the "complicated situation" emerged in Dagestan, he said, "the whole country came to its rescue."[168] Apart from the military and MChS, Putin recalled that "doctors from all over the country and from Moscow went there."[169] Moscow-based medics who had been dispatched to the region began to pack up, saying that COVID hospitals were returning to their pre-COVID stance, and the local health minister expressed hope that within a month the region would begin lifting restrictions.[170] At the end of June, the national health minister announced that the situation in Dagestan had stabilized, with "ten times fewer people hospitalized" compared to when the federal government intervened.[171]

The Dagestan case was emblematic of the struggle facing many regions. Regional health-care systems were severely taxed by the COVID outbreak and regional authorities kept real numbers concealed in the initial period. The case of Dagestan was used to laud federal intervention, but in other ways, such regions remained on the backburner. For example, when vaccine production began, the hard-hit republic received just 800 doses in mid-December.[172] It is also telling that when the acting head of Dagestan was sickened with COVID in December, he was not treated in Dagestan but instead transferred to a Moscow hospital.[173]

As Dagestan appeared to be coming out of its period of acute crisis in June, other regions were still hobbling along. Throughout the summer, as cases rose, authorities had little appetite to implement the sorts of restrictions that could slow the spread. When summer outbreaks turned into a full-fledged second wave in the fall, Putin again put the onus on regional leaders. Even if there was no national lockdown in the fall, there were regional restrictions.[174] As regions checked internal borders, implemented curfews, enforced mask mandates, and canceled non-urgent surgeries, Putin's office continued to promise "special measures" of assistance upon request.[175]

When news reports reemerged of overburdened regions with long waits for access to critical equipment and even patients being locked out of hospitals, Kremlin officials placed responsibility on regional heads and promised they were "responding to every piece of published information."[176] "We are following the situation in every territory, we are helping, and we will help," Putin said in comments aimed at regional heads, before again urging them to "please, don't forget about your responsibility."[177] Putin called on the central government to provide additional monetary assistance to the regions and to investigate systemic shortcomings.[178] He promised to deal "separately and directly" with failing regions.[179] And he apparently even dispatched medical teams based on citizen complaints.[180]

As local websites showed video of COVID patients forced to lie on chairs in hospital hallways,[181] Kremlin spokesman Peskov acknowledged "failures" in some regions, adding that "the president is aware of that" and the federal government was responding.[182] By mid-November, seventeen regions were at 90 percent bed capacity and the National Health Ministry was dispatching medics as well as auditors to several struggling regions.[183] Prime Minister Mishustin ordered regional leaders to "assume direct control" over the situation and Peskov referred to "an absolutely unacceptable crisis situation" in certain regions.[184]

Despite this, Putin continued to deflect. He denied the need for a comprehensive national plan, the Kremlin insisting that "the need to introduce tougher restrictive and isolation measures varies from region to region."[185] Putin regularly defended this devolution, explaining that in such a large country, "we must exercise a selective approach to what's happening in the territories."[186] He maintained in the fall that the federal government had always played the "dominant role"[187] but explained that adopting a "one-size-fits-all solution" would have led to either economic or health failures.[188] A "common template," Putin said, would be "not only inefficient, but even sometimes harmful."[189] His spokesperson also pressed the point that regional policies were "strictly controlled and coordinated by the government headquarters" and that Putin "personally took part in that work."[190]

As in the spring, government officials were periodically asked why Putin's role in the pandemic response was less prominent than was typical. The response was that Putin was taking an active role behind the scenes.[191] In late October, for instance, Prime Minister Mishustin found himself in the awkward spot of vouching for his boss. "Since the first days of the pandemic Vladimir Vladimirovich [Putin] was doing everything possible for all of us to cope with it: he both was helping the government, was making strategic decisions, and was in constant touch with doctors," Mishustin said.[192] In December, the Kremlin spokesperson again reassured reporters that Putin continued to be fully informed about the COVID situation which, he added, "is a matter [for] the crisis center."[193]

This deferral of responsibility was particularly convenient at a time when more and more citizens were experiencing pandemic fatigue. While China's leaders had the political security and confidence to continue imposing restrictions months, even years, after COVID had begun, the Russian government's attitude was more circumspect. This was visible when owners of more than 40 St. Petersburg bars and restaurants said they would refuse to abide by a municipal decree to close down at the end of December.[194] An additional 200 were reportedly considering joining in the protest. When asked whether the government would intervene, Peskov replied that "the Kremlin can't interfere in that" and encouraged local authorities to seek a compromise.[195]

With all the building public angst, Putin did not shy away from or downplay the year's hardships in his annual New Year's address, instead trying to rally his people around them. "We went through this year together, with dignity, as the united people who cherish ancestral traditions should," he said, before comparing the fight against COVID to the one against Nazis in World War II he had just celebrated in the summer.[196] Putin expressed empathy with those sickened by COVID and promised "the fight against it does not stop for a minute."[197]

Even as he empathized, Putin maintained a tough technocratic image, adamant that the path out of COVID was to follow the science. From the start, Putin publicly insisted the response be based on "the positions of the medical and scientific community"[198] and that the government would hew closely to "doctors' recommendations."[199] Throughout the year, and unlike what we would see from democratic populists, Putin periodically downplayed cheery prognoses by referencing sober warnings from "experts and scientists."[200] He insisted regional leaders follow "recommendations from specialists,"[201] as did his spokesman in his absence.[202] Though Putin publicly celebrated Sputnik's emergency use authorization,[203] he spent the development period distancing himself from it, saying he only knew what he had read "in the media."[204]

Putin's public pledge to abide by expert guidance continued throughout the first year of the pandemic.[205] But when he sought to avoid the toughest measures, including renewed lockdowns during the fall wave, he began to intentionally choose a new sort of expert. This was evident when Putin, in December, spoke to the Presidential Council for Civil Society and Human Rights about the need to balance health restrictions with human rights. "At a time when all countries are trying to balance the unavoidable but forced restrictions with the necessary freedoms, expert evaluation provided by our Council has been and remains absolutely relevant," Putin said.[206]

Putin's strategy of (selectively) following the science and putting the responsibility on the regions yielded short-term losses. His approval rating fell steadily from 69 percent in February to 63 percent in March before nose diving.[207] Only half of respondents in late April believed the national government was doing "everything needed and everything they can,"[208] and by early May, Putin's approval rating was at its lowest level since he took power twenty years earlier.[209] Pollsters reported frustration among locals who watched Putin celebrate Russian foreign aid in the COVID sphere even as Russia's own medical system struggled.[210] His spokesperson dismissed these indicators in a way only a non-democrat could: "You should not think about your ratings—because if you think about your ratings, you won't be able to take responsible decisions."[211] The passage of his constitutional amendments provided sufficient reassurance that Putin had used his powers and strategy to weather the disaster.

PROPAGANDA AND SCAPEGOATS: OPPORTUNITIES AND LIMITS OF WRITING THE NARRATIVE IN A HYBRID REGIME

Putin's ratings might have been far worse if it weren't for his government's efforts to control the coronavirus narrative. While the Chinese efforts to control information were much further reaching (and warranted their own section), Russian authorities did use their powers to influence information flow in three important ways. First, agents of the government were employed to directly manipulate the message and heighten the image of responsiveness. More specifically, the government created a one-stop-shop coronavirus hotline where the public could call in to request assistance or seek advice.[212] Under the auspices of RosCongress Foundation, which bills itself as a "socially oriented non-financial development institution" established by Putin, the hotline was branded "In This Together."[213] Residents could call in to offer or ask for assistance with attaining everything from medicine and groceries to trash collection, and they could receive advice on subjects that spanned from economic support to "psychological and spiritual guidance." State media reported that by late March, more than 450 organizations and businesses had joined.[214]

These efforts were part of a second project to control the message at home and abroad. At the start of March, Russia's Human Rights Commissioner dismissed social media reports of high levels of viral spread, warning Russians "not to give way to panic and [to] trust official sources" instead.[215] Putin alleged the "provocative fake news" was being largely spread from abroad[216] and Russia's media watchdog, Roskomnadzor, announced it would block access to social media posts spreading COVID disinformation.[217] A new communication center would "identify and refute" fake news.[218]

From early February, state television and government officials were balancing between accusing foreign countries of engaging in "deliberate misinformation" about Russia's COVID response,[219] and countering foreign accusations that they were the ones spreading misinformation.[220] When it came to charges of misinformation, Western reporters were alleged to be using negative press on Russia "to divert the public's attention from domestic issues."[221] Russia's deputy foreign minister accused Western media and think tanks of serving as "propaganda mouthpieces" of Western states.[222] In response, the government threatened to take away journalists' Russian accreditation and fine them for threatening public order.[223]

As they attacked foreign sources of alleged misinformation, Russian officials sought to shield themselves from charges that Russia was actually fueling disinformation abroad. Officials openly denied foreign claims that Russia was intent on sewing panic and undermining governmental responses in the West.[224] Foreign Ministry officials again decried this as an "immoral attempt to conceal their own problems" and divert attention away from their own policy failures, accusations parroted in the state-controlled press.[225]

Of course, many of the attacks were targeted at their own citizens. By late March, officials claimed they were identifying five to six deliberate misinformation campaigns every day and said violators could face fines of up to 3 million rubles ($37,320) or even imprisonment.[226] In one case, the independent Ekho Moskvy radio station was charged $3,750 for reporting positivity and death rates far higher than official numbers.[227] As noted above, there were also reports of inundated and frustrated medical professionals and others being fired or dragged before prosecutors for publicly complaining about conditions, threatened with five years' imprisonment for spreading fake news.[228] Not incidentally, Russian authorities found the suspension of large public gatherings convenient for shutting down various types of protests as well.[229]

A third method the state employed to help shape the narrative was to punish those lower-level authorities seen as failing in the fight against COVID—employing the same pressure release as Chinese leaders. As in China, high-level officials punishing their subordinates were hoping to both exonerate themselves for response shortcomings and to demonstrate they were there to right the path. This approach was encapsulated by comments from Putin, who warned on state television that his directions should be carried out in a timely manner and, if not, "I'll see this as criminal negligence with all that it entails."[230] "You just have to act more actively and more quickly," Putin said with the confidence of a leader far from the fight.[231] Meanwhile, Prime Minister Mishustin blamed regional leaders for local medical conditions that "can hardly be described as satisfactory."[232]

These threats were enough to convince regional officials and hospital heads facing a COVID tsunami that covering up illnesses and deaths was the best way to avoid punishment.[233] There were various ways to evade blame. Sometimes regional leaders purposely avoided uploading statistics that were damning.[234] Other times, they sought to avoid conditions that would generate unfavorable statistics in the first place. For instance, throughout the first year of the pandemic, there were accusations that authorities in some regions refused people tests for fear they would drive up positivity rates.[235] And sometimes they were caught actually manipulating the data. In one case, a governor was recorded telling lower-level officials to "change the figures or they will think badly about our region."[236]

Over the course of 2020, this political leader was proven correct as officials were periodically fired or forced to resign. This happened in the early weeks of the pandemic, when the health ministers of at least two regions stepped down for failing "to make prompt decisions on fighting the spread" of COVID.[237] Accountability went all the way to the top, with at least four regional leaders (from the Komi Republic, Nenets Autonomous Region, Arkhangelsk Region, and Far East Kamchatka Territory) resigning in the first week of April, under fire for their insufficient COVID response.[238] Speaking to a pro-Kremlin news agency, the head of Russia's Institute of Socioeconomic and Political Research commented that "amid the epidemic situation, the quality of regional management requires greater responsibility."[239]

As Putin blamed response shortcomings on regions' "sloppiness,"[240] and his health minister condemned those regions that had deceptively "painted an idealistic picture" of their state of readiness, more resignations came.[241] By the end of April, a reported ten regional health ministers had resigned, with at least two others forced out less ceremoniously.[242] The pressure continued throughout the year and extended to municipal heads accused of hiding the true rate of COVID as well.[243]

Regional leaders were almost set up for failure. High infection rates drew unwanted attention, but so did low ones. Putin himself cast doubts on regions with lower infection levels during the fall wave, saying the data raised questions about the "quality of diagnostics and timely detection of the disease as well as hospital and in-home patient care."[244]

Some observers noted that by pushing responsibility onto lower-level officials, Putin "violated a fundamental contract with governors and bureaucrats—the state's middle management—who actually keep the system running."[245] But Putin did not take aim at only officials. As his government warned of "severe penalties" for price-fixing by manufacturers and sellers of needed medical equipment,[246] Putin and other government officials routinely reminded common citizens of their obligation.

Sometimes these words seemed meant to chide those who "reacted to the self-isolation regime negligently," as one state television presenter put it.[247] Other times, they were more like parental urgings to, in Putin's words, "show maximum responsibility for yourselves and those who are near you."[248] "In order to secure a victory, each and every one of us has to behave responsibly," said an official heading the government's response.[249] A Russian bill introduced in March equated quarantine violations to acts of terrorism and stipulated that deaths resulting from such negligence could be punishable by five to seven years in prison.[250] Local reporting in November noted that Russian police had fined more than 1.1 million people for violating restrictions since the start of the pandemic, bringing in at least $22.35 million in revenue.[251]

SYSTEMIC LEGITIMACY: RUSSIAN SUCCESS
AND THE DECLINE OF THE WEST

Russia may have walked a tortured path through the pandemic, but officials there took evident joy in highlighting the failures of Western democracies in a clear effort to highlight how Russia's system of governance had proven superior.[252] This was best exemplified in the unrolling of Russia's vaccine which, as noted earlier, was the world's first to be cleared by a government (though many said prematurely).

But the vaccine boast was just one incident in a long pattern in which Russian officials repeated claims that their COVID response was superior to that in the West, in good part thanks to Russia's rejection of the Western political model. Officials, sometimes using questionable statistics, regularly claimed that their situation was "more favorable"[253] or "not as acute"[254] as in much of Western Europe. State news praised Russia as a "haven of calm" relative to Europe.[255] The United States was depicted as a "living nightmare,"[256] that the overseas Russians were desperate to flee.[257] Putin credited Russia's "much more stable"[258] health-care situation, and its "much lower,"[259] "way lower,"[260] and "one of the world's lowest"[261] fatality counts, to what the Kremlin said was an advantage in per capita health personnel, as well as medical facilities "unparalleled anywhere else in the world."[262]

The comparisons struck a chord with opposition activists, who accused their government of "constantly lying about coronavirus,"[263] as well as doctors, only one-quarter of whom said the authorities had taken all necessary measures to fight the pandemic.[264] Where shortcomings were too obvious to hide, as with deficits in PPE and hand sanitizer, the Kremlin spokesperson noted that "all countries of the world are now short of all these."[265] Kremlin officials emphasized that "no country in the world could be ready"[266] for the virus and that every country was facing a "very difficult"[267] situation. Even as Putin offered his condolences for deaths, he reminded Russians their country had "one of the lowest indicators."[268] "One can confidently say that we have dealt with these problems worthily and in part maybe even better than other countries," he concluded.[269] At least one poll showed most Russians bought this message, with 70 percent agreeing at year's end that the state health-care system had successfully handled the pandemic.[270]

Russian leaders hoped to invest some of this political capital in their long-running project of upending the Western-dominated world order and, specifically, democratic primacy. State media hammered the West, and especially the United States and the United Kingdom, for "blatant carelessness" and racism in their response.[271] Meanwhile, the foreign minister condemned on state television "the classical system of liberal democracy," which he said gave "absolute priority to everything individual" and had "seriously exhausted itself."[272] The head of Russia's Security Council similarly equated "new Western values" with "individualism, ego-centrism, a cult of delights" and said they were leading to "disunity, indifference and disarray in the face of a looming danger."[273] More sweepingly, the head of Putin's ruling United Russia party said that Western-dominated "principles of globalization" had failed the test.[274]

While individualism had run amuck in the West, according to Putin, Russians would not tolerate "putting their personal unlimited freedom above the interests and freedoms of other people."[275] The problem, Putin said, went beyond culture and dug right into liberal institutions. Putin pointed directly at the United States and what he saw as the failings of pluralism, where "group [or] party interests are prioritized over the interests of the whole society, the interests of the people in this case." "If the people elect supreme authorities," Putin continued, "then these supreme authorities are mandated by the people and have the right to build their work so as to guarantee the interests of an absolute majority of the country's population."[276]

Another problem was that Western states lacked sufficient control and assertiveness, according to Putin.[277] Even as Putin claimed that his policies of decentralization had become a model for other countries around the world, he emphasized that Russia's central authorities and regional leaders worked "as one team."[278] He contrasted this with the U.S. "management system." "I doubt someone in our government or somewhere in a region could say: We won't do as the government say[s] or as the president says," Putin chided.[279] "Only a capable state can act efficiently in a crisis," the president added, reminding listeners of his efforts to strengthen state institutions "after the decay, and at times total devastation, in the 1990s."[280] The prime minister parroted this commentary, saying that in contrast to the West, in Russia "the necessary means and resources were provided without delay" and "state and the society were united."[281]

In addition to fatality rates, Russian officials pointed to their testing ramp up as evidence of their superiority.[282] Throughout April, the state press claimed Russia had placed second in the world in the number of tests completed.[283] Between mid-April and mid-May, the number of tests performed grew three times to six million, according to state sources.[284] This number grew two and a half times to 15 million one month later, these same sources claimed.[285] "Our country is a global leader in terms of the number of tests performed," Mishustin declared, adding that "leading European countries" were following the Russian lead.[286] They made no mention of test quality; in spring and summer, observers suggested Russian tests were of questionable reliability.[287] Nor did they highlight their record of producing and disseminating PPE, a chronic weakness the government struggled to rectify during the spring wave.[288]

As various Western states resorted to lockdowns to slow down the fall wave, Putin viewed this decision as another failed policy that Russia could exploit. "Just look what's happening in certain countries: they're reinstating strict restrictions, shutting down manufacturing enterprises, etc.," Putin said, with an obvious eye toward EU countries. "Our situation is a lot better, but the only reason why is the efficient measures taken by us in a timely and effective manner."[289] In his comments, Putin ignored the sharply rising case rate and fatality count in Russia, absent such restrictions. Instead, the Kremlin spokesperson added plainly that the pandemic exposed how the entire Western-dominated international system "leaves something to be desired."[290]

Finally, the Kremlin sought to demonstrate that Russian economic policy was more prudent than in the west. By late November, Putin claimed Russia had spent 4.5 percent of its GDP to mitigate the impact of COVID.[291] This included hundreds of millions of dollars spent bolstering the health-care sector,[292] but also social support, from unemployment,[293] poverty reduction measures, and special benefits for families with children[294] to breaks on consumer loans and mortgage payments.[295] Mishustin reassured Russians amidst fall budget shortfalls that the government would meet "all social guarantees and obligations that President Vladimir Putin has identified."[296]

But when analysts compared Russian spending to others, including the United States, which had already spent 11 percent of its GDP on the pandemic by mid-May, the Kremlin bristled.[297] Putin claimed that other countries spent more simply because their recession was far worse.[298] He pointed to a much smaller GDP contraction in Russia,[299] as well as an unemployment level (6 percent officially, up to 10 percent unofficially) that was "not as dramatic as in many other countries"[300] where, he said, "it just skyrocketed."[301] Both Putin and his spokesman also contrasted Russia's "pinpoint measures" with the "cheap populism"[302] in the West, where they described cash flows that "just burned in the furnace."[303]

CONCLUSION

Stuck somewhere just on the democratic side of the line dividing democracy and authoritarianism, Putin's Russia seemed set up for failure when the pandemic arrived. Looking at Russia's record, it is easy to see Russia's enormous shortcomings. These included, ironically, a deficit of effective central control. Putin built his astounding political career on the promise of returning Russia to a vertical power structure. But when disaster struck, he backed quietly away from this framework.

Why he did this was understandable. As a quasi-authoritarian populist who had built the image of a wise, apolitical technocrat doing what was right for the country and its people, Putin could not afford to single-handedly launch the aggressive COVID policies he asked others to implement. At least, he could not do so without either facing a political backlash or clamping down on the remaining democratic liberties he had allowed in his country.

Like China's leaders, Putin's foray into the pandemic was more of a dodge. But when he finally did get involved, he, just like China's leaders, encouraged tough measures. The key difference was that these measures were enforced by leaders in Beijing, in the China case, but by local leaders in the Russian one. Putin and Xi both promoted the COVID response, which they believed would bring their states long-term security and prosperity. But they did so in fundamentally different ways.

Putin was performing a delicate dance, balancing the shortcut of devolutionary delegation with the task of top-down delegation. While both Xi and Putin took on the role of distant commander during the pandemic, Putin, subject to more democratic pressures, was far more visible, even during the roughest periods. As the more visible leader, he made persistent appeals to follow science throughout the spring, but he lacked the resolve and firm control over the narrative needed to pull the trigger on aggressive policies. When things got rough for a second round in the fall, political pressures left Putin lacking the strength needed to sustain the tough policies Xi held to for years. Perhaps if COVID had arrived in 2022, after Putin had begun his war in Ukraine and eliminated the last vestiges of freedom at home, he may have pursued a more aggressive strategy, as in China.

Russia's performance in the first year of the pandemic, based on its infection and death rates, was lackluster at best, owing largely to its decrepit medical system but also to its high level of decentralization. But the very fact that Putin attempted to show himself taking the lead on COVID is testament to the power of populism and democratic pressures. Xi clearly did not feel the same burden to be front and center. In a competitive authoritarian regime like Russia's, Putin could afford to brandish his populist roots and simultaneously concur with the unpopular need to follow science. A more democratic populist, like the one running the United States, had no such luxury. And, as a result, that country was left with a far different outcome.

NOTES

1. Andrew Higgins, "A Doctor Who Accused Russia of Underreporting Virus Totals Is Detained: [Foreign Desk]," *New York Times*, April 5, 2020, A6.

2. Ibid.; Andrew Higgins, "After Months of Denial, Russia Admits the Virus Is Taking Hold," *New York Times* (Online), April 10, 2020.

3. ITAR-TASS, "More Than 100 Medical Staff Test Positive for Coronavirus in Russia's St. Petersburg," April 17, 2020; BBC, "Coronavirus in Russia: 20 April 2020," *BBC Monitoring Former Soviet Union - Political Supplied by BBC Worldwide Monitoring*, April 20, 2020.

4. "Coronavirus in Russia: 20 April 2020."

5. "Covid-19 Roundup: Russia 30 April 2020," *BBC Monitoring Former Soviet Union - Political Supplied by BBC Worldwide Monitoring*, April 30, 2020.

6. Thomas Grove and Ann M. Simmons, "Three Doctors in Russia Have Fallen out of Hospital Windows; the Incidents Occurred as More Medical Professionals Are Speaking out About the Stress of Treating Coronavirus," May 7, 2020, https://www.wsj.com/articles/three-doctors-in-russia-have -fallen-out-of-hospital-windows-11588887817.

7. Isabelle Khurshudyan, "In Russia, Rising Concern for Health-Care Workers," *The Washington Post*, May 7, 2020, A14; BBC, "Covid-19 Roundup: Russia 16 May 2020," *BBC Monitoring Former Soviet Union - Political Supplied by BBC Worldwide Monitoring*, May 16, 2020.

8. Grove and Simmons, "Three Doctors in Russia Have Fallen out of Hospital Windows; the Incidents Occurred as More Medical Professionals Are Speaking out About the Stress of Treating Coronavirus"; BBC, "Covid-19 Roundup: Russia 4 May 2020," *BBC Monitoring Former Soviet Union - Political Supplied by BBC Worldwide Monitoring*, May 4, 2020; "Covid-19 Roundup: Russia 26 April 2020," *BBC Monitoring Former Soviet Union - Political Supplied by BBC Worldwide Monitoring*, April 26, 2020.

9. ITAR-TASS, "Russia Ranks Coronavirus among Dangerous Diseases Along with HIV and Plague," February 2, 2020.

10. "State of Emergency Declared in Two Districts in Russia's Far East," February 2, 2020; "Russia Opens Quarantine Points in Border Areas with China," February 2, 2020; Newswire, "Emergency Declared in 3rd District in Russia's Primorye Territory to Address Spread of Coronavirus," *Russia & CIS General Newswire*, February 3, 2020.

11. ITAR-TASS, "Russia Taking All Necessary Prophylactic Measures against Coronavirus - Official," February 3, 2020; "Russia to Prolong Existing Restrictions against Coronavirus until April 1 - Official," February 26, 2020; Newswire, "Entry to Russia for Chinese Citizens to Be Suspended Starting Feb 20 (Part 2)," *Russia & CIS General Newswire*, February 18, 2020; "Russia Restricting Foreign Arrivals from S. Korea on March 1 (Part 2)," *Russia & CIS General Newswire*, February 28, 2020; "Russia to Restrict Air Traffic with Italy, Germany, France, Spain from March 13 - Coronavirus HQ (Part 2)," *Russia & CIS General Newswire*, March 11, 2020; ITAR-TASS, "Russia Imposes Entry Ban for Foreigners from March 18 to May 1 over Coronavirus Risks," March 16, 2020.

12. Newswire, "Rospotrebnadzor Chief: 366 Observation Facilities Prepared in Russia for Coronavirus Quarantine," *Russia & CIS General Newswire*, February 29, 2020; BBC, "Coronavirus in Russia: 5 March 2020," *BBC Monitoring Former Soviet Union - Political Supplied by BBC Worldwide Monitoring*, March 5, 2020; Newswire, "Six Coronavirus Cases Registered in Russia since Mid-Feb - Rospotrebnadzor," *Russia & CIS General Newswire*, March 3, 2020.

13. ITAR-TASS, "No Plans to Impose Tough Quarantine in Russia, Crisis Center Says," March 22, 2020.

14. BBC, "Coronavirus in Russia: 23 March 2020," *BBC Monitoring Former Soviet Union - Political Supplied by BBC Worldwide Monitoring*, March 23, 2020.

15. Elena Teslova, "Moscow Mayor Imposes Home Quarantine for People over 65," Andalou Agency, March 23, 2020, https://www.aa.com.tr/en/asia-pacific/moscow-mayor-imposes-home-quar-antine-for-people-over-65/1775599.

16. BBC, "BBCM Russia Watchlist for 23 March," *BBC Monitoring Former Soviet Union - Political Supplied by BBC Worldwide Monitoring*, March 23, 2020; ITAR-TASS, "Russia's Entry Ban Not to Be Applicable to CIS, Abkhazian, South Ossetian Nationals," March 23, 2020; BBC, "BBCM Russia Watchlist for 23 March"; ITAR-TASS, "Russia Fully Halts International Flights Amid Coronavirus," March 27, 2020.

17. BBC, "Coronavirus in Russia: 30 March 2020," *BBC Monitoring Former Soviet Union - Political Supplied by BBC Worldwide Monitoring*, March 30, 2020.

18. ITAR-TASS, "Governor of Russia's Kaliningrad Region Announces Lockdown Starting on March 31," March 30, 2020.

19. "Russia's Yamalo-Nenets Region Goes on Lockdown over Coronavirus - Authorities," March 31, 2020.

20. Ibid.

21. ITAR-TASS, "TASS: Kremlin Not Considering Possibility of Declaring Emergency Situation in Russia Amid Coronavirus Outbreak - Spokesman," April 1, 2020; Newswire, "Number of People in Self-Isolation Due to Coronavirus Situation Almost Doubles in Russia - Poll," *Russia & CIS General Newswire*, April 8, 2020.

22. "Covid-19 Growth Rates May Slow Down in Russia by May - Health Ministry's Chief Epidemiologist (Part 2)," *Russia & CIS General Newswire*, March 27, 2020.

23. Higgins, "A Doctor Who Accused Russia of Underreporting Virus Totals Is Detained: [Foreign Desk]"; Maxim Trudolyubov, "Late in the Game, Russia Steps up to Covid-19," *New York Times* (Online), April 7, 2020.

24. BBC, "Coronavirus in Russia: 13 April 2020," *BBC Monitoring Former Soviet Union - Political Supplied by BBC Worldwide Monitoring*, April 13, 2020; Higgins, "After Months of Denial, Russia Admits the Virus Is Taking Hold."

25. ITAR-TASS, "Russia Ranks About 50th in Cases of COVID-19 Per 100,000 Residents - Official," April 28, 2020.

26. "Russia Passes Spain to Rank Second in Coronavirus Cases Globally," May 12, 2020.

27. Robyn Dixon, "Putin Tells Russia Coronavirus Is in Retreat. Critics Face Crackdowns for Saying It's Far from Over: Some Activists and Medical Professionals Claim Russia Is Covering up the Extent of the Pandemic," *The Washington Post* (Online), June 27, 2020; ITAR-TASS, "Mortality in Russia in January-April 2020 Down on 2019 - Deputy PM," May 29, 2020; BBC, "Covid-19 Roundup: Russia 28 May 2020," *BBC Monitoring Former Soviet Union - Political Supplied by BBC Worldwide Monitoring*, May 28, 2020; "Russia Region Accused of Grossly Underreporting Covid Deaths," *BBC Monitoring Former Soviet Union - Political Supplied by BBC Worldwide Monitoring*, November 18, 2020; "Russia's Covid-19 Statistics Questioned," *BBC Monitoring Former Soviet Union - Political Supplied by BBC Worldwide Monitoring*, May 27, 2020; "Covid-19 Roundup: Russia 31 October 2020," *BBC Monitoring Former Soviet Union - Political Supplied by BBC Worldwide Monitoring*, October 31, 2020.

28. "Covid-19 Roundup: Russia 12 June 2020," *BBC Monitoring Former Soviet Union - Political Supplied by BBC Worldwide Monitoring*, June 12, 2020; "Covid-19 Roundup: Russia 9 July 2020," *BBC Monitoring Former Soviet Union - Political Supplied by BBC Worldwide Monitoring*, July 9, 2020; "Covid-19 Roundup: Russia 8 August 2020," *BBC Monitoring Former Soviet Union - Political Supplied by BBC Worldwide Monitoring*, August 8, 2020; "Covid-19 Roundup: Russia 7 November 2020," *BBC Monitoring Former Soviet Union - Political Supplied by BBC Worldwide Monitoring*, November 7, 2020; "Covid-19 Roundup: Russia 9 November 2020," *BBC Monitoring Former Soviet Union - Political Supplied by BBC Worldwide Monitoring*, November 9, 2020; "Russia's Excess Deaths 'Five Times Higher' Than Official Covid Death Toll," *BBC Monitoring Former Soviet Union - Political Supplied by BBC Worldwide Monitoring*, November 23, 2020; Newswire, "Russia Sees Overall Mortality Grow by over 150% Year-on-Year in Nov 2020 - Rosstat," *Russia & CIS General Newswire*, December 28, 2020.

29. ITAR-TASS, "Russia Has One of World's Lowest Coronavirus Mortality Rates - Health Minister," April 22, 2020; "Coronavirus Death Rate in Russia Does Not Exceed 1% - Consumer Rights Watchdog Chief," April 28, 2020; "Russia's Coronavirus Death Rate Lower Than in the World - Deputy Prime Minister," May 20, 2020; Newswire, "Coronavirus Death Rates 7.4 Times Lower in Russia Than in World as a Whole - Deputy PM Golikova," *Russia & CIS General Newswire*, May 11, 2020.

30. "No Regions in Russia Remain Unaffected by New Coronavirus as 1st Case Recorded in Republic of Altai," *Russia & CIS General Newswire*, April 16, 2020.

31. BBC, "Covid-19 Roundup: Russia 18 June," *BBC Monitoring Former Soviet Union - Political Supplied by BBC Worldwide Monitoring*, June 18, 2020.

32. "Covid-19 Roundup: Russia 27 April 2020," *BBC Monitoring Former Soviet Union - Political Supplied by BBC Worldwide Monitoring*, April 27, 2020; Newswire, "Russia May Begin Easing Coronavirus Restrictions after May 12 - Rospotrebnadzor Head (Part 2)," *Russia & CIS General Newswire*, April 27, 2020.

33. BBC, "Coronavirus in Russia: 13 April 2020"; "Coronavirus in Russia: 14 Apr 2020," *BBC Monitoring Former Soviet Union - Political Supplied by BBC Worldwide Monitoring*, April 14, 2020; ITAR-TASS, "Emergencies Ministry Teams Disinfect About 1,000 Social Facilities across Russia," April 8, 2020. Just days later, the ministry announced 3,300 Ministry of Defence staff had tested positive since March, 2,910 of whom were either military personnel or cadets in training. Presidential Bulletin, "Russia - April 8," *Russia & CIS Presidential Bulletin*, April 8, 2020; ITAR-TASS, "Russia's Emergencies Ministry Disinfects 20,900 Transport Buildings, 4,100 Km of Roads," May 17, 2020.

34. Newswire, "Over 5,000 Military Medics Might Be Engaged in Fighting Coronavirus Epidemic in Russia by Mid-May - Shoigu," *Russia & CIS General Newswire*, April 17, 2020; Esmerk, "Russia: Ministry Constructing Medical Center for 160 Patients in Novosibirsk," *M-Brain Russia News*, April 10, 2020, LexisNexis; BBC, "Covid-19 Roundup: Russia 24 April 2020," *BBC Monitoring Former Soviet Union - Political Supplied by BBC Worldwide Monitoring*, April 24, 2020; "Covid-19 Roundup: Russia 30 April 2020"; "Covid-19 Roundup: Russia 4 June 2020," *BBC Monitoring Former Soviet Union - Political Supplied by BBC Worldwide Monitoring*, June 4, 2020; "Covid-19 Roundup: Russia 17 December 2020," *BBC Monitoring Former Soviet Union - Political Supplied by BBC Worldwide Monitoring*, December 17, 2020; "Covid-19 Roundup: Russia 24 December 2020," *BBC Monitoring Former Soviet Union - Political Supplied by BBC Worldwide Monitoring*, December 24, 2020; ITAR-TASS, "Armed Forces Dispatched to Fight Coronavirus Outbreak at Russia's Largest Gold Mine," May 18, 2020; Newswire, "Group of Military Medics, Engineers, Chemists Created in Russia's Novosibirsk, Kemerovo Regions," *Russia & CIS General Newswire*, March 26, 2020.

35. BBC, "Covid-19 Roundup: Russia 24 April 2020"; "Covid-19 Roundup: Russia 30 April 2020"; Presidential Bulletin, "Russia - June 15," *Russia & CIS Presidential Bulletin*, June 15, 2020; ITAR-TASS, "Russia's Health Ministry Sends Medics to Kamchatka to Help Combat Coronavirus Infection," June 5, 2020.

36. BBC, "Coronavirus in Russia: 23 March 2020."

37. Robyn Dixon, "In Russia, Facial Surveillance and Threat of Prison Being Used to Make Coronavirus Quarantines Stick: Russia's Tough Approach to Policing Its Coronavirus Rules Undermines Social Trust, Activists Say," *The Washington Post* (Online), March 25, 2020; Justin Sherman, "Russia's Fight against the Coronavirus May Give Putin Even More Power," Ibid., June 2.

38. Isabelle Khurshudyan, "Coronavirus Is Testing the Limits of Russia's Surveillance State: Moscow Held Back on Requiring Digital Bar Codes to Leave Home, but Other Regions Are Pushing Ahead with Mobile Tracking," Ibid., April 5.

39. ITAR-TASS, "Russia's Far Eastern Region Introduces Digital Passes to Curb Coronavirus," April 6, 2020; BBC, "Coronavirus in Russia: 14 Apr 2020"; "Coronavirus in Russia: 16 April 2020," *BBC Monitoring Former Soviet Union - Political Supplied by BBC Worldwide Monitoring*, April 16, 2020.

40. ITAR-TASS, "Russia Proposes Three-Stage Lockdown Exit Strategy," May 6, 2020.

41. "Russia's Second Stage of Exiting Lockdown to Open Educational Facilities, Allow Walks," May 6, 2020.

42. "Readiness as the New Reality: How COVID-19 Made Russia's Healthcare System Shift Gears," May 26, 2020.

43. Ibid.

44. ITAR-TASS, "Minister Says Russia's Infectious Diseases Service Was Not Fully Prepared for Pandemic," October 13, 2020; "All Medical Institutions in Russia Must Be Ready to Treat Coronavirus Patients - Minister," April 15, 2020.

45. BBC, "Covid-19 Roundup: Russia 17 June 2020," *BBC Monitoring Former Soviet Union - Political Supplied by BBC Worldwide Monitoring*, June 17, 2020; Grove and Simmons, "Three

Doctors in Russia Have Fallen out of Hospital Windows; the Incidents Occurred as More Medical Professionals Are Speaking out About the Stress of Treating Coronavirus."

46. Dixon, "Putin Tells Russia Coronavirus Is in Retreat. Critics Face Crackdowns for Saying It's Far from Over: Some Activists and Medical Professionals Claim Russia Is Covering up the Extent of the Pandemic."

47. ITAR-TASS, "Nearly 500 Doctors Die from Coronavirus in Russia - Healthcare Watchdog," June 18, 2020.

48. "Russia's Healthcare System Proved to Be Flexible and Ready to Mobilize - Putin," June 28, 2020.

49. BBC, "Covid-19 Roundup: Russia 28 June 2020," *BBC Monitoring Former Soviet Union - Political Supplied by BBC Worldwide Monitoring*, June 28, 2020.

50. ITAR-TASS, "Putin: Russia to Hold Victory Day Parade on Red Square and in Other Cities on June 24," May 26, 2020.

51. Newswire, "Putin Hopes Improved Coronavirus Situation Will Allow Russia to Focus on Long-Term Agenda (Part 2)," *Russia & CIS General Newswire*, May 14, 2020; Presidential Bulletin, "Russia - May 22," *Russia & CIS Presidential Bulletin*, May 22, 2020; ITAR-TASS, "Masks to Remain Mandatory in Russia for the Next Month or Two - Watchdog Chief," May 25, 2020.

52. Andrew Higgins, "Hit Hard by Coronavirus, Russia Holds a Mostly Mask-Free Victory Parade," *New York Times* (Online), June 24, 2020; Anton Troianovski, "In Russia, the Lockdown Is Over. But Putin Stays in His Bubble," *New York Times*, October 2, 2020, A1.

53. BBC, "Covid-19 Roundup: Russia 12 June 2020."

54. "Covid-19 Roundup: Russia 15 June 2020," *BBC Monitoring Former Soviet Union - Political Supplied by BBC Worldwide Monitoring*, June 15, 2020.

55. Presidential Bulletin, "Russia - June 1," *Russia & CIS Presidential Bulletin*, June 1, 2020.

56. ITAR-TASS, "Russia's Sanitary Security Measures at Voting Stations Well Thought out - Who," June 30, 2020.

57. Ann M. Simmons, "Russia Sets July 1 Vote on Constitutional Changes Allowing Putin to Extend His Rule; Outcome Could Allow President Potentially to Stay in Office until 2036, Surpassing Soviet Dictator Josef Stalin's Nearly Three Decades in Power," *Wall Street Journal* (Online), June 1, 2020; Presidential Bulletin, "Russia - June 3," *Russia & CIS Presidential Bulletin*, June 3, 2020.

58. Andrew Higgins, "Russia Voting Affirms a Foregone Conclusion: [Foreign Desk]," *New York Times*, July 2, 2020, A18; ITAR-TASS, "Russia's Central Election Commission Approves Results of Constitutional Vote," July 3, 2020.

59. Newswire, "Second Covid-19 Wave in Russia on Same Scale as First One Unlikely - Health Minister Murashko (Part 2)," *Russia & CIS General Newswire*, July 3, 2020; BBC, "Covid-19 Roundup: Russia 10 July 2020," *BBC Monitoring Former Soviet Union - Political Supplied by BBC Worldwide Monitoring*, July 10, 2020; ITAR-TASS, "Russia's Coronavirus Infection Curve Going Down, but It's Not Time to Relax - Kremlin," July 17, 2020; BBC, "Covid-19 Roundup: Russia 22 September 2020," *BBC Monitoring Former Soviet Union - Political Supplied by BBC Worldwide Monitoring*, September 22, 2020; ITAR-TASS, "COVID-19 Situation in Russia to Improve Due to Introduced Measures - Putin," September 24, 2020; "Number of Severe COVID-19 Cases in Russia Decreases - Health Minister," September 24, 2020; "No Direct Grounds to Impose Further Coronavirus Lockdowns in Russia - Sanitary Watchdog," September 28, 2020.

60. Newswire, "Russia's Southern Regions See Increase in Coronavirus Cases after Start of Tour Season," *Russia & CIS General Newswire*, August 5, 2020; ITAR-TASS, "Russia Remains at 40th Place on COVID-19 Incidence Per 100,000 People - Watchdog," September 14, 2020.

61. BBC, "Covid-19 Roundup: Russia 31 October 2020"; Newswire, "Rospotrebnadzor Epidemiologist Says Rise in New Covid-19 Cases in Russia Due to More Testing," *Russia & CIS General Newswire*, November 16, 2020.

62. ITAR-TASS, "Putin Calls Efficient Russia's Battle against Coronavirus," September 15, 2020.

63. BBC, "Covid-19 Roundup: Russia 17 October 2020," *BBC Monitoring Former Soviet Union - Political Supplied by BBC Worldwide Monitoring*, October 17, 2020.

64. ITAR-TASS, "No Wholesale Harsh Restrictions Amid COVID-19 Pandemic in Russia Are Due - Putin," October 21, 2020; BBC, "Covid-19 Roundup: Russia 21 October 2020," *BBC Monitoring Former Soviet Union - Political Supplied by BBC Worldwide Monitoring*, October 21, 2020.

65. "Covid-19 Roundup: Russia 31 October 2020."

66. Ann M. Simmons, "Russia's Covid Surge Exacts a Heavy Toll on Its Emergency Responders; a Shortage of Paramedics Pushes Wait Times for Ambulances to 24 Hours as the Virus Continues to Reach New Highs," *Wall Street Journal* (Online), November 7, 2020.

67. Robyn Dixon, "In Russia, Sick People Often Treat Themselves. That's Not Helping in the Coronavirus Fight: Cases in the Country Are Spiking Sharply. One Reason May Be a Long-Held Suspicion of Doctors," *The Washington Post* (Online), October 23, 2020; Simmons, "Russia's Covid Surge Exacts a Heavy Toll on Its Emergency Responders; a Shortage of Paramedics Pushes Wait Times for Ambulances to 24 Hours as the Virus Continues to Reach New Highs"; Esmerk, "Russia: Coronavirus Treatment Rules on Outpatient Basis Changed," *M-Brain Russia News*, November 9, 2020, LexisNexis.

68. Newswire, "Peskov Denies Enhanced Quarantine Measures, Another Self-Isolation Period in Russia Being Discussed (Part 2)," *Russia & CIS General Newswire*, September 17, 2020; "Russia's Coronavirus Response System, Available Hospital Beds Make It Possible to Avoid Lockdown for Now - Kremlin (Part 2)," *Russia & CIS General Newswire*, October 12, 2020; "Kremlin Views Coronavirus Situation in Russia as 'Quite Serious' (Part 2)," *Russia & CIS General Newswire*, October 26, 2020; BBC, "Covid-19 Roundup: Russia 6 November 2020," *BBC Monitoring Former Soviet Union - Political Supplied by BBC Worldwide Monitoring*, November 6, 2020.

69. "Covid-19 Responses: Russia Advises over 60s to Avoid Public Spaces," *BBC Monitoring Former Soviet Union - Political Supplied by BBC Worldwide Monitoring*, September 28, 2020.

70. "Covid-19 Roundup: Russia 2 October 2020," *BBC Monitoring Former Soviet Union - Political Supplied by BBC Worldwide Monitoring*, October 2, 2020; "Covid-19 Roundup: Russia 10 October 2020," *BBC Monitoring Former Soviet Union - Political Supplied by BBC Worldwide Monitoring*, October 10, 2020; "Covid-19 Roundup: Russia 19 October 2020," *BBC Monitoring Former Soviet Union - Political Supplied by BBC Worldwide Monitoring*, October 19, 2020; "Covid-19 Roundup: Russia 10 November 2020," *BBC Monitoring Former Soviet Union - Political Supplied by BBC Worldwide Monitoring*, November 10, 2020.

71. ITAR-TASS, "No Sense in Imposing Face Mask Requirement across Entire Russia - Health Minister," November 27, 2020.

72. "Russia Not Planning New Coronavirus Restrictions - Crisis Center," November 23, 2020.

73. Georgi Kantchev, "Russia Begins to Roll out Its Sputnik V Coronavirus Vaccine; Doctors, Teachers and Social Workers in Moscow Are among the First to Receive the Shot," *Wall Street Journal* (Online), December 5, 2020; ITAR-TASS, "No Plans to Introduce Strict Quarantine in Russia for Winter Holidays, Kremlin Says," December 14, 2020.

74. BBC, "Covid-19 Roundup: Russia 29 December 2020," *BBC Monitoring Former Soviet Union - Political Supplied by BBC Worldwide Monitoring*, December 29, 2020.

75. Newswire, "Coronavirus Situation Stabilizing in Russia, yet Differs from One Region to Another - Rospotrebnadzor Head Popova," *Russia & CIS General Newswire*, December 15, 2020.

76. ITAR-TASS, "Daily Coronavirus Figures Vary across Russia, Says Chief Sanitary Doctor," November 23, 2020.

77. BBC, "Covid-19 Roundup: Russia 6 December 2020," *BBC Monitoring Former Soviet Union - Political Supplied by BBC Worldwide Monitoring*, December 6, 2020; "Covid-19 Roundup: Russia 25 December 2020," *BBC Monitoring Former Soviet Union - Political Supplied by BBC Worldwide Monitoring*, December 25, 2020.

78. ITAR-TASS, "Deputy PM Says Russia Did Not Impose New Lockdown Due to Readiness to Fight Pandemic," December 28, 2020.

79. BBC, "Covid-19 Roundup: Russia 11 December 2020," *BBC Monitoring Former Soviet Union - Political Supplied by BBC Worldwide Monitoring*, December 11, 2020; "Covid-19 Roundup: Russia 19 December 2020," *BBC Monitoring Former Soviet Union - Political Supplied by BBC Worldwide Monitoring*, December 19, 2020.

80. Andrew Higgins, "New Data Triples Russia's Death Toll," *New York Times* (Online), December 29, 2020, "New Data Triples Russia's COVID-19 Death Toll," *New York Times* (Online), December 29, 2020.

81. Newswire, "Covid-19 Situation in Russia Becoming More Complicated, Is Manageable - Peskov (Part 2)," *Russia & CIS General Newswire*, November 24, 2020.

82. Presidential Bulletin, "Russia - December 17," *Russia & CIS Presidential Bulletin*, December 17, 2020.

83. Ibid.; BBC, "Covid-19 Roundup: Russia 20 November 2020," *BBC Monitoring Former Soviet Union - Political Supplied by BBC Worldwide Monitoring*, November 20, 2020; ITAR-TASS, "Potential of Russia's Health Service System Grows - Putin," December 2, 2020.

84. Newswire, "Coronavirus Morbidity on Decline in Russia - Health Ministry," *Russia & CIS General Newswire*, December 29, 2020.

85. Presidential Bulletin, "Russia - December 17."

86. Andrew E. Kramer, "Russia Is Slow to Administer Virus Vaccine Despite Kremlin's Approval," *New York Times* (Online), November 24, 2020; BBC, "Covid-19 Roundup: Russia 26 December 2020," *BBC Monitoring Former Soviet Union - Political Supplied by BBC Worldwide Monitoring*, December 26, 2020.

87. ITAR-TASS, "No Risk of Further Spread of Coronavirus in Russia - Rospotrebnadzor," January 31, 2020.

88. Newswire, "Matviyenko: No Panic Should Be Caused over Coronavirus Spread, Russia Keeps Situation under Control," *Russia & CIS General Newswire*, January 30, 2020.

89. Andrew Higgins, "As Russia Braces for Coronavirus, Putin Lets Underlings Take the Heat," *New York Times* (Online), March 30, 2020.

90. Newswire, "Threat of Novel Coronavirus Importation to Russia Exists - Peskov," *Russia & CIS General Newswire*, January 31, 2020.

91. "Russia Taking Large-Scale, Systemic Efforts to Avert Coronavirus Risk, Develop Vaccine - Peskov," *Russia & CIS General Newswire*, February 5, 2020.

92. ITAR-TASS, "Threat of Coronavirus Spread in Russia Minimized, Says PM," March 12, 2020.

93. "Russia Has All Tools to Maintain Financial Stability - PM," March 12, 2020.

94. "Russia's Measures Can Compensate for Negative Economic Processes - Kremlin," March 13, 2020.

95. Newswire, "Despite Unfavorable Conditions, Russia to Fulfill All Social Commitments - Matviyenko," *Russia & CIS General Newswire*, March 14, 2020.

96. ITAR-TASS, "Russia Sets up Council Coordinating Anti-Coronavirus Efforts - PM," March 14, 2020; Russia, "First Meeting of the Government Coordination Council to Control the Incidence of Coronavirus Infection in Russia," *The Russian Government*, March 16, 2020, http://government.ru /en/news/39164/.

97. ITAR-TASS, "Russia Will Step up Fight against Coronavirus, Pledges Putin," March 18, 2020.

98. BBC, "Russian TV News: Russia Anti-Virus Efforts, 'Pandemic of Fakes', UK 'Inaction'," *BBC Monitoring Former Soviet Union - Political Supplied by BBC Worldwide Monitoring*, March 18, 2020.

99. ITAR-TASS, "No Reason to Panic Due to Coronavirus in Russia - Deputy PM," March 17, 2020; "Situation with Spread of Coronavirus in Russia Is under Control - President Putin," March 17, 2020.

100. BBC, "Russia-Backed Crimea Leader Briefs Putin on Coronavirus Measures," *BBC Monitoring Former Soviet Union - Political Supplied by BBC Worldwide Monitoring*, March 20, 2020.

101.   Isabelle Khurshudyan, "Russia's Low Count Raises Skepticism, Even with Moscow's Mayor," *The Washington Post*, March 25, 2020, A14; BBC, "Russia-Backed Crimea Leader Briefs Putin on Coronavirus Measures."

102.   Higgins, "As Russia Braces for Coronavirus, Putin Lets Underlings Take the Heat."

103.   ITAR-TASS, "Putin: Russia Contains Coronavirus Spread but Cannot Block Threat," March 25, 2020.

104.   "Russia Has Means to Solve Problems in Any Coronavirus Scenario - Putin," April 8, 2020.

105.   BBC, "Covid-19 Politics: Putin Says Russia May Survive Crisis with 'Minimal Loses'," *BBC Monitoring Former Soviet Union - Political Supplied by BBC Worldwide Monitoring*, April 7, 2020; Newswire, "Putin Hopes Coronavirus in Russia Can Be Overcome Earlier Than in 3 Months," *Russia & CIS General Newswire*, March 26, 2020.

106.   "Putin: No Need to Issue General Order to All Businesses across Russia to Limit Operations (Part 2)," *Russia & CIS General Newswire*, April 3, 2020.

107.   Andrew Higgins, "Putin, Russia's Man of Action, Is Passive, Even Bored, in the Coronavirus Era," *New York Times* (Online), April 30, 2020.

108.   Trudolyubov, "Late in the Game, Russia Steps up to Covid-19."

109.   Higgins, "As Russia Braces for Coronavirus, Putin Lets Underlings Take the Heat."

110.   Ann M. Simmons, "Coronavirus Forces Putin to Delay Vote That Could Keep Him in Power; Referendum Originally Planned for April Is Final Hurdle to Allowing Russia's President to Potentially Stay in Office until 2036," *Wall Street Journal* (Online), March 25, 2020; BBC, "PM Says Russia Should Replicate Moscow's Virus Measures," *BBC Monitoring Former Soviet Union - Political Supplied by BBC Worldwide Monitoring*, March 27, 2020.

111.   Presidential Bulletin, "Russia - December 28," *Russia & CIS Presidential Bulletin*, December 28, 2020.

112.   Trudolyubov, "Late in the Game, Russia Steps up to Covid-19."

113.   Newswire, "Putin Signs Decree on Measures to Ensure Sanitary-Epidemiological Wellbeing of People on Territory of Russia Amid Coronavirus (Part 2)," *Russia & CIS General Newswire*, April 2, 2020.

114.   BBC, "Russia to Lose 38bn Dollars Because of Oil Price Slump - Minister," *BBC Monitoring Former Soviet Union - Political Supplied by BBC Worldwide Monitoring*, March 23, 2020; Newswire, "Situation Thus Far Not Developing in Best Way, Russia to See Budget Deficit in 2020 - Siluanov," *Russia & CIS General Newswire*, March 18, 2020; ITAR-TASS, "Russia's PM Orders to Prepare a Priority Actions Plan Due to Coronavirus," March 16, 2020.

115.   "Putin Orders Permanent Monitoring of Russia's Economic Situation," March 29, 2020; Simmons, "Coronavirus Forces Putin to Delay Vote That Could Keep Him in Power; Referendum Originally Planned for April Is Final Hurdle to Allowing Russia's President to Potentially Stay in Office until 2036."

116.   Anton Troianovski, "As Coronavirus Overruns Russia, Doctors Are Dying on the Front Lines," *New York Times* (Online), May 14, 2020.

117.   ITAR-TASS, "Russia's Chechnya Closes Administrative Borders Amid Coronavirus Outbreak," March 28, 2020; BBC, "Coronavirus in Russia: 30 March 2020"; "Coronavirus in Russia: 11 April 2020," *BBC Monitoring Former Soviet Union - Political Supplied by BBC Worldwide Monitoring*, April 11, 2020.

118.   "Coronavirus in Russia: 3 April 2020," *BBC Monitoring Former Soviet Union - Political Supplied by BBC Worldwide Monitoring*, April 3, 2020.

119.   "Coronavirus in Russia: 7 April 2020," *BBC Monitoring Former Soviet Union - Political Supplied by BBC Worldwide Monitoring*, April 7, 2020.

120.   Presidential Bulletin, "Russia - April 8."

121.   correspondent Fred Weir Special, "As Russia Reopens, Putin Takes a Back Seat to Local Leaders," *The Christian Science Monitor*, June 22, 2020; BBC, "Covid-19 Roundup: Russia 13 May 2020," *BBC Monitoring Former Soviet Union - Political Supplied by BBC Worldwide Monitoring*, May 13, 2020.

122. "Coronavirus in Russia: 3 April 2020."

123. Newswire, "Russia Should Ensure Quickest Possible Economic Recovery after Coronavirus Epidemic - Putin," *Russia & CIS General Newswire*, April 7, 2020.

124. Ann M. Simmons and Georgi Kantchev, "Putin Extends Stay-at-Home Order through April in Russia; Despite Measures Taken by Federal and City Authorities, Leader Says It Wasn't Possible 'to Turn the Tide' of the Spread of Coronavirus," *Wall Street Journal* (Online), April 2, 2020; ITAR-TASS, "Public Order, Security in Russia to Be Safeguarded in Pandemic - Putin," April 3, 2020.

125. Presidential Bulletin, "Russia - April 8."

126. Newswire, "Coronavirus Problem Spreading into Russia's Provinces - Putin (Part 2)," *Russia & CIS General Newswire*, April 17, 2020.

127. Presidential Bulletin, "Russia - April 28," *Russia & CIS Presidential Bulletin*, April 28, 2020.

128. "Russia - April 8."

129. BBC, "Coronavirus in Russia: 7 April 2020"; Troianovski, "In Russia, the Lockdown Is Over. But Putin Stays in His Bubble."

130. Presidential Bulletin, "Russia - April 27," *Russia & CIS Presidential Bulletin*, April 27, 2020.

131. BBC, "Covid-19 Roundup: Russia 26 April 2020."

132. Ann M. Simmons, "In Russia, Putin Wrestles with Economic Impact of Coronavirus; What Was Tipped to Be Marquee Year for Kremlin Leader Has Turned into One of Toughest Challenges of His 20-Year Reign," *Wall Street Journal* (Online), May 5, 2020.

133. Presidential Bulletin, "Russia - April 17," *Russia & CIS Presidential Bulletin*, April 17, 2020.

134. "Russia - April 28."

135. "Russia - April 13," *Russia & CIS Presidential Bulletin*, April 13, 2020.

136. "Russia - April 17."

137. "Russia - June 3."

138. "Russia - September 29," *Russia & CIS Presidential Bulletin*, September 29, 2020.

139. ITAR-TASS, "Putin Says Coronavirus Situation in Russia Is Improving," June 4, 2020.

140. Presidential Bulletin, "Russia - June 9," *Russia & CIS Presidential Bulletin*, June 9, 2020.

141. "Russia - December 10," *Russia & CIS Presidential Bulletin*, December 10, 2020.

142. BBC, "Russian TV News: Government Caps Food Prices, United Russia's Volunteers," *BBC Monitoring Former Soviet Union - Political Supplied by BBC Worldwide Monitoring*, December 15, 2020.

143. Ann M. Simmons, "Moscow, Center of Russia's Coronavirus Crisis, Emerges from Lockdown; Infections Remain High as City Authorities Begin Reopening and Putin Prepares for Parade, Referendum," *Wall Street Journal* (Online), June 9, 2020.

144. Presidential Bulletin, "Russia - April 28."

145. Troianovski, "As Coronavirus Overruns Russia, Doctors Are Dying on the Front Lines"; BBC, "Covid-19 Roundup: Russia 1 May 2020," *BBC Monitoring Former Soviet Union - Political Supplied by BBC Worldwide Monitoring*, May 1, 2020; "Covid-19 Roundup: Russia 8 May 2020," *BBC Monitoring Former Soviet Union - Political Supplied by BBC Worldwide Monitoring*, May 8, 2020; "Covid-19 Roundup: Russia 15 June 2020."

146. "Covid-19 Roundup: Russia 10 June 2020," *BBC Monitoring Former Soviet Union - Political Supplied by BBC Worldwide Monitoring*, June 10, 2020.

147. Ibid.

148. BBC, "Covid-19 Roundup: Russia 27 May 2020," *BBC Monitoring Former Soviet Union - Political Supplied by BBC Worldwide Monitoring*, May 27, 2020; Presidential Bulletin, "Russia - May 27," *Russia & CIS Presidential Bulletin*, May 27, 2020.

149. Imago, "People Watch a Victory Day Military Parade Marking the 75th Anniversary of the Victory over Nazi Germany in World War II," *Imago*, June 24, 2020, https://www.imago-images.com /st/0101806535.

150. BBC, "Russia: Dagestan Media Highlights 8-14 Jun 20," *BBC Monitoring Former Soviet Union - Political Supplied by BBC Worldwide Monitoring*, July 7, 2020.

151. ITAR-TASS, "Coronavirus Cases Double in Russia's Dagestan - Watchdog," April 4, 2020.

152. Isabelle Khurshudyan, "In Dagestan, a Covid Recount Adds to Questions on Russia's Overall Numbers: Russia Boasts of a Low Mortality Rate. But in Dagestan, Pneumonia and Other Causes Were Not Part of Pandemic Totals," *The Washington Post* (Online), August 3, 2020.

153. Anton Troianovski, "As Virus Spreads in Russia's Caucasus, Rumors Swirl over Strongman's Health," *New York Times* (Online), May 22, 2020.

154. ITAR-TASS, "Russia's Coronavirus Cases Growth on the Decline for the Past Three Days," April 24, 2020.

155. BBC, "Covid-19 Roundup: Russia 10 May 2020," *BBC Monitoring Former Soviet Union - Political Supplied by BBC Worldwide Monitoring*, May 10, 2020.

156. Presidential Bulletin, "Russia - May 18," *Russia & CIS Presidential Bulletin*, May 18, 2020.

157. Ibid.

158. Khurshudyan, "In Dagestan, a Covid Recount Adds to Questions on Russia's Overall Numbers: Russia Boasts of a Low Mortality Rate. But in Dagestan, Pneumonia and Other Causes Were Not Part of Pandemic Totals."

159. Presidential Bulletin, "Russia - May 18."

160. Ibid.

161. Ibid.

162. BBC, "Covid-19 Roundup: Russia 23 May 2020," *BBC Monitoring Former Soviet Union - Political Supplied by BBC Worldwide Monitoring*, May 23, 2020.

163. "Covid-19 Roundup: Russia 19 May 2020," *BBC Monitoring Former Soviet Union - Political Supplied by BBC Worldwide Monitoring*, May 19, 2020; "Covid-19 Response: Russia Sends Emergency Virus Support to Dagestan," *BBC Monitoring Former Soviet Union - Political Supplied by BBC Worldwide Monitoring*, May 19, 2020.

164. "Covid-19 Roundup: Russia 22 May 2020," *BBC Monitoring Former Soviet Union - Political Supplied by BBC Worldwide Monitoring*, May 22, 2020.

165. Newswire, "Government Allots About 2 Bln Rubles to Build Medical Centers in Russia's Dagestan - Mishustin," *Russia & CIS General Newswire*, May 28, 2020; "Children's Hospital Chief Physician, Ambulance Paramedic Die of Covid-19 in Buinaksk in Russia's Dagestan," *Russia & CIS General Newswire*, May 27, 2020.

166. BBC, "Russia: Dagestan Head Says Covid-19 Situation 'under Control'," *BBC Monitoring Former Soviet Union - Political Supplied by BBC Worldwide Monitoring*, May 28, 2020.

167. Ibid.

168. Newswire, "Putin Sees Russia's Strength in Its Multiethnic Nature," *Russia & CIS General Newswire*, June 14, 2020.

169. Ibid.

170. BBC, "Covid-19 Roundup: Russia 20 June 2020," *BBC Monitoring Former Soviet Union - Political Supplied by BBC Worldwide Monitoring*, June 20, 2020.

171. ITAR-TASS, "Coronavirus Situation in Russia's Dagestan Stabilized - Minister," June 30, 2020.

172. BBC, "Russia: Dagestan Media Highlights 7-13 Dec 20," *BBC Monitoring Former Soviet Union - Political Supplied by BBC Worldwide Monitoring*, December 23, 2020.

173. Ibid.

174. Newswire, "Russia Not Considering Coronavirus-Related Lockdown for Now - Peskov," *Russia & CIS General Newswire*, October 2, 2020; BBC, "Covid-19 Roundup: Russia 1 October 2020," *BBC Monitoring Former Soviet Union - Political Supplied by BBC Worldwide Monitoring*, October 1, 2020.

175. ITAR-TASS, "Medical Workers Can Be Redistributed between Russia's Regions to Fight Pandemic - Kremlin," October 12, 2020; "COVID-19 Situation in Russia under Control - Peskov," October 23, 2020; BBC, "Covid-19 Response: Russia's Regions Tighten Restrictions

Amid New Spike," *BBC Monitoring Former Soviet Union - Political Supplied by BBC Worldwide Monitoring*, October 9, 2020; ibid.; BBC, "Covid-19 Roundup: Russia 15 October 2020," *BBC Monitoring Former Soviet Union - Political Supplied by BBC Worldwide Monitoring*, October 15, 2020.

176. Presidential Bulletin, "Russia - October 28," *Russia & CIS Presidential Bulletin*, October 28, 2020; BBC, "Covid-19 Roundup: Russia 27 October 2020," *BBC Monitoring Former Soviet Union - Political Supplied by BBC Worldwide Monitoring*, October 27, 2020.

177. Presidential Bulletin, "Russia - October 28."

178. Ibid.

179. Ibid.

180. BBC, "Covid-19 Roundup: Russia 31 October 2020."

181. "Covid-19 Roundup: Russia 2 November 2020," *BBC Monitoring Former Soviet Union - Political Supplied by BBC Worldwide Monitoring*, November 2, 2020.

182. "Covid-19 Roundup: Russia 5 November 2020," *BBC Monitoring Former Soviet Union - Political Supplied by BBC Worldwide Monitoring*, November 5, 2020.

183. "Covid-19 Roundup: Russia 12 November 2020," *BBC Monitoring Former Soviet Union - Political Supplied by BBC Worldwide Monitoring*, November 12, 2020; "Covid-19 Roundup: Russia 8 November 2020," *BBC Monitoring Former Soviet Union - Political Supplied by BBC Worldwide Monitoring*, November 8, 2020.

184. Presidential Bulletin, "Russia - November 13," *Russia & CIS Presidential Bulletin*, November 13, 2020; BBC, "Covid-19 Roundup: Russia 12 November 2020."

185. ITAR-TASS, "Russia Does Not Have a Comprehensive COVID-19 Restrictions Plan - Kremlin," November 16, 2020.

186. Presidential Bulletin, "Russia - May 6," *Russia & CIS Presidential Bulletin*, May 6, 2020.

187. ITAR-TASS, "Putin Says Coordination Was a Key Factor in the Fight against COVID-19 in Russia," September 5, 2020.

188. BBC, "Covid-19 Roundup: Russia 5 September," *BBC Monitoring Former Soviet Union - Political Supplied by BBC Worldwide Monitoring*, September 5, 2020.

189. Presidential Bulletin, "Russia - April 8."

190. Newswire, "Peskov Denies Enhanced Quarantine Measures, Another Self-Isolation Period in Russia Being Discussed (Part 2)."

191. Presidential Bulletin, "Russia - November 19," *Russia & CIS Presidential Bulletin*, November 19, 2020.

192. ITAR-TASS, "Putin Did Everything for Russia to Cope with Pandemic from Day One, Russian PM Says," October 22, 2020.

193. "Putin Fully Informed About COVID-19 Situation in Russia - Kremlin," December 2, 2020.

194. BBC, "Covid-19 Roundup: Russia 8 December 2020," *BBC Monitoring Former Soviet Union - Political Supplied by BBC Worldwide Monitoring*, December 8, 2020.

195. Presidential Bulletin, "Russia - December 9," *Russia & CIS Presidential Bulletin*, December 9, 2020.

196. Newswire, "Russia Went through Hardships in 2020, Needs Unity - Putin," *Russia & CIS General Newswire*, December 31, 2020.

197. Ibid.

198. Newswire, "Putin: Russia Still Hasn't Passed Peak of Coronavirus Epidemic, Should Avoid Mistakes Made by Others," *Russia & CIS General Newswire*, April 7, 2020; ITAR-TASS, "Public Order, Security in Russia to Be Safeguarded in Pandemic - Putin."

199. "Russia Has Means to Solve Problems in Any Coronavirus Scenario - Putin."

200. "Russia Managed to Slow Down Pace of Coronavirus Epidemiology Spread, Says Putin," April 28, 2020.

201. Presidential Bulletin, "Russia - May 6."

202. "Russia - October 27," *Russia & CIS Presidential Bulletin*, October 27, 2020.

203. Kramer, "Russia Is Slow to Administer Virus Vaccine Despite Kremlin's Approval"; BBC, "Covid-19 Roundup: Russia 11 August 2020," *BBC Monitoring Former Soviet Union - Political Supplied by BBC Worldwide Monitoring*, August 11, 2020.

204. Presidential Bulletin, "Russia - July 29," *Russia & CIS Presidential Bulletin*, July 29, 2020.

205. "Russia - December 2," *Russia & CIS Presidential Bulletin*, December 2, 2020.

206. "Russia - December 10."

207. Higgins, "A Doctor Who Accused Russia of Underreporting Virus Totals Is Detained: [Foreign Desk]."

208. BBC, "Covid-19 Roundup: Russia 30 April 2020."

209. Intellinews, "Putin Eases Russia's Coronavirus Lockdown Restrictions," *Intellinews - Russia This Week*, May 11, 2020, https://www.intellinews.com/putin-eases-russia-s-coronavirus-lockdown-restrictions-182927/.

210. Yaroslav Trofimov and Thomas Grove, "Putin's Global Ambitions Are Upended by Coronavirus's Heavy Toll in Russia; Russian President's Efforts to Showcase the Country's Strength Abroad Backfired Amid Virus Troubles at Home," *Wall Street Journal* (Online), June 6, 2020.

211. Newswire, "Effective Healthcare System Allowed Russia to Deal with Coronavirus - Peskov," *Russia & CIS General Newswire*, June 10, 2020.

212. "Russia to Soon Launch Phone Hotline, Online System to Inform Citizens of Covid-19 Situation - Mishustin," *Russia & CIS General Newswire*, March 16, 2020.

213. RosCongress, "Russian National Helpline," *RosCongress*, March 19, 2021, https://roscongress.org/en/blog/hotline/.

214. ITAR-TASS, "More Than 450 Organizations Join Russia-Wide 'We Are Together' Help Campaign," March 23, 2020.

215. "Russia's Human Rights Chief Dismisses Rumors on Coronavirus Spread in Moscow," March 2, 2020.

216. "Nothing Critical About Coronavirus in Russia, Fake News Come from Abroad - Putin," March 4, 2020.

217. BBC, "Coronavirus in Russia: 5 March 2020"; ITAR-TASS, "Roscomnadzor Says Ready to Block Websites Spreading Fake New on Coronavirus in Russia," March 18, 2020.

218. Newswire, "Center to Identify Fake News Included in Council for Resisting Coronavirus in Russia," *Russia & CIS General Newswire*, March 30, 2020.

219. BBC, "Coronavirus in Russia: 7 Feb 20," *BBC Monitoring Former Soviet Union - Political Supplied by BBC Worldwide Monitoring*, February 7, 2020.

220. ITAR-TASS, "US' Allegations About Russia's Spreading Misinformation About Coronavirus Seen as Fake," February 22, 2020.

221. "Western Media Spread Fake News of Russia's COVID Death Toll to Distract Public Attention," May 13, 2020.

222. "Western Media Are Mouthpieces Spreading Coronavirus Falsehoods against Russia - Ryabkov," April 17, 2020.

223. "Roskomnadzor Studies Articles in Western Media for Fakes About Coronavirus in Russia," May 14, 2020; Newswire, "Future of FT, NYT in Russia to Depend on Whether They Retract Russia Covid-19 Death Toll Articles - Foreign Ministry," *Russia & CIS General Newswire*, May 14, 2020; "Foreign Media May Lose Accreditation in Russia for Fakes - State Duma Commission," *Russia & CIS General Newswire*, May 28, 2020.

224. Tony Romm, "State Department Blames 'Swarms of Online, False Personas' from Russia for Wave of Coronavirus Misinformation Online," *The Washington Post* (Online), March 5, 2020.

225. BBC, "Russian TV News: Russia Ready for Covid-19, EU 'Fails', UK Spreads 'Fake News'," *BBC Monitoring Former Soviet Union - Political Supplied by BBC Worldwide Monitoring*, March 20, 2020; ITAR-TASS, "Diplomat Slams as Fake News Eu's Saying Russia Spreads False Information About Coronavirus," March 19, 2020.

226. "5-6 Misinformation Campaigns About Coronavirus Exposed Daily in Russia," March 20, 2020; "Russia Introduces Large Fines for Spreading Fake News on Coronavirus," March 30, 2020.

227. BBC, "Covid-19 Roundup: Russia 19 June," *BBC Monitoring Former Soviet Union - Political Supplied by BBC Worldwide Monitoring*, June 19, 2020.

228. Dixon, "Putin Tells Russia Coronavirus Is in Retreat. Critics Face Crackdowns for Saying It's Far from Over: Some Activists and Medical Professionals Claim Russia Is Covering up the Extent of the Pandemic"; BBC, "Coronavirus in Russia: 7 April 2020"; "Covid-19 Roundup: Russia 30 April 2020"; "Covid-19 Roundup: Russia 22 May 2020"; Robyn Dixon, "Russian Medical Workers Say Coronavirus Is Ravaging Their Ranks. But Hospital Chiefs Are Silent: Medical Personnel Complain That a Lack of Protective Equipment Leaves Them in Peril as the Pandemic Advances across Russia," *The Washington Post* (Online), April 22, 2020; BBC, "Coronavirus in Russia: 20 April 2020"; Grove and Simmons, "Three Doctors in Russia Have Fallen out of Hospital Windows; the Incidents Occurred as More Medical Professionals Are Speaking out About the Stress of Treating Coronavirus"; BBC, "Covid-19 Roundup: Russia 4 July 2020," *BBC Monitoring Former Soviet Union - Political Supplied by BBC Worldwide Monitoring*, July 4, 2020.

229. "Coronavirus in Russia: 11 March 2020," *BBC Monitoring Former Soviet Union - Political Supplied by BBC Worldwide Monitoring*, March 11, 2020; ITAR-TASS, "Task Force Requests Restrictions on Public Gatherings in Russia over Coronavirus," March 11, 2020; BBC, "BBCM Russia Watchlist for 11 March," *BBC Monitoring Former Soviet Union - Political Supplied by BBC Worldwide Monitoring*, March 11, 2020; Newswire, "Moscow City Hall Denies Open Russia Authorization of Opposition Rally," *Russia & CIS General Newswire*, March 13, 2020.

230. BBC, "Coronavirus in Russia: 13 April 2020."

231. Presidential Bulletin, "Russia - April 17."

232. "Russia - April 22," *Russia & CIS Presidential Bulletin*, April 22, 2020.

233. Dixon, "Russian Medical Workers Say Coronavirus Is Ravaging Their Ranks. But Hospital Chiefs Are Silent: Medical Personnel Complain That a Lack of Protective Equipment Leaves Them in Peril as the Pandemic Advances across Russia."

234. Khurshudyan, "In Dagestan, a Covid Recount Adds to Questions on Russia's Overall Numbers: Russia Boasts of a Low Mortality Rate. But in Dagestan, Pneumonia and Other Causes Were Not Part of Pandemic Totals."

235. BBC, "Covid-19 Roundup: Russia 7 October 2020," *BBC Monitoring Former Soviet Union - Political Supplied by BBC Worldwide Monitoring*, October 7, 2020.

236. "Russia's Covid-19 Statistics Questioned."

237. Esmerk, "Russia: Health Ministers in Omsk and Samara Regions Step Down," *M-Brain Russia News*, April 1, 2020, LexisNexis.

238. BBC, "Why Are Russia's Governors Resigning?" *BBC Monitoring Former Soviet Union - Political Supplied by BBC Worldwide Monitoring*, April 3.

239. Ibid.

240. Dixon, "Russian Medical Workers Say Coronavirus Is Ravaging Their Ranks. But Hospital Chiefs Are Silent: Medical Personnel Complain That a Lack of Protective Equipment Leaves Them in Peril as the Pandemic Advances across Russia."

241. ITAR-TASS, "Russia Allocates Funds to Ensure All Regions Are Ready to Combat COVID-19 - Minister," April 20, 2020.

242. BBC, "Covid-19 Roundup: Russia 29 April 2020," *BBC Monitoring Former Soviet Union - Political Supplied by BBC Worldwide Monitoring*, April 29, 2020; Esmerk, "Russia: Ministry of Health Appoints Acting Minister of Astrakhan Region," *M-Brain Russia News*, April 8, 2020, LexisNexis; BBC, "Coronavirus in Russia: 10 April 2020," *BBC Monitoring Former Soviet Union - Political Supplied by BBC Worldwide Monitoring*, April 10, 2020; Esmerk, "Russia: New Minister of Health in Komi Republic," *M-Brain Russia News*, April 24, 2020, LexisNexis.

243. BBC, "Covid-19 Roundup: Russia 20 July 2020," *BBC Monitoring Former Soviet Union - Political Supplied by BBC Worldwide Monitoring*, July 20, 2020.

244. ITAR-TASS, "Russia's Coronavirus Situation Manageable, Although Difficult in Some Regions - Putin," November 18, 2020.

245. Higgins, "Putin, Russia's Man of Action, Is Passive, Even Bored, in the Coronavirus Era."

246. BBC, "Coronavirus in Russia: 7 Feb 20."

247. "Russian TV News: Russia's Covid-19 Spread Accelerating, US 'Nightmare'," *BBC Monitoring Former Soviet Union - Political Supplied by BBC Worldwide Monitoring*, April 11, 2020.

248. ITAR-TASS, "Battle against Coronavirus in Russia Continues, Putin Cautions," September 28, 2020.

249. "Russia's Coronavirus Situation Is Stabilizing - Watchdog Chief," December 25, 2020.

250. "Russia to Classify Deliberate Coronavirus Contamination as Terrorism or Sabotage," March 25, 2020.

251. BBC, "Covid-19 Security: Russia to Vaccinate over 400,000 Soldiers," *BBC Monitoring Former Soviet Union - Political Supplied by BBC Worldwide Monitoring*, November 27, 2020.

252. Presidential Bulletin, "Russia - July 22," *Russia & CIS Presidential Bulletin*, July 22, 2020; ITAR-TASS, "Russia's Daily COVID-19 Rate Is 8 Per 100,000 People - Watchdog Chief," October 13, 2020; "Russia Managed to Avoid Panic, Crime Situation Deterioration During Pandemic - Ex-Premier," June 9, 2020; Newswire, "Putin Says Russia Exiting Coronavirus Situation with Confidence, in Contrast with U.S (Part 2)," *Russia & CIS General Newswire*, June 14, 2020; ITAR-TASS, "Russia Was Better Prepared for COVID-19 Pandemic Than Majority - Security Council," July 13, 2020.

253. BBC, "Kremlin Says Covid-19 Situation Better in Russia Than Other States," *BBC Monitoring Former Soviet Union - Political Supplied by BBC Worldwide Monitoring*, March 10, 2020.

254. ITAR-TASS, "Coronavirus Cases in Russia Rise to 438 over Past Day - Prime Minister," March 23, 2020.

255. BBC, "Russian TV News: Russia's Covid-19 Measures; UK, US Struggling," *BBC Monitoring Former Soviet Union - Political Supplied by BBC Worldwide Monitoring*, March 24, 2020.

256. "Russian TV News: Russia's Covid-19 Spread Accelerating, US 'Nightmare'."

257. ITAR-TASS, "Number of People Willing to Return to Russia from US Increases Amid Unrest - Diplomat," June 6, 2020.

258. Presidential Bulletin, "Russia - October 27."

259. ITAR-TASS, "Russia's Coronavirus Death Rate Lower Than in Other States - Expert," April 20, 2020.

260. Presidential Bulletin, "Russia - July 13," *Russia & CIS Presidential Bulletin*, July 13, 2020.

261. BBC, "Covid-19 Roundup: Russia 27 August 2020," *BBC Monitoring Former Soviet Union - Political Supplied by BBC Worldwide Monitoring*, August 27, 2020.

262. "Pro-Kremlin TV Talk Show Praises Russia's Covid-19 Response," *BBC Monitoring Former Soviet Union - Political Supplied by BBC Worldwide Monitoring*, March 25, 2020.

263. ITAR-TASS, "Number of Coronavirus Cases in Russia Rises from 34 to 45 - Officials," March 13, 2020.

264. BBC, "Covid-19 Roundup: Russia 7 July 2020," *BBC Monitoring Former Soviet Union - Political Supplied by BBC Worldwide Monitoring*, July 7, 2020.

265. Newswire, "Kremlin Admits Certain Shortage of Means of Individual Protection against Coronavirus in Russia," *Russia & CIS General Newswire*, March 20, 2020.

266. ITAR-TASS, "Russia's Health Workers, Coronavirus Prevention Headquarter Working Very Well - Kremlin," March 31, 2020.

267. BBC, "Putin Says Coronavirus Outbreak in Russia 'Getting Worse'," *BBC Monitoring Former Soviet Union - Political Supplied by BBC Worldwide Monitoring*, April 1, 2020.

268. Newswire, "Russia Has Been Able to Protect Its Citizens from Coronavirus in General - Putin (Part 2)," *Russia & CIS General Newswire*, June 28, 2020.

269. BBC, "Covid-19 Roundup: Russia 17 December 2020."

270. "Covid-19 Roundup: Russia 22 December 2020," *BBC Monitoring Former Soviet Union - Political Supplied by BBC Worldwide Monitoring*, December 22, 2020.

271. "Russian TV Weekly Highlights: Covid-19 - Reassurance About Russia, Attacks on US," *BBC Monitoring Former Soviet Union - Political Supplied by BBC Worldwide Monitoring*, April 20, 2020.

272. ITAR-TASS, "Ideas Promoted by Russia before Pandemic Become More Popular - Lavrov," April 25, 2020.

273. "Pandemic Unmasks Negative Implications of New Western Values - Russia's Security Chief," June 17, 2020.

274. "Globalization Principles Fail to Work Amid Pandemic - Chairman of Russia's Ruling Party," July 14, 2020.

275. Presidential Bulletin, "Russia - April 28."

276. Newswire, "Putin Says Russia Exiting Coronavirus Situation with Confidence, in Contrast with U.S (Part 2)."

277. Presidential Bulletin, "Russia - May 27."

278. "Russia - May 6."

279. Newswire, "Putin Says Russia Exiting Coronavirus Situation with Confidence, in Contrast with U.S (Part 2)."

280. Presidential Bulletin, "Russia - October 23," *Russia & CIS Presidential Bulletin*, October 23, 2020.

281. ITAR-TASS, "Russia's Measures against COVID-19 Were Timely and Correct, Prime Minister Says," July 22, 2020.

282. "Over One Million Coronavirus Tests Conducted in Russia - Watchdog," April 9, 2020; BBC, "Coronavirus in Russia: 10 April 2020"; Presidential Bulletin, "Russia - April 28."

283. ITAR-TASS, "Russia Conducts over 1.5 Mln Coronavirus Tests, Ranked Second in the World," April 15, 2020; BBC, "Covid-19 Responses: Putin Discusses 'Epidemiological Situation' in Russia," *BBC Monitoring Former Soviet Union - Political Supplied by BBC Worldwide Monitoring*, April 21, 2020.

284. ITAR-TASS, "Over 6 Mln Coronavirus Tests Conducted in Russia, Says Watchdog," May 14, 2020.

285. "Over 15 Mln Tests for COVID-19 Held in Russia," June 15, 2020.

286. Newswire, "Russia to Continue Covid-19 Testing - Mishustin," *Russia & CIS General Newswire*, June 15, 2020.

287. BBC, "Covid-19 Roundup: Russia 26 June," *BBC Monitoring Former Soviet Union - Political Supplied by BBC Worldwide Monitoring*, June 26, 2020; Robyn Dixon, "In Russia's Pandemic Struggles, Even Putin Couldn't Speed Bonuses to Health Workers: The Country Has the Third-Largest Number of Confirmed Covid-19 Cases, but Its Counting System Raises Question About Relatively Low Death Rates," *The Washington Post* (Online), May 27, 2020.

288. "Russian Medical Workers Say Coronavirus Is Ravaging Their Ranks. But Hospital Chiefs Are Silent: Medical Personnel Complain That a Lack of Protective Equipment Leaves Them in Peril as the Pandemic Advances across Russia"; Fred Weir, "Coronavirus Shortages Give Russia's Charity Sector a New Spark," *The Christian Science Monitor*, June 9, 2020; BBC, "Covid-19 Responses: Russia Minister Admits 'Big Deficit' of Protective Suits," *BBC Monitoring Former Soviet Union - Political Supplied by BBC Worldwide Monitoring*, April 7, 2020; "Coronavirus in Russia: 11 April 2020"; "Coronavirus in Russia: 14 Apr 2020"; "Covid-19 Roundup: Russia 28 April 2020," *BBC Monitoring Former Soviet Union - Political Supplied by BBC Worldwide Monitoring*, April 28, 2020; "Coronavirus in Russia: 11 April 2020"; "Covid-19 Roundup: Russia 21 May 2020," *BBC Monitoring Former Soviet Union - Political Supplied by BBC Worldwide Monitoring*, May 21, 2020; ITAR-TASS, "Putin: Russia Managed to Avoid Critical Disruptions in PPE Supplies for Healthcare Workers," June 3, 2020; Presidential Bulletin, "Russia - June 3."

289. "Russia - September 24," *Russia & CIS Presidential Bulletin*, September 24, 2020.

290. "Russia - April 13."

291. ITAR-TASS, "Russia Allocates 4.5% of GDP to Mitigate Consequences of Pandemic - Putin," November 21, 2020.

292. BBC, "Covid-19 Roundup: Russia 27 April 2020"; "Coronavirus in Russia: 15 April 2020," *BBC Monitoring Former Soviet Union - Political Supplied by BBC Worldwide Monitoring*, April 15, 2020; "Russia Allocates 420m Dollars to Regional Hospitals," *BBC Monitoring Former Soviet*

Union - Political Supplied by BBC Worldwide Monitoring, March 30, 2020; "Coronavirus in Russia: 23 March 2020"; ITAR-TASS, "Russia's Government to Use $67.09 Mln to Purchase of 1,200 Ambulances," April 2, 2020.

293.   BBC, "Covid-19 Roundup: Russia 10 September 2020," *BBC Monitoring Former Soviet Union - Political Supplied by BBC Worldwide Monitoring*, September 10, 2020; Presidential Bulletin, "Russia - October 19," *Russia & CIS Presidential Bulletin*, October 19, 2020.

294.   BBC, "Covid-19 Roundup: Russia 28 May 2020"; Newswire, "Russia's Unemployment Situation Not 'Threatening' - Labor Minister," *Russia & CIS General Newswire*, May 13, 2020.

295.   Georgi Kantchev, "Russia Cuts Interest Rates to Post-Soviet Low; Central Bank's Rate Cut Comes as Economic Pain Penetrates All Sectors of Russian Society," *Wall Street Journal* (Online), June 19, 2020.

296.   Newswire, "Russia's Draft Budget Turns out to Be Tense Amid Covid-19 - Mishustin (Part 2)," *Russia & CIS General Newswire*, October 26, 2020.

297.   Thomas Grove and Georgi Kantchev, "Russia's Economy Suffers Double Hit from Oil Slump and Coronavirus; as Infections Grow, Russia Finds a Shortfall in Oil Revenue Hurts Its Ability to Offer the Kind of Emergency Support Provided in the West," May 20, 2020, https://www.wsj.com /articles/russias-economy-suffers-double-hit-from-oil-slump-and-coronavirus-11589976001.

298.   ITAR-TASS, "Russia to Spend 4.5% of GDP on Support for Economy, Households in 2020, Says Putin," October 29, 2020.

299.   "Economic Recession Due to Pandemic Not So Deep in Russia as in Other Countries, Says Putin," September 10, 2020.

300.   Presidential Bulletin, "Russia - June 15."

301.   "Russia - June 3"; BBC, "Covid-19 Roundup: Russia 1 June 2020," *BBC Monitoring Former Soviet Union - Political Supplied by BBC Worldwide Monitoring*, June 1, 2020; "Covid-19 Roundup: Russia 4 June 2020."

302.   ITAR-TASS, "All of Russia's Organizations Concerned Worked Effectively During Pandemic - Peskov," December 27, 2020.

303.   Ibid.

Chapter 6

The United States

The Abyss of Democratic Populism

Medical workers may have been the heroes in every COVID battle waged around the world. But the odds of getting out the message that COVID was a life-and-death fight differed by country. This is precisely where regime type should provide some clarity. In authoritarian China, we saw doctors hushed and punished for spreading word online. In semi-authoritarian Russia, we saw doctors' organizations fined and threatened for speaking and acting more publicly. And in the democratic United States, we should have found uninhibited doctors not only speaking out publicly but also gaining the eager ear of policymakers and the broader populace looking for guidance on how to stop the pandemic in its tracks.

Yet this is not how the American story played out. Desperate American frontline medical workers, inundated with patients and lacking sufficient PPE, got sick just like their counterparts in China and Russia. They begged the public to contribute to their meager stockpile of protective equipment and put up crowdfunding petitions to pay medical bills.[1] They even sued their employers for failing to protect them.[2] But they did not win over the public with their words and deeds.

Instead, many Americans targeted their anger at the medical establishment that had supported painful lockdowns in the name of saving lives. Public health officials, physically threatened and facing their own lawsuits over local closures, chose resignation.[3] Cheering the crowds on was the president of the United States, who quipped, if it were up to the doctors, they may say, "Let's keep it shut down . . . let's shut down the entire world, and when we shut it down, that would be wonderful and let's keep it shut for a couple of years."[4] America's democratic populist president relentlessly worked to ensure the medical experts would take a backseat to his preferred COVID policies of business-as-usual.

With the exception of a few weeks in spring 2020, President Trump's approach from the first reports of COVID until the end of his presidency was to downplay the disease and question the approach, and even the very science, championed by his own experts. As the U.S. overview in chapter 3 underscores, the calamitous U.S. response to COVID came as a shock to many observers who had predicted the United States would be one of the most capable at handling a pandemic.

The U.S. struggle to (not) deal with COVID can be encapsulated in the excruciating battle over testing. As COVID began spreading in the winter, the Centers for Disease Control and Prevention (CDC) demanded all health facilities use its test, which would be analyzed in one of just eight labs around the country.[5] But when word circulated that the CDC tests were faulty, the Food and Drug Administration (FDA) bowed before angry governors and began approving independent tests.[6] As Vice President Pence promised that any American with doctors' orders could be tested, desperate medical centers turned to small, independent (though still unapproved) labs to help them meet demand.[7] New York's governor, who had begun independently contracting with twenty-eight private area labs, complained, "We're not in a position where we can rely on the CDC or the FDA."[8]

With all of the furor over testing, Trump in mid-March overpromised, pledging to churn out by the end of the month 5 million tests to be administered at thousands of testing sites.[9] Yet one month later, only 3.3 million residents had been tested since the very start of the outbreak. Contrary to Trump's boast that the United States had "the most advanced and robust testing system anywhere in the world,"[10] the U.S. testing rate was far under that of other advanced economies.[11] The German government, for instance, was testing twice the number every day despite having a population four times smaller.[12] One independent senator from Maine lashed out at the administration, calling the lack of a national testing strategy a "dereliction of duty."[13]

Ramping up testing without the initiative—or force—of the federal government proved difficult in part because of weaknesses in the supply chain and hesitation among market actors to invest in producing a test of questionable profitability.[14] There were also concerns over who would pay for the testing; most health insurers only agreed in mid-March to cover the tab.[15]

With these and other challenges, Trump walked the line between promises to use his powers vis-à-vis the Defense Production Act to increase production of one scarce component (swabs) and shifting the testing responsibility to governors.[16] "Testing is a local thing," Trump said in mid-April. "Governors must be able to step up and get the job done. We will be with you ALL THE WAY!"[17] The reaction from the head of the National Governors Association, a moderate Republican from Maryland, was sharp. "To try to push this off to say that the governors have plenty of testing, and they should just get to work on testing, somehow we aren't doing our job, is just absolutely false," Governor Larry Hogan said.[18]

But the Trump administration's handling of the testing dilemma and the tit-for-tat accusations between the administration and the governors were emblematic of Trump's general approach to COVID policy. As a populist seeking to garner positive attention and deflect negative narratives concerning his pandemic response, Trump made big promises at the same time that he claimed he had no real obligation to act in the first place.

The conflicting stances could be seen in a series of exchanges in April in which he transferred blame from his office to his political opponents. Trump tweeted that testing demand was driven by "Radical Left, Do Nothing Democrats," and he accused the media, as well as Hogan and other angry governors, of a "complete failure to understand the scope of the testing abilities we've brought on line."[19] "It's going to be up to the states to use that capability," he added. "Everything is perfect."[20] When the following week Trump unveiled a new "blueprint" for increased testing capacity, he maintained the federal role would be limited to "strategic direction and technical assistance" and "supplier of last resort." [21]

Trump struggled to come through on lofty promises to establish mass drive-thru testing sites, leaving the population with insufficient tests to manage rapid viral spread.[22] Spinning this failure, Trump alternated between boasting about his record on testing and questioning the utility of the tests in the first place. "Now there are big believers in testing, and then there are some governors that don't feel as strongly about it at all, you understand, that they feel much differently about it," he said in March.[23] "The whole concept of tests aren't necessarily great," Trump said in May.[24] What tests did, Trump began to argue, was create a false negative perception of his administration's COVID response. "In a way, by doing all of this testing, we make ourselves look bad," he said.[25] This became a talking point for lower-level allies, who blamed rising case numbers on increased testing.[26]

Perhaps in a non-democracy, Trump could have pressed this claim more effectively. But facing widespread skepticism, he instead awkwardly wobbled between calling tests useless and exaggerating his effectiveness in getting tests to the population. "America leads the world in testing," Trump said in mid-May. "We have met the moment and we have prevailed."[27] Around that time, the U.S. testing rate of 16.4 tests per 1,000 people was significantly below the 36-state OECD average of 23.1.[28] As Trump spoke in May, the United States had tested the equivalent of 2.74 percent of its population, compared with 15.4 percent in Iceland, 4.3 percent in Italy, 3.4 percent in

Germany and almost 3 percent in neighboring Canada.[29] Independent analysts warned the country would need 900,000 tests per day (8 percent of the population per month) to effectively detect case clusters.[30] The United States was testing less than half as many.[31]

Throughout the summer, Trump continued to reject pressures to remedy testing-related supply chain issues by invoking the Defense Production Act.[32] As he did so, the country fell further behind. By the time the United States hit about 800,000 tests a day in August, state medical leaders said the jump in summer travel and related virus spread necessitated far more capacity.[33] Colorado Gov. Jared Polis (D) summarized the situation as viewed from below: "The national testing scene is a complete disgrace."[34]

The criticism sparked by the summer COVID spike and ongoing testing problems prompted Trump to turn even more aggressively against testing. "The number of ChinaVirus cases goes up, because of GREAT TESTING," Trump tweeted at the end of June.[35] The obvious resolution, he told a group of supporters, was to "slow the testing down."[36] Although the CDC estimated up to 40 percent of all COVID cases were asymptomatic but still highly infectious, the organization suddenly fell into line in August, reversing testing guidelines for close contacts who, if they had no symptoms, "do not necessarily need a test."[37] These changes led to an outcry from public health experts, the sort that could be swiftly silenced in China and hobbled in Russia. The CDC relented, reverting to its previous, more cautious guidance within a month.[38]

Lacking the testing needed to trace and stop the virus from the beginning, COVID spread rapidly throughout the country. The case count rose from just 2,900 on March 16, when the federal government promised to stop the spread, to 13,000 just a few days later.[39] By the end of May, the number of cases and deaths in the United States was the highest in the world, with the 1.7 million confirmed cases almost equal to the total from the next six countries, even though the U.S. population was just over half of theirs.[40] One month later, in late June, the United States reported 2.5 million cases, though the CDC acknowledged the true number could be as much as ten times higher.[41]

These numbers skyrocketed during the summer and fall surges. By August, the United States had 5 million cases, climbing to 8 million in October.[42] By the time election day came in November, daily cases surpassed 115,000.[43] It took just ten days to move from a case count of 9 million to 10 million, and just another week to climb to 11 million.[44] In the last month of 2020, daily case counts were in the 200,000 range, with a yearly high of 252,000 on December 17.[45] By that point, COVID had long since gone from most severely impacting residents of long-term care facilities to infecting a broad swathe of society, including rural areas largely spared in the earlier outbreak.[46] As one state-level CDC director commented, "Now, the kitchen table is a place of risk."[47]

With increased cases came more deaths. It took two months from the first U.S. death at the end of February for the country to surpass 3,700 deaths.[48] But by April, more than 1,000 people were dying every single day.[49] And this death count was, in the words of the CDC, invariably an "underestimation" as a result of under-testing and false negatives—something non-democracies had no monopoly on.[50] In fact, the CDC reported that until early April it was only counting COVID deaths after a lab test confirmed coronavirus in the deceased patient.[51] In some states, even COVID-positive patients who died could be omitted from the official COVID count if they had no respiratory symptoms or if they died of an acute event such as a stroke or heart attack.[52] By June, overwhelmed by case numbers, less than half of states were actually following federal recommendations that they report probable cases of morbidity and fatality.[53]

Excess death statistics indicated that the number of people dying from COVID was considerably higher than official reports indicated.[54] By late May, the per capita death rate in the United States stood at nearly seven times higher than the global average.[55] By mid-summer, it was four times the per capita rate of Germany and 300 times the number reported in China.[56] As fall kicked off, the United States, which accounted for just over 4 percent of the world's population, recorded more than 20 percent of global COVID deaths.[57] Just after the November elections, U.S. deaths surpassed 200,000, and by mid-December, there were an average of 2,000 deaths per day, with peaks of over 3,400.[58]

As grim as all this news was, there was one area where the United States appeared to shine: its economic support for the population. Of the three countries studied, it was the United States that by far spent the most as opposing political players, the president and Congress, one-upped each other. Between March and April, the U.S. Congress passed four bipartisan spending bills worth about $3 trillion.[59] In total, the United States is estimated to have spent in 2020 approximately 15.7 percent of its GDP on these fiscal stimulus measures.[60] This figure emerged as a result of political wrangling between parties and governmental branches, often absent from the leadership of the president, who nonetheless sought to take credit for popular spending outcomes.[61]

DEMOCRATIC POPULISM: LEADERSHIP, MESSAGING, AND INSTITUTIONAL CHALLENGES IN A POST-FACTUAL WORLD

The U.S. case demonstrates how the experiences of leadership and public relations become fused under conditions of democratic populism. In China,

Xi's dominance over the media landscape allowed him to quietly ensure that the message he championed would be vociferously broadcast around the country. In Russia, where Putin's control over messaging was weaker, the president was compelled to make more of a show of his leadership with the knowledge that the dominant state press would maintain his line. But in the United States, where Trump was in constant conflict with independent media, the president spent much of the pandemic focused more on message than substance. Trump's leadership was, for most of the pandemic year, characterized by railing against potential opponents and attacking his own institutions as the causes of policy shortcomings.

It should be said from the start that there were certainly institutional faults that set the United States up for a crippling fight with COVID (a phenomenon not unique to the U.S. case). Among these was a "just-in-time" medical system in which the business model of America's hospitals—more than three-quarters of which are private[62]—ensured most beds and critical equipment stayed consistently full even in normal times.[63] Just as U.S. hospitals had almost no surge capacity and little interest in preparing for infectious disease,[64] the public health sector was stretched thin, having faced years of workforce and budget cuts.[65] The same was true for the federal government's medical arsenal, known as the National Strategic Stockpile, spread across more than 1,300 locations around the country.[66] After distributing critical supplies during the 2009 H1N1 influenza outbreak, the stockpile was never fully replenished.[67] The stockpile also suffered from the political waves that tossed it back and forth between various offices in the Department of Health and Human Services (DHHS) and the Department of Homeland Security (DHS), creating confusion and complicating coordination for end users at the state level.[68]

In short, America's system designated mitigation and preparedness to the decrepit basement of health policy, accounting for only 3 percent of the country's $3.6 trillion in yearly health spending.[69] Having a democratic populist leader in charge during the pandemic only magnified these institutional weaknesses. Unlike Xi and Putin, who presided over the state response, albeit from a safe distance, Trump continually questioned that response, both at the local level and at the federal one he was supposed to be running. More specifically, Trump made numerous statements that were inconsistent with the available science that his own advisors were relaying to Americans. He also attacked his own institutions as incompetent, both directly through his words and by creating new alternative bodies (discussed below).

With a few notable exceptions, including launching the travel ban, Trump's early strategy was to downplay the emerging COVID outbreak rather than discuss it.[70] Unable to hide the news as capably as the Chinese, Trump instead countered it. He promised that the country was "in great shape"[71] and suggested about the new virus, much to his scientific advisors' chagrin, that "when it gets a little warmer, it miraculously goes away."[72] As the number of cases grew, Trump mysteriously calculated that "within a couple of days" the total would be "close to zero."[73] COVID, he said, was "like a flu" for which "we're totally prepared." His flu comments would resurface frequently as he compared the new disease to the annual virus. "So last year 37,000 Americans died from the common Flu," Trump tweeted. "At this moment there are 546 confirmed cases of CoronaVirus, with 22 deaths. Think about that!"[74]

Trump's reassurances not only flew in the face of science. They also ran counter to the message he was given and, apparently, fully accepted. In this way, his early response pattern was similar to that of his Chinese authoritarian counterpart. Already in January, Trump had been informed by his national security adviser that COVID "will be the biggest national security threat you face in your presidency."[75] Behind the scenes, Trump acknowledged to an investigative reporter that COVID was "more deadly than even your strenuous flus."[76] Yet when the head of DHHS warned of a coming swell of infections, Trump claimed publicly that the number would actually fall to "just one or two people over the next short period of time."[77] Two weeks later, as the virus rapidly grew into a pandemic, Trump dismissed the reported lethality of the virus based on his own "hunch."[78]

When Trump's conversation with an investigative reporter went public months later, he admitted to downplaying COVID so as not "to create a panic."[79] He tried to do this in the spring by portraying his country as invincible, far superior to parts of Europe whose trajectory local experts warned the United States would follow in just weeks.[80] "We are doing a great job and we have 40 people right now, 40, compare that with other countries that have many, many times that amount," he said.[81] "The virus will not have a chance against us," Trump said after closing the border to Europeans. "No nation is more prepared or more resilient than the United States."[82]

Trump's string of comments drew fire from governors, including from his own party, who complained that his words "sometimes conflict with the information we're getting from the rest of the administration." "It's critically important that the message is straightforward and fact-based for the public," the Governors Association head said in March.[83] Trump allies repeated this refrain throughout the spring, encouraging the president "to give the experts the microphone and the platform as much as possible."[84]

Compelled by spiraling case numbers and a UN pandemic declaration, Trump in mid-March suddenly reversed a two-month program of deemphasizing the disease. He turned to reframing COVID from a non-issue to a profound threat necessitating strong leadership—and, in more typical democratic fashion, began showing himself as uniquely capable of governing through crisis. "I felt it was a pandemic long before it was called a pandemic," he stated.[85]

In a major sign of this change, Trump announced a fifteen-day plan to stop the spread of the virus, including urging Americans to stay home.[86] There would be no federal order, but his administration, like Putin's in Russia, encouraged states to follow the national lead. At this point, Trump made COVID a focal point of his presidency. In his new role, Trump, like Xi, referred to COVID as "an invisible enemy" and rebranded himself as a "wartime president."[87] The term "invisible enemy" came up in his press briefings and statements more than ninety times in 2020.

Trump also praised his "very early decision to close the 'borders' from China—against the wishes of almost all."[88] And he boasted that he had a "natural ability" to understand the medical issues at play in ways that shocked doctors around him.[89] In a span of just a few weeks, he went from dismissing the virus to claiming that any death count under 200,000 would mean "we all together have done a very good job."[90]

Unlike the semi-democratic Putin, who sought to portray himself as the distant general, Trump inserted himself directly into the center of the government's COVID response. The White House's Coronavirus Task Force daily press briefings served as Trump's stage from where he could demonstrate his leadership to the American people.[91] To bolster the image of a strong military leader, Trump arrived at a coronavirus task force press conference wearing a navy "U.S.A." hat and took center stage at coronavirus task force briefings.[92] According to one analysis, Trump spoke for more than twenty-eight hours during the thirty-five briefings held between mid-March and late April, the period in which Trump acknowledged COVID was a national emergency.[93] By comparison, Pence, who presided over the task force, spoke for less than six hours, and the government's top infectious disease doctor, Anthony Fauci, had the microphone for only two.[94]

As a democratic populist, Trump felt the need to insert himself directly into the response. He also felt compelled to challenge unpopular aspects of the response pushed by his own public health officials. Sometimes this was done by modeling contradictory behavior. For instance, through the first half of March, as public health officials pushed for social distancing, Trump continued shaking hands in public and refused the recommendation to quarantine after contact with a positive individual.[95] He explained, disregarding his own administration's public health warnings of asymptomatic spread, "We have no symptoms whatsoever."[96]

The president also demonstrated his disapproval of wearing face masks to slow the spread. In early April, as Trump announced that all Americans were advised to wear cloth masks, he emphasized that mask use would be "voluntary" and that "I don't think I'm going to be doing it."[97]

Trump explained,

> I don't know, somehow sitting in the Oval Office behind that beautiful Resolute
> Desk—the great Resolute Desk—I think wearing a face mask as I greet presi-
> dents, prime ministers, dictators, kings, queens, I don't know. Somehow, I don't
> see it for myself.

Trump's defiance of mask recommendations continued even after two aides
tested positive in May, after which Trump appeared maskless saying, "I
don't worry about things. I do what I have to do."[98] Later that month, Trump
refused to wear a mask at a mask-producing plant, defying an order from the
Michigan governor and the Ford company where the masks were being produced. He explained, "I didn't want to give the press the pleasure of seeing
it."[99] Trump typically appeared maskless in public and frequently disregarded
social distancing at White House events, which were held regardless of rising
positivity rates.[100] Some of his events, including indoor rallies, were held even
in defiance of local public health regulations.[101]

Beyond modeling a disregard for his administration's best science, Trump
openly questioned it, offering simple—and sometimes dangerous—solutions
to a complicated viral disaster. In one high-profile example of this, Trump
incorrectly claimed at a March press conference that anti-malaria drugs had
been approved by the FDA to treat COVID, calling the drugs a potential
"game changer."[102] His comments prompted a rebuff from the FDA head,
who warned that treating patients with chloroquine "may do more harm than
good."[103] But the damage was done: after a surge of "off-label" prescribing
of chloroquine and hydroxychloroquine, the FDA acquiesced and moved on
a plan that would essentially allow patients to take those drugs on an experi-
mental basis as they continued to be studied, despite known heart risks.[104]

Instead, the White House ordered millions of hydroxychloroquine tablets
to be sent from the federal stockpile to states and retail pharmacies for use.[105]
Democratic institutions were rocked by the moves but recovered. Under
intense outside criticism and armed with studies that questioned the effectiveness of the anti-malarials and highlighted potential safety risks from taking them, the FDA revoked its emergency use authorization in mid-June.[106]
Despite this, Trump and his family continued to publicly promote the remedies (at one point publicly stating he was taking them prophylactically).[107]

Even as this debate played out over the spring, Trump searched for hope
in still less conventional places. In one of the most notorious incidents that
marked the president's intent to spread hope over science, Trump suggested
the possibility of killing the virus by using ultraviolet lights or injecting disinfectant into people.[108] "I see the disinfectant, where it knocks [the virus] out in
a minute—one minute—and is there a way we can do something like that, by

injection inside, or almost a cleaning," he mused at a task force press conference. "Because you see it gets in the lungs and it does a tremendous number
on the lungs. So it would be interesting to check that."[109]

Trump's participation in the press briefings was curtailed after his disinfectant comments. His explanation for his subsequent absence was that
briefings were not useful. "What is the purpose of having White House News
Conferences when the Lamestream Media asks nothing but hostile questions,
& then refuses to report the truth or facts accurately," Trump tweeted. "They
get record ratings, & the American people get nothing but Fake News. Not
worth the time & effort!"[110]

These outbursts were reminiscent of others that occurred throughout
Trump's time in the coronavirus task force briefings (and other press briefings before that). They involved furious reactions to reporters engaged in
fact-checking (according to one journalistic analysis, one-quarter of the president's statements during the daily task force briefing were factually incorrect).[111] "You are a third-rate reporter. And what you just said is a disgrace,"
Trump said to one reporter. "You will never make it."[112] "You just asked
your question in a very nasty tone," he said to another (one of several times
I found the president calling out a reporter's "nasty" question or tone). "And
you should say, 'Congratulations. Great job'—instead of being so horrid in
the way you ask a question," he added.[113]

The image Trump created, an amalgam of a ruling general and a hapless underdog, fit well with the populist characteristics he espoused. In this vision, Trump
was suffering under the elites, who blamed him for things beyond his control and
punished him in spite of his policy victories. "We've done good," Trump said
in March, just as states were preparing to launch their own states of emergency.
"But no matter what we do, it will never be good for the press. Because they're
using this to try and win an election."[114] Two weeks later, he aimed his comments
at critical governors, saying, "I want them to be appreciative. I don't want them
to say things that aren't true. I want them to be appreciative. We've done a great
job."[115] The term "great job" came up more than 380 times in my analysis of
Trump's 2020 press briefings and statements on the pandemic.

Even when Trump no longer dominated the daily task force briefings, he
continued to speak out on the coronavirus response at other White House
events.[116] And as he pushed states to reopen in late April and early May, he
alternated between being the general rallying his troops ("We have to be warriors. We can't keep our country closed down for years," he said)[117] and the
doubter, incorrectly calling children "immune" to COVID.[118] He fought for
what he saw as the silent majority that wanted to get back to work with little
concern for the minority slated to suffer most. "Will some people be affected
badly? Yes. But we have to get our country open, and we have to get it open
soon."[119]

When Trump found he could not benefit from COVID, he again tried to ignore it. This was the pattern for much of the summer and fall, when most of Trump's comments on COVID reverted to his downplaying of the virus. The one exception to this was the vaccine rollout. While 37 percent of Americans initially said they would not take the vaccine, Trump sang praise on his administration for helping attain the "monumental national achievement" of rapidly developing a vaccine.[120] "People that aren't necessarily big fans of Donald Trump are saying, 'Whether you like him or not, this is one of the greatest miracles in the history of modern-day medicine' or any other medicine—any other age of medicine," Trump said.[121]

Notably, while Xi and Putin leaned into science and bureaucratic expertise to distance themselves from the harsh response, Trump, confronting more immediate political threats, moved in the opposite direction: he worked to distance himself from experts. The coronavirus task force itself included high-level scientists. But as these experts continued to push for more stringent policies that Trump did not support, the president began to directly and publicly castigate them.[122] Xi and Putin spread misinformation through their state-controlled press, but Trump preferred to spread it through Twitter.

Perhaps the most notorious target was the CDC, which might have been expected to run the pandemic response. The CDC was an easy target because, like Trump, it initially overestimated its ability to manage that threat.[123] It was also responsible for the initial testing lag, having favored its own botched tests over viable foreign testing options, a decision that left the United States without a working test for more than a month and a half (till late February).[124] Trump's sidelining of the premier infectious disease agency, which held its last news briefing on March 9,[125] drew rebuke from independent scientists, who wrote that "punishing the agency by marginalizing and hobbling it is not the solution."[126]

Over the spring, Trump and his aides attacked the CDC for its testing failures,[127] but they also cast doubts on fatality statistics[128] and questioned the agency's guidance, even tweeting messages accusing the CDC of "lying" about the virus.[129] But Trump went beyond a war of words. In April, the government issued a $10.2 million contract to a private company to provide data the CDC was already giving.[130] The new coronavirus reporting system launched in July would cut the CDC out by routing real-time virus data collection (e.g., number of cases, hospital bed capacity) through a private contractor rather than through the CDC, which historically held that role.[131]

The CDC's real crime appears not to have been testing shortcomings, given Trump's own doubts about testing, but the inconvenient messages coming out of the CDC from early on. This included a February warning by a CDC official that the virus would likely have a profound impact on everyday life, a message that caused the stock market to plummet.[132] It also included warnings that contradicted Trump's rosy pronouncements, including on the risks of using antimalarial medications to treat COVID, as well as recommendations that all Americans wear masks in public and that religious institutions alter their services to reduce viral spread.[133] Later CDC comments over the spread of COVID in children, insufficient testing, and limited vaccine distribution also prompted backlash from the administration.[134]

In response, the CDC faced relentless pressure from Trump and his loyalists in other state institutions, who accused the CDC of disseminating "political content" rather than scientific knowledge.[135] Comments ranged from the mild, such as that the CDC "made a mistake"[136] or was "undermining the President,"[137] to the noxious, including accusations by an assistant secretary of DHHS that government scientists were guilty of "sedition" and that Trump supporters should prepare for an armed insurrection.[138] The president's most vehement rejection came when the CDC recommended absentee voting in the run-up to the November presidential election, something Trump tweeted would "LEAD TO THE END OF OUR GREAT REPUBLICAN PARTY."[139]

Counter-attacks by Trump appeared to work, causing the CDC to change some of its public recommendations, at least until pushback from the public health and medical community sometimes led to subsequent reversals.[140] Such frequent changes, which often took place without proper explanation, created the impression that the agency was acting arbitrarily or, worse still, based on political motivations.[141] The chief scientific officer at the Association of American Medical Colleges noted that as a result of the CDC's pandemic flip-flopping its "credibility and effectiveness have been damaged."[142] From the inside, one CDC epidemiologist lamented, "I never would have expected the level of political interference we're seeing now. It's so sad."[143]

Trump's proclivity to attack state institutions extended to even his administration's own task force, whose experts pushed policies Trump did not support.[144] Late in the spring, Trump questioned whether the task force was still necessary and favored other working groups, including an economic task force known as the "Opening Our Country Council"; his son-in-law's "shadow task force"; and what became known as the "doctors group,"[145] composed of individuals pushing back against what they saw as the reckless approach of task force health experts.[146] The number of task force meetings in May and June declined as specific pandemic-related responsibilities were divvied out to individual agencies.[147] In late July, with virus numbers exploding and his popularity falling, Trump announced a resumption of task force briefings, but he continued to steer clear of task force meetings through the fall.[148]

Even after allowing the task force to meet again, Trump took aim at it, this time by bringing on "alterative fact" experts—aptly credentialed non-specialists who would agree with the president's views on the pandemic.[149] Most significant was the appointment of a loyal doctor, Scott Atlas, a radiologist with little knowledge of disease spread. Atlas frequently clashed with task force epidemiologists, questioning their analysis in ways that Fauci complained "spread confusion" and gave license to those who discounted public health measures.[150] Outside experts said Atlas was peddling "junk science"[151] while a former CDC chief of staff warned more bluntly, "He's telling the world lies from a bully pulpit, from a position of power, and I believe people died because of that."[152]

Most often, Trump attacked lead task force individuals. Such assaults reached a crescendo during the summer, when the White House put out a list of examples said to be Fauci's grave errors, and Trump took to Fox to denigrate Fauci, saying he "is a nice man, but he's made a lot of mistakes."[153] Fauci was guilty of repeatedly countering Trump's central message that everything was under control, both in Congress and on news programs. Fauci's words, commenting the government was "failing"[154] and acknowledging "I don't think you can say we're doing great," eventually led the White House to cancel some of his media appearances.[155]

In the fall, as Fauci referred to one infamous Rose Garden event as a "super spreader" and called "very troublesome" Trump's reemergence on the campaign trail after his COVID diagnosis, Trump's condemnations took on a more vicious tone.[156] "People are tired of hearing Fauci and all these idiots," Trump said in October. "Fauci is a disaster."[157] Trump had emerged from his own hospitalization, characterized by extraordinarily comprehensive treatment for a very serious infection, determined to go back to downplaying COVID. "FEELING GREAT!" he tweeted, adding that Americans "are learning to live with COVID."[158]

The attacks, censorship, and misinformation invariably muddied the message coming from governmental institutions about the seriousness of the pandemic and how to best respond to it.[159] But democratic institutions also created space to push back. Deborah Birx, the task force's coordinator, for instance, during the summer wave pressed for governors and mayors to issue mask mandates and put in place additional restrictions, despite the president's opposition, and his assertions the pandemic was under control.[160] The FDA, which had been repeatedly pressured by Trump over the course of the pandemic, issued new safety standards for vaccines that would make any vaccine rollout prior to election day highly unlikely. The CDC, which had earlier acquiesced to White House demands for less testing of asymptomatic individuals, reversed course on this guidance and expanded its definition of "close contact."[161]

Trump's troubled relationship with science bled over into the development of a vaccine aimed at ending the COVID threat. Over the objections of his scientific advisors, Trump in the spring promised to have a vaccine ready for distribution "over the next few months."[162] He declared himself in charge of the "Operation Warp Speed"[163] vaccine project, promising hundreds of millions of vaccine doses would be ready to go out by the end of the year.[164] Trump's highly political approach drove fears that the approval process would involve dangerous shortcuts.[165] Even as the FDA launched a public campaign to convince residents the vaccine was based on science, Trump was promising to have a vaccine ready around election day and tweeting charges that "The deep state, or whoever, over at the FDA" was purposely slowing progress.[166] When the FDA drafted new standards for emergency use authorization meant to increase public confidence, Trump attacked them as a "political move" and threatened to block them.[167] The White House chief of staff later threatened the FDA head to clear the vaccine or resign.[168]

What is clear is that in the case of the democratic populist under examination here, leadership and messaging were closely intertwined. This is unsurprising; the democratic executive's bully pulpit is both a place to lead and frame, both by word and example. Populism, however, infused into this already unfavorable mix a fundamental distrust and antagonism toward competitors, including from within the state apparatus. This, in turn, further deteriorated the likelihood that the president would make a concerted and politically costly effort to stem the unfolding disaster.

THE POWER OF DELEGATION: TRUMP'S MOVE TOWARD EXTREME DECENTRALIZATION

Trump's leadership and messaging shortcomings were exacerbated by a political system that facilitated passing the buck on response. As Trump was posturing and pontificating from above, he assigned lower-level actors in state and local governments with the gargantuan task of actually dealing with COVID. This devolutionary policy was, in some ways, similar to what we witnessed in semi-authoritarian Russia. Unlike in Putin's case, however, Trump faced greater political pressure and less political power, which, in turn, meant more effort at deflection but less ability to effectively scapegoat. As a democratic populist, far more likely to face political challenges than a more authoritarian one would, Trump worked to largely wash his hands of the pandemic by making it clear that ultimate accountability lay not in the president's office, as in Russia and China, but in the governors' mansions. He chose devolutionary delegation.

The U.S.'s decentralized approach to COVID was visible from the beginning of the outbreak when, absent federal intervention or guidance, efforts to combat the threat varied by state and locality, with some state and local governments closing down entire communities while others took practically no precautions at all.[169] In mid-March, New York became the first state to close schools and other public spaces within a one-mile radius of a hard-hit subur-ban town.[170] While the federal government appeared poised to take the lead in the response with the declaration of a national emergency on March 13,[171] it quickly became clear that Trump's intention was to dump the responsibility for response further down the line.

The president's political dodging was facilitated by a disaster system characterized by a measurable degree of ambiguity. Disaster response in the United States is typically a local and state issue, with the addition of federal assets when state and regional resources are insufficient. In other words, the U.S. disaster system is built on a pattern of mutual (state/local) and federal aid, a strategy that has been shown effective when there are only a small handful of disasters at any one time.[172] In the case of the pan-demic, however, the system began to break down. There were simply too few resources to go around, as the brief discussion of the national stockpile above illustrates.

But the Trump administration's failings went beyond resources and under-scored the crippling effects of poor coordination and national leadership, sometimes purposeful. For instance, when Trump issued quarantines for those arriving from China in the first weeks of the outbreak, local and state officials were given little to no direction for how and where to quarantine travelers in what amounted to the first federal health quarantine in more than fifty years.[173] When the president called on state leaders to "Do the best you can to get what you can actually get,"[174] the Chicago mayor described the lack of directives: "It was kind of like, either silence, or 'Do the best you can,' which was obviously not acceptable."[175] "The way this was rolled out is concerning. This is not the kind of thing you want to do on the fly because that creates chaos," lamented Hawaii's lieutenant governor.

The lesson that many states took from their early experience was that they were on their own. This meant creating state and local restrictions without any federal direction. Several states, for instance, began limiting occupancy in public spaces, closing down bars and restaurants, and banning gatherings of more than twenty-five people.[176] By the time Trump declared a national emergency on March 13, three-fifths of U.S. states had already declared their own states of emergency.[177]

Trump's March 16 urging of shutdowns came almost eight weeks after the virus had first been detected in the United States.[178] But even after the national emergency declaration, it was clear there would be no highly central-ized federal response. "The governors, locally, are going to be in command," Trump said. "We will be following them, and we hope they can do the job, and I think they will."[179] The governors assigned to lead the fight were over-whelmed. "We're all building the airplane as we fly it right now," said one. "It would be nice to have a national strategy."[180] Leaders at the municipal level felt this leadership void acutely, demanding not "advice" from the top, but "clear directives."[181]

With Trump instead demanding governors take the lead role, the Republican chair of the National Governors Association acknowledged "a lot of tension and frustration [among] the governors."[182] The Democratic governor of Virginia was more blunt, comparing the situation to being at war when "our leader says you all need to get your own weapons at the state level to defeat this." The New York governor complained, "This is a national problem, and there are no national rules." Such worries fueled unusual scrutiny of the White House from Republican senators as well.[183]

Despite Trump's heavy presence in the media, he forced state and local leaders to wrestle with the politically fraught issue of whether and how to implement lockdowns.[184] With no unified national position, states all went their own way. This rankled governors, particularly the more aggressive ones. "You can't have a patchwork quilt of policies," the New York governor said, adding that if New York closed stores but neighboring New Jersey did not, the virus would be unimpacted, but New York would have "just sent thousands of vehicles over to New Jersey, flooding stores."[185] Fauci himself complained later that, unlike European countries that were almost entirely shut down during the first wave, the collection of divergent policies in the United States left only around half the country actually shut down.[186]

The devolution of restrictive powers exposed rifts between state and local leaders as well. In one example from early in the pandemic, the Republican mayor of hard-hit Sioux City, South Dakota, publicly urged the governor to issue a "shelter-in-place order" that he, as mayor, lacked the authority to implement.[187] South Dakota's governor instead held a press conference where she said, "the people themselves are primarily responsible for their safety . . . They are the ones that are entrusted with expansive freedoms."[188] Without strong federal guidance, state-local conflicts played out around the country.

State and local leaders were asking for more than a common policy, though. They also urgently needed goods and personnel, with the head of the Governor's Association demanding the White House "take the lead" in providing medical equipment. "We're way behind the curve," he said.[189] During a March 16 call with governors, Trump warned them not to depend on federal deliveries of PPE or other essential medical equipment which, he said, they needed to obtain themselves. This led to a back-and-forth, where Trump called on NY governor Cuomo to "do more"[190] and the governor responded via Twitter: "I have to do more? No—YOU have to do something! You're supposed to be the President."[191]

New York's governor was not the only leader overwhelmed. Almost 90 percent of the mayors responding to a national preparedness survey conducted in March by the U.S. Conference of Mayors said they faced a shortage of test kits and PPE, with 85 percent saying they had an inadequate number of ventilators.[192] "We've got part of the federal stockpile, but most of this response has been driven by mayors and governors," one mayor commented. "Anything we get from the federal government is a bonus, but we're not sitting around waiting for it to be the solution."[193]

The urgency was clearest in New York City, which became the epicenter of the pandemic's first high-growth phase in the United States. New York's mayor asked for a military deployment. Rebutting Trump's stance that the government was sending substantial help, the mayor complained, "We are very much on our own at this point."[194] Other governors pleaded for federal action to ensure the delivery of critical medical supplies. As one told the president during a conference call in which Trump called the federal government a "great backup," "We don't need a backup. We need a Tom Brady."[195]

While the government did disseminate some materials and deploy small teams of medical personnel to hotspots, as outlined in chapter 3, these efforts amounted to a trickle compared to what was needed. The U.S. Army Corps of Engineers facilitated the conversion of dozens of existing facilities to handle increased patient loads.[196] National Guard troops were used to help deliver supplies and disinfect public areas under the control of local governors.[197] Thousands of Public Health Service personnel would be dispatched over the course of the pandemic to assist in hospitals and nursing homes.[198] And the federal government occasionally facilitated surge testing in highly impacted areas.[199]

But the bulk of the response was still on the backs of local authorities, and much of the federal aid to states was overstated and insufficient. In one example, the military dispatched the 1,000-bed USNS Comfort hospital ship to hard-hit New York in order to relieve area hospitals of non-COVID patients, a delivery that Trump called a "70,000-ton message of hope and solidarity to the incredible people of New York."[200] But in this grand show of force, reports quickly emerged of a botched rescue. The Comfort and other temporary hospitals run by the military were limited by a failure to coordinate with local hospitals, the military's employment of narrow treatment eligibility criteria, and a lack of specialized equipment in the temporary facilities.[201]

In another high-profile federal intervention, the federal government worked with several private contractors to deliver urgently needed medical supplies to hot spots around the country. Project Airbridge, launched with great fanfare in March, reportedly conducted 122 flights at a cost of $91 million during its first six weeks of operations.[202] Trump praised the initiative: "The big planes—they are very big, very powerful—and they are loaded to the gills with supplies," he said.[203] But the actual amount of relief delivered was difficult to pin down. For instance, Vice President Pence claimed the Project was delivering 22 million masks per day, while FEMA said the number was 2.2

million. There was also consternation that the deal was commercial in nature, with insufficient oversight amidst allegations of over-charging.[204]

Promises of outside help could not address the fundamental issues emerging from a lack of coordination. As medical groups complained of their inability to acquire key medical equipment, one of the most vivid images of this was governors engaged in bidding wars with one another for scarce medical goods.[205] "Price gouging is a tremendous problem and it's only getting worse," Governor Cuomo said. "I'm competing against every other state, and in some cases, against other countries around the world."[206] Private healthcare companies trying to get their hands on N95s saw prices shoot up from $.30 per mask before the outbreak to between $3 and $15 per mask after.[207] The U.S. attorney general warned that profiteers and hoarders of medical masks would "be hearing a knock on your door."[208] As in other countries, U.S. authorities found the pandemic resulted in a stream of fraudulent claims for cures and preventative treatments, as well as the sale of fake products.[209]

By mid-April, some governors, accepting they were largely on their own, began mulling their own collective strategy.[210] Some, including Florida, Texas, Rhode Island, and later, New York, put in place mandatory self-quarantines for those arriving from hard-hit states, going so far as to have police set up checkpoints and stop out-of-state vehicles with warnings to adhere to the rules.[211] Even Trump threatened a federal quarantine of New York City, causing mass confusion.[212] Legal advocates, including the American Civil Liberties Union (ACLU), warned many of these moves—and especially Trump's quarantine threat—were constitutionally questionable at best.[213]

This was not the last time Trump called for populist policies that brought charges of constitutional overreach. When Trump demanded a rapid reopening of all states in mid-April, even as the virus continued to circulate widely, he was again attacked for assuming powers he did not have. "The president of the United States calls the shots" when it comes to reopening," Trump said, alleging that news reports claiming such powers rested with governors were intended to stir "conflict and confusion."[214] "It is the decision of the President, and for many good reasons."[215] The claim drew shock from governors, one remarking, "We don't have a king, we have an elected president." When Trump backed down, he demanded that governors "take charge"[216] and promised to "hold the governors accountable" if there were no speedy reopenings.[217] By late April, more than a dozen states had released reopening plans, winning praise from the president.[218]

As some states opened, neighboring states, counties, and cities were again frustrated that their own restrictions were becoming an exercise in futility.[219] "We don't exist within a bubble," one mayor explained. "We would be asking people to keep making sacrifices in the name of public health when people in other communities are not and continue to spread the virus into our community."[220] Local emergency managers pleaded for a "national-level plan,"[221] as overly vague federal guidance, interpreted differently by various entities, became meaningless.[222]

While the president's early pandemic policy was centered on encouraging local decision-making, his tolerance for local action did not extend to states cautious about opening up. Already in mid-April Trump was calling on citizens to "liberate" themselves if governors did not end restrictions, adding weight to the demands of protesters in states such as Michigan, Minnesota, and Virginia.[223] While the president lacked the power to mandate reopening, his Justice Department did intervene to support religious institutions fighting off restrictions[224] and Trump claimed he would "override" any governors who refused to comply with a new order he issued allowing places of worship to immediately open.[225]

The reopening led to soaring positivity and hospitalization rates at the very start of the summer.[226] For instance, Arizona, which had been the first state to fully reopen, experienced an 800 percent increase in cases up until early July, as well as praise from the White House.[227] Meanwhile, the Trump administration had still not complied with federal legislation demanding it create a national testing strategy, instead having just a draft plan that left testing largely at the discretion of state leaders.[228] Using different tests with varying levels of accuracy, some states offered testing to any resident, while others limited tests to symptomatic individuals.[229]

Nor, despite pressure from business groups and others, did the president provide a national standard on mask usage that could allow local officials to mandate masks where the spread was high.[230] Instead, Trump looked away from case spikes, repeatedly musing that "at some point, that's going to sort of just disappear."[231]

Without national rules on restrictions, mayors fighting local surges faced off with governors demanding an end to all restrictions.[232] Often, there was a heavy partisan component to these struggles. Some (especially Republican) governors restrained from restrictions while allowing their (largely Democratic) mayors to implement their own and bear the political fallout.[233] In Texas, for instance, the governor warned mayors that new restrictions would "force Texans into poverty."[234] Salt Lake City's mayor lamented "state pressure to reopen the economy without the guidance of the public-health data."[235] In turn, some states sued their own municipalities for imposing restrictions.[236] "It feels like we're fighting our own state to keep our citizens safe," commented one Democratic mayor in Georgia.[237]

As local, state, and national governments continued to clash over what constituted an acceptable level of public health restrictions, courts became ever more embroiled in the debate. The Wisconsin governor, whose "Safer at Home" order had been struck down by the state's Supreme Court earlier in the pandemic, was compelled to try again during the summer wave.[238] On the southern border, a state appeals court blocked an El Paso County judge's stay-at-home order issued as patients were sent out of Texas to receive care.[239] And the Supreme Court struck down temporary restrictions on religious organizations imposed by the governors of New York and California.[240]

One of the largest issues to emerge in the opening saga concerned when and how to reopen schools. This debate brought an additional layer to the state-local dynamic, pitting governors against school superintendents. In South Carolina, the Republican school superintendent lashed out at her Republican governor, who had called for a full reopening, saying that "South Carolina is still a long way from Washington, D.C." and would not bow to the president and his allies.[241] School reopenings also, unsurprisingly, ended up in the courts. In Florida, for instance, a judge blocked the governor's order requiring that school districts reopen.[242]

Amidst the fall wave, state and local officials were even forced to square off directly with the president, who disregarded the health policies he claimed were theirs to make. On the campaign trail, Trump held large rallies where maskless participants abandoned social distancing to hear his assurances that they were "very quickly" returning to "normal life."[243] When he held a large rally in a Duluth, Minnesota airport, local officials responsible for enforcing their health codes chose to look the other way rather than rile up the president and his supporters.[244] "We will not incite an incident by unilaterally taking physical action to close the event," the airport's executive director told his board members.[245]

After the elections passed, the president continued to play down the risks of COVID and promised that no national lockdown would be on the table under "any circumstances."[246] This left state and local governments to wrestle with rising cases on their own, often without the authority to do much about them. In Indiana, for instance, the state health agency released an announcement that counties and cities could impose "ANY additional health emergency restriction they determine necessary," but officials on the ground were skeptical.[247] "People are well aware of the fact that anything I do I have no enforcement for," said one Indiana county's health officer.[248]

As the federal government prepared to distribute vaccines to the states, the CDC made a set of recommendations for prioritizing certain groups, but—as with the rest of the COVID response—states were free to choose their own priorities.[249] When Trump came under fire in the last days of the year for leading an unexpectedly slow federal distribution, he responded with his traditional deflection: "It is up to the States to distribute the vaccines once brought to the designated areas by the Federal Government."[250]

State leaders felt like this set them up for failure, complaining that the federal government severely underspent on vaccine distribution.[251] By early

December, plagued by supply chain issues and difficulties in preparing and staffing vaccine clinics, the projected number of vaccine doses for distribution by the end of the month fell from 300 million to less than 40 million.[252] By the end of the year, just 2.6 million doses had been administered, despite more than 12 million having been delivered.[253]

Trump's pattern of delegating authority while undermining local decisions set the stage for a painful response for which the president had no intention of taking responsibility. In abdicating accountability to those lower down, Trump performed in some ways like his more authoritarian populist counterparts. Unlike in China, however, the U.S. president did not infuse massive national assets into struggling regions, hesitating to take measures to ameliorate the situation that were squarely within his own power. While Putin's federal response paled relative to China's, it was arguably a step above the U.S. one. At the very least, Putin took ownership of the disaster in ways his U.S. counterpart refused.

SCAPEGOATING BY A DEMOCRATIC POPULIST

Trump looked far and wide in his efforts to defray blame. This included using opaque references to what he claimed was a better, or at least not worse, situation in the United States compared to other parts of the globe (COVID, he noted, was "not under control any place in the world").[254] The tactic also involved more direct redirection of blame, with the president repeatedly referring to a "foreign virus" and emphasizing that it was "not our fault."[255] When he declared a national emergency amidst a shortage of testing and monitoring resources, Trump also sought to place responsibility squarely on previous administrations. "I don't take responsibility at all," he said.[256] He later backed up this assertion by referencing H1N1 deaths as evidence of Obama's "incompetence."[257] When the economy crashed, Trump similarly looked outward, saying, "It's China's fault."[258]

As alluded to in the previous section, the tactic of placing blame on a predecessor or foreign country was gradually replaced as the virus spread and domestic leaders more sharply attacked Trump's national response. Unlike in more authoritarian states, Trump could not directly punish lower-level authorities. Instead, he worked to cast them as incompetent and nefarious, and himself as the humble servant, with the hope that voters would take the cue and mete out accountability themselves.

In the day-to-day, Trump primarily aimed his fire at those who were relentless in their criticism of his administration rather than, as in the case of Putin, at those who were failing in their response. Over the spring, he consistently passed the baton on to governors. When asked one week after the national emergency declaration why he was not doing more to get PPE and tests to the states, Trump redirected the questions: "Governors are supposed to be doing a lot of this work . . . The federal government's not supposed to be out there buying vast amounts of items and then shipping. You know, we're not a shipping clerk."[259] Trump persistently underscored that the role of his federal government was "to back you [governors] up should you fail" and expressed resentment that governors were "blaming the Federal Government for their own shortcomings."[260] "The complainers should have been stocked up and ready long before this crisis hit," Trump said.[261] "Long before this pandemic arrived, they should have been on the open market, just buying."[262]

When Trump wasn't blaming, he was portraying himself as the undeserving subject of gubernatorial recriminations—the populist underdog. This was most clear in the case of New York governor Andrew Cuomo, whose state was hit hardest in the initial wave and who desperately pleaded for more federal assistance. "We're building them hospitals. We're building them medical centers. And he was complaining," Trump said. "I'm not blaming him or anything else but he shouldn't be talking about us."[263] Trump's conflict with Cuomo was replicated in other parts of the country, causing him to respond: "To my face, they're very nice, but then sometimes, I guess, they assume I don't watch them or something," Trump said.[264] "They can't say, 'Oh, gee, we should get this, we should get that.'"[265]

One less advertent, and far more common, method of blame involved taking a hands-off approach, allowing lower-level leaders to take the blame from their own constituents. For instance, rather than using his position to press states to lock down, Trump provided broad guidance and told state governors and business leaders to make their own decisions on who should not be at work, as well as who could return to work and public spaces, and under what conditions.[266] Constituents would then blame any tough measures on the state government rather than the president.

To accomplish this goal, Trump politicized the pandemic in ways totally foreign to the non-democratic cases, where the effort was on ensuring people that their political leaders were all of one mind. Already in February, Trump was framing the COVID outbreak in partisan terms, claiming that some Democrats were "trying to gain political favor by saying a lot about this."[267] He also shot out at the mainstream media for "doing everything possible to make the [Coronavirus] look as bad as possible."[268] His message was picked up by sympathetic conservative media hosts who attacked Democrats for "weaponizing an infectious disease" that they charged was no worse than "the common cold."[269] Trump's more conservative wing of the Republican party from the get-go expressed the feeling that the virus was primarily a political phenomenon aimed at hurting the right.[270]

Even after Trump's pivot away from conspiracies and to a more sober, expert-informed tone on the virus in mid-March, his administration remained inconsistent.[271] As highlighted above, Trump made comments that vacillated between demanding a military-style approach to a grave danger, on the one hand, and serving as the country's most high-profile skeptic, on the other. These comments created space for politicians to continue making claims that the pandemic was political in nature, even as the body count rapidly climbed.

Two particular issues highlight the high level of pandemic politicization: the spring reopening and the use of masks. Despite assurances that governors would "need to make the decisions that are right for their particular state,"[272] Trump's reopening blueprint, coupled with his urging that "our country has to get open, and it will get open,"[273] set the stage for conflict. By dangling a carrot but leaving governors responsible for lowering it to their people, Trump effectively positioned state and local leaders charged with ensuring public health as the villains. An "open it up" caucus in the Republican Party quickly formed and took to conservative media.[274] "If the U.S. economy collapses, the world economy collapses. And trying to burn down the village to save it is foolish," said one Republican lawmaker on Fox News.[275] Another declared starkly on radio: "In the choice between the loss of our way of life as Americans and the loss of life, of American lives, we have to always choose the latter."[276]

The reopening was predictably partisan, Republican states moving further and faster to reopen than their Democratic counterparts.[277] In some cases, including in Georgia, Tennessee, and Utah, the governors defied or side-stepped medical advisors in ending restrictions.[278] They also clashed with worried workers, threatening that those who refused to go back could lose unemployment benefits or their jobs.[279] Trump egged them on, criticizing states not reopening due to a rise in cases as not "going fast enough."[280] "There just seems to be no effort on certain blue states to get back into gear, and the people aren't going to stand for it," Trump said in mid-May. "They want our country open. I want our country open, too."[281]

Administration officials published opinion pieces arguing that the health risks of COVID had to be balanced with "the health, social and economic costs of keeping Main Streets across the United States closed for business,"[282] as Trump rowdily charged that "The Democrats are moving slowly, all over the U.S.A., for political purposes."[283] His tweets resounded with phrases such as "REOPEN THE COUNTRY!" and "TRANSITION TO GREATNESS."[284]

In early May, small but highly visible protests in favor of immediate reopening picked up pace, spreading to cities across the country. Occasionally, they were marked by the threat of violence, with military-clad protesters carrying guns as they confronted police.[285] In words reminiscent of the language he used to describe those taking part in a 2017 white supremacist rally in Virginia, Trump responded by calling the participants to one of these gun-toting, pro-opening rallies "very good people, but they are angry. They want their lives back again, safely!"[286] Nor were these one-off incidents. After federal and state officials thwarted a plot to kidnap the governor of Michigan, motivated by the belief that the state government was illegally depriving Michiganders of their constitutional rights, Trump's coronavirus adviser tweeted out a call for Michigan residents to once again "rise up" against the measures.[287]

Just as reopenings became a political hot potato on a grand scale, so did masks at a much more micro level. Mask mandates emerged as a political flash point, seen by some as a collective responsibility and by others as a baseless infringement on their personal freedoms.[288] With Trump suggesting masking was below his dignity and questioning its usefulness, significant sectors of the population followed in step. This led even Republican governors to back down from masking requirements, with the Republican governor of Ohio commenting that the president should have set an example: "I would have liked to have seen the president do that."[289]

As skyrocketing summer cases led many Republican leaders to break with Trump and at last urge their constituents to wear masks,[290] the White House reacted by hedging: "The president has said he has no problem with masks, that he encourages people to make whatever decision is best for their safety and to follow what their local jurisdictions say."[291] The partisan nature of masking up was unmistakable at that point. Of the roughly half of Americans claiming to wear a mask anytime they left home, Democrats were twice as likely (71 percent) as Republicans (35 percent).[292] Only in mid-July, during a visit at Walter Reed National Military Medical Center, did Trump, for the first time in three months, don a mask in public, saying that they "have a time and place."[293]

Whether emboldened by the second wave in the fall or by changing political calculations, some Republican governors tightened their policies after the November elections.[294] When the outgoing Republican governor of Utah implemented a mask mandate as part of his state of emergency days after the election, he posted a video on Twitter in which he used freedom as a reason for following the mandate: "Individual freedom is certainly important, and it is our rule of law that protects that freedom."[295] Trump's Surgeon General, three weeks after the election, echoed this voice, calling masks "an instrument of freedom."[296]

These episodes demonstrate how scapegoating takes a fundamentally different form under conditions of democratic, as opposed to authoritarian, populism. Unable to dismiss or formally punish lower-level political leaders, Trump instead spent much of his leadership and messaging attacking them with the aim of inciting public pressure that would ultimately lead to state and local policy changes or even the termination of the applicable authorities. Notably, these efforts were not about admonishing officials whose pandemic policies were ineffective at saving lives, but those whose policies—often driven more by science than politics—countered the president's agenda and message.

CONCLUSION

Democratic populists are better known for manufacturing and instrumentalizing crises than managing disasters. The U.S. record during the first year of the pandemic underscores the propensity for populists to abandon difficult struggles and pass on responsibility for the resulting devastation to others. But it also demonstrates the various methods populists can utilize in their efforts to gain politically from an unfolding disaster.

Trump, like his authoritarian counterparts, approached the pandemic with inward trepidation and outward denial. It was a hot potato that the president skirted away from for as long as he could. But in a boisterous democracy, Trump's ability to deny or play down the emerging outbreak was highly constrained. From a vibrant media and organized civil society to outspoken political opponents, there were just too many eyes on him.

It was these eyes that likely convinced Trump, unlike Xi and Putin, that he had to be front and center once he was forced to confront the disaster, like his authoritarian counterparts, by encouraging states to shut down. Sensing the potential gains from this move, which Trump hoped would last closer to days than weeks or months, the president adopted the somber demeanor and rhetoric of a general. But while Trump felt compelled to become the face of the COVID response, he could not afford to be the one imposing pain on his citizens—particularly when he faced upcoming elections and lacked the power to bring a quick end to the threat: that unenviable task he delegated down the line to state and local officials.

Even as he sought to be the face of the U.S. response, Trump questioned the grim, science-based assessments and recommendations coming from both inside and outside his own governmental institutions. Rather than heeding his experts' advice as his more authoritarian counterparts did, Trump soon returned to challenging them and downplaying the disaster. The atmosphere quickly became cantankerous as Trump was slammed with a barrage of complaints over the federal government's lack of leadership. The president tried to deflect, spreading blame outwards, and reverted back to the simple line that the pandemic was not so bad after all—and that economic revival had to be the priority. Politicization of the virus, from the start, intensified with the process of reopening. When decreased restrictions led to a summer and fall wave of death, Trump again questioned the severity of the disease.

By the end of Trump's tenure, COVID reached deep into rural America, overwhelming the already fragile medical infrastructure in Trump's political heartland.[297] Fuming from his 2020 electoral loss, Trump by year's end had grown nearly silent on the pandemic, with the exception of his celebration of the vaccine, for which he took partial credit.[298] The head of the Governors Association recalled a horrific fall during which "in the worst part of the battle, the general was missing in action."[299] "Words matter a lot, and what we have here is a failure to communicate—and worse than that, the effective communication of policies, of myths, of confusion," concluded one former CDC director. "It's stunning."[300]

Trump's COVID rhetoric helped deepen a bitter societal rift on everything COVID, from restrictions and mask use to stimulus payments.[301] His words also had important impacts on lower-level policy. One CDC report found that when governors, mayors, and the president announced the need for restrictions, people heeded them—particularly when they came from the president, indicating the seriousness of the situation.[302] Indeed, governors in Republican states such as Florida and Georgia began taking the stay-at-home suggestion seriously only once the president switched to his "wartime" posturing.[303] Similarly, when Trump chose to downplay the pandemic, his views were echoed by others, including numerous governors and his own vice president, who, as head of the coronavirus task force, assured Americans in late April that in less than a month "we will largely have this coronavirus epidemic behind us."[304]

The U.S. performance in the first year of the pandemic was an unmitigated failure that shocked observers at home and abroad. As a result, the U.S. case was held up as the poster child of populism's failure. Yet, as we've seen in the previous two chapters, populism is not inevitably a weakness. In the next chapter, I reach for some tentative cross-case conclusions and explore how these cases relate to the broader population of countries struggling against the pandemic.

NOTES

1. Brittany Shammas et al., "Mounting Cases Push Hospitals to Brink," *The Washington Post*, December 17, 2020, A1.

2. Amy Goldstein, "Health-Care Chain Sued by Hospital Workers," *The Washington Post*, August 21, 2020, A7.

3. Lenny Bernstein, Rachel Weiner, and Joel Achenbach, "Virus Guidance Ignored as Case Numbers Rise," Ibid., A1; Rachel Weiner and Ariana Eunjung Cha, "Amid Threats and Political Pushback, Public Health Officials Are Leaving Posts," Ibid., June 23, A5.

4. White House, "Remarks by President Trump, Vice President Pence, and Members of the Coronavirus Task Force in a Fox News Virtual Town Hall," *White House Archives*, March 24, 2020, https://trumpwhitehouse.archives.gov/briefings-statements/remarks-president-trump-vice-president-pence-members-coronavirus-task-force-fox-news-virtual-town-hall/.

5. Geoffrey A. Fowler, Lenny Bernstein, and Laurie McGinley, "California Seeks out Patient's Contacts," *The Washington Post*, February 28, 2020, A1.

6. Carolyn Y. Johnson, Laurie McGinley, and Lena H. Sun, "Faulty CDC Test Delays Ability to Monitor Disease's Spread in United States," Ibid., February 26; William Wan et al., "Spreading Coronavirus Kills First U.S. Patient," Ibid., March 1, 2020, A1.

7. Seung Min Kim, Maria Sacchetti, and Brady Dennis, "Every American Can Be Tested for Virus, Pence Promises," Ibid., March 4, A8; Carolyn Y. Johnson et al., "Labs Step up as Americans Clamor for More Testing," Ibid., November 5, 2022, A10.

8. Amy Goldstein, Laurie McGinley, and Yasmeen Abutaleb, "Trump Says Drive-through Testing Sites Are in the Works," Ibid., March 14, 2020, A4.

9. Philip Rucker et al., "As Deaths Mounted, Trump Fixated on Stalled Economy," Ibid., May 3, A1.

10. White House, "Remarks by President Trump in a Press Briefing on COVID-19 Testing," *White House Archives*, May 11, 2020, https://trumpwhitehouse.archives.gov/briefings-statements/remarks-president-trump-press-briefing-COVID-19-testing/.

11. Philip Rucker, Josh Dawsey, and Yasmeen Abutaleb, "In Trump Plan, Governors Take on Burdens of Testing, Reopening," *The Washington Post*, April 17, 2020, A1.

12. Ibid.

13. Isaac Stanley-Becker, Toluse Olorunnipa, and Seung M. Kim, "Trump Fomenting Defiance of Strictures," April 18, 2022, A1.

14. Steven Mufson, Yasmeen Abutaleb, and Juliet Eilperin, "States Plead for Federal Testing Help Amid Push to Reopen," *The Washington Post*, April 18, 2020, A7.

15. Amy Goldstein, "Most Insurers Will Waive Costs for Tests, but Not Sick Visits or Treatment," Ibid., March 14, A13; Rachel Weiner, "Demand Strains Testing Capacity as Infections Soar," Ibid., July 2, A1.

16. Shane Harris, Felicia Sonmez, and Mike DeBonis, "Governors from Both Parties Contradict Trump on Testing," Ibid., April 20, A4.

17. Ibid.

18. Ibid.

19. Karen DeYoung, "As Restrictions Begin to Ease, Battle over Testing Deepens," Ibid., April 21; Karen DeYoung, Miriam Berger, and Katie Mettler, "Governors Chart Different Paths as They Consider Reopening States' Activities," Ibid., April 22.

20. White House, "Remarks by President Trump, Vice President Pence, and Members of the Coronavirus Task Force in Press Briefing," *White House Archives*, April 7, 2020, https://trumpwhitehouse.archives.gov/briefings-statements/remarks-president-trump-vice-president-pence-members-coronavirus-task-force-press-briefing-21/.

21. Mike DeBonis, Chris Mooney, and Juliet Eilperin, "U.S. Testing 'Blueprint' Keeps Onus on States," *The Washington Post*, April 28, 2020, 2020, A1.

22. Elizabeth Dwoskin et al., "Promised Drive-through Testing Sites Haven't Materialized," Ibid., March 28, A17; Rucker et al., "As Deaths Mounted, Trump Fixated on Stalled Economy."

23. White House, "Remarks by President Trump, Vice President Pence, and Members of the Coronavirus Task Force in Press Briefing," *White House Archives*, March 24, 2020, https://trumpwhitehouse.archives.gov/briefings-statements/remarks-president-trump-vice-president-pence-members-coronavirus-task-force-press-briefing-9/.

24. "Remarks by President Trump in Meeting with Republican Members of Congress," *White House Archives*, May 8, 2020, https://trumpwhitehouse.archives.gov/briefings-statements/remarks-president-trump-meeting-republican-members-congress/.

25. "Remarks by President Trump and Vice President Pence at a Meeting with Governor Reynolds of Iowa," *White House Archives*, May 6, 2020, https://trumpwhitehouse.archives.gov/briefings-statements/remarks-president-trump-vice-president-pence-meeting-governor-reynolds-iowa/.

26. Frances Stead Sellers and Ben Guarino, "Many States Falling Short on Efforts to Trace Contacts," *The Washington Post*, June 15, 2020, A1.

27. White House, "Press Briefing by Press Secretary Kayleigh McEnany," *White House Archives*, May 12, 2020, https://trumpwhitehouse.archives.gov/briefings-statements/press-briefing-press-secretary-kayleigh-mcenany-051220/; Anne Gearan et al., "As States Get Testing Funds, Trump Paints Rosy Picture," *The Washington Post*, May 12, 2020, A1.

28. Anne Gearan and Felicia Sonmez, "As U.S. Cases Top 1 Million, Testing Rate Is Below Average," Ibid., April 29, A4.

29. Gearan et al., "As States Get Testing Funds, Trump Paints Rosy Picture."

30. Steve Thompson, Juliet Eilperin, and Brady Dennis, "A Boost in Tests, but Lack of Takers," Ibid., May 18.

31. Amy Goldstein, "Administration Pledges More Equipment but Still Puts Testing Onus on States," Ibid., May 25, A9.

32. Weiner, "Demand Strains Testing Capacity as Infections Soar"; Rachel Weiner and William Wan, "Backlogs in Test Results Hobble Virus Response," Ibid., July 13; Philip Rucker et al., "A Lost Summer: How Trump Fell Short in Confronting the Virus," Ibid., August 9.

33. Rucker et al., "A Lost Summer: How Trump Fell Short in Confronting the Virus."

34. Derek Hawkins, Felicia Sonmez, and Hannah Knowles, "Officials Sound Familiar Alarms as Cases Surge," Ibid., July 20, A3.

35. Toluse Olorunnipa, Josh Dawsey, and Yasmeen Abutaleb, "Major Surge in Infections Exposes U.S. Failures," Ibid., June 28, A1.

36. Yasmeen Abutaleb, Taylor Telford, and Josh Dawsey, "Experts Upset by Trump's Virus Testing Comments," Ibid., June 22.

37. Amy Goldstein and H. Sun Lena, "Abrupt Change in U.S. Testing Guidelines Worries Public Health Experts," Ibid., August 27, A9.

38. Kevin O'Reilly, "Why CDC Was Right to Revise Coronavirus Testing Guidelines," *American Medical Association*, September 23, 2020, https://www.ama-assn.org/delivering-care/public-health/why-cdc-was-right-revise-coronavirus-testing-guidelines.

39. Fowler, Bernstein, and McGinley, "California Seeks out Patient's Contacts"; Toluse Olorunnipa, Seung Min Kim, and Scott Wilson, "Trump Voices New U.S. Containment Guidelines," Ibid., March 17, 2020; Katie Zezima et al., "Restrictions Rise, Along with Number of Cases," Ibid., March 20.

40. Joe Davidson, "Former CDC Director Freiden Says U.S. Has Become a 'Laggard' in Global Health," Ibid., May 30, A8.

41. Anne Gearan, Brittany Shammas, and Lateshia Beachum, "White House Says Virus Is under Control Despite Surges," Ibid., June 30; Lena H. Sun and Joel Achenbach, "CDC: Coronavirus May Have Infected 24 Million in U.S.," Ibid., June 26, A1.

42. Derek Hawkins, Marisa Iati, and Jacqueline Dupree, "U.S. Case Count Soars Past 5 Million," Ibid., August 10, A2; Toluse Olorunnipa, "Trump Messaging Sows Confusion in Outbreak Response," Ibid., July 14, A5; Anne Gearan, Marisa Iati, and Jacqueline Dupree, "U.S. Passes 4 Million Cases; Pace of Infections Doubles," Ibid., July 24, A9; Toluse Olorunnipa and Erica Werner, "Partisan Gridlock Hardens Amid Surging Pandemic and Stalling Economy," Ibid., October 18, A14; William Wan and Jacqueline Dupree, "U.S. Breaks Record for Daily Cases," Ibid., October 24, A1; Joel Achenbach et al., "Hospitals Nationwide See Flood of Patients," Ibid., October 27.

43. Lenny Bernstein et al., "Coronavirus Cases Shatter Records, Straining Health Care," Ibid., November 6, A3.

44. Robert Barnes, "Latest COVID Surge Is Breaking Records," Ibid., November 9, A2; Paulina Firozi and Hannah Knowles, "States Impose Tougher Restrictions as U.S. Virus Cases Surpass 11 Million," Ibid., November 16, A7.

45. Moriah Balingit, "School Leaders Face Closures Again as Cases Rise," Ibid., November 22; Brittany Shammas and Reis Thebault, "Fauci Warns of 'Surge Upon a Surge' as Air Travel Hits Highs During Holidays," Ibid., December 29.

46. Karin Brulliard, "Transmission Surges, Fueled by Parties and Game Nights," Ibid., November 13, A4; "Outbreak Reaches Final Frontier - Sparsely Populated U.S. Counties," *The Washington Post*, October 29, 2020, A16; Debbie Cenziper, Peter Whoriskey, and Joel Jacobs, "Government Puts Nursing Home Toll at over 25,000, but Data Is Incomplete," Ibid., June 2, A23.

47. Brulliard, "Transmission Surges, Fueled by Parties and Game Nights."

48. Wan et al., "Spreading Coronavirus Kills First U.S. Patient"; Matt Zapotosky, Kim Bellware, and Jacqueline Dupree, "U.S. Deaths Pass 3,700; Officials Say Worst Is yet to Come," Ibid., April 1, A4.

49. Matt Zapotosky, Isaac Stanley-Becker, and John Wagner, "Single-Day Death Toll in U.S. Tops 1,000 as Trump Insists Country Will Recover," Ibid., April 3, A3.

50. Emma Brown, Beth Reinhard, and Aaron C. Davis, "Experts: Americans Are Dying but Aren't Being Included in Count," Ibid., April 6, A1.

51. Emma Brown, Beth Reinhard, and Reis Thebault, "States Vary in Deciding Which Deaths Count toward Virus Toll," Ibid., April 17.

52. Ibid.

53. Beth Reinhard et al., "Many States Aren't Giving Their 'Probables' Data to CDC," Ibid., June 9, A14.

54. Emma Brown et al., "U.S. Deaths Surged Early in Pandemic," Ibid., April 28, A1; Andrew B. Tran, Leslie Shapiro, and Emma Brown, "Pandemic's Overall Death Toll in U.S. Likely Surpassed 100,000 Weeks Ago," Ibid., June 3, A25; Reis Thebault et al., "Spike in Non-Virus Deaths Suggests Delay in Seeking Care," Ibid., July 3, A10.

55. DeBonis, Mooney, and Eilperin, "U.S. Testing 'Blueprint' Keeps Onus on States"; Tran, Shapiro, and Brown, "Pandemic's Overall Death Toll in U.S. Likely Surpassed 100,000 Weeks Ago"; Davidson, "Former CDC Director Freiden Says U.S. Has Become a 'Laggard' in Global Health."

56. Marc Fisher and Chris Dixon, "'Too Many': U.S. Toll Nears 150,000," Ibid., July 30, A1.

57. Ariana Eunjung Cha, Loveday Morris, and Michael Birnbaum, "Experts Not Sure Why COVID-19 Death Rates Have Dropped," Ibid., October 11, A18.

58. Shammas and Thebault, "Fauci Warns of 'Surge Upon a Surge' as Air Travel Hits Highs During Holidays"; Marc Fisher, Shayna Jacobs, and Poe Kelley, "As Toll Nears 250,000, We Remain Entrenched," Ibid., November 19, A1; Jenna Johnson, Amy B. Wang, and Josh Dawsey, "Biden Calls for Shared Sacrifice to Conquer Virus," Ibid., November 26.

59. Erica Werner, Jeff Stein, and Rachael Bade, "McConnell Details Stance on Relief Bill," Ibid., July 7, A13.

60. Phil Dean, "The Unprecedented Federal Fiscal Policy Response to the COVID-19 Pandemic and Its Impact on State Budgets," *Kem C. Garner Policy Institute*, May 2022, https://gardner.utah.edu/wp-content/uploads/Fiscal-Stimulus-May2022.pdf?x71849.

61. Erica Werner et al., "House Moves toward Passing Virus Relief Package," *The Washington Post*, March 14, 2020, A12; Erica Werner, Jeff Stein, and Mike DeBonis, "White House Seeks $1 Trillion Stimulus," Ibid., March 19, A1; Zezima et al., "Restrictions Rise, Along with Number of Cases"; Leon LaBrecque, "The Cares Act Has Passed: Here Are the Highlights," March 29, 2020, 2020; Robert Costa and Philip Rucker, "With Public's Money, Trump Casts Himself as Crisis Patron," *The Washington Post*, April 11, 2020, A1; Mike DeBonis, Erica Werner, and Jeff Stein, "Administration, Congressional Negotiators Close to Deal on Economic Relief," Ibid., March 13, A10; Derek Hawkins and Marisa Iati, "Calif. Is Third State to Exceed 10,000 Deaths," Ibid., August 9, A3; Tony Romm, Erica Werner, and Jeff Stein, "Trump's Orders Deemed 'Paltry'," Ibid., August 10, A1; Eli Rosenberg and Heather Long, "Unemployed Americans Feel Sting of Abandonment," Ibid., August 28; Jeff Stein and Tony Romm, "President Trump's Attempt to Bypass Congress on Stimulus Is Offering Only Limited Economic Relief," Ibid., August 23; Heather Long, "Details of Trump's Executive Actions Paint a Less Generous Picture of Aid," Ibid., August 10, A16; Erica

Werner and Rachael Bade, "In Move That May Revive Talks, Trump Calls for Major Relief Bill," Ibid., September 17, A18.

62. Taressa Fraze et al., "Public Hospitals in the United States, 2008," *Healthcare Cost and Utilization Project*, September, 2020, https://www.hcup-us.ahrq.gov/reports/statbriefs/sb95.pdf.

63. Christopher Rowland and Ariana Eunjung Cha, "Expected Patient Surge Threatens to Flood U.S. Hospitals," *The Washington Post*, March 16, 2020, A10; Christopher Rowland, "More Lifesaving Ventilators Are Available, but Hospitals Can't Afford Them," Ibid., March 19, A8.

64. Jenn Abelson et al., "Boom-and-Bust Pandemic Funding Hurt Preparedness," Ibid., May 3, A1.

65. Sellers Frances Stead, "Experts: Public Health Is Underfunded," Ibid., March 13, A14; C. Janes and William Wan, "Ailing Public Health Units Further Stifled Amid Pandemic," Ibid., September 1, A9.

66. Amy Goldstein, Sun H. Lena, and Beth Reinhard, "States' Needs Overwhelm Unprepared Stockpile," Ibid., March 29, A1.

67. Beth Reinhard and Emma Brown, "Face Masks in National Stockpile Have Not Been Substantially Replenished since 2009," Ibid., March 10; Goldstein, Lena, and Reinhard, "States' Needs Overwhelm Unprepared Stockpile"; Amy Goldstein, "Stockpile of Emergency Medical Supplies Is Moving Back under HHS Control," Ibid., June 19, A10.

68. Jon Swaine, Robert O'Harrow, and Aaron C. Davis, "HHS Official Shifted Stockpile's Focus," Ibid., May 5, A1; HHS, "Strategic National Stockpile (Sns)," *U.S. Department of Health and Human Services*, September 5, 2023, https://chemm.hhs.gov/sns.htm; Goldstein, "Stockpile of Emergency Medical Supplies Is Moving Back under HHS Control"; Goldstein, Lena, and Reinhard, "States' Needs Overwhelm Unprepared Stockpile."

69. Janes and Wan, "Ailing Public Health Units Further Stifled Amid Pandemic."

70. David Nakamura, Yasmeen Abutaleb, and Josh Dawsey, "Pressure Mounts on Trump to Launch Coordinated Response to Epidemic," Ibid., January 31, A19; Ashley Parker, Yasmeen Abutaleb, and Lena H. Sun, "How the Trump Administration Squandered Its Response Time," Ibid., March 8, A1.

71. Yasmeen Abutaleb and Josh Dawsey, "Trump's Praise of Xi Alarms Advisers," Ibid., February 17.

72. Glenn Kessler, "Tracking the President's False or Misleading Claims About Threat from the Virus," Ibid., March 22, A4.

73. Philip Rucker and Anne Gearan, "Trump Announces 30-Day Ban on All Travel from Europe Amid Pandemic," Ibid., March 12, A14; Kessler, "Tracking the President's False or Misleading Claims About Threat from the Virus."

74. Rucker et al., "A Lost Summer: How Trump Fell Short in Confronting the Virus."

75. Robert Costa and Philip Rucker, "I Wanted to Always Play It Down," Ibid., September 10.

76. Ibid.

77. Toluse Olorunnipa, Josh Dawsey, and Yasmeen Abutaleb, "Trump Taps Pence to Lead Emerging Coronavirus Effort," Ibid., February 27.

78. Ashley Parker, Josh Dawsey, and Yasmeen Abutaleb, "For Trump, This Pandemic Is All About the Numbers - and They Aren't Good," Ibid., March 13.

79. Josh Dawsey, Felicia Sonmez, and Paul Kane, "Trump Tries to Limit Damage from Revelations He Minimized Virus Threat," Ibid., September 10, A4.

80. Anne Gearan and Toluse Olorunnipa, "Economic Aid Deal Brokered Amid Expanding Nationwide Tumult Trump Declares a National Emergency," Ibid., March 14, A1.

81. Ibid.

82. Katie Zezima et al., "Who Declares Virus a Global Pandemic," Ibid., March 12.

83. Rucker et al., "A Lost Summer: How Trump Fell Short in Confronting the Virus."

84. Ashley Parker, "White House Looks to Move Trump Away from Spotlight," Ibid., April 28, A7.

85. Kessler, "Tracking the President's False or Misleading Claims About Threat from the Virus."

86. Olorunnipa, Kim, and Wilson, "Trump Voices New U.S. Containment Guidelines."

87. Toluse Olorunnipa, Nick Miroff, and Dan Lamothe, "Trump Invokes Wartime Powers to Bolster U.S. Response," Ibid., March 19, A6; Philip Rucker, "Governors Led as President Minimized Pandemic," Ibid., March 17, A1.

88. Olorunnipa, Miroff, and Lamothe, "Trump Invokes Wartime Powers to Bolster U.S. Response."

89. David Nakamura, "On CDC Tour, Trump Plays Medical Expert by Second-Guessing the Professionals," Ibid., March 8, A5.

90. Ian Duncan and Felicia Sonmez, "Trump Extends Distancing Guidelines," Ibid., March 30, A1.

91. Olorunnipa, Dawsey, and Abutaleb, "Trump Taps Pence to Lead Emerging Coronavirus Effort"; Lenny Bernstein et al., "First Person-to-Person Transmission Confirmed in U.S. Who Labels Virus a Global Emergency," Ibid., January 31; Nakamura, Abutaleb, and Dawsey, "Pressure Mounts on Trump to Launch Coordinated Response to Epidemic."

92. Philip Rucker and Ashley Parker, "Uneven Performance by Trump in 'Wartime President' Role," Ibid., March 21, A5.

93. Philip Bump and Ashley Parker, "Trump Briefings Full of Attacks, Boasts but Little Empathy," Ibid., April 27, A6.

94. Ibid.

95. Rucker et al., "A Lost Summer: How Trump Fell Short in Confronting the Virus"; David A. Fahrenthold, Anne Gearan, and Lee Michelle Ye Hee, "Trump Is Still Shaking Hands, and He Hasn't Been Tested," Ibid., March 14, A8.

96. White House, "Remarks by President Trump, Vice President Pence, and Members of the Coronavirus Task Force in Press Conference," *White House Archives*, March 13, 2020, https://trumpwhitehouse.archives.gov/briefings-statements/remarks-president-trump-vice-president-pence-members-coronavirus-task-force-press-conference-3/.

97. Ibid.

98. White House, "Remarks by President Trump in Meeting with Republican Members of Congress."

99. Anne Gearan, "Trump Skips Mask in Plant Visit, Defying Ford's Request and Michigan Law," *The Washington Post*, May 22, 2020, A7.

100. Toluse Olorunnipa, Yasmeen Abutaleb, and Josh Dawsey, "Trump Shifts Focus from Virus to Jobs and Law and Order," Ibid., June 6, A4; David Nakamura, "Trump Overrides Virus Precautions Set up for His Own Events," Ibid., August 8, A7; Josh Dawsey and Yasmeen Abutaleb, "White House Set for Packed Party Season Despite Virus," Ibid., December 2, A3.

101. Anne Gearan and Josh Dawsey, "President's Latest Indoor Rally Defies State Health Rules," Ibid., September 15, A6.

102. Zezima et al., "Restrictions Rise, Along with Number of Cases."

103. David Nakamura, "Amid Pandemic, Trump Is Making Promises He Can't Keep," Ibid., A4.

104. Christopher Rowland, "Hospitals, Doctors Wiping out Supplies of Unproven Coronavirus Treatment," Ibid., March 21, A5; Christopher Rowland, Jon Swaine, and Josh Dawsey, "Spurred by Trump, Unproven Drug Regimen Is Fast-Tracked," Ibid., March 27, A1; Karen DeYoung, "U.S. Passes 50,000 Deaths, More Than Quarter of Global Toll," Ibid., April 25, A6.

105. Christopher Rowland, Debbie Cenziper, and Lisa Rein, "White House Efforts to Sidestep FDA Revealed," Ibid., November 2, A19.

106. Toluse Olorunnipa, Ariana Eunjung Cha, and Laurie McGinley, "Drug Promoted by Trump as 'Game Changer' Increasingly Linked to Deaths," Ibid., May 16, A7; Laurie McGinley and Carolyn Y. Johnson, "FDA Pulls Emergency Approval for Antimalarial Drugs Promoted by Trump," Ibid., June 16.

107. Anne Gearan et al., "Trump Says He's Taking Unproven Medication," Ibid., May 19, A1; Carol Morello, "New Cases Rise in Midwest as They Plateau in Sun Belt," Ibid., July 29, A9; Rachel Lerman, Katie Shepherd, and Taylor Telford, "Twitter Penalizes Trump Jr., Citing Misinformation on Coronavirus," Ibid., A18.

108. Philip Rucker et al., "Outcry, Warnings over Trump's New Cure Idea," Ibid., April 25, A1.

109. White House, "Remarks by President Trump, Vice President Pence, and Members of the Coronavirus Task Force in Press Conference."

110. Bump and Parker, "Trump Briefings Full of Attacks, Boasts but Little Empathy."

111. Ibid.

112. White House, "Remarks by President Trump, Vice President Pence, and Members of the Coronavirus Task Force in Press Conference."

113. White House, "Remarks by President Trump, Vice President Pence, and Members of the Coronavirus Task Force in Press Briefing."

114. David Nakamura, Josh Dawsey, and David A. Fahrenthold, "After Downplaying Risks, Trump Pivots to Precautions," *The Washington Post*, March 15, 2020, A11.

115. White House, "Remarks by President Trump, Vice President Pence, and Members of the Coronavirus Task Force in Press Briefing."

116. Gearan and Sonmez, "As U.S. Cases Top 1 Million, Testing Rate Is Below Average."

117. White House, "Remarks by President Trump at Signing of a Proclamation in Honor of National Nurses Day," *White House Archives*, May 6, 2020, https://trumpwhitehouse.archives.gov/briefings-statements/remarks-president-trump-signing-proclamation-honor-national-nurses-day/.

118. Carol Morello, "Health Experts Issue Urgent Call for Change of Course as U.S. Economy Tanks," *The Washington Post*, July 31, 2020, A6.

119. White House, "Remarks by President Trump in Roundtable Discussion on Supporting Native Americans | Phoenix, Az," *White House Archives*, May 5, 2020, https://trumpwhitehouse.archives.gov/briefings-statements/remarks-president-trump-roundtable-discussion-supporting-native-americans-phoenix-az/.

120. David Nakamura, "Competing Events Highlight Trump's, Biden's Different Approaches to Pandemic," *The Washington Post*, December 9, 2020, A22; Christopher Rowland, "Vaccine Politics, Skewed by Trump's Polarizing Approach, Will Complicate Biden's Path to a Unified Pandemic Response," Ibid., December 13, A7.

121. White House, "Remarks by President Trump at the Operation Warp Speed Vaccine Summit," *White House Archives*, December 8, 2020, https://trumpwhitehouse.archives.gov/briefings-statements/remarks-president-trump-operation-warp-speed-vaccine-summit/.

122. Lenny Bernstein et al., "CDC Offers Scant Guidelines for Reopening Safely," *The Washington Post*, May 15, 2020, A1; Laurie McGinley and Yasmeen Abutaleb, "White House Effort to Undermine Fauci Criticized," Ibid., July 14, A5; Yasmeen Abutaleb, Josh Dawsey, and Laurie McGinley, "White House Sidelines an Increasingly Candid Fauci," Ibid., July 12, A1.

123. David William, "How CDC Stumbled in Race for a Virus Test," Ibid., December 28.

124. Ibid.

125. Ashley Parker et al., "Scientists at Trump's Side Have to Toe a Difficult Line," Ibid., April 23.

126. Lenny Bernstein, Josh Dawsey, and Yasmeen Abutaleb, "Friction between White House, CDC Hobbles Response," Ibid., May 16, A5.

127. Felicia Sonmez and Darryl Fears, "Trump Aide Raises Tensions with CDC," Ibid., May 18, A1.

128. Brown, Reinhard, and Thebault, "States Vary in Deciding Which Deaths Count toward Virus Toll."

129. Olorunnipa, "Trump Messaging Sows Confusion in Outbreak Response."

130. Bernstein, Dawsey, and Abutaleb, "Friction between White House, CDC Hobbles Response."

131. Lena H. Sun and Amy Goldstein, "Disappearance of Virus Data from CDC Website Spurs Outcry," Ibid., July 17, A11.

132. Bernstein, Dawsey, and Abutaleb, "Friction between White House, CDC Hobbles Response."

133. Ibid.; Lena H. Sun, "Administration Officials Seek Greater Control over CDC Coronavirus Reports," Ibid., September 13, A16; Lena H. Sun and Josh Dawsey, "Church Choir Warning Removed from CDC Reopening Guidance," Ibid., May 29, A2.

134. "CDC Walks a Tightrope as Pandemic Meets Politics," *The Washington Post*, July 10, 2020, A6; Derek Hawkins and Marisa Iati, "CDC Warns of Risks to Children as Some Schools Attempt to Resume Classes," Ibid., August 17.

135. Sun, "Administration Officials Seek Greater Control over CDC Coronavirus Reports."

136. Amy Goldstein and Sean Sullivan, "CDC Chief: Most Won't Get Vaccine Till Mid-'21," Ibid., September 17, A1.

137. Sun and Dawsey, "CDC Walks a Tightrope as Pandemic Meets Politics"; Hawkins and Iati, "CDC Warns of Risks to Children as Some Schools Attempt to Resume Classes."

138. Yasmeen Abutaleb and Josh Dawsey, "HHS Official Apologizes for Accusing Scientists of 'Sedition'," Ibid., September 16, A11.

139. Michelle Y. H. Lee, "CDC Voting Safety Guidelines Endorse Mail, Early Balloting," Ibid., July 8, A9.

140. Lena H. Sun, "CDC Reverses Itself after New Advice on Testing Draws Sharp Criticism," Ibid., September 19, A7; Toluse Olorunnipa, "To Trump, Economy Determines Discourse," Ibid., May 8, A1; Bernstein et al., "CDC Offers Scant Guidelines for Reopening Safely"; Isaac Stanley-Becker, William Wan, and Ben Guarino, "States Reopening Lack Benchmarks for Reimposing Rules," Ibid., May 16, A7; Laura Meckler and Rachel Weiner, "Delayed CDC Guidelines Offer Low-Key Guide to Reopening," Ibid., May 20, A8.

141. Sun and Dawsey, "CDC Walks a Tightrope as Pandemic Meets Politics."

142. Lena H. Sun and Joel Achenbach, "Political Jabs, Errors Erode Trust in CDC at Key Time," Ibid., September 29, A1.

143. Ibid.

144. Bernstein et al., "CDC Offers Scant Guidelines for Reopening Safely."

145. Ashley Parker, Yasmeen Abutaleb, and Josh Dawsey, "Lots of Players, but No Consensus on a Game Plan," Ibid., April 12.

146. Matt Zapotosky and John Wagner, "Trump Reverses, Says Task Force to Convene 'Indefinitely'," Ibid., May 7, A6.

147. Olorunnipa, Abutaleb, and Dawsey, "Trump Shifts Focus from Virus to Jobs and Law and Order."

148. Toluse Olorunnipa and Josh Dawsey, "Bad Numbers Push Trump to Bring Back Virus Briefing," Ibid., July 21, A1; Ashley Parker et al., "Amid Election Fight, Trump Tunes out Spike in Cases," Ibid., November 15.

149. Yasmeen Abutaleb et al., "Distrust, Lethargy Worsening within Virus Task Force," Ibid., October 20.

150. Yasmeen Abutaleb et al., "How Trump's Pandemic Missteps Led to a Dark Winter," Ibid., December 20.

151. Abutaleb et al., "Distrust, Lethargy Worsening within Virus Task Force."

152. Abutaleb et al., "How Trump's Pandemic Missteps Led to a Dark Winter."

153. Abutaleb, Dawsey, and McGinley, "White House Sidelines an Increasingly Candid Fauci"; McGinley and Abutaleb, "White House Effort to Undermine Fauci Criticized."

154. Mike DeBonis, Erica Werner, and Seung Min Kim, "Testing Lag Ignites Political Uproar as Trump Insists Process Is 'Very Smooth'," Ibid., March 13, A13.

155. Abutaleb, Dawsey, and McGinley, "White House Sidelines an Increasingly Candid Fauci."

156. David Nakamura, Josh Dawsey, and Yasmeen Abutaleb, "As Infections Rise, Trump Again Attacks Fauci's Guidance," Ibid., October 14, A6.

157. Michael Scherer and Josh Dawsey, "Trump: People Tired of 'Fauci and All These Idiots'," Ibid., October 20, A1.

158. Matt Viser and Sean Sullivan, "Virus Again Front and Center in Campaigns," Ibid., October 7.

159. Bernstein et al., "CDC Offers Scant Guidelines for Reopening Safely"; McGinley and Abutaleb, "White House Effort to Undermine Fauci Criticized."

160. Morello, "Health Experts Issue Urgent Call for Change of Course as U.S. Economy Tanks"; Laurie McGinley et al., "Government Scientists Pushing Back against President," Ibid., November 2, A4.

161. "Government Scientists Pushing Back against President."

162. Philip Rucker, Yasmeen Abutaleb, and Ashley Parker, "Messaging Undermines U.S. Efforts on Virus," Ibid., March 4, A1.

163. Anne Gearan, Felicia Sonmez, and Erica Werner, "Administration Describes Dash for a Vaccine Usable by January," Ibid., May 1, A4.

164. Carolyn Y. Johnson et al., "Trump's Vaccine Timeline Doubted," Ibid., May 16, A1; Gearan, Sonmez, and Werner, "Administration Describes Dash for a Vaccine Usable by January."

165. Isaac Stanley-Becker, "Promises of Fast Vaccine Risk Warping Views Further," Ibid., May 21, A1.

166. Laurie McGinley, Yasmeen Abutaleb, and Lena H. Sun, "Health Officials Ramp up Effort to Convince Public That Vaccine Decisions Will Be Based on Science, Not Politics," Ibid., August 9, A6; Laurie McGinley, Carolyn Y. Johnson, and Josh Dawsey, "Trump Accuses 'Deep State' at FDA of Delaying Virus Vaccines, Treatments," Ibid., August 23, A8.

167. Amy Goldstein and Laurie McGinley, "Trump Calls FDA's Plan for Tougher Vaccine Standards a 'Political Move'," Ibid., September 24, A4; Laurie McGinley, Yasmeen Abutaleb, and Josh Dawsey, "White House Challenges FDA Vaccine Standards," Ibid., September 26, A1; Laurie McGinley and Carolyn Y. Johnson, "FDA Set to Back Higher Standard for Vaccine," Ibid., September 23; Goldstein and McGinley, "Trump Calls FDA's Plan for Tougher Vaccine Standards a 'Political Move'."

168. Yasmeen Abutaleb, Laurie McGinley, and Carolyn Y. Johnson, "Disparaged by Trump, Scientists Deliver," Ibid., December 15, A1.

169. Katie Zezima et al., "Pandemic Takes a Dramatic Toll as Institutions, Routines Shut Down," Ibid., March 14.

170. Ben Guarino et al., "Schools Close, National Guard Deployed to Help New York Suburb Stem Spread of Coronavirus," Ibid., March 11.

171. Zezima et al., "Pandemic Takes a Dramatic Toll as Institutions, Routines Shut Down"; Joel Achenbach et al., "Pandemic Exposes America's Flaws and Fissures," Ibid., July 20.

172. Frances Stead-Sellers and Abigail Hauslohner, "Growing Shortages of Health-Care Workers Strain Hospitals," Ibid., July 27, A10.

173. Siobhán O'Grady et al., "'They've Been through a Lot': More Americans Flee Wuhan," Ibid., February 6, A1; Lena H. Sun et al., "A Scramble to Execute U.S. Order on Travel," Ibid., February 4.

174. White House, "Remarks by President Trump and Vice President Pence in a Video Teleconference with Governors on COVID-19," *White House Archives*, March 19, 2020, https://trump-whitehouse.archives.gov/briefings-statements/remarks-president-trump-vice-president-pence-video-teleconference-governors-COVID-19/.

175. Dungca Nicole, Jenn Abelson, and John Sullivan, "'They Didn't Move Fast Enough'," *The Washington Post*, March 30, 2020, A1.

176. Nick Miroff et al., "States, Cities Close Businesses, Take Strict Measures as Cases Rise," Ibid., March 16.

177. Nicole, Abelson, and Sullivan, "They Didn't Move Fast Enough."

178. Rucker, "Governors Led as President Minimized Pandemic."

179. White House, "Remarks by President Trump, Vice President Pence, and Members of the Coronavirus Task Force in Press Briefing."

180. Robert Costa and Aaron Gregg, "Trump's Lagging Response Widens Rift with City and State Leaders," *The Washington Post*, March 23, 2020, 2020, A1.

181. Jose Del Real, Julie Zauzmer, and Ava Wallace, "Seeking Answers, without Clear Guidance from Officials," Ibid., March 16, A11.

182. Rucker, "Governors Led as President Minimized Pandemic."

183. Seung M. Kim and Toluse Olorunnipa, "Some GOP Senators Want Greater Federal Role in Testing," Ibid., April 22, A6.

184. Philip Rucker, "Trump Takes Spotlight but Leaves Key Calls Largely to States, Cities," Ibid., March 25, A11.

185. Griff Witte et al., "Across the Nation, Disparity in Containment Policy Is Vast," Ibid., March 18, A12.

186. Carol Morello, "Hearing Underscores U.S. Failure to Halt Virus," Ibid., August 1, A9.

187. Griff Witte, "A New Hot Spot, but No Statewide Stay-Home Call," Ibid., April 14, A1.

188. Ibid.

189. Costa and Gregg, "Trump's Lagging Response Widens Rift with City and State Leaders."

190. White House, "Remarks by President Trump, Vice President Pence, and Members of the Coronavirus Task Force in Press Briefing."

191. Olorunnipa, Kim, and Wilson, "Trump Voices New U.S. Containment Guidelines."

192. Nick Miroff, "In Survey, U.S. Mayors Cite Need for Supplies," Ibid., March 28, A3.

193. Ibid.

194. Costa and Gregg, "Trump's Lagging Response Widens Rift with City and State Leaders."

195. Robert Costa et al., "Governors Frustrated with Offer of 'Backup'," Ibid., March 27.

196. Paul Sonne and Missy Ryan, "As Beds Go Unfilled, States Scale Back Army Corps Makeshift Hospitals," Ibid., April 25.

197. Dan Lamothe, "Pentagon Combats Conspiracy Theories as National Guard Assists in Response," Ibid., March 24, A4; Matt Zapotosky, John Wagner, and Amanda Coletta, "Trump Announces CDC Guidance That All Americans Wear Cloth Masks," Ibid., April 4, A3.

198. Federal, "On the Frontlines of COVID Response This Agency Makes Safety Paramount," *The Federal Times*, July 17, 2020, https://www.federaltimes.com/management/2020/07/17/on-the-front-lines-of-COVID-response-this-agency-makes-safety-paramount/.

199. Amy Goldstein, "Federal Officials Organize Large-Scale Testing in 3 Cities in Hard-Hit Sun Belt," *The Washington Post*, July 8, 2020, A9.

200. White House, "Remarks by President Trump at Naval Station Norfolk Send-Off for U.S.Ns Comfort | Norfolk, Va," *White House Archives*, March 28, 2020, https://trumpwhitehouse.archives.gov/briefings-statements/remarks-president-trump-naval-station-norfolk-send-off-usns-comfort-norfolk-va/.

201. Jada Yuan and Ben Guarino, "The Military's Medical 'Relief Valves' Remain Mostly Empty in New York," *The Washington Post*, April 12, 2020, 2020, A7.

202. Amy Brittain, Isaac Stanley-Becker, and Nick Miroff, "Oft-Praised 'Airbridge' Flights Miss Their Mark," Ibid., May 10, A1.

203. White House, "Remarks by President Trump, Vice President Pence, and Members of the Coronavirus Task Force in Press Briefing."

204. Brittain, Stanley-Becker, and Miroff, "Oft-Praised 'Airbridge' Flights Miss Their Mark"; Amy Brittain and Isaac Stanley-Becker, "Senators Seek Project Airbridge Probe," Ibid., June 10, A2.

205. Olorunnipa, Dawsey, and Abutaleb, "Major Surge in Infections Exposes U.S. Failures."

206. Shayna Jacobs et al., "Trump Approves Aid to N.Y. As State Braces for Shutdown," Ibid., March 23, A12.

207. Jeanne Whalen et al., "States and Hospitals Compete for Scarce Medical Supplies," Ibid., March 25, A18.

208. Matt Zapotosky, "Barr Warns against Hoarding Masks, Drugs That Trump Touted," Ibid., March 26, A6; Zapotosky, Stanley-Becker, and Wagner, "Single-Day Death Toll in U.S. Tops 1,000 as Trump Insists Country Will Recover."

209. Laurie McGinley, "FDA Suspends Most Inspections of Foreign Manufacturers," Ibid., March 11, A19; Matt Zapotosky, "Justice Department Seeks New Emergency Judicial Powers," Ibid., March 24, A12.

210. Lena H. Sun, William Wan, and Yasmeen Abutaleb, "Plans to Contain Virus Emerge in Bottom-up Effort," Ibid., April 11, A1.

211. Colby Itkowitz and Marissa J. Lang, "Death Toll Surges Past 2,000 in U.S," Ibid., March 29; Luz Lazo and Katherine Shaver, "Checkpoints Targeting out-of-State Drivers Draw Scrutiny," Ibid., April 15, A8; Joel Achenbach, Rachel Weiner, and C. Janes, "Experts Push for New Tack on Virus," Ibid., August 2, A1.

212. Itkowitz and Lang, "Death Toll Surges Past 2,000 in U.S."

213. Lazo and Shaver, "Checkpoints Targeting out-of-State Drivers Draw Scrutiny."

214. White House, "Remarks by President Trump, Vice President Pence, and Members of the Coronavirus Task Force in Press Briefing"; Tim Craig and Brady Dennis, "States Explore Plans to Reopen," *The Washington Post*, April 14, 2020, A1.

215. "States Explore Plans to Reopen."

216. White House, "Remarks by President Trump in Press Briefing," *White House Archives*, April 14, 2020, https://trumpwhitehouse.archives.gov/briefings-statements/remarks-president-trump-press-briefing/.

217. Ibid.

218. Anne Gearan, "With Shifting Advice, Trump Sows Confusion on Opening," *The Washington Post*, April 24, 2020, A7.

219. Karin Brulliard and Rachel Weiner, "Fragmented Virus Rules Stir Tensions," Ibid., July 28, A1; C. Janes, Isaac Stanley-Becker, and Rachel Weiner, "In States across the U.S., Cases Still on Rise," Ibid., June 11.

220. Griff Witte, "States Are Reopening. Cities Aren't," Ibid., May 2.

221. Brulliard and Weiner, "Fragmented Virus Rules Stir Tensions."

222. Todd C. Frankel, "States' Different Definitions of a Fever Highlight Lack of a National Strategy," Ibid., May 16, A5; Lori Aratani, "With Few Hygiene Rules in Place, Airlines, Airports Adopt Their Own," Ibid., June 28, A21; Chris Mooney, Sarah Kaplan, and Juliet Eilperin, "States, Not Science, Get to Define 'Outbreak,' Hampering Efforts to Curb Virus," Ibid., October 8, A12.

223. Stanley-Becker, Olorunnipa, and Kim, "Trump Fomenting Defiance of Strictures."

224. Matt Zapotosky, "Justice Dept. Seems to Side with Church in Lawsuit over Drive-in Services," *The Washington Post*, April 15, 2020, A4.

225. White House, "Remarks by President Trump on Protecting Seniors with Diabetes," *White House Archives*, May 26, 2020, https://trumpwhitehouse.archives.gov/briefings-statements/remarks-president-trump-protecting-seniors-diabetes/.

226. Janes, Stanley-Becker, and Weiner, "In States across the U.S., Cases Still on Rise."

227. Anne Gearan and Jacqueline Dupree, "Trump Hails Arizona - as It Grapples with a Huge Spike," Ibid., August 6, A6.

228. Rachel Weiner and Rosalind S. Helderman, "States Are 'on Their Own' as They Try to Expand Testing," Ibid., June 12, A9.

229. Ibid.

230. Paul Kane, "Businesses Seek Nationwide Rules to Face Pandemic," Ibid., July 5, A2.

231. Arelis R. Hernández, Stead S. Frances, and Ben Guarino, "Texas, Florida Walk Back Reopenings," Ibid., June 27, A1; Joel Achenbach et al., "As Hot Spots Erupt, Researchers Warn of 2nd Wave in South," Ibid., May 21; Anne Gearan, Derek Hawkins, and Siobhán O'Grady, "States' Early Reopenings Fueled 50% Rise in Cases in June," Ibid., July 2, A6; Gearan, Shammas, and Beachum, "White House Says Virus Is under Control Despite Surges."

232. Anne Gearan, Scott Wilson, and Annie Gowen, "As Limits Return, Fauci Raises Alarm," Ibid., July 1, A1; Robert Barnes and Derek Hawkins, "Rush to Reopen Caused Case Spikes, Officials Say," Ibid., July 6, A2.

233. Isaac Stanley-Becker and C. Janes, "Pockets of U.S. Still Resisting Urgent Mantra to Stay at Home," Ibid., April 3, A1; Witte et al., "Across the Nation, Disparity in Containment Policy Is Vast."

234. Griff Witte, "Growing Chorus Pushes for Renewed Shutdown Orders," Ibid., July 10, A1.

235. Isaac Stanley-Becker and Rachel Weiner, "In Deciding to Reopen, Some Governors Reject Counsel of Their Medical Experts," Ibid., April 24, A7.

236. Rachel Weiner, "Republican Governors Begin to Soften on Mask Mandates," Ibid., July 11, A5; Abigail Hauslohner and Haisten Willis, "Georgia Bars Municipalities from Mandating Masks as More States Now Require Them," *The Washington Post* (Online), July 16, 2020.

237. "Georgia Bars Municipalities from Mandating Masks as More States Now Require Them."

238. Achenbach, Weiner, and Janes, "Experts Push for New Tack on Virus."

239. Hannah Knowles, "States Enacting New Virus Measures," Ibid., November 15, A3.

240. Jacqueline Alemany, "Leading Health Experts Call for Greater Precautions," Ibid., November 20; Robert Barnes, "Supreme Court Sides with California Church Protesting Virus Restrictions," Ibid., December 4, A11.

241. Moriah Balingit, "Even Where Trump Is Popular, Some School Leaders Reject Push to Reopen Classrooms," Ibid., July 26, A4.

242. Valerie Strauss, "Fla. Judge Blocks School Reopening Order; State Appeals Case," Ibid., August 25, A3.

243. Michael Scherer and Josh Dawsey, "Trump Claims Coronavirus Is 'Ending' as Infections Spike," Ibid., October 27, A6.

244. Shawn Boburg, "Trump Flouted Safety Pact for Minn. Rally, Records Show," Ibid., October 26, A1.

245. Ibid.

246. Knowles, "States Enacting New Virus Measures."

247. Todd C. Frankel, "Ind. County Health Leaders: Politics Hinders COVID-19 Fight," Ibid., October 30, A18.

248. Ibid.

249. Christopher Rowland et al., "Major Firms Lobbying for Workers' Spot on Vaccine List," Ibid., December 21, A1.

250. Jenna Johnson, Amy B. Wang, and C. Janes, "Biden Assails Trump's Efforts to Fight Pandemic," Ibid., December 30.

251. Lena H. Sun, "States Say They Lack Funds to Dispense a Virus Vaccine," Ibid., October 30, A3.

252. Isaac Stanley-Becker, "Vaccination Totals Lag Amid Snags, Confusion," Ibid., December 31, A1; Christopher Rowland et al., "Vaccine Rollout Smaller Than Pledged," Ibid., December 6.

253. Stanley-Becker, "Vaccination Totals Lag Amid Snags, Confusion."

254. White House, "Remarks by President Trump, Vice President Pence, and Members of the Coronavirus Task Force in Press Briefing."

255. Toluse Olorunnipa and Anne Gearan, "Facing a Global Crisis, Trump Doubles Down on His Go-It-Alone Approach," *The Washington Post*, March 13, 2020, A19.

256. White House, "Remarks by President Trump, Vice President Pence, and Members of the Coronavirus Task Force in Press Conference."

257. Heather Long et al., "Staffing, Antiquated Technology Slow the Delivery of Virus Relief," *The Washington Post*, April 18, 2020, A1.

258. White House, "Remarks by President Trump in Press Briefing | September 16, 2020," *White House Archives*, September 16, 2020, https://trumpwhitehouse.archives.gov/briefings-statements/remarks-president-trump-press-briefing-september-16-2020/; Morello, "Health Experts Issue Urgent Call for Change of Course as U.S. Economy Tanks."

259. Nakamura, "Amid Pandemic, Trump Is Making Promises He Can't Keep."

260. Costa and Gregg, "Trump's Lagging Response Widens Rift with City and State Leaders."

261. Philip Rucker and Robert Costa, "Trump's Crisis Response Short on Consistency, Long on Blame," Ibid., April 3.

262. White House, "Remarks by President Trump, Vice President Pence, and Members of the Coronavirus Task Force in Press Briefing."
263. White House, "Remarks by President Trump, Vice President Pence, and Members of the Coronavirus Task Force in a Fox News Virtual Town Hall."
264. White House, "Remarks by President Trump, Vice President Pence, and Members of the Coronavirus Task Force in Press Briefing."
265. White House, "Remarks by President Trump, Vice President Pence, and Members of the Coronavirus Task Force in a Fox News Virtual Town Hall."
266. Ashley Parker and Philip Rucker, "Trump Seems Poised to Let Others Lead on Reopening," *The Washington Post*, May 18, 2020, A1.
267. Anne Gearan, Seung Min Kim, and Erica Werner, "Trump: Rivals Hype Crisis for Political Gain," Ibid., February 29.
268. Paul Farhi, "Western Journalists Are Pushed out of China," Ibid., September 17, C1.
269. Ibid.
270. Robert Costa, "Some in Gop Remain Skeptical of Illness's Reach and Official Reaction," Ibid., March 18, A18.
271. Ibid.
272. White House, "Remarks by President Trump, Vice President Pence, and Members of the Coronavirus Task Force in Press Briefing."
273. White House, "Remarks by President Trump in Press Briefing."
274. Mike DeBonis, "'Open It up' Bloc in Gop Attacks Restrictions as Others in Party Urge Caution," *The Washington Post*, April 18, 2020, A4.
275. Ibid.
276. Ibid.
277. Griff Witte et al., "Warily, U.S. Cracks Doors Open," Ibid., April 26, A1.
278. Stanley-Becker and Weiner, "In Deciding to Reopen, Some Governors Reject Counsel of Their Medical Experts."
279. Tony Romm, "Return to Work or Risk Jobless Aid, States Warn," Ibid., May 5.
280. Toluse Olorunnipa, Griff Witte, and Lenny Bernstein, "Trump Applauds States Reopening Ahead of Guidance," Ibid., A1.
281. White House, "Remarks by President Trump in a Press Briefing on COVID-19 Testing."
282. Alex M. II Azar, "We Have to Reopen - for Health Reasons," *The Washington Post*, May 22, 2020, A21.
283. Michael Scherer and Ashley Parker, "As Trump Pushes Reopening, Democrats Embrace Caution," Ibid., May 23, A6.
284. Ibid.
285. Craig Timberg, Elizabeth Dwoskin, and Moriah Balingit, "Protests Spread, Fueled by Economic Woes and Internet Subcultures," Ibid., May 3, A1.
286. Anne Gearan and John Wagner, "Trump Calls Michigan Protesters 'Very Good People'," Ibid., A4.
287. Griff Witte, Meryl Kornfield, and Hannah Denham, "Calif. Pulls 'Emergency Brake' as States Race against Virus," Ibid., November 7; Matt Zapotosky, Barrett Devlin, and Abagail Hauslohner, "13 Charged in Plot to Seize Mich. Governor," Ibid., October 9, A1.
288. Marc Fisher, Clarence Williams, and Lori Rozsa, "Across Nation, Masks Are the Latest Political, Cultural Divide," Ibid., April 20.
289. Griff Witte, Ariana Eunjung Cha, and Josh Dawsey, "In Resisting Masks, U.S. Lost Early Virus Weapon," Ibid., July 29.
290. Philip Rucker and Seung M. Kim, "Gop Leaders Break with Trump on Masks as Cases Climb," Ibid., July 1, A7.
291. Ibid.
292. Ibid.
293. Toluse Olorunnipa, "In About-Face, Trump Dons Mask at Walter Reed," Ibid., July 13, A2.

294. Brady Dennis, Jacqueline Dupree, and Marisa Iati, "Surge Shows No Sign of Easing," Ibid., November 11, A1.

295. Ibid.

296. Alemany, "Leading Health Experts Call for Greater Precautions."

297. Shammas et al., "Mounting Cases Push Hospitals to Brink."

298. Johnson, Wang, and Dawsey, "Biden Calls for Shared Sacrifice to Conquer Virus"; Abutaleb et al., "How Trump's Pandemic Missteps Led to a Dark Winter."

299. "How Trump's Pandemic Missteps Led to a Dark Winter."

300. Ibid.

301. Matt Zapotosky et al., "Poll: Americans Deeply Wary of Opening Economy," Ibid., May 6; Scott Clement and Dan Balz, "Poll: Many Governors Praised; Some Republicans Panned over Reopening," Ibid., May 13, A10; Gearan, Sonmez, and Werner, "Administration Describes Dash for a Vaccine Usable by January"; Scott Clement and Dan Balz, "Poll: Most Still Favor Curbing Outbreak over Reopening," Ibid., June 2, A3.

302. William Wan and Philip Bump, "Decrees Influenced Choices to Stay Home, Study Suggests," Ibid., April 14, A11.

303. Stanley-Becker and Janes, "Pockets of U.S. Still Resisting Urgent Mantra to Stay at Home."

304. Felicia Sonmez, Paige W. Cunningham, and Meryl Kornfield, "Mixed Signals on Virus Orders," Ibid., April 27.

Chapter 7

Beyond the Cases

Populism, COVID, and the Broader World

Over the past few decades, the rising tide of populism around the globe has been the source of great consternation for believers in the democratic ideal. The reason is clear: populism and demagoguery appear to go hand in hand. And as Aristophanes, an ancient Greek playwright, said in the fifth century BC, "A demagogue must be neither an educated nor a honest man; he has to be an ignoramus and a rogue."[1] This is certainly not the recipe for sound policy.

The failed U.S. response to COVID seems to validate this sentiment. The top political leader of the United States made it a practice of denying basic science and the expert views of his own administration. Instead, he chose the path of political expediency, wishing away an untimely disaster that bore down on his country in an election year. If democrats' short time horizons leave them tethered to public opinion regardless of the season, President Trump's re-election goals had him on a particularly tight leash as he reckoned with the evolving pandemic. It is difficult to say whether Trump would have acted differently if the pandemic had struck earlier in his presidency, but his focus on short-term policy gains throughout his administration suggests the answer is no. That Trump ultimately paused for a few weeks from his populist denialism in order to encourage action is testament to the durability of democratic institutions under unfavorable leadership conditions. But his refusal to commit himself to tough measures in the longer term, and his swift abandonment of science when COVID demonstrated its staying power, highlights the deadly risks of populism.

Yet the other two cases in this book provide a deeper and more complex picture of populism's potential. China's authoritarian regime prior to populism had a history of denying threats or only haphazardly dealing with them.[2] But since the rise of populists to the top of China's Communist Party, we

195

have seen a transformation in responsiveness. This began under President Hu Jintao, whose regime eventually took the 2003 SARS outbreak, as well as other disasters such as the 2008 Sichuan earthquake, seriously.[3] Under populism, we have begun to see a fairly predictable Chinese disaster template: denial, acknowledgment, response, and cleanup (often interspersed with a dose of scapegoating for those alleged to be responsible). With the rise of an even more populist president Xi, China's COVID policy reflected a more extreme version of this pattern. China's authoritarian nature continues to leave it a laggard in the early phases of disaster. But the injection of populism has led to a real desire to secure policy success once the disaster can no longer be covered up.

Perhaps the most interesting case in this collection is Russia, where we could so clearly see the populist semi-authoritarian leader painstakingly balance the authoritarian need to appear resolute with the democratic desire to tread cautiously. Like Trump, President Putin downplayed but did not hide the rising threat and then explicitly left it to lower-level leaders to ostensibly run the disaster response as they saw fit. But like Xi, Putin made it very clear that he was ultimately in charge and would assist, but also punish, those perceived to be failing in their ability to deal with the disaster at hand.

From a bird's-eye view, we can see that these cases had predictable results. Even after accounting for various calculation errors and tricks, the populist country with the highest morbidity and mortality rates was the United States; the one with the lowest was China. And Russia, with a much poorer infrastructure than the United States, ranked in between, though leaning much closer to the dismal U.S. record.

These detailed case studies, however, highlight how the numbers tell only a small part of the story. A closer examination allows us to see the mechanisms that contribute to populism's powerful impact for both good and ill. Populism is more than demagoguery. It is a force that can transform the basic functioning of regimes. And the ways in which it does so are predictable.

First, populism does have a penchant for breaking the bonds between policymakers and the expert advisors they typically rely on to make informed choices. But only, as we have seen through these cases, when the preferences of populist leaders and experts are out of sync. That is most likely in democracies, where populist politicians bent on simple, quick, and pain-free policies encounter resistance from strong, independent institutions. It is less likely in states whose institutions already work at the behest of the leader in charge and where the leaders have a greater degree of political security and, hence, patience—conditions more likely in a highly authoritarian regime.

As the U.S. leader ridiculed and dismissed experts, the Chinese and Russian ones followed their recommendations, publicly lauding them as sound policy. To populists, expert advice is the proverbial bitter pill; it may make you gag going down, but it will eventually make you stronger. In the United States, Trump resisted taking the pill, then coughed it up soon after trying to swallow it. He then turned against the medicine, saying that everyone would get better without it. In China, by contrast, Xi not only took that bitter pill, but he also framed it as the only wise choice for long-term health and forced everyone to take it despite the pain it caused. Finally, in Russia, Putin accepted the medicine but dispatched others to administer it until he reasoned his populace had had enough. He then turned to other, less noxious supposed remedies—in this case, touting alternative experts who encouraged a cautious return to everyday life.

Second, populist leaders in each of these countries calibrated their leadership based on the institutional constraints and opportunities surrounding them. In all three cases, we saw an uncharacteristic silence from the three populist presidents during COVID's initial spread. After this, the leaders began to separate along two dimensions: leadership style and delegation of responsibility. President Trump, facing the greatest political threats from an established opposition party, independent media, and civil society organizations, felt compelled to be the face of disaster response at its spring peak. This was reflected in the prominent role he took during daily press briefings, where he spent hours pontificating on the pandemic at the expense of his experts, whom he frequently contradicted. But as Trump ran the PR side of this national disaster, he shifted almost all response duties to state and local leaders, clearing himself of accountability for the human costs of failure. This was a quintessential case of devolutionary delegation.

In China, Xi took the opposite approach. Instead of playing to the cameras, Xi took to governing from a high tower. While Xi largely limited his public appearances to periodic celebrations of improving conditions, the state media assured the Chinese public that Xi was in charge, issuing orders and constantly assessing the situation from above. With no opposition parties or significant threats from the media and civil society, Xi could afford to stand further away from the painful disaster response while still demonstrating his leadership. It was a top-down delegation of power, where Xi's immediate subordinates were dispatched to implement a harsh, but lifesaving, response on the ground.

In Russia, Putin had to reckon with a polity where he dominated but did not all-out control the political stage. This meant the risk of opposition in the streets and even, though a long shot, in state institutions. As a result, Putin struck a middle ground. Most of the daily COVID management was performed by subordinates in the government; the brunt of the response was delegated to regional leaders. Unlike in China, democratic elements ensured Putin kept a higher public profile, but unlike in the United States, he sought to project a greater degree of power. What this meant in practice was a hybrid form of delegation: three parts devolutionary, as Putin pushed most lower-level officials to make their own tough decisions, to one part top-down, as Putin regularly appeared on television in a show of power to hear out, commend, and lecture regional governors over their response.

Third, in all three of these cases, the populists in charge relied heavily on scapegoating to bolster their own legitimacy. For Trump, this followed from his devolutionary delegation, which allowed him to pin policy shortcomings (initially measured in morbidity and mortality rates and later in reopening rates) directly on state and local leaders. Lacking the ability to remove these officials, Trump instead attacked their leadership in the hope of seeing them pressured, or eventually removed, from below. Trump may have even had the perverse incentive of seeing political enemies fail in their response, though apart from his blistering rebukes, I saw no sign that this affected material support from the federal government, which, in any case, was relatively paltry. This may be because Trump rapidly turned to defining failure not in terms of containing COVID and limiting sickness and death, but in terms of the speed of economic reopening.

For Xi, a top-down delegation meant large-scale national intervention, but it also created space for scapegoating lower-level officials. While I could not find a rolling tally of concrete numbers, the regular reporting in the state press of punishments and dismissals for those accused of failing in their anti-pandemic duties suggests the number is high. With China having continued its zero-COVID policy long after most other countries, such scapegoating continued late into 2022, at which point Xi suddenly reversed his country's COVID stance.[4]

In Russia, where the mixed delegation pattern was accompanied by a smaller, more targeted national role than in China, there is evidence of regional and local leaders and administrators being punished and dismissed, but the reports are less common. This could reflect the greater need by Putin to balance the image of strength with a more diplomatic role in maintaining political loyalty throughout his state.

Fourth, populists work to control the information flow, but the degree to which they can successfully do so can impact their response. As hard as President Trump worked to direct the narrative, through his dominance during government press briefings and his own Twitter campaign, democratic institutions deprived him of the ability to accomplish this goal. He was, however, able to gain the support of certain sectors of the media, primarily on the right (including, most infamously, Fox News). Despite repeatedly lashing out and trying to discredit reporters, the free flow of information in the United States kept pressure on the president to act. This had pivotal effects, including causing him or governmental institutions to walk back policies that experts largely agreed were unsound, from the premature termination of coronavirus taskforce briefings to FDA and CDC authorizations and recommendations.

Perhaps more surprisingly, President Xi also found himself under public pressure around the start of the pandemic. With traditional media almost fully controlled by the state, these critical forces primarily rose up in social media accounts that flourished despite the actions of Chinese censors. Such pressures helped illuminate the viral spread and galvanize the government into action. Over the course of the pandemic, the government continued to work aggressively to control the narrative, partly by blocking and punishing those publishing unflattering reports online. They had some success in this endeavor; the images many Chinese regularly saw were official depictions of the Chinese government and citizens working together to stop the spread.

In Russia, where the state dominated the most prominent media, including television, but allowed for a degree of freedom in other outlets, Putin's regime used information to highlight the good but also allowed it to expose the bad. Those negatives were blamed on lapses in local leadership and sometimes led to punishments. But, as in China, the Kremlin's information campaign aimed to highlight the very sporadic nature of problems, and how such issues were quickly isolated and addressed (especially with the intervention of Moscow). The freer flow of information in Russia makes utilization of this semi-transparent tactic more difficult in the long term and may have contributed to Putin's "return to normalcy" campaign even in the midst of a brutal fall wave.

It is important to note that in each of these cases, politics loomed large and appears to have had a profound impact on the need for this "return to normalcy." For Trump, one barrier to an aggressive COVID response was his impending reelection bid. By hitting during an election year, COVID likely shortened Trump's time horizon even beyond what is typical in a democracy. Indeed, Trump reluctantly began to take the outbreak seriously when he still had hopes that his "15 days to stop the spread" might be enough to get over the pandemic hump and flatten the curve. When instead he was asked to prolong stay-at-home recommendations, he balked, then did so unenthusiastically before championing the abandonment of COVID restrictions altogether. Given the enormous scale of the COVID disaster, the populist U.S. president fighting for reelection gambled that the best he could do was fall back on the simple solution: ignore the outbreak until a vaccine came along.

Putin, though largely in control of political and civil life, was not totally immune to the sorts of public pressure and political goals Trump was dealing with. COVID threatened to interfere with two projects Putin had been working on for years. The first was his patriotic-nationalist campaign, which regularly pushed through Victory Day parades celebrating the culmination of World War II. The second was his Constitutional referendum, which would serve to both cement his nationalist credentials and lengthen the period in which he could maintain power. By allowing for the opening up of public spaces in early summer, Putin could oversee a grand 75th-year anniversary celebration of the Soviet victory during World War II and legally expand his own reign. Once Russians had a taste of reopening, Putin never pushed hard for renewed restrictions.

The biggest political obstacle facing Xi and the single-party state over which he dominated was more molehill than mountain. The "two sessions" annual meeting of the National People's Congress (NPC) and the National Committee of the Chinese People's Political Consultative Conference (CPPCC) was initially scheduled for March. When Xi declared the country safe enough for the event to take place in late May, he reassured his citizens that China was still on track to reach his goal of a "moderately prosperous society" through economic growth and poverty eradication. In a piece in the state-run Xinhua news outlet, the editors declared the "two sessions" an essential "window to observe China's development and an embodiment of Chinese democracy," as well as a forum to "oversee overall plans, unify minds, and increase national cohesion to achieve the country's important goals and tasks."[5] But the editors also noted that holding the meeting showed the country's "significant achievements in epidemic prevention and control." The "two sessions" may have been both part goal and part method to demonstrate success.

Finally, in all of these cases, leaders repeatedly sought to demonstrate that their "successful" COVID response reflected the superiority of both their personal leadership and the country they led. In the United States, this involved inaccurately boasting of superior testing and other response capabilities relative to those of other countries, while obfuscating and downplaying rising COVID case numbers. In both China and Russia, it went beyond inter-country comparisons and took the shape of inter-civilizational contrasts. For both of them, the poor response in the West, and in the United States in particular, was evidence of liberal democracy's failure and, in turn, authoritarian's promise.

In summary, an important lesson from these cases is how populism impedes crisis response on the part of democrats who lack the power and time needed to implement the painful measures essential to achieving long-term stability. This approach puts populist democratic leaders at war with their own experts and institutions, pushes them to delegate responsibility rather than take it, and feeds into the politicization of disasters in an effort to make opponents back down. The outcome, at least in a protracted disaster (whether a disease outbreak or major hurricane and its aftermath), can be a policy that focuses more on messaging than actually doing the tough job of effective disaster management.

Those who hold more loosely to the democratic template should similarly want disasters to go away, but their behaviors should differ thanks to the time and power they have at their disposal. More secure in office, and arguably facing greater expectations for action based on the strength of their political position, hybrid leaders have an incentive to align themselves more closely with the experts and respond more aggressively than democrats. Limited political competition in these states gives hybrid leaders a need to stay in the light but not hog it, and an incentive to outsource the response but maintain the mantle of leadership, thereby necessitating a somewhat higher degree of central mobilization. Facing a similar predicament as democrats, however, hybrid leaders should resist the sorts of aggressive measures that might cost them political support. The Russian case highlights how even small doses of freedom and competition can cause partially democratic leaders to back away from making tough decisions.

It is non-democratic populists who hold the greatest potential to respond. Unlike other non-democrats, non-democratic populists can be jolted into action by a perceived need to maintain public legitimacy. With an extraordinarily high degree of control over the state and security in office, these leaders can afford to align themselves with state experts and pursue costly steps in the name of long-term success. The lack of political competition gives them no need to stay in the light, but instead to come out only when it (at last) casts a favorable glow upon them.

COVID RESPONSE BEYOND 2020

This, at any rate, is the takeaway from year one, the most critical year in the pandemic disaster and the year that marked the first (pre-vaccine) phase of the response. Rarely do disasters last so long—days or weeks is more typical, and all it usually takes to see the phenomena described here begin to play out. But the longer-term nature of this pandemic allows us to reach back and ask: If authoritarian populism seems to have an edge on democratic populism, is this finding enduring over an extended period of time? The answer to this question is key to helping us gauge potential responses to other extended disasters, including those triggered by climate change, which will invariably have a profound impact on policymaking in the future.

One observation we can make based on these cases over the course of 2020 is that those with the most and least to lose politically seemed to hold tightest to the policies they pursued. In other words, once democratic and authoritarian populists set the course and stake their legitimacy on a particular approach, it can be politically difficult for them to backpedal and search out a new, potentially more effective route.

For Trump, this meant continually dismissing the threat even as thousands were dying per day. For Xi, it meant strict adherence to draconian policies even when alternatives, through vaccinations, had become available. It was in the semi-democratic case of Russia that we actually saw more flexibility in approach, though not necessarily for the betterment of the population. Instead, authoritarian strength appears to have convinced Putin to encourage a somewhat aggressive approach early in the pandemic, but existing democratic pressures compelled him to subsequently back down.

What we can observe is that nearly three years into the pandemic, as 2022 neared an end, the U.S. case count had reached around 100 million, with deaths at nearly 1.1 million.[6] Russia had more than 21 million cases and nearly 400,000 reported deaths. And China, before it abandoned its zero-COVID policy, had nearly 260,000 cases and just over 5,000 reported deaths. In terms of both per capita cases and per capita death count, the United States had the worst record of the three and China the best.

But truly answering the question of longer-term policy across all three of these cases is impossible since the United States (perhaps demonstrating the advantage of democracy as a corrective mechanism) saw a change in leadership at the start of 2021, after President Trump lost his 2020 election bid. He was succeeded by President Joe Biden, a non-populist. To what degree did this impact the U.S. COVID situation?

Nearly one year to the day after Trump's November 2020 electoral loss, the United States was facing about 75,000 new daily infections, falling to about half that another year later (2022), though with large fluctuations in between as a result of increasingly virulent new strains.[7] As 2022 drew to a close, about 400 people were dying from COVID per day in the United States. While it is clear that the case count and death count declined sharply under the new administration, it is likely this was a function of increased vaccine availability and previous exposure rather than any major policy change. Under Biden, health experts claimed science had returned to the fore of the government's COVID policy, which involved vastly increased access to tests and vaccines, so that 75 percent of Americans had at least one shot after his first year in office.[8] But they also complained that the president was overly focused on vaccinations as an easy answer, avoiding politically tougher steps, such as encouraging all states to have mask mandates during virulent outbreaks. In other words, it is difficult to gauge how Biden would have responded in the first critical phase of the pandemic, though certainly his rhetoric suggests he would have been more aggressive. Biden openly campaigned on calls for a mask mandate, for instance, arguing "It's not about your rights. It's about your responsibilities."[9]

The vaccination campaign was much more halting in Russia, where the world's first approved vaccine was greeted with skepticism. Putin himself proved reluctant to take the shot he had celebrated, only accepting it months after it became available. By mid-2021, despite an adequate supply of the domestic vaccine, only 15 percent of the general population had received at least one shot, a rate almost four times lower than in the United States.[10] As case rates continued to shoot up in late 2021, Putin expressed exasperation at the unwillingness of Russians to vaccinate. "These are intelligent people with a good education. I can't understand what's going on," Putin said. "We have a reliable and efficient vaccine. I want to emphasize again, there are only two choices: get sick or get vaccinated."[11]

Meanwhile, cases spiked to the point that in fall 2021, Putin issued orders for greater restrictions, though only fairly mild ones, including limiting hours for certain public venues and lengthening isolation times for those infected.[12] Yet he maintained his use of devolutionary delegation, leaving the toughest decisions and implementation to lower-level officials. By that point, Russia's mortality rate was the highest in Europe and the second highest in Asia (after populist India). COVID continued to shake Russia even as Putin launched his war against Ukraine in February 2022. By the following summer, with just 52 percent of the population vaccinated, the government ended all existing restrictions, including mask mandates.[13] A few months later, the country was back to 50,000-plus new daily cases.[14] By October, it was nearing 250,000 daily infections, and a total of nearly 400,000 had died since the start of the pandemic.[15]

Contrast these cases with China, where President Xi continued to consolidate his hold on power despite the pandemic. One and a half years after Chinese authorities approved their vaccine, widespread hesitancy amidst safety questions left only about 20 percent of the over-sixty population vaccinated.[16] This factor was both a cause and an effect of the zero-COVID strategy, which convinced some who were already hesitant to take the shot that lockdowns offered the safest route to continued health. But it also prompted the government to launch a major vaccination drive, including new monetary incentives to get vaccinated. It apparently had an impact. As China approached the three-year anniversary of COVID's emergence, 90 percent of Chinese had been vaccinated, with Chinese state media claiming the rate was 86 percent for the elderly population, though questions remained over both the true numbers and the Chinese vaccine's effectiveness on new variants.[17]

Still, China's leaders doggedly clung to their zero-COVID policy. Tens of millions in 2022 faced days or weeks of lockdowns, causing economic insecurity and raising public discontent.[18] At the 2022 Communist Party congress, where Xi cemented his leadership by winning a third term unseen since Mao Zedong, Xi continued to call his zero-COVID policy "a people's war to stop the spread of the virus."[19] While Xi's zero-COVID policies certainly saved lives in the short run, maintaining the course, which Xi staked his legitimacy on, had severe long-term disadvantages. Three years after the start of the pandemic, China's economy remained battered by the stop-go pattern of lockdowns.

The longer-term trajectory of these cases thus highlights the reticence of democratic and semi-democratic leaders to adopt harsh measures but also the willingness of authoritarian populists to stick with such tough measures thanks to their political strength. It also shows, however, that there can be too much of a good thing. Xi clung to zero-COVID as the "most economic and effective" policy for China, emphasizing that more than 1 million Chinese would have died of COVID without it.[20] But for many in China, who long commended the government's tough take on COVID, the accumulating costs of unemployment and periodic food shortages caused by the lockdowns had triggered a groundswell of discontent within three years of the pandemic's start.[21]

This frustration boiled over in late 2022, following an apartment fire in the northwest city of Urumqi in which nearly a dozen people died, a disaster many blamed on harsh COVID restrictions.[22] Protests rapidly spread to China's main cities, including Shanghai and Beijing, and led authorities to make a sudden, unceremonious about-face on Xi's stubbornly touted policy.[23] As if a switch had been flicked, COVID restrictions were lifted, and residents of China resumed normal life. The predictable result was an explosion of infections and, with relatively low booster shot uptake among the elderly, a reported surge in deaths.[24] The Chinese government once again relied on shady accounting methods to drastically lower the official casualty rates,[25] but evidence from hospitals and crematoriums suggested that the policy reversal had a catastrophic impact.[26]

The China case raises red flags as to how we should define success. Did China's leaders save lives for the first three years of the pandemic or merely delay the inevitable? Many observers attacked China's zero-COVID policy not for its inability to stem infections but for the authorities' failure to utilize the time provided by sporadic harsh lockdowns to invest in the country's medical infrastructure and prepare it for an eventual and safe, full-fledged reopening.[27] Another critique, more germane to this book, would be that populist authoritarian regimes can be just as fickle and prone to detrimental policy reversals as their democratic counterparts—albeit with a sizable window of opportunity to act.

The latter appraisal is rooted in the argument, emphasized in this book, that populist authoritarians are sensitive to public pressure. In fact, populism is the very quality that makes such leaders sensitive and responsive to public concerns in the first place. While institutional strength buys populist authoritarians space to maneuver (and in China, this was an astounding period of years), the publics in whose interests they claim to act wield far more influence than those publics living under non-populist authoritarians. This, it turns out, can be a double-edged sword. In the case of China's COVID response, public opposition to zero-COVID was evident from the start, but Xi was apparently convinced he had enough time to win the COVID war he claimed to be waging, and then enjoy the legitimacy of victory. Instead, mounting public pressures eventually prompted him to suddenly and prematurely declare victory on COVID and rely on more traditional authoritarian methods (censorship, crackdowns on dissent) as he marketed his about-face as a triumph.

It is critical to emphasize that the about-face we saw in the China case is consistent with the argument in this book. While populist democrats facing public pressure have very limited space for tough responses, authoritarian populists have more time to show that the pain they inflicted was for the greater good. But this timeline is not infinite. Eventually, like their democratic populist counterparts, they can face so much pressure that they opt for the easy way out. The insulating effect of authoritarianism is somewhat akin to a dam: it does a remarkable job retaining the swelling waters, but only for so long.

Still, the China case raises important questions. If Chinese leaders were willing to stake their legitimacy on tough and costly measures to stymie a disaster, why did they lack the foresight or initiative needed to make structural changes during their aggressive, multi-year response that would allow for a safe loosening of the anti-COVID regime over time? One likely answer to this may be overconfidence on the part of the Chinese leadership that their political strength guaranteed them sufficient time to gradually implement programs (including more effective vaccination and booster campaigns) that would yield a happier ending to the COVID story. The November 2022 protests unexpectedly and drastically cut this timeline short.

Another plausible answer is that Xi was so focused on his political objectives of winning a third term as China's leader that his COVID policy suffered from acute myopia. This would suggest populist authoritarians suffer from limitations similar to those of their populist counterparts in democracies, where immediate political concerns can overshadow long-term policy planning.

Evidence for a more definitive answer in the China case may emerge in the months or years after this book has been printed. This very unsatisfying conclusion is a dilemma that seems almost inherent in any study of contemporary events.

This dilemma is also likely exacerbated by the particular nature of this study. The goal of this book has been to make a compelling theoretical argument and immerse readers in a detailed study that has the power to illuminate mechanisms, processes, and outcomes in ways that large, quantitative studies cannot. Delving into three cases allows us to uncover insights into complicated phenomena, but it comes with the inevitable question of generalizability. As such, this book is only a first step in a much larger research program.

BEYOND THE UNITED STATES, RUSSIA, AND CHINA

While a larger quantitative study might miss many of the nuances and details presented here, it could help systematically test these and additional hypotheses. In this section, I seek to couch the findings of this study in others that have recently emerged.

Absent controls for regime type, some of the emergent literature has found that during COVID outbreaks, populist governments were less aggressive in their implementation of health measures and mobility restrictions than non-populists governments.[28] One of the reasons for this, consistent with what I have found in the democratic case in this book, is that populists are more likely to hedge their bets with vague policies and have a habit of searching out blame for a disaster rather than building unity in response to it.[29] As populists attack their own institutions, including those housing and promoting expertise, their response levels are lower and excess mortality rates are higher than in non-populist regimes.[30]

Unfortunately, these specific studies do not differentiate between populist democrats and authoritarians, leaving the interplay between these variables unclear. On the flip side, there are also studies that have looked at COVID response based on regime type but absent controls for populism. These findings have also been mixed. While democrats' institutional constraints sometimes left them at a disadvantage,[31] there is evidence that democracies had stronger health-care systems to begin with, allowing them to do a better job reducing deaths.[32] Yet another advantage, perhaps ironically, stemmed from the ability of democrats to ultimately clamp down on the freedom of their populations to stop the viral spread.[33] It is notable that some of the most effective democracies were those in which power was more centralized, including South Korea and Taiwan.[34] This is, again, consistent with the argument in this book that response effectiveness hinges in good part on power and time horizons, both of which can be altered through emergency measures during states of emergency.

Yet doing so can be perilous for many reasons. According to another study, democratic populists may actually hold an advantage over non-democratic populists in their response effectiveness when democratic pressures and institutions capably correct for populists' worst policy preferences (something the U.S. case provides modest evidence in support of).[35] Still, the authors of this study acknowledged that the "deliberative process of decision-making" and "reluctance to encroach on privacy and personal freedom" reduce democracies' disaster response effectiveness compared with authoritarians, which seems to obfuscate the initial findings.[36]

As informative as such quantitative studies are, they do carry the potential risk of missing critical aspects of the regime in ways that diminish their explanatory value. For instance, the authors who found democratic populists more effective than non-democratic populists actually referred to China's response as "technocratic," which I would argue misses the populist roots of China's response policy.[37] Other anecdotes that they use to bulwark their case similarly raise questions. For instance, they point to the Philippines, under the hybrid populist president Rodrigo Duterte, as another case of non-democratic populist response failure. There, Duterte downplayed the virus before pursuing a "militaristic lockdown" that clumsily worsened the pandemic by leading to the jailing (with no social distancing) of tens of thousands of lockdown violators.[38] The Philippines president thus responded with the assertiveness afforded to a less democratic leader, as argued in this book, but also with an element of incompetence that likely worsened the response outcome. It is difficult to chalk the latter weakness up exclusively to regime type, however.

While these large-N quantitative studies are thus laudable, they also come with important caveats. One such caveat that I have addressed only in passing relates to the operationalization of the dependent variable: the best measure of response success seems to be morbidity and mortality rates. Unfortunately, data on COVID rates are highly dependent on official government statistics and, as we've seen in this book, can be distorted as a result of manipulation but also a lack of capacity. The pandemic demonstrated the difficulty of gauging COVID spread in even strong and fairly well-off states. This phenomenon is magnified in the context of the large number of states scoring lower on the UN's Human Development Index, raising potential questions about the validity of emerging quantitative studies.

The case of Nicaragua is one of many that highlights this dilemma. The published COVID rates in this populist non-democracy suggested an effective response. In actuality, human rights advocates and health workers, citing inconsistency in data, slammed the government's response and accused it of severely concealing the true extent of COVID spread.[39]

It's important to note that the methodological problem of data reliability can surface in all regime types. In other words, while we might presume the less democratic the regime, the murkier the numbers, this does not always hold. In authoritarian China, for instance, early figures were widely disputed but subsequent (low) numbers attracted much less consternation. The same goes for nearby authoritarian Vietnam, where independent analysts on the ground corroborated the government's official low rate of infections.[40] But other populist authoritarians, including Venezuela's Nicolás Maduro, spewed out entirely false numbers in the face of much higher rates. According to one nongovernmental group of medical workers monitoring COVID deaths, the true number of medical worker fatalities alone at one point exceeded the official total death rate.[41]

While democratic mechanisms can help reduce the risk of faulty figures, they cannot entirely eliminate it. Moving closer to democracy, populist semi-democratic Turkish president Recep Tayyip Erdoğan followed the all-too-frequent practice of reporting COVID deaths only if a patient with COVID symptoms had actually tested positive which, given a dearth of reliable tests, resulted in relatively low death rates.[42] But even in more democratic, populist-run India, early estimates from summer 2020 suggested official test results were undercounting morbidity rates by up to twenty times,[43] and by mid-2022, the WHO estimated India's actual 2020–2021 COVID death count may have been almost ten times higher than the official estimate of 481,000.[44] Government officials retorted, in words that could easily have come from any non-democratic denier, that the WHO's report was "fallacious, ill-informed and mischievous in nature."[45]

All of this makes a large-N study of disaster performance during COVID much more difficult. A bird's-eye view of the numbers might lead us to conclude that Nicaragua, India, and Venezuela performed reasonably well. But we can see from tentative data collected by nongovernmental observers that these numbers are a mirage. And looking past the numbers, it is clear that COVID policies in these countries, including Maduro's repression-driven response, where government officials denounced people who may have had contact with COVID as "bioterrorists" and intimidated medical professional who questioned the state's actions,[46] were problematic.

These sorts of glimpses into a broader subset of cases, even anecdotally, can help highlight the strengths and weaknesses of the argument presented in this book, as well as identify potential additional variables.

Perhaps the most intriguing of the democratic cases is India, the world's largest democracy and a country omitted from this study due to its relatively low HDI (India ranks 132nd on that global indicator). Populist prime minister Modi, initially blamed for denying community transmission much like his U.S. counterpart,[47] took surprisingly aggressive actions—a strict lockdown for the entire country—in the face of dire predictions of 50 million severely sick Indians by July 2020 alone.[48] The multi-week lockdown was reinstated multiple times, ultimately stretching from late March until June.

Modi's aggressive response, surprising for a democratic populist, was matched by major investments in fiscal stimuli, amounting to an estimated 10 percent of GDP in the first months of the pandemic.[49] But it also proved ephemeral, much as Trump's less comprehensive fifteen-day strategy had been. After what many considered a premature rollback of restrictions, infections spiked.[50] Intent on keeping India open, high-level officials then pressured scientists at influential state institutions to downplay risks. While his government buried the science, Modi credited himself for having "saved humanity from a big disaster."[51] Modi's record was subject to a bristling rebuke by *The Lancet* medical journal, which accused him of severely under-counting cases and prematurely washing his hands of the pandemic.[52] As Modi freed the country and carried on with large-scale religious celebrations and political rallies, cases and deaths exploded.

While surprising at first, what we see in the India case, a generally free but blemished populist-led democracy (with a combined Freedom House politi-cal and civil rights score of 5), was actually reflected in other populist-led countries with similar regime characteristics. This includes Poland (combined score of 4) and Hungary (combined score of 5), ranked by Freedom House as just on the democratic side of a hybrid regime.

In both of these cases, which have significantly higher HDIs than India, the early response was broadly praised. In Poland, where the government was commended for being both quick and thorough, the country launched a quite strict national lockdown which extended from March to May.[53] The same went for Hungary, which launched a lockdown before many others in the region and was similarly extolled for its very positive outcomes early on.[54]

It is important to point out that, as in India, in neither case was COVID good for the already waning democracy. The outbreak hit Poland during a presidential campaign, allowing the government to further tilt an already uneven playing field. More specifically, the governing party's ban on public events greatly reduced the visibility of opposition candidates, even as the incumbent president continued to hold public meetings and press conferences that received overwhelmingly positive coverage from public television and radio stations over which his government held heavy sway.[55]

In Hungary, where Prime Minister Viktor Orbán oversaw a longer and more precipitous shift away from democracy than Poland prior to 2020, COVID presented an opportunity for an even sharper break from democratic checks and balances. The ruling party, Fidesz, used the pandemic to further curtail immigration and asylum policies before passing in late March its infa-mous Coronavirus Act, allowing the government to rule by decree with no set termination period (though it was eventually rescinded in June).[56] Orbán slammeá any criticism of the Act as an unjust politicization of the pandemic, aimed at sullying his crisis response and bringing down the government. He used his dominance over state media to present his measures as popular and promote nationalism. More akin to the leader of a hybrid regime, Orbán used these measures to implement harsh lockdowns and present himself as the face of the tough restrictions (following expert advice). Any policy failures were blamed on opposition leaders at the local level.

These cases suggest that democratic populists can pursue aggressive steps to address a crisis and are not necessarily impediments to effective policy. But they are also a reminder that short-term wins can be eroded as democratic pressures (for instance, to relax health regulations) build over time and that populist democrats are prone to taking non-democratic shortcuts to try to maximize their gains.

Following from this, and consistent with the lessons from this book, these cases also suggest that democratic populists may be more aggressive in crisis response when they are actually less democratic. Hungary's leadership, in particular, demonstrated what we might expect to see not in a populist democracy but in a populist country at the more democratic edge of a hybrid regime: a leader with the confidence and powers to oversee aggressive actions but for a limited time and weary of accepting responsibility for policy failure.

This trend is clear in other cases that move a few steps further from democracy. Sri Lanka, another populist partial democracy that brings us closer to the authoritarian side of the spectrum (with a combined Freedom House score of 8 compared to Hungary's 5), pursued an aggressive intervention, much as the Hungarians did following their Coronavirus Act. The Sri Lankans also simultaneously used the pandemic as an excuse to further reduce democratic liberties. Human rights observers reported arbitrary arrests, physical assaults, and even death threats to those critical of the regime's response.[57] With the military at the helm, citizens complained of a securitization of the crisis, leading to the arrest of tens of thousands for violating curfew (reminiscent of the Philippines case noted above) and a contact tracing process run by the distrusted intelligence services. While most saw a successful pandemic response early on based on case and fatality numbers alone, others complained the cost came in the form of increased nationalist ideology and the scapegoating of minorities, especially Muslims.[58]

Edging up against the authoritarian side of hybrid regimes, close to Russia, Turkish president Erdoğan eventually issued a month-long nationwide lockdown followed by mask mandates, including fines for those who did not comply.[59] With greater political control than Orbán, Erdoğan did not merely blame failures on local members of the opposition. Instead, as in Russia, authorities actively impeded lower-level rivals' efforts to protect the population from the virus, fining media outlets for critical coverage and shutting down local field hospitals and soup kitchens that challenged the central government's legitimacy and messaging.[60]

Taken together, these cases highlight the propensity of hybrid regimes, or seriously flawed democracies, to demonstrate elements of both democratic populist and authoritarian populist approaches to disaster. There appears to be a tendency for less democratic populist rulers to act more aggressively for a period, making clampdowns on democracy both a tool to do this and a goal to strengthen public support. The threat that disasters can push states already deviating from democracy even further from democratic norms is neither a surprise nor is it unique to this subset of regimes. With the start of the pandemic, one prominent NGO found that at least eighty countries, varying from non-democracies to full-fledged democracies, witnessed a deterioration in democratic freedoms.[61]

CONSIDERING ADDITIONAL VARIABLES

While I would argue that the theory laid out in this book is persuasive, and can help explain variation among many cases, there are clear discrepancies even in the small population of cases I have introduced here. Venezuela, for example, was governed by a populist who presided over what Freedom House labels a closed regime, so we might have expected a more aggressive response than what played out. What, then, separates Venezuela's Maduro from China's Xi in their response given this similarity?

This question deserves much more attention. One potential answer may be that the predictive ability of populism and regime type could be enhanced by specifying the particular nature of the regime. As noted at the start of this book, different types of non-democracies can behave quite differently. Maduro's Venezuela, though perhaps similarly closed to Xi's China, looked more like a personalistic regime than a single-party one.[62] And Maduro acted in ways quite similar to another personalistic non-democrat, Belarus president Alexander Lukashenko, who derided fears of COVID as "psychosis" and claimed it could be beaten by vodka, sauna time, or rigorous exercise.[63]

However, specific regime type is probably insufficient on its own. Populism remains an important variable. In another single-party regime, just across the border from China, Vietnamese authorities—who were notably not classified as populists—were initially credited with a highly capable response.[64] Their actions focused on lower cost preventative measures, including contact tracing and targeted quarantines, rather than the higher-cost measures implemented by China. But, unlike in populist China and consistent with the premise of this book, Vietnam's elites were also wary of implementing costly lockdowns as the virus spread throughout 2021.[65] The outcome was far more COVID spread in Vietnam than in China, where zero-COVID remained the strategy of choice.

This comparison brings to center stage another variable critical to this story: development level. This book sought to control for development and capacity, as measured by HDI. Pointedly, China's HDI rank, 79th in the world, is considerably higher than that of Vietnam's (at 115th), which might also account for the difference in policies.[66] Economic development also featured in other populist non-democracies, including Nicaragua, where President Daniel Ortega downplayed the risks of COVID and resisted tight restrictions, arguing that the economic impacts would be just too painful for his developing country.[67] Here we saw a populist dictator who initially shrank away from the public view as expected but, as a result of resource limitations (Nicaragua ranks 126th in HDI), actually objected to calls for quarantines.

This might help explain some differences among hybrid regimes as well. In relatively poor Guatemala (ranking 135th in HDI), for example, the state simply lacked money for supplies and medical staff salaries.[68] Another informative lesson comes from the cases of Hungary (with an HDI ranking of 46) and Sri Lanka (73), described above, compared with another hybrid populist regime, Indonesia (114). While the first two countries initially responded aggressively to COVID, Indonesia's populist president Joko Widodo was criticized for a slow and confusing response, including a lack of clarity on the need for social distancing.[69] Widodo found it politically advantageous to adopt an anti-scientific approach similar to Trump and Brazil's Jair Bolsonaro, while taking a backseat to the response (run by his health minister) more akin to Putin.[70] He briefly supported a vague stay-at-home policy before pressuring local elites to relax restrictions to keep the economy functioning.[71] While Indonesia's record was not horrendous on a global scale, it performed among the worst of southeast Asian countries, surprising given its geographical advantages to stopping a disease.[72] Lack of capacity could explain the discrepancy between the cases.

HDI on its own, however, also does not tell the full story. Consider, for instance, the non-populist, non-democratic case of Iran, which ranks in HDI close to China (76th in the world). There, authorities first denied the scope and intensity of the unfolding disaster (as is typical) but then refrained from spending the amount needed to keep people from going out.[73] Restrictions that were imposed by the central government were rapidly rolled back, despite rebounding case numbers. Throughout 2020, Iran suffered from repeated surges and lacked the leadership or willingness to spend the needed resources to stop them. This, according to the argument in this book, might not have happened if the Iranian leaders were populist in nature. In other words, the Iranians followed precisely the pattern we would have expected from non-populist authoritarians, regardless of HDI.

Of course, there are other important variables, beyond regime type, populism, and HDI, that may account for differences in COVID policy and should be considered in the next stage of research. Take, for instance, political culture. Perhaps it was the U.S. culture of individualism and China's collectivist culture, rather than populist democracy and authoritarianism, that so weightily impacted COVID policy. Indeed, the United States is among the most individualist countries in the world, for instance, trailed by Russia and then, much closer to the collectivist side of this spectrum, China.[74] Other countries that score high on collectivist characteristics, including Taiwan, South Korea, and Singapore, performed well during COVID. Clearly, individualism is not the only explanation for shortcomings, though. Highly collectivist Indonesia, for instance, also had a relatively poor track record during COVID. The same goes for Venezuela and Portugal, two countries that rank low in individualism but struggled to contain the virus. A more thorough investigation of this variable might lead to new insights.

Another potential determinant of success is experience dealing with the specific form of disaster investigated here, a virulent disease outbreak. Just over a decade and a half before COVID-19 emerged, some of the top COVID performers had been hit by a similar outbreak (SARS). The experience they gained from their response may have helped. Yet it is worth remembering that China itself faced many similar early obstacles to COVID as it had with SARS under its then populist leader.[75] And while China, Hong Kong, and Taiwan were especially hard hit by SARS and responded effectively in 2020,[76] Canada—a non-populist democracy—was also hit with a spike in cases but, as a result of political factors, failed to make major adjustments that would have left it safer when COVID struck.[77]

Finally, one might posit that the ideology (left-wing versus right-wing) of the populist in charge matters. Anecdotal evidence suggests that is not the case. On the left, we have discussed both China (which excelled in its response) and Venezuela (which performed poorly). To that, we can add another left-wing populist, Mexico's president Andrés Manuel López Obrador, who oversaw a country with an astounding 600,000 excess deaths in 2020.[78] Very much like his right-wing counterparts in the United States and Brazil, Obrador habitually dismissed the threat of COVID (and also ignored his "mini-COVID" diagnosis, disregarded his own government's health recommendations, and publicly lauded unproven over-the-counter treatments as sufficient).[79] Like the others, Obrador also demonstrated a similar lack of central leadership, forcing states to deal with the crisis in the absence of a comprehensive federal strategy.[80]

Importantly, the cases noted here—and, indeed, in much of the world— also highlight the difficulty of gauging success in a disaster that continues to play out over an extended period, as will be the case with many climate change-driven threats.

In fact, over time, both democracies and non-democracies have found that early successes do not necessarily portend certain victory. The cases of China and Vietnam, where domestic publics gave strong marks to their leaders for fighting COVID in 2020 before experiencing great disappointments in subsequent years, are just two that highlight the fickle nature of triumph in the disaster setting.[81] The same goes for the Polish case discussed above. A fall wave brought a sharp rise in hospitalizations and renewed restrictions in both countries, where authorities were weary of launching a second lockdown and only did so after a long period of hesitation.[82] (In somewhat less democratic Hungary, the outcome was similar.)[83] Israel's populist prime minister experienced much the same.[84] Democratic and hybrid regimes seem to suffer most from short-sightedness, but as the smattering of non-democratic cases discussed demonstrate, populist authoritarians are not fully immune from such pressures.

In order to explore the relevance of my argument to the sorts of disasters we can expect to encounter as the climate continues to change, I close by briefly reflecting on how closely the COVID experiences in the three countries studied here match that of other disasters they have faced. In the United States, unsurprisingly, the populist president had a track record that preceded COVID (and, importantly, Trump's 2020 reelection campaign) of playing down disasters to the detriment of the population. This was abundantly clear when Hurricane Maria devastated the U.S. territory of Puerto Rico in 2017. President Trump, under public pressure, flew into the capital, San Juan, and assured Americans that the damage had been minimal and the federal response stellar ("A+").[85] As Trump playfully tossed out rolls of paper towels to a crowd of his supporters, he drastically downplayed both the physical damage and the death toll, calling the official tally of sixteen a success. Estimates would eventually show the number of dead to be closer to 3,000. As with COVID (but notably years before his reelection campaign had begun), Trump responded to these reported figures not with humility but with anger, calling them an attempt by his political opponents "to make me look as bad as possible."

Contrast Trump's dismissive, politically polarizing approach to disaster with President Putin's personal handling of the 2010 wildfires that broke out across Russia. Putin dominated national media coverage, portraying himself as in control of the situation, much as he did with other disasters.[86] He emerged on site, dressed down, to sit with victims, whom he connected and empathized with using colloquial references.[87] Putin, like Trump, looked for others to blame but settled on local and regional authorities, who were forced to resign.[88] In contrast to the U.S. president, who felt that acknowledging the scope of the problem was a sign of weakness, the semi-authoritarian Russian president felt the need, and perhaps the opportunity, to show himself in charge of the response and recovery while personally visiting impacted villages.

Finally, Xi has also sought to use major disasters to promote his personal image. Under his rule, state media shifted from a long-standing practice of hiding leaders during times of trouble to actually showing them off.[89] In recent floods, for instance, state media depicted Xi as the one on the ground and in charge, if after a short delay (much as with COVID).[90] Sidelining his own premier (also sloshing through flood waters), Xi was the one to issue "important instructions" in response.[91]As with COVID, Xi simultaneously demanded that local leaders act to "take the lead in fighting the floods" but, unlike in the more democratic cases, his words and actions appeared more resolute.[92] Rather than pass the buck politically, Xi was shown in the Chinese press to be taking on more of a commanding role ("he ordered authorities at all levels to promptly organize") and ordering top-down intervention ("The People's Liberation Army and the People's Armed Police Force must actively assist local authorities in emergency rescue and relief work," he said.).

In short, what we have seen in this book is consistent with the behavior these populist leaders have demonstrated in other disasters and appears to be indicative of how they are likely to deal with future ones. On the one hand, the democratic populists have been dismissive of monumental threats perceived to be politically dangerous in the short term. On the other hand, more authoritarian populists have felt the need to deal with threats in exchange for a hike in long-term legitimacy. This could offer lessons on what to expect as climate change-driven disasters continue to arise.

As an exploratory study, the goal of this book has been to generate debate and prompt readers to think more deeply about how populism interacts with regime type in ways that profoundly affect politics and policy. My cases were chosen to explore how the argument presented might, or might not, play out in three very different cases. A next step might be to conduct a series of studies testing this argument on different sets of cases that hew more closely to standard comparative (most similar or different systems) case designs, keeping in mind the need to control for some of the variables noted above. One, for instance, might explore populist versus non-populist disaster responses in both presidential and parliamentary democracies. Another might look at populist versus non-populist disaster responses in, for instance, both single-party and personalistic non-democracies. Of course, with more reliable data, quantitative studies could bolster the generalizability of future findings. This field is quite ripe for exploration.

CONCLUSION

This concluding chapter, including a brief exploration of additional cases, suggests that there is much we still do not know about what determines the effectiveness of disaster response. What is clear from this book, however, is that the interplay between populism and regime type can potentially have a powerful impact.

Under conditions of democracy, populism appears to have its most deleterious effects. Populism can effectively pull democratic leaders away from either costly but effective policies or the very democratic institutions designed to ensure they act in the public good. Those democratic populists who are inclined to respond aggressively to a severe crisis may find they can only do so by ameliorating their time horizon dilemma, something easiest done by increasing executive authority and seizing control over the emerging narrative. Ironically, democratic populists seem most willing to act aggressively (at least for a spell) once they have stepped far enough away from democracy that it no longer threatens them.

Populists at the helm of hybrid regimes with adequate resources have both the incentive to respond but also far more limited space to maneuver than the non-democrats so many aspire to be. It is the lingering mechanisms of democracy that most limit these populists, subject to the (albeit weakly) institutionalized pressures of their populace. This can lead to tough but short measures; hybrid populists may desire to see themselves as captains of a great rescue ship, but they face pressure to declare victory far earlier than do non-democratic populists.

Interestingly, just as democratic populists feel they can only act with more authoritarian power, it is populism that provides already authoritarian leaders with the incentive to take costly actions in the name of the public good. Absent populism, dictators are more likely to shirk at investing the considerable resources needed to protect their people. As the discussion in this chapter has indicated, however, populism on its own is likely insufficient to move non-democrats to action. Leaders must also possess the essential capacity needed to effectively respond. Without that, they may decide they are better off dismissing a disaster than grappling with it absent the tools they need.

As I have made clear in this final chapter, this study is designed to be the first step of a much broader research agenda. Looking at additional cases, controlling for additional variables and considering a wider array of disaster types are critical for understanding the degree to which the findings detailed here are generalizable. Those studies, in turn, will provide vital lessons that could help us better prepare for a quickly changing world where disasters are projected to become far more common.

In closing, I want to emphasize that the goal of this book is by no means to suggest that populist non-democracies are a normatively "good" thing. For starters, China's authoritarianism bears responsibility for allowing the COVID-19 virus to fester early on, endangering its own citizens and then the entire world.[93] It seems far less likely that the COVID outbreak would have turned into a full-fledged pandemic if the virus had been initially identified in a stable democratic country characterized by the free flow of information, strong institutions, and accountable political leaders.

Moreover, even as we acknowledge that populist non-democrats can be inclined to take the tough actions needed to effectively deal with a disaster, their effectiveness can come at great cost, from civil liberties infringements to scapegoating certain ethnic, racial, or class groups. China's early response may have had highly positive outcomes when measured in human health, but it has certainly been a disaster for human rights, both political and economic.

On that note, there are a plethora of cases, from New Zealand and South Korea to Germany, that indicate how democracies can also manage disasters highly effectively and without the same degree of human rights abuses. So long, that is, as the populists are not in charge.

In short, if one is looking for a regime most capable of dealing with an emerging disaster, authoritarianism is not the obvious answer. But populist authoritarianism clearly has advantages over non-populist authoritarianism and, in many ways, populist democracy. As we look forward to an increasingly unstable global environment, in which disaster responsiveness becomes an ever more valuable political good, these lessons are surely worth considering.

NOTES

1. Aristophanes, *The Knights, the Complete Greek Drama* (New York: Random House, 1938).

2. Yi Kang, *Disaster Management in China in a Changing Era, Springer Briefs in Political Science* (Berlin: Springer-Verlag Berlin Heiderlberg, 2015).

3. Thung-hong Lin, "Governing Disaster: Political Institutions, Social Inequality and Human Vulnerability," in *2012 Annual Meeting of Taiwanese Sociological Association* (2012); Bin Xu, "Durkheim in Sichuan: The Earthquake, National Solidarity, and the Politics of Small Things," *Social Psychology Quarterly* 72 (2009): 5–8; Yanzhong Huang, "The SARS Epidemic and Its Aftermath in China: A Political Perspective," in *Learning from SARS: Preparing for the Next Disease Outbreak: Workshop Summary*, ed. Katherine Oberholtzer, et al. (Washington, DC: The National Academies Press, 2004); Yihong Liu, *Crisis Rhetoric and Policy Change in China: Toward a Dynamic Process Model of Crisis Exploitation*, ed. Ultrecht University (Ultrecht, Netherlands, 2019).

4. William Zheng, "Dozens of Chinese Officials Punished over Latest Wave of Covid-19 Cases," *South China Morning Post*, March 22, 2022.

5. Xinhua, "Understanding the Two Sessions: Why Must China Hold the Two Sessions?" *Xinhua General News Service*, March 22, 2020.

6. WorldOMeter, "Coronavirus Cases," *WorldOMeter*, https://www.worldometers.info/coronavirus/#countries.

7. Nate Rattner and Robert Towey, "After Weeks of Declines, U.S. Covid Cases Have Stalled at a High Level: 'The Ers Are Packed'," *CNBC*, November 11, 2021; KFF, "Global COVID-19 Tracker," *KFF*, January 20, 2023, https://www.kff.org/coronavirus-covid-19/issue-brief/global-covid-19-tracker/.

8. Selena Simmons-Duffin and Pien Huang, "A Year in, Experts Assess Biden's Hits and Misses on Handling the Pandemic," *National Public Radio*, January 18, 2022, https://www.npr.org/sections/health-shots/2022/01/18/1073292913/a-year-in-experts-assess-bidens-hits-and-misses-on-handling-the-pandemic.

9. Christina Wilkie, "Joe Biden Calls for a Nationwide Mask Mandate as He Pushes His Plan to Combat Coronavirus," *CNBC*, August 13, 2020.

10. Daria Litvinova, "Putin Reveals He Was Vaccinated with Russia's Sputnik V," *Associated Press News*, June 30, 2021; Amanda B. Pariseault, "Current Status of COVID-19 Vaccines Rollout Nationwide: July 2021 Update for the Attorney General Community," *National Association of Attorneys General*, August 10, 2021, https://www.naag.org/attorney-general-journal/current-status-of -covid-19-vaccines-rollout-nationwide-july-2021-update-for-the-attorney-general-community/.

11. Charles Maynes, "With Record-High Deaths, Moscow and Other Parts of Russia Enter a Partial Lockdown," *National Public Radio*, October 28, 2021, https://www.npr.org/2021/10/28 /1049976625/moscow-russia-covid-deaths-lockdown.

12. Paul Stronski, "Russia's Response to Its Spiraling COVID-19 Crisis Is Too Little, Too Late," *Carnegie Endowment for International Peace*, October 28, 2021, https://carnegieendowment.org /2021/10/28/russia-s-response-to-its-spiraling-covid-19-crisis-is-too-little-too-late-pub-85677.

13. Reuters, "Russia Scraps Remaining COVID Restrictions," *Reuters*, July 1, 2022.

14. "Russia Reports 50,000 COVID-19 Cases for Second Day Running," *Reuters*, September 3, 2022.

15. IHME, "COVID-19 Results Briefing," *Institute for Health Metrics and Evaluation*, December 15, 2022, https://www.healthdata.org/sites/default/files/covid_briefs/62_briefing_Russian_Federation.pdf; WorldOMeter, "COVID-19 Coronavirus Pandemic," *WorldOMeter*, January 21, https:// www.worldometers.info/coronavirus/.

16. Dennis Normile, "'An Undebatable Political Decision': Why China Refuses to End Its Harsh Lockdowns," *Science*, April 15, 2022, https://www.science.org/content/article/undebatable-political -decision-why-china-refuses-to-end-its-harsh-lockdowns.

17. William Yang, "No Way out in Sight for China's Zero-COVID Strategy," *Deutsche Welle*, October 19, 2022, https://www.dw.com/en/no-way-out-in-sight-for-chinas-zero-covid-strategy/a -63489794; Ken Moritsugu, "Afraid of Needles? China Using Inhalable COVID-19 Vaccine," *Associate Press News*, October 26, 2022.

18. William Yang, "COVID: Why Is Discontent Growing over Shanghai's Lockdown?" *Deutsche Welle*, April 18, 2022, https://www.dw.com/en/china-why-is-public-discontent-growing -over-shanghais-covid-lockdown/a-61504275; J. Stephen Morrison, Scott Kennedy, and Yanzhong Huang, "China's Zero-Covid: What Should the West Do?" *Center for Strategic and International Studies*, June 27, 2022, https://www.csis.org/analysis/chinas-zero-covid-what-should-west-do.

19. Yvette Tan, Tessa Wong, and Stephen McDonell, "China Congress: Xi Jinping Doubles Down on Zero-Covid as Meeting Opens," *BBC*, October 16, 2022.

20. Bloomberg, "Why China Is Sticking with Its 'Covid Zero' Strategy," *Bloomberg*, September 23, 2022.

21. Lijia Zhang, "How Will China's 'Zero-Covid' Policy Affect Public Support for the Government? It's Complicated," *South China Morning Post*, October 29, 2022.

22. Tessa Wong and Nathan Williams, "China Covid: Protests Continue in Major Cities across the Country," *BBC*, November 27, 2022.

23. Stephen McDonell, "China Covid: Xi's Face-Saving Exit from His Signature Policy," Ibid., December 5.

24. Editorial, "China's New Covid Nightmare Could Become a Global Catastrophe," *The Washington Post* (Online), December 20, 2022.

25. Thomas Mackintosh, "China Covid: Five Deaths under Country's New Counting Method," *BBC*, December 20, 2022.

26. Kathryn Armstrong, "China Covid: Who Warns About under-Representing Covid Deaths," Ibid., January 4.

27. Economist, "A Wave of Covid-19 Reveals Flaws in China's Health System," *The Economist*, December 19, 2022, https://www.economist.com/china/2022/12/19/a-wave-of-covid-19-reveals -flaws-in-chinas-health-system.

28. Kerim Can Kavakli, "Did Populist Leaders Respond to the COVID-19 Pandemic More Slowly? Evidence from a Global Sample," *Bocconi University*, 2020, https://covidcrisislab.unibocconi.eu/sites/default/files/media/attach/Kerim-Can-Kavakli.pdf.

29. Marcus Mietzner, "Populist Anti-Scientism, Religious Polarisation, and Institutionalised Corruption: How Indonesia's Democratic Decline Shaped Its COVID-19 Response," *Journal of Current Southeast Asian Affairs* 39, no. 2 (2020): 230; Laura Cervi, Fernando García, and Carles Marín-Lladó, "Populism, Twitter, and COVID-19: Narrative, Fantasies, and Desires," *Social Sciences* 10, no. 8 (2021): 15.

30. Michael Bayerlein et al., "Populism and COVID-19: How Populist Governments (Mis) Handle the Pandemic," *V-Dem Institute Working Paper* 121 (2021).

31. Ilan Alon, Matthew Farrell, and Shaomin Li, "Regime Type and COVID-19 Response," *FIIB Business Review* 9, no. 3 (2020): 157; David Stasavage, "Democracy, Autocracy, and Emergency Threats: Lessons for COVID-19 from the Last Thousand Years," *International Organization* 74, no. S1 (2020): 2.

32. Bayerlein et al., "Populism and COVID-19: How Populist Governments (Mis) Handle the Pandemic."

33. José Antonio Cheibub, Ji Yeon Jean Hong, and Adam Przeworski, "Rights and Deaths: Government Reactions to the Pandemic," *Social Science Research Network*, July 7, 2020, http://dx.doi.org/10.2139/ssrn.3645410.

34. Stasavage, "Democracy, Autocracy, and Emergency Threats: Lessons for COVID-19 from the Last Thousand Years," 6.

35. Gabriel Cepaluni, Michael Dorsch, and Semir Dzebo, *Populism, Political Regimes, and COVID-19 Deaths*, ed. Social Science Research Network (Social Science Research Network: Social Science Research Network, 2021).

36. Ibid.

37. Ibid.

38. Ibid.

39. HRW, "Nicaragua: Doctors Fired for Covid-19 Comments," *Human Rights Watch*, June 23, 2020, https://www.hrw.org/news/2020/06/23/nicaragua-doctors-fired-covid-19-comments; Mateo Jarquín and Salvador Martí i Puig, "Nicaragua: Denying the Health Crisis and the Political Crisis," in *COVID-19's Political Challenges in Latin America*, ed. Michelle Fernandez and Carlos Machado (Switzerland: Springer, 2021), 41.

40. Nectar Gan, "How Vietnam Managed to Keep Its Coronavirus Death Toll at Zero," *CNN*, May 30, 2020, https://www.cnn.com/2020/05/29/asia/coronavirus-vietnam-intl-hnk.

41. Luke Taylor, "The Venezuelan Health-Care Workers Secretly Collecting COVID Stats," *Nature*, August 25, 2021, https://www.nature.com/articles/d41586-021-02276-1.

42. Orla Guerin, "Coronavirus: How Turkey Took Control of Covid-19 Emergency," *BBC*, May 29, 2020.

43. Jean Drèze, "India Is in Denial About the COVID-19 Crisis," *Scientific American*, August 25, 2020, https://www.scientificamerican.com/article/india-is-in-denial-about-the-covid-19-crisis/.

44. Soutik Biswas, "Why India's Real Covid Toll May Never Be Known," *BBC*, May 5, 2022.

45. Ibid.

46. NYT, "As U.S. Schools Move to Reopen Despite Covid-19, Teachers Threaten to Strike," *New York Times*, August 21, 2020, https://www.nytimes.com/2020/08/19/world/covid-19-coronavirus.html.

47. Drèze, "India Is in Denial About the COVID-19 Crisis."

48. Vaishnavi Chandrashekar, "1.3 Billion People. A 21-Day Lockdown. Can India Curb the Coronavirus?" *Science.org*, March 31, 2020, https://www.science.org/content/article/13-billion-people-21-day-lockdown-can-india-curb-coronavirus; Ipchita Bharali et al., "India's Policy Response to COVID-19," *The Center for Policy Impact in Global Health*, June, 2020, http://centerforpolicyimpact.org/our-work/the-4ds/indias-policy-response-to-covid-19/.

49. Maurice Kugler and Shakti Sinha, "The Impact of COVID-19 and the Policy Response in India," *Brookings Institution*, July 13, 2020, https://www.brookings.edu/blog/future-development/2020/07/13/the-impact-of-covid-19-and-the-policy-response-in-india/.

50. Griff Witte et al., "Surge in Caseload Driven by Poorer Nations - and U.S.," *The Washington Post*, July 15, 2020, A1.

51. Karan Deep Singh, "As India's Lethal Covid Wave Neared, Politics Overrode Science," *New York Times*, September 14, 2021.

52. Lancet, "India's COVID-19 Emergency," 397, no. 10286 (2021).

53. Tomasz Zalewski, "Poland Divided over Elections and COVID Restrictions," *Atlantic Council*, May 13, 2020, https://www.atlanticcouncil.org/blogs/new-atlanticist/poland-divided-over-elections-and-covid-restrictions/; Tadeusz Jędrzejczyk and Łukasz Balwicki, "Poland Country Snapshot: Public Health Agencies and Services in the Response to COVID-19," *European Observatory on Health Systems and Policies*, March 1, 2022, https://eurohealthobservatory.who.int/news-room/articles/item/poland-country-snapshot-public-health-agencies-and-services-in-the-response-to-covid-19.

54. Martin McKee, "Learning from Success: How Has Hungary Responded to the COVID Pandemic?," *GeroScience* 42, no. 5 (2020).

55. Joanna Fomina, "Poland: How Populists Have Exploited the Coronavirus," *Carnegie Endowment for International Peace*, April 28, 2020, https://carnegieendowment.org/2020/04/28/poland-how-populists-have-exploited-coronavirus-pub-81648.

56. Márton Bene and Zsolt Boda, "Hungary: Crisis as Usual - Populist Governance and the Pandemic," in *Populism and the Politicization of the COVID-19 Crisis in Europe*, ed. Giuliano Bobba and Nicolas Hubé (Springer Nature, 2021), 91–5.

57. HRW, "Sri Lanka: Increasing Suppression of Dissent," *Human Rights Watch*, August 8, 2020, https://www.hrw.org/news/2020/08/08/sri-lanka-increasing-suppression-dissent; UN, "Bachelet Dismayed at Restrictions on Human Rights Ngos and Arrests of Activists in India," *United Nations Office of High Commissioner for Human Rights*, October 20, 2020, https://www.ohchr.org/en/press-releases/2020/10/bachelet-dismayed-restrictions-human-rights-ngos-and-arrests-activists-india?LangID=E&NewsID=26398.

58. Ahilan Kadirgamar, "Sri Lanka: Elections, Polarized Politics, and the Pandemic," *Carnegie Endowment for International Peace*, April 28, 2020, https://carnegieendowment.org/2020/04/28/sri-lanka-elections-polarized-politics-and-pandemic-pub-81649.

59. Kaya Genç, "COVID-19 in Turkey: A Nation on Edge," 397, no. 10287 (2021).

60. Soner Cagaptay and Deniz Yuksel, "Turkey's COVID-19 Response," *The Washington Institute*, June 4, 2020, https://www.washingtoninstitute.org/policy-analysis/turkeys-covid-19-response; Senem Aydin-Düzgit, "Turkey: Deepening Discord and Illiberalism Amid the Pandemic," *Carnegie Endowment for International Peace*, April 28, 2020, https://carnegieendowment.org/2020/04/28/turkey-deepening-discord-and-illiberalism-amid-pandemic-pub-81650.

61. Adam Taylor, "As Pandemic Rages, Democracy and Human Rights Are Backsliding Worldwide," *The Washington Post*, October 4, 2020, A28.

62. Alexander Baturo and Jakob Tolstrup, "Personalism and Personalist Regimes: Theory and Comparative Perspective," *European Consortium for Political Research*, 2020, https://ecpr.eu/Events/Event/PanelDetails/7660.

63. Charles Maynes, "Belarus Leader Says He Survived Coronavirus," *VOA News*, July 29, 2020, https://www.voanews.com/a/covid-19-pandemic_belarus-leader-says-he-survived-coronavirus/6193613.html.

64. Emma Willoughby, "An Ideal Public Health Model? Vietnam's State-Led, Preventative, Low-Cost Response to COVID-19," *Brookings Institution*, June 29, 2021, https://www.brookings.edu/blog/order-from-chaos/2021/06/29/an-ideal-public-health-model-vietnams-state-led-preventative-low-cost-response-to-covid-19/#:~:text=The%20world%20noticed%20Vietnam's%20success,effort%20to%20stop%20the%20virus.

65. Luu Duc Toan Huynh, "What Vietnam's Localized Lockdown Policy Showed: It Did Not Work and Was Too Late," *Policy Debates* 57, no. 9 (2022): 1882–92.

66. UNDP, "Human Development Insights," *Human Development Reports*, https://hdr.undp.org/data-center/country-insights#/ranks.

67. Jarquín and Martí i Puig, "Nicaragua: Denying the Health Crisis and the Political Crisis," 37–9.

68. Amnesty, "Guatemala's Health Workers Are Endangered by COVID-19, but Also by Their Government," *Amnesty International*, July 3, 2020, https://www.amnesty.org/en/latest/news/2020/07/trabajadoras-salud-guatemala-corren-peligro-covid19/.

69. Eve Warburton, "Indonesia: Polarization, Democratic Distress, and the Coronavirus," *Carnegie Endowment for International Peace*, April 28, 2020, https://carnegieendowment.org/2020/04/28/indonesia-polarization-democratic-distress-and-coronavirus-pub-81641.

70. Mietzner, "Populist Anti-Scientism, Religious Polarisation, and Institutionalised Corruption: How Indonesia's Democratic Decline Shaped Its COVID-19 Response," 227, 31.

71. Ibid., 232.

72. Joshua Kurlantzick, "How Jokowi Failed the Test of COVID-19 in Indonesia," *World Politics Review*, June 9, 2020, https://www.worldpoliticsreview.com/amid-lackluster-response-by-jokowi-indonesia-reels-from-covid-19/.

73. Marzieh Nojomi, Maziar Moradi-Lakeh, and Farshad Pourmalek, "COVID-19 in Iran: What Was Done and What Should Be Done," *Medical journal of the Islamic Republic of Iran* 35, no. 97 (2021).

74. Hofstede, "Compare Countries," *Hofstede Insights*, https://www.hofstede-insights.com/fi/product/compare-countries/.

75. Huang, "The SARS Epidemic and Its Aftermath in China: A Political Perspective"; Guoxin Xing, "Hu Jintao's Political Thinking and Legitimacy Building: A Post-Marxist Perspective," *Asian Affairs: An American Review* 36, no. 4 (2009): 213–26; WHO, "SARS: How a Global Epidemic Was Stopped," *World Health Organization Regional Office for the Western Pacific*, 2006, https://iris.who.int/handle/10665/207501.

76. "Summary of Probable SARS Cases with Onset of Illness from 1 November 2002 to 31 July 2003," *World Health Organization*, July 24, 2015, https://www.who.int/publications/m/item/summary-of-probable-sars-cases-with-onset-of-illness-from-1-november-2002-to-31-july-2003.

77. Lisa Gorman and Christopher Stoney, "Missed Opportunities: Public Health Disaster Management in Canada," *Journal of Public Management & Social Policy* 22, no. 2 (2015): 12.

78. Economist, "Omicron Comes to Mexico, a Place That Never Really Shut Down," *The Economist*, January 22, 2022, https://www.economist.com/the-americas/2022/01/22/omicron-comes-to-mexico-a-place-that-never-really-shut-down.

79. Bruna Cavalcanti, "Mexico in the Face of Covid-19: In-between Actions and Inefficiency," in *COVID-19's Political Challenges in Latin America*, ed. Michelle Fernandez and Carlos Machado (Switzerland: Springer, 2021); Sandra Weiss, "Mexico 'Flying Blind' in Pandemic Response," *Deutsche Welle*, August 18, 2020, https://www.dw.com/en/mexico-coronavirus-cases-update/a-54615046; André Borges and Lucio Rennó, "Brazilian Response to Covid-19: Polarization and Conflict," in *COVID-19's Political Challenges in Latin America*, ed. Michelle Fernandez and Carlos Machado (Switzerland: Springer, 2021).

80. Cavalcanti, "Mexico in the Face of Covid-19: In-between Actions and Inefficiency"; Borges and Rennó, "Brazilian Response to Covid-19: Polarization and Conflict."

81. Huong Le Thu, "Delta Variant Outbreak Challenges Vietnam's COVID-19 Response Strategy," *Brookings Institution*, August 11, 2021, https://www.brookings.edu/blog/order-from-chaos/2021/08/11/delta-variant-outbreak-challenges-vietnams-covid-19-response-strategy/.

82. Zalewski, "Poland Divided over Elections and COVID Restrictions"; Jędrzejczyk and Balwicki, "Poland Country Snapshot: Public Health Agencies and Services in the Response to COVID-19."

83. Márton Jász, "Pandemic Started Exactly One Year Ago in Hungary," *Hungary Today*, April 3, 2021, https://hungarytoday.hu/pandemic-started-exactly-one-year-ago-in-hungary/.

84. Joshua Mitnick, "Israel's Cautionary Coronavirus Tale," *Foreign Policy*, July 22, 2020, https://foreignpolicy.com/2020/07/22/israel-coronavirus-second-wave-netanyahu/.

85.   David Nakamura and Ashley Parker, "'It Totally Belittled the Moment': Many Look Back in Dismay at Trump's Tossing of Paper Towels in Puerto Rico," *The Washington Post*, 13 September, 2018.

86.   Eva Bertrand, "Constructing Russian Power by Communicating During Disasters: The Forest Fires of 2010," *Problems of Post-Communism* 59, no. 3 (2012): 32–4, 37–8.

87.   "Disaster, Communication and Legitimization of Power in Russia: The Case of the Forest Fires in Summer 2010," *The Soviet and Post-Soviet Review* 40 (2013): 266–9, 77.

88.   Egor Lazarev et al., "Trial by Fire: A Natural Disaster's Impact on Support for the Authorities in Rural Russia," *World Politics* 66, no. 4 (2014): 649, 61.

89.   Kang, *Disaster Management in China in a Changing Era*, 38.

90.   Katsujikoon Nakazawa, "China Portrays 'Xi the Great,' Tamer of Floods," *Nikkei Asia*, August 27, 2020.

91.   David Bandurski, "As Disaster Strikes, Xi Takes the Headlines," *China Media Project*, July 21, 2021, https://chinamediaproject.org/2021/07/21/as-disaster-strikes-xi-takes-the-headlines/.

92.   Xinhua, "Xi Stresses Prioritizing People's Safety, Property in Flood Prevention, Control," *Xinhua General News Service*, July 21, 2021.

93.   Yaqiu Wang, "China's Covid Success Story Is Also a Human Rights Tragedy," *Human Rights Watch*, January 26, 2021, https://www.hrw.org/news/2021/01/26/chinas-covid-success-story-also-human-rights-tragedy.

Bibliography

Abelson, Jenn, Dana Priest, John Sullivan, and Nicole Dungca. "Boom-and-Bust Pandemic Funding Hurt Preparedness." *The Washington Post*, May 3, 2020, A1.

Abutaleb, Yasmeen, and Josh Dawsey. "HHS Official Apologizes for Accusing Scientists of 'Sedition'." *The Washington Post*, September 16, 2020, A11.

———. "Trump's Praise of Xi Alarms Advisers." *The Washington Post*, February 17, 2020, A1.

Abutaleb, Yasmeen, Josh Dawsey, and Laurie McGinley. "White House Sidelines an Increasingly Candid Fauci." *The Washington Post*, July 12, 2020, A1.

Abutaleb, Yasmeen, Josh Dawsey, Ellen Nakashima, and Greg Miller. "70 Days of Denial, Delays and Dysfunction." *The Washington Post*, April 5, 2020, A1.

Abutaleb, Yasmeen, Laurie McGinley, and Carolyn Y. Johnson. "Disparaged by Trump, Scientists Deliver." *The Washington Post*, December 15, 2020, A1.

Abutaleb, Yasmeen, Ashley Parker, Josh Dawsey, and Philip Rucker. "How Trump's Pandemic Missteps Led to a Dark Winter." *The Washington Post*, December 20, 2020, A1.

Abutaleb, Yasmeen, Philip Rucker, Josh Dawsey, and Robert Costa. "Distrust, Lethargy Worsening within Virus Task Force." *The Washington Post*, October 20, 2020, A1.

Abutaleb, Yasmeen, Taylor Telford, and Josh Dawsey. "Experts Upset by Trump's Virus Testing Comments." *The Washington Post*, June 22, 2020, A1.

Abutaleb, Yasmeen, and Rachel Weiner. "Experts Wary of Early Reopenings as Federal Distancing Rules End." *The Washington Post*, May 1, 2020, A4.

Abutaleb, Yasmeen, and Erica Werner. "HHS Tells Congress It May Need $136 Million More." *The Washington Post*, February 4, 2020, A15.

Achenbach, Joel, Karin Brulliard, Brittany Shammas, and Jacqueline Dupree. "Hospitals Nationwide See Flood of Patients." *The Washington Post*, October 27, 2020, A1.

Achenbach, Joel, Brittany Shammas, and Jacqueline Dupree. "As Cases Spike, Death Toll Inches Up." *The Washington Post*, October 31, 2020.

Achenbach, Joel, William Wan, Karin Brulliard, and C. Janes. "Pandemic Exposes America's Flaws and Fissures." *The Washington Post*, July 20, 2020, A1.

Achenbach, Joel, Rachel Weiner, Karin Brulliard, and Isaac Stanley-Becker. "As Hot Spots Erupt, Researchers Warn of 2nd Wave in South." *The Washington Post*, May 21, 2020.

Achenbach, Joel, Rachel Weiner, and C. Janes. "Experts Push for New Tack on Virus." *The Washington Post*, August 2, 2020, A1.

AFP. "As World Cowers, China Glimpses Coronavirus Aftermath." *Agence France Presse - English*, March 18, 2020.

———. "China Censored Virus News for Weeks, Say Researchers." *Agence France Presse - English*, March 3, 2020.

———. "China Charges Xi Critic with 'Subversion', Say Activists." *Agence France Presse - English*, March 9, 2020.

———. "China Expels US Journalists in Biggest Crackdown in Years." *Agence France Presse - English*, March 17, 2020.

———. "China Exports Plunge on Coronavirus Epidemic." *Agence France Presse - English*, March 7, 2020.

———. "China Inflation Slips but Stays High on Virus, Food Worries." *Agence France Presse - English*, March 10, 2020.

———. "China Leadership Admits 'Shortcomings' in Virus Response." *Agence France Presse - English*, February 3, 2020.

———. "China Ordered to Slash State Media Staff in US." *Agence France Presse - English*, March 2, 2020.

———. "China President Makes Rare Visit to Meet Virus Workers, Patients." *Agence France Presse - English*, February 10, 2020.

———. "China Reports 27 New Virus Deaths, Lowest Rise in Cases since January." *Agence France Presse - English*, March 8, 2020.

———. "China Reports Rise in Imported Virus Cases." *Agence France Presse - English*, March 3, 2020.

———. "China Seeks to Recast Itself from Virus Pariah to Helping Hand." *Agence France Presse - English*, March 5, 2020.

———. "China Stutters Back to Work as Virus Deaths Soar." *Agence France Presse - English*, February 10, 2020.

———. "China Threatens Retaliation over US 'Bullying' of State Media." *Agence France Presse - English*, March 3, 2020.

———. "China to Cut Banks' Reserve Requirement to Combat Virus Fallout." *Agence France Presse - English*, March 13, 2020.

———. "China's Xi Pays First Visit to Virus Epicentre Wuhan." *Agence France Presse - English*, March 10, 2020.

———. "Death of Whistleblower Ignites Calls for Political Reform in China." *Agence France Presse - English*, February 9, 2020.

———. "How China Turned the Tide on the Coronavirus." *Agence France Presse - English*, March 13, 2020.

———. "'I Can Never Be Happy Again': Grieving Wuhan Families Say China Is Blocking Coronavirus Lawsuits." *Agence France Presse - English*, September 17, 2020.

———. "Italy Locks Down as China Signals Major Progress in Own Virus Fight." *Agence France Presse - English*, March 10, 2020.

———. "New Normal in Virus-Hit China: High-Tech Tracking and Fever Checks." *Agence France Presse - English*, March 4, 2020.

———. "People at Centre of China's Virus Outbreak Say Time to End Lockdown." *Agence France Presse - English*, March 8, 2020.

Ahlbom, Tove, and Marina Povitkina. "'Gimme Shelter': The Role of Democracy and Institutional Quality in Disaster Preparedness." *V-Dem Institute Working Paper* 35 (August 2016).

Akimov, Valery, and Boris Porfiriev. "The Institutional Framework and Governance Model of Russia's Crisis Policy: Disaster Focus." In *Crises in Russia : Contemporary Management Policy and Practice from a Historical Perspective*, edited by Boris Porfiriev and Greg Simons, 63–80. Burlington: Ashgate, 2012.

Aldrich, Daniel P., and Kevin Crook. "Strong Civil Society as a Double-Edged Sword." *Political Research Quarterly* 61, no. 3 (September 2008): 379–89.

Alemany, Jacqueline. "Leading Health Experts Call for Greater Precautions." *The Washington Post*, November 20, 2020, A3.

Alon, Ilan, Matthew Farrell, and Shaomin Li. "Regime Type and COVID-19 Response." *FIIB Business Review* 9, no. 3 (2020): 152–60.

Amnesty. "Guatemala's Health Workers Are Endangered by COVID-19, but Also by Their Government." Amnesty International, July 3, 2020, https://www.amnesty.org/en/latest/news/2020/07/trabajadoras-salud-guatemala-corren-peligro-covid19/.

Aratani, Lori. "With Few Hygiene Rules in Place, Airlines, Airports Adopt Their Own." *The Washington Post*, June 28, 2020, A21.

Aratani, Lori, and Lena H. Sun. "U.S. Screenings for Pathogen Expanded to Atlanta and Chicago Gateways." *The Washington Post*, January 23, 2020, A14.

Aristophanes. *The Knights, the Complete Greek Drama*. New York: Random House, 1938.

Armstrong, Kathryn. "China Covid: Who Warns About under-Representing Covid Deaths." *BBC*, January 4, 2022.

Aron, Leon. "Yeltsin Russia's Rogue Populist." *The Washington Post*, June 3, 1990.

Aschwanden, Christie. "The False Promise of Herd Immunity for COVID-19." *Nature* 587, no. 7832 (October 21 2020): 26–28.

Ashworth, Scott. "Electoral Accountability: Recent Theoretical and Empirical Work." *Annual Review of Political Science* 15 (2012): 183–201.

Avelino, George, David S. Brown, and Wendy Hunter. "The Effects of Capital Mobility, Trade Openness, and Democracy on Social Spending Inlatin America, 1980–1999." *American Journal of Political Science* 49, no. 3 (July 2005): 625–41.

Awad, Atif, and Ishak Yussof. "Democracy and Human Development Nexus: The African Experience." *Journal of Economic Cooperation and Development* 37, no. 2 (2016): 1–34.

Aydin-Düzgit, Senem. "Turkey: Deepening Discord and Illiberalism Amid the Pandemic." Carnegie Endowment for International Peace, April 28, 2020, https://carnegieendowment.org/2020/04/28/turkey-deepening-discord-and-illiberalism-amid-pandemic-pub-81650.

Azar, Alex M. II. "We Have to Reopen - for Health Reasons." *The Washington Post*, May 22, 2020, A21.

Babones, Salvatore. "Xi Jinping: Communist China's First Populist President." Forbes, October 20, 2017, https://www.forbes.com/sites/salvatorebabones/2017/10/20/populism-chinese-style-xi-jinping-cements-his-status-as-chinas-first-populist-president/?sh=520241c2152e.

Balingit, Moriah. "Even Where Trump Is Popular, Some School Leaders Reject Push to Reopen Classrooms." *The Washington Post*, July 26, 2020, A4.

———. "School Leaders Face Closures Again as Cases Rise." *The Washington Post*, November 22, 2020.

Bandurski, David. "As Disaster Strikes, Xi Takes the Headlines." China Media Project, July 21, 2021, https://chinamediaproject.org/2021/07/21/as-disaster-strikes-xi-takes-the-headlines/.

Bang, Henrik, and David Marsh. "Populism: A Major Threat to Democracy?" *Policy Studies* 39, no. 3 (2018): 352–63.

Barnes, Robert. "Latest COVID Surge Is Breaking Records." *The Washington Post*, November 9, 2020, A2.

———. "Supreme Court Sides with California Church Protesting Virus Restrictions." *The Washington Post*, December 4, 2020, A11.

Barnes, Robert, and Derek Hawkins. "Rush to Reopen Caused Case Spikes, Officials Say." *The Washington Post*, July 6, 2020, A2.

Baturo, Alexander, and Jakob Tolstrup. "Personalism and Personalist Regimes: Theory and Comparative Perspective." European Consortium for Political Research, 2020, https://ecpr.eu/Events/Event/PanelDetails/7660.

Bayerlein, Michael, Vanessa Alexandra Boese, Scott Gates, Katrin Kamin, and Syed Mansoob Murshed. "Populism and COVID-19: How Populist Governments (Mis) Handle the Pandemic." *V-Dem Institute Working Paper* 121 (2021).

BBC. "BBCM Russia Watchlist for 11 March." *BBC Monitoring Former Soviet Union - Political Supplied by BBC Worldwide Monitoring*, March 11, 2020.

————. "BBCM Russia Watchlist for 23 March." *BBC Monitoring Former Soviet Union - Political Supplied by BBC Worldwide Monitoring*, March 23, 2020.

————. "China Discouraging Marriage, Funeral Gatherings Amid Outbreak." *BBC Monitoring Asia Pacific - Political Supplied by BBC Worldwide Monitoring*, January 31, 2020.

————. "China Experts Identify 'New Coronavirus' in Pneumonia Outbreak." *BBC Monitoring Asia Pacific*, January 9, 2020.

————. "Chinese Media Criticise Wuhan Handling of Virus Outbreak." *BBC Worldwide Monitoring*, January 23, 2020.

————. "Chinese Media Deny Cover up, Rumours on Coronavirus Outbreak." *BBC Monitoring Asia Pacific - Political Supplied by BBC Worldwide Monitoring*, January 21, 2020.

————. "Coronavirus in Russia: 10 April 2020." *BBC Monitoring Former Soviet Union - Political Supplied by BBC Worldwide Monitoring*, April 10, 2020.

————. "Coronavirus in Russia: 11 April 2020." *BBC Monitoring Former Soviet Union - Political Supplied by BBC Worldwide Monitoring*, April 11, 2020.

————. "Coronavirus in Russia: 11 March 2020." *BBC Monitoring Former Soviet Union - Political Supplied by BBC Worldwide Monitoring*, March 11, 2020.

————. "Coronavirus in Russia: 13 April 2020." *BBC Monitoring Former Soviet Union - Political Supplied by BBC Worldwide Monitoring*, April 13, 2020.

————. "Coronavirus in Russia: 14 April 2020." *BBC Monitoring Former Soviet Union - Political Supplied by BBC Worldwide Monitoring*, April 14, 2020.

————. "Coronavirus in Russia: 15 April 2020." *BBC Monitoring Former Soviet Union - Political Supplied by BBC Worldwide Monitoring*, April 15, 2020.

————. "Coronavirus in Russia: 16 April 2020." *BBC Monitoring Former Soviet Union - Political Supplied by BBC Worldwide Monitoring*, April 16, 2020.

————. "Coronavirus in Russia: 20 April 2020." *BBC Monitoring Former Soviet Union - Political Supplied by BBC Worldwide Monitoring*, April 20, 2020.

————. "Coronavirus in Russia: 23 March 2020." *BBC Monitoring Former Soviet Union - Political Supplied by BBC Worldwide Monitoring*, March 23, 2020.

————. "Coronavirus in Russia: 3 April 2020." *BBC Monitoring Former Soviet Union - Political Supplied by BBC Worldwide Monitoring*, April 3, 2020.

————. "Coronavirus in Russia: 30 March 2020." *BBC Monitoring Former Soviet Union - Political Supplied by BBC Worldwide Monitoring*, March 30, 2020.

————. "Coronavirus in Russia: 5 March 2020." *BBC Monitoring Former Soviet Union - Political Supplied by BBC Worldwide Monitoring*, March 5, 2020.

————. "Coronavirus in Russia: 7 April 2020." *BBC Monitoring Former Soviet Union - Political Supplied by BBC Worldwide Monitoring*, April 7, 2020.

————. "Coronavirus in Russia: 7 February 20." *BBC Monitoring Former Soviet Union - Political Supplied by BBC Worldwide Monitoring*, February 7, 2020.

————. "Covid-19 Politics: Putin Says Russia May Survive Crisis with 'Minimal Loses'." *BBC Monitoring Former Soviet Union - Political Supplied by BBC Worldwide Monitoring*, April 7, 2020.

————. "Covid-19 Response: Russia Sends Emergency Virus Support to Dagestan." *BBC Monitoring Former Soviet Union - Political Supplied by BBC Worldwide Monitoring*, May 19, 2020.

————. "Covid-19 Response: Russia's Regions Tighten Restrictions Amid New Spike." *BBC Monitoring Former Soviet Union - Political Supplied by BBC Worldwide Monitoring*, October 9, 2020.

————. "Covid-19 Responses: Putin Discusses 'Epidemiological Situation' in Russia." *BBC Monitoring Former Soviet Union - Political Supplied by BBC Worldwide Monitoring*, April 21, 2020.

————. "Covid-19 Responses: Russia Advises over 60s to Avoid Public Spaces." *BBC Monitoring Former Soviet Union - Political Supplied by BBC Worldwide Monitoring*, September 28, 2020.

————. "Covid-19 Responses: Russia Minister Admits 'Big Deficit' of Protective Suits." *BBC Monitoring Former Soviet Union - Political Supplied by BBC Worldwide Monitoring*, April 7, 2020.

———. "Covid-19 Roundup: Russia 24 April 2020." *BBC Monitoring Former Soviet Union - Political Supplied by BBC Worldwide Monitoring*, April 24, 2020.
———. "Covid-19 Roundup: Russia 26 April 2020." *BBC Monitoring Former Soviet Union - Political Supplied by BBC Worldwide Monitoring*, April 26, 2020.
———. "Covid-19 Roundup: Russia 27 April 2020." *BBC Monitoring Former Soviet Union - Political Supplied by BBC Worldwide Monitoring*, April 27, 2020.
———. "Covid-19 Roundup: Russia 28 April 2020." *BBC Monitoring Former Soviet Union - Political Supplied by BBC Worldwide Monitoring*, April 28, 2020.
———. "Covid-19 Roundup: Russia 29 April 2020." *BBC Monitoring Former Soviet Union - Political Supplied by BBC Worldwide Monitoring*, April 29, 2020.
———. "Covid-19 Roundup: Russia 30 April 2020." *BBC Monitoring Former Soviet Union - Political Supplied by BBC Worldwide Monitoring*, April 30, 2020.
———. "Covid-19 Roundup: Russia 1 May 2020." *BBC Monitoring Former Soviet Union - Political Supplied by BBC Worldwide Monitoring*, May 1, 2020.
———. "Covid-19 Roundup: Russia 4 May 2020." *BBC Monitoring Former Soviet Union - Political Supplied by BBC Worldwide Monitoring*, May 4, 2020.
———. "Covid-19 Roundup: Russia 6 May 2020." *BBC Monitoring Former Soviet Union - Political Supplied by BBC Worldwide Monitoring*, May 6, 2020.
———. "Covid-19 Roundup: Russia 8 May 2020." *BBC Monitoring Former Soviet Union - Political Supplied by BBC Worldwide Monitoring*, May 8, 2020.
———. "Covid-19 Roundup: Russia 10 May 2020." *BBC Monitoring Former Soviet Union - Political Supplied by BBC Worldwide Monitoring*, May 10, 2020.
———. "Covid-19 Roundup: Russia 13 May 2020." *BBC Monitoring Former Soviet Union - Political Supplied by BBC Worldwide Monitoring*, May 13, 2020.
———. "Covid-19 Roundup: Russia 16 May 2020." *BBC Monitoring Former Soviet Union - Political Supplied by BBC Worldwide Monitoring*, May 16, 2020.
———. "Covid-19 Roundup: Russia 19 May 2020." *BBC Monitoring Former Soviet Union - Political Supplied by BBC Worldwide Monitoring*, May 19, 2020.
———. "Covid-19 Roundup: Russia 21 May 2020." *BBC Monitoring Former Soviet Union - Political Supplied by BBC Worldwide Monitoring*, May 21, 2020.
———. "Covid-19 Roundup: Russia 22 May 2020." *BBC Monitoring Former Soviet Union - Political Supplied by BBC Worldwide Monitoring*, May 22, 2020.
———. "Covid-19 Roundup: Russia 23 May 2020." *BBC Monitoring Former Soviet Union - Political Supplied by BBC Worldwide Monitoring*, May 23, 2020.
———. "Covid-19 Roundup: Russia 27 May 2020." *BBC Monitoring Former Soviet Union - Political Supplied by BBC Worldwide Monitoring*, May 27, 2020.
———. "Covid-19 Roundup: Russia 28 May 2020." *BBC Monitoring Former Soviet Union - Political Supplied by BBC Worldwide Monitoring*, May 28, 2020.
———. "Covid-19 Roundup: Russia 1 June 2020." *BBC Monitoring Former Soviet Union - Political Supplied by BBC Worldwide Monitoring*, June 1, 2020.
———. "Covid-19 Roundup: Russia 4 June 2020." *BBC Monitoring Former Soviet Union - Political Supplied by BBC Worldwide Monitoring*, June 4, 2020.
———. "Covid-19 Roundup: Russia 10 June 2020." *BBC Monitoring Former Soviet Union - Political Supplied by BBC Worldwide Monitoring*, June 10, 2020.
———. "Covid-19 Roundup: Russia 11 June 2020." *BBC Monitoring Former Soviet Union - Political Supplied by BBC Worldwide Monitoring*, June 11, 2020.
———. "Covid-19 Roundup: Russia 12 June 2020." *BBC Monitoring Former Soviet Union - Political Supplied by BBC Worldwide Monitoring*, June 12, 2020.
———. "Covid-19 Roundup: Russia 15 June 2020." *BBC Monitoring Former Soviet Union - Political Supplied by BBC Worldwide Monitoring*, June 15, 2020

———. "Covid-19 Roundup: Russia 17 June 2020." *BBC Monitoring Former Soviet Union - Political Supplied by BBC Worldwide Monitoring*, June 17, 2020.

———. "Covid-19 Roundup: Russia 18 June." *BBC Monitoring Former Soviet Union - Political Supplied by BBC Worldwide Monitoring*, June 18, 2020.

———. "Covid-19 Roundup: Russia 19 June." *BBC Monitoring Former Soviet Union - Political Supplied by BBC Worldwide Monitoring*, June 19, 2020.

———. "Covid-19 Roundup: Russia 20 June 2020." *BBC Monitoring Former Soviet Union - Political Supplied by BBC Worldwide Monitoring*, June 20, 2020.

———. "Covid-19 Roundup: Russia 26 June." *BBC Monitoring Former Soviet Union - Political Supplied by BBC Worldwide Monitoring*, June 26, 2020.

———. "Covid-19 Roundup: Russia 28 June 2020." *BBC Monitoring Former Soviet Union - Political Supplied by BBC Worldwide Monitoring*, June 28, 2020.

———. "Covid-19 Roundup: Russia 4 July 2020." *BBC Monitoring Former Soviet Union - Political Supplied by BBC Worldwide Monitoring*, July 4, 2020.

———. "Covid-19 Roundup: Russia 7 July 2020." *BBC Monitoring Former Soviet Union - Political Supplied by BBC Worldwide Monitoring*, July 7, 2020.

———. "Covid-19 Roundup: Russia 9 July 2020." *BBC Monitoring Former Soviet Union - Political Supplied by BBC Worldwide Monitoring*, July 9, 2020.

———. "Covid-19 Roundup: Russia 10 July 2020." *BBC Monitoring Former Soviet Union - Political Supplied by BBC Worldwide Monitoring*, July 10, 2020.

———. "Covid-19 Roundup: Russia 20 July 2020." *BBC Monitoring Former Soviet Union - Political Supplied by BBC Worldwide Monitoring*, July 20, 2020.

———. "Covid-19 Roundup: Russia 8 August 2020." *BBC Monitoring Former Soviet Union - Political Supplied by BBC Worldwide Monitoring*, August 8, 2020.

———. "Covid-19 Roundup: Russia 11 August 2020." *BBC Monitoring Former Soviet Union - Political Supplied by BBC Worldwide Monitoring*, August 11, 2020.

———. "Covid-19 Roundup: Russia 14 August 2020." *BBC Monitoring Former Soviet Union - Political Supplied by BBC Worldwide Monitoring*, August 14, 2020.

———. "Covid-19 Roundup: Russia 27 August 2020." *BBC Monitoring Former Soviet Union - Political Supplied by BBC Worldwide Monitoring*, August 27, 2020.

———. "Covid-19 Roundup: Russia 5 September." *BBC Monitoring Former Soviet Union - Political Supplied by BBC Worldwide Monitoring*, September 5, 2020.

———. "Covid-19 Roundup: Russia 10 September 2020." *BBC Monitoring Former Soviet Union - Political Supplied by BBC Worldwide Monitoring*, September 10, 2020.

———. "Covid-19 Roundup: Russia 22 September 2020." *BBC Monitoring Former Soviet Union - Political Supplied by BBC Worldwide Monitoring*, September 22, 2020.

———. "Covid-19 Roundup: Russia 1 October 2020." *BBC Monitoring Former Soviet Union - Political Supplied by BBC Worldwide Monitoring*, October 1, 2020.

———. "Covid-19 Roundup: Russia 2 October 2020." *BBC Monitoring Former Soviet Union - Political Supplied by BBC Worldwide Monitoring*, October 2, 2020.

———. "Covid-19 Roundup: Russia 7 October 2020." *BBC Monitoring Former Soviet Union - Political Supplied by BBC Worldwide Monitoring*, October 7, 2020.

———. "Covid-19 Roundup: Russia 10 October 2020." *BBC Monitoring Former Soviet Union - Political Supplied by BBC Worldwide Monitoring*, October 10, 2020.

———. "Covid-19 Roundup: Russia 15 October 2020." *BBC Monitoring Former Soviet Union - Political Supplied by BBC Worldwide Monitoring*, October 15, 2020.

———. "Covid-19 Roundup: Russia 17 October 2020." *BBC Monitoring Former Soviet Union - Political Supplied by BBC Worldwide Monitoring*, October 17, 2020.

———. "Covid-19 Roundup: Russia 19 October 2020." *BBC Monitoring Former Soviet Union - Political Supplied by BBC Worldwide Monitoring*, October 19, 2020.

———. "Covid-19 Roundup: Russia 21 October 2020." *BBC Monitoring Former Soviet Union - Political Supplied by BBC Worldwide Monitoring,* October 21, 2020.

———. "Covid-19 Roundup: Russia 27 October 2020." *BBC Monitoring Former Soviet Union - Political Supplied by BBC Worldwide Monitoring,* October 27, 2020.

———. "Covid-19 Roundup: Russia 29 October 2020." *BBC Monitoring Former Soviet Union - Political Supplied by BBC Worldwide Monitoring,* October 29, 2020.

———. "Covid-19 Roundup: Russia 31 October 2020." *BBC Monitoring Former Soviet Union - Political Supplied by BBC Worldwide Monitoring,* October 31, 2020.

———. "Covid-19 Roundup: Russia 2 November 2020." *BBC Monitoring Former Soviet Union - Political Supplied by BBC Worldwide Monitoring,* November 2, 2020.

———. "Covid-19 Roundup: Russia 5 November 2020." *BBC Monitoring Former Soviet Union - Political Supplied by BBC Worldwide Monitoring,* November 5, 2020.

———. "Covid-19 Roundup: Russia 6 November 2020." *BBC Monitoring Former Soviet Union - Political Supplied by BBC Worldwide Monitoring,* November 6, 2020.

———. "Covid-19 Roundup: Russia 7 November 2020." *BBC Monitoring Former Soviet Union - Political Supplied by BBC Worldwide Monitoring,* November 7, 2020.

———. "Covid-19 Roundup: Russia 8 November 2020." *BBC Monitoring Former Soviet Union - Political Supplied by BBC Worldwide Monitoring,* November 8, 2020.

———. "Covid-19 Roundup: Russia 9 November 2020." *BBC Monitoring Former Soviet Union - Political Supplied by BBC Worldwide Monitoring,* November 9, 2020.

———. "Covid-19 Roundup: Russia 10 November 2020." *BBC Monitoring Former Soviet Union - Political Supplied by BBC Worldwide Monitoring,* November 10, 2020.

———. "Covid-19 Roundup: Russia 12 November 2020." *BBC Monitoring Former Soviet Union - Political Supplied by BBC Worldwide Monitoring,* November 12, 2020.

———. "Covid-19 Roundup: Russia 13 November 2020." *BBC Monitoring Former Soviet Union - Political Supplied by BBC Worldwide Monitoring,* November 13, 2020.

———. "Covid-19 Roundup: Russia 20 November 2020." *BBC Monitoring Former Soviet Union - Political Supplied by BBC Worldwide Monitoring,* November 20, 2020.

———. "Covid-19 Roundup: Russia 6 December 2020." *BBC Monitoring Former Soviet Union - Political Supplied by BBC Worldwide Monitoring,* December 6, 2020.

———. "Covid-19 Roundup: Russia 8 December 2020." *BBC Monitoring Former Soviet Union - Political Supplied by BBC Worldwide Monitoring,* December 8, 2020.

———. "Covid-19 Roundup: Russia 11 December 2020." *BBC Monitoring Former Soviet Union - Political Supplied by BBC Worldwide Monitoring,* December 11, 2020.

———. "Covid-19 Roundup: Russia 17 December 2020." *BBC Monitoring Former Soviet Union - Political Supplied by BBC Worldwide Monitoring,* December 17, 2020.

———. "Covid-19 Roundup: Russia 19 December 2020." *BBC Monitoring Former Soviet Union - Political Supplied by BBC Worldwide Monitoring,* December 19, 2020.

———. "Covid-19 Roundup: Russia 22 December 2020." *BBC Monitoring Former Soviet Union - Political Supplied by BBC Worldwide Monitoring,* December 22, 2020.

———. "Covid-19 Roundup: Russia 24 December 2020." *BBC Monitoring Former Soviet Union - Political Supplied by BBC Worldwide Monitoring,* December 24, 2020.

———. "Covid-19 Roundup: Russia 25 December 2020." *BBC Monitoring Former Soviet Union - Political Supplied by BBC Worldwide Monitoring,* December 25, 2020.

———. "Covid-19 Roundup: Russia 26 December 2020." *BBC Monitoring Former Soviet Union - Political Supplied by BBC Worldwide Monitoring,* December 26, 2020.

———. "Covid-19 Roundup: Russia 29 December 2020." *BBC Monitoring Former Soviet Union - Political Supplied by BBC Worldwide Monitoring,* December 29, 2020.

———. "Covid-19 Security: Russia to Vaccinate over 400,000 Soldiers." *BBC Monitoring Former Soviet Union - Political Supplied by BBC Worldwide Monitoring,* November 27, 2020.

———. "Kremlin Says Covid-19 Situation Better in Russia Than Other States." *BBC Monitoring Former Soviet Union - Political Supplied by BBC Worldwide Monitoring*, March 10, 2020.

———. "Navalny Questions Official Line on Coronavirus in Russia." *BBC Monitoring Former Soviet Union - Political Supplied by BBC Worldwide Monitoring*, March 13, 2020.

———. "PM Says Russia Should Replicate Moscow's Virus Measures." *BBC Monitoring Former Soviet Union - Political Supplied by BBC Worldwide Monitoring*, March 27, 2020.

———. "Pro-Kremlin TV Talk Show Praises Russia's Covid-19 Response." *BBC Monitoring Former Soviet Union - Political Supplied by BBC Worldwide Monitoring*, March 25, 2020.

———. "Putin Says Coronavirus Outbreak in Russia 'Getting Worse'." *BBC Monitoring Former Soviet Union - Political Supplied by BBC Worldwide Monitoring*, April 1, 2020.

———. "Russia Allocates 420m Dollars to Regional Hospitals." *BBC Monitoring Former Soviet Union - Political Supplied by BBC Worldwide Monitoring*, March 30, 2020.

———. "Russia Region Accused of Grossly Underreporting Covid Deaths." *BBC Monitoring Former Soviet Union - Political Supplied by BBC Worldwide Monitoring*, November 18, 2020.

———. "Russia Restricts Flights to China Amid Coronavirus Outbreak." *Political Supplied by BBC Worldwide*, January 31, 2020.

———. "Russia to Lose 38bn Dollars Because of Oil Price Slump - Minister." *BBC Monitoring Former Soviet Union - Political Supplied by BBC Worldwide Monitoring*, March 23, 2020.

———. "Russia: Dagestan Head Says Covid-19 Situation 'under Control'." *BBC Monitoring Former Soviet Union - Political Supplied by BBC Worldwide Monitoring*, May 28, 2020.

———. "Russia: Dagestan Media Highlights 7–13 December 20." *BBC Monitoring Former Soviet Union - Political Supplied by BBC Worldwide Monitoring*, December 23, 2020.

———. "Russia: Dagestan Media Highlights 8–14 Jun 20." *BBC Monitoring Former Soviet Union - Political Supplied by BBC Worldwide Monitoring*, July 7, 2020.

———. "Russia's Covid-19 Statistics Questioned." *BBC Monitoring Former Soviet Union - Political Supplied by BBC Worldwide Monitoring*, May 27, 2020.

———. "Russia's Excess Deaths 'Five Times Higher' Than Official Covid Death Toll." *BBC Monitoring Former Soviet Union - Political Supplied by BBC Worldwide Monitoring*, November 23, 2020.

———. "Russia-Backed Crimea Leader Briefs Putin on Coronavirus Measures." *BBC Monitoring Former Soviet Union - Political Supplied by BBC Worldwide Monitoring*, March 20, 2020.

———. "Russian TV News: Government Caps Food Prices, United Russia's Volunteers." *BBC Monitoring Former Soviet Union - Political Supplied by BBC Worldwide Monitoring*, December 15, 2020.

———. "Russian TV News: Russia Anti-Virus Efforts, 'Pandemic of Fakes', UK 'Inaction'." *BBC Monitoring Former Soviet Union - Political Supplied by BBC Worldwide Monitoring*, March 18, 2020.

———. "Russian TV News: Russia Ready for Covid-19, EU 'Fails', UK Spreads 'Fake News'." *BBC Monitoring Former Soviet Union - Political Supplied by BBC Worldwide Monitoring*, March 20, 2020.

———. "Russian TV News: Russia's Covid-19 Measures; UK, US Struggling." *BBC Monitoring Former Soviet Union - Political Supplied by BBC Worldwide Monitoring*, March 24, 2020.

———. "Russian TV News: Russia's Covid-19 Spread Accelerating, US 'Nightmare'." *BBC Monitoring Former Soviet Union - Political Supplied by BBC Worldwide Monitoring*, April 11, 2020.

———. "Russian TV Weekly Highlights: Covid-19 - Reassurance About Russia, Attacks on US." *BBC Monitoring Former Soviet Union - Political Supplied by BBC Worldwide Monitoring*, April 20, 2020.

———. "TV Says Russia 'Ready' for Coronavirus." *Political Supplied by BBC Worldwide Monitoring*, January 28, 2020.

———. "Why Are Russia's Governors Resigning?" *BBC Monitoring Former Soviet Union - Political Supplied by BBC Worldwide Monitoring*, April 3.

Bechtel, Michael M., and Jens Hainmueller. "How Lasting Is Voter Gratitude? An Analysis of the Short- and Long-Term Electoral Returns to Beneficial Policy." *American Journal of Political Science* 55, no. 4 (October 2011): 852–68.

Béland, Daniel. "Right-Wing Populism and the Politics of Insecurity: How President Trump Frames Migrants as Collective Threats." *Political Studies Review* 18, no. 2 (2020): 162–77.

Bene, Márton, and Zsolt Boda. "Hungary: Crisis as Usual - Populist Governance and the Pandemic." In *Populism and the Politicization of the COVID-19 Crisis in Europe*, edited by Giuliano Bobba and Nicolas Hubé, 87–100. Springer Nature, 2021.

Bermingham, Finbarr, and Orange Wang. "China's Coronavirus Recovery Plan Falls Back on Old Playbook of Debt and Construction." *South China Morning Post*, June 15, 2020.

———. "China's Economic Rebound Shows Upside to 'Stringent Lockdowns, Testing, Tracking', Analysts Say." *South China Morning Post*, October 19, 2020.

Bernstein, Lenny, Joel Achenbach, A. Hinojosa, and Carolyn Y. Johnson. "Coronavirus Cases Shatter Records, Straining Health Care." *The Washington Post*, November 6, 2020, A3.

Bernstein, Lenny, Josh Dawsey, and Yasmeen Abutaleb. "Friction between White House, CDC Hobbles Response." *The Washington Post*, May 16, 2020, A5.

Bernstein, Lenny, and Lena H. Sun. "Gaps Remain in U.S. Preparation." *The Washington Post*, January 23, 2020, A14.

Bernstein, Lenny, Lena H. Sun, Siobhán O'Grady, and Yasmeen Abutaleb. "First Person-to-Person Transmission Confirmed in U.S. Who Labels Virus a Global Emergency." *The Washington Post*, January 31, 2020, A1.

Bernstein, Lenny, William Wan, Josh Dawsey, and Holly Bailey. "CDC Offers Scant Guidelines for Reopening Safely." *The Washington Post*, May 15, 2020, A1.

Bernstein, Lenny, Rachel Weiner, and Joel Achenbach. "Virus Guidance Ignored as Case Numbers Rise." *The Washington Post*, 2020, A1.

Bertrand, Eva. "Constructing Russian Power by Communicating During Disasters: The Forest Fires of 2010." *Problems of Post-Communism* 59, no. 3 (May–June 2012): 31–40.

———. "Disaster, Communication and Legitimization of Power in Russia: The Case of the Forest Fires in Summer 2010." *The Soviet and Post-Soviet Review* 40 (2013): 260–86.

Bharali, Ipchita, Preeti Kumar, Sakthivel Selvaraj, Mao Wenhui, Osondu Ogbuoji, and Gavin Yamey. "India's Policy Response to COVID-19." The Center for Policy Impact in Global Health, June, 2020, http://centerforpolicyimpact.org/our-work/the-4ds/indias-policy-response-to-covid-19/.

Birkland, Thomas. *Lessons of Disaster: Policy Change after Catastrophic Events*. Washington, DC: Georgetown University Press, 2006.

Biswas, Soutik. "Why India's Real Covid Toll May Never Be Known." *BBC*, May 5, 2022.

Bjørnskov, Christian. "Populism: Three Approaches to an International Problem." *Economic Affairs* 39 (2019): 273–81.

Bloomberg. "Why China Is Sticking with Its 'Covid Zero' Strategy." *Bloomberg*, September 23, 2022.

Boburg, Shawn. "Trump Flouted Safety Pact for Minn. Rally, Records Show." *The Washington Post*, October 26, 2020, A1.

Bolin, Bob. "Race, Class, Ethnicity, and Disaster Vulnerability." In *Handbook of Disaster Research*, edited by Rodríguez Havidán, Enrico L. Quarantelli, and Russell R. Dynes, 181–203. Springer, 2007.

Bollfrass, Alexander K. "The Half-Lives of Others: The Democratic Advantage in Nuclear Intelligence Assessment." Princeton University, 2017.

Bonansinga, Donatella. "'A Threat to Us': The Interplay of Insecurity and Enmity Narratives in Left-Wing Populism." *The British Journal of Politics and International Relations* 24, no. 3 (2022): 511–25.

Bonikowski, Bart, Daphne Halikiopoulou, Eric Kaufmann, and Matthijs Rooduijn. "Populism and Nationalism in a Comparative Perspective: A Scholarly Exchange." *Nations and Nationalism* 25, no. 1 (2019): 58–81.

Borges, André, and Lucio Rennó. "Brazilian Response to Covid-19: Polarization and Conflict." Chap. 2 In *COVID-19's Political Challenges in Latin America*, edited by Michelle Fernandez and Carlos Machado, 9–22. Springer, 2021.

Bradsher, Keith. "Slowed by the Coronavirus, China Inc. Struggles to Reopen." *New York Times (Online)*, February 17, 2020.

———. "The World Is Turning to Bailouts, but China Is Holding Back: [Business/Financial Desk]." *New York Times*, April 10, 2020, B7.

Bradsher, Keith, and Vindu Goel. "China's Economy Shrinks 6.8 Percent, Ending Four Decades of Growth: [Business/Financial Desk]." *New York Times*, April 17, 2020, B6.

Brittain, Amy, and Isaac Stanley-Becker. "Senators Seek Project Airbridge Probe." *The Washington Post*, June 10, 2020, A2.

Brittain, Amy, Isaac Stanley-Becker, and Nick Miroff. "Oft-Praised 'Airbridge' Flights Miss Their Mark." *The Washington Post*, May 10, 2020, A1.

Brown, Emma, Beth Reinhard, and Aaron C. Davis. "Experts: Americans Are Dying but Aren't Being Included in Count." *The Washington Post*, April 6, 2020, A1.

Brown, Emma, Beth Reinhard, and Reis Thebault. "States Vary in Deciding Which Deaths Count toward Virus Toll." *The Washington Post*, April 17, 2020, A1.

Brown, Emma, Andrew B. Tran, Beth Reinhard, and Monica Ulmanu. "U.S. Deaths Surged Early in Pandemic." *The Washington Post*, April 28, 2020, A1.

Brulliard, Karin. "Outbreak Reaches Final Frontier - Sparsely Populated U.S. Counties." *The Washington Post*, October 29, 2020, A16.

———. "Transmission Surges, Fueled by Parties and Game Nights." *The Washington Post*, November 13, 2020, A4.

Brulliard, Karin, and Rachel Weiner. "Fragmented Virus Rules Stir Tensions." *The Washington Post*, July 28, 2020, A1.

Buckley, Chris. "China's Nationalists Sneer at U.S. Troubles: [Foreign Desk]." *New York Times*, December 14, 2020, A10.

Buckley, Chris, and Javier C. Hernández. "As Fears of Pandemic Grow, China Puts 20 Million on Lockdown: [Foreign Desk]." *New York Times*, January 24, 2020, A1.

Buckley, Chris, David D. Kirkpatrick, Amy Qin, and Javier C. Hernández. "25 Days That Changed the World: How COVID-19 Slipped China's Grasp." *New York Times (Online)*, December 30, 2020.

Buckley, Chris, Amy Qin, and Wee Sui-Lee. "In China's War on the Coronavirus, a Community Is Besieged." *New York Times (Online)*, February 28, 2020.

Buckley, Chris, and Myers Steven Lee. "China Kept World in Dark as Outbreak Rippled." *New York Times*, February 2, 2020, A1.

———. "Chinese Officials Race to Contain Public Fury over Virus Management: [Foreign Desk]." *New York Times*, January 28, 2020, A8.

Bueno de Mesquita, Bruce, James D. Morrow, Randolph M. Siverson, and Alastair Smith. "Policy Failure and Political Survival: The Contribution of Political Institutions." *Journal of Conflict Resolution* 43, no. 2 (April 1999): 147–61.

Bump, Philip, and Ashley Parker. "Trump Briefings Full of Attacks, Boasts but Little Empathy." *The Washington Post*, April 27, 2020, A6.

Bur, Jessie. "On the Front Lines of COVID Response, This Agency Makes Safety Paramount." *Federal Times*, July 17, 2020, https://www.federaltimes.com/management/2020/07/17/on-the-front-lines-of-covid-response-this-agency-makes-safety-paramount/.

Burrett, Tina. "Charting Putin's Shifting Populism in the Russian Media from 2000 to 2020." *Politics and Governance* 8, no. 1 (2020): 193–205.

Busygina, Irina. "Are Post-Soviet Leaders Doomed to Be Populist? A Comparative Analysis of Putin and Nazarbayev." In *Multifaceted Nationalism and Illiberal Momentum at Europe's Eastern Margins*, 133–49. Routledge, 2021.

Cagaptay, Soner, and Deniz Yuksel. "Turkey's COVID-19 Response." The Washington Institute, June 4, 2020, https://www.washingtoninstitute.org/policy-analysis/turkeys-covid-19-response.

Carothers, Thomas. "Stepping Back from Democratic Pessimism." Carnegie Endowment for International Peace, February 25, 2009, http://www.carnegieendowment.org/publications/index.cfm?fa=view&id=22781.

Cassani, Andrea. "Social Services to Claim Legitimacy: Comparing Autocracies' Performance." *Contemporary Politics* 23, no. 3 (2017): 348–68.

Casula, Philipp. "Sovereign Democracy, Populism, and Depoliticization in Russia: Power and Discourse During Putin's First Presidency." *Problems of post-Communism* 60, no. 3 (2013): 3–15.

Cavalcanti, Bruna. "Mexico in the Face of Covid-19: In-between Actions and Inefficiency." Chap. 3 In *COVID-19's Political Challenges in Latin America*, edited by Michelle Fernandez and Carlos Machado, 23–33. Springer, 2021.

Cenziper, Debbie, Peter Whoriskey, and Joel Jacobs. "Government Puts Nursing Home Toll at over 25,000, but Data Is Incomplete." *The Washington Post*, June 2, 2020, A23.

Cepaluni, Gabriel, Michael Dorsch, and Semir Dzebo. "Populism, Political Regimes, and COVID-19 Deaths." edited by Social Science Research Network. Social Science Research Network, 2021.

Cervi, Laura, Fernando García, and Carles Marín-Lladó. "Populism, Twitter, and COVID-19: Narrative, Fantasies, and Desires." *Social Sciences* 10, no. 8 (2021): 294.

Chaguaceda, Armando, and Claudia González. "Russia: Citizen Demonstrations in an Electoral Autocracy." *V-Dem Institute Working Paper* 30 (May 2020).

Chandrashekar, Vaishnavi. "1.3 Billion People: A 21-Day Lockdown. Can India Curb the Coronavirus?" Science.org, March 31, 2020, https://www.science.org/content/article/13-billion-people-21-day-lockdown-can-india-curb-coronavirus.

Cheibub, José Antonio, Ji Yeon Jean Hong, and Adam Przeworski. "Rights and Deaths: Government Reactions to the Pandemic." Social Science Research Network, July 7, 2020, http://doi.org/10.2139/ssrn.3645410.

Churchill, Owen. "China Imposes Limits on 6 More US-Based News Outlets, Including ABC, LA Times, Newsweek and Bloomberg Industry Group." *South China Morning Post*, October 27, 2020.

Clardie, Justin. "Protests in Russia's Regions: The Influence of Regional Governance." *Social Science Quarterly* 103, no. 1 (2022): 5–17.

Clement, Scott, and Dan Balz. "Poll: Many Governors Praised; Some Republicans Panned over Reopening." *The Washington Post*, May 13, 2020, A10.

———. "Poll: Most Still Favor Curbing Outbreak over Reopening." *The Washington Post*, June 2, 2020, A3.

Conger, Kate. "Twitter Deletes Accounts Linked to Chinese Misinformation Efforts: [Business/Financial Desk]." *New York Times*, June 12, 2020, B4.

Costa, Robert. "Some in Gop Remain Skeptical of Illness's Reach and Official Reaction." *The Washington Post*, March 18, 2020, A18.

Costa, Robert, and Aaron Gregg. "Trump's Lagging Response Widens Rift with City and State Leaders." *The Washington Post*, March 23, 2020, 2020, A1.

Costa, Robert, and Philip Rucker. "'I Wanted to Always Play It Down'." *The Washington Post*, September 10, 2020, A1.

———. "With Public's Money, Trump Casts Himself as Crisis Patron." *The Washington Post*, April 11, 2020, A1.

Costa, Robert, Laura Vozzella, Josh Dawsey, and David Nakamura. "Governors Frustrated with Offer of 'Backup'." *The Washington Post*, March 27, 2020, A1.

Craig, Tim, and Brady Dennis. "States Explore Plans to Reopen." *The Washington Post*, April 14, 2020, A1.

Cremonesi, Cristina, and Eugenio Salvati. "Populism and the 2014 European Elections: A Comparative Study of Party Speeches by the Leaders of Movimento Cinque Stelle and United Kingdom Independence Party." *Journal of Comparative Politics* 12, no. 2 (July 2019): 18–37.

CRFB. "The Fiscal Response to COVID-19 Will Be Larger Than the Great Recession Response." Committee for a Responsible Federal Budget, December 22, 2020, https://www.crfb.org/blogs/fiscal-response-covid-19-will-be-larger-great-recession-response.

Critchlow, Donald T. *In Defense of Populism: Protest and American Democracy.* Philadelphia: University of Pennsylvania Press, 2020.

CSIS. "Cheap Talk: China's Central Bank Still Struggles to Speak to Markets." Center for Strategic and International Studies, February 8, 2021, https://www.csis.org/analysis/cheap-talk-chinas-central-bank-still-struggles-speaks-markets.

Davidson, Joe. "Agency Leadership Vacancies Take a Toll on Crisis Response." *The Washington Post*, April 16, 2020, A8.

———. "Former CDC Director Freiden Says U.S. Has Become a 'Laggard' in Global Health." *The Washington Post*, May 30, 2020, A8.

Dawsey, Josh, and Yasmeen Abutaleb. "White House Set for Packed Party Season Despite Virus." *The Washington Post*, December 2, 2020, A3.

Dawsey, Josh, Felicia Sonmez, and Paul Kane. "Trump Tries to Limit Damage from Revelations He Minimized Virus Threat." *The Washington Post*, September 10, 2020, A4.

Deacon, Robert. "Public Good Provision under Dictatorship and Democracy." *Public Choice* 139 (2013): 241–62.

Dean, Phil. "The Unprecedented Federal Fiscal Policy Response to the COVID-19 Pandemic and Its Impact on State Budgets." Kem C. Garner Policy Institute, May 2022, https://gardner.utah.edu/wp-content/uploads/Fiscal-Stimulus-May2022.pdf?x71849.

DeBonis, Mike. "'Open It up' Bloc in Gop Attacks Restrictions as Others in Party Urge Caution." *The Washington Post*, April 18, 2020, A4.

DeBonis, Mike, Chris Mooney, and Juliet Eilperin. "U.S. Testing 'Blueprint' Keeps Onus on States." *The Washington Post*, April 28, 2020, 2020, A1.

DeBonis, Mike, Erica Werner, and Seung Min Kim. "Testing Lag Ignites Political Uproar as Trump Insists Process Is 'Very Smooth'." *The Washington Post*, March 13, 2020, A13.

DeBonis, Mike, Erica Werner, and Jeff Stein. "Administration, Congressional Negotiators Close to Deal on Economic Relief." *The Washington Post*, March 13, 2020, A10.

Del Real, Jose, Julie Zauzmer, and Ava Wallace. "Seeking Answers, without Clear Guidance from Officials." *The Washington Post*, March 16, 2020, A11.

Deng, Iris. "China's Internet Watchdog Tightens Online Controls with New App to Squash Rumours." *South China Morning Post*, August 13, 2020.

Dennis, Brady. "As Virus Cases Surge, U.S. Prepares for a Grim Week." *The Washington Post*, March 24, 2020, A4.

Dennis, Brady, Jacqueline Dupree, and Marisa Iati. "Surge Shows No Sign of Easing." *The Washington Post*, November 11, 2020, A1.

Desilver, Drew. "Despite Global Concerns About Democracy, More Than Half of Countries Are Democratic." Pew Research Center, May 14, 2019, https://www.pewresearch.org/fact-tank/2019/05/14/more-than-half-of-countries-are-democratic/.

Devinney, Timothy M., and Christopher A. Hartwell. "Varieties of Populism." *Global Strategy Journal* 10, no. 1 (2020): 32–66.

DeYoung, Karen. "As Restrictions Begin to Ease, Battle over Testing Deepens." *The Washington Post*, April 21, 2020, A4.

———. "U.S. Passes 50,000 Deaths, More Than Quarter of Global Toll." *The Washington Post*, April 25, 2020, A6.

DeYoung, Karen, Miriam Berger, and Katie Mettler. "Governors Chart Different Paths as They Consider Reopening States' Activities." *The Washington Post*, April 22, 2020, A4.

Diamond, Larry. "Economic Development and Democracy Reconsidered." Chap. 6 In *Reexamining Democracy*, edited by Gary Marks and Larry Diamond, 93–139. Newbury Park: Sage, 1992.

Diamond, Larry Jay. "Thinking About Hybrid Regimes." *Journal of Democracy* 13, no. 2 (April 2002): 21–35.

Dickman, Samuel L., David U. Himmelstein, and Steffie Woolhandler. "Inequality and the Health-Care System in the USA." *The Lancet* 389, no. 10077 (April 8 2017): 1431–41.

Dixon, Robyn. "Russian Medical Workers Say Coronavirus Is Ravaging Their Ranks: But Hospital Chiefs Are Silent: Medical Personnel Complain That a Lack of Protective Equipment Leaves Them in Peril as the Pandemic Advances across Russia." *The Washington Post (Online)*, April 22, 2020.

———. "In Russia, Facial Surveillance and Threat of Prison Being Used to Make Coronavirus Quarantines Stick: Russia's Tough Approach to Policing Its Coronavirus Rules Undermines Social Trust, Activists Say." *The Washington Post (Online)*, March 25, 2020.

———. "In Russia's Pandemic Struggles, Even Putin Couldn't Speed Bonuses to Health Workers: The Country Has the Third-Largest Number of Confirmed Covid-19 Cases, but Its Counting System Raises Question About Relatively Low Death Rates." *The Washington Post (Online)*, May 27, 2020.

———. "In Russia, Sick People Often Treat Themselves. That's Not Helping in the Coronavirus Fight: Cases in the Country Are Spiking Sharply. One Reason May Be a Long-Held Suspicion of Doctors." *The Washington Post (Online)*, October 23, 2020.

Dou, Eva. "China Skips Trials to Roll out Vaccine." *The Washington Post*, August 25, 2020, A18.

———. "In Vaccine Trials, Mixed Results for China's Sinovac." *The Washington Post*, November 19, 2020, A14.

Doucouliagos, Hristos, and Mehmet Ali Ulubasoglu. "Democracy and Economic Growth: A Meta-Analysis." *American Journal of Political Science* 52, no. 1 (January 2008): 61–83.

———. "Putin Tells Russia Coronavirus Is in Retreat. Critics Face Crackdowns for Saying It's Far from Over: Some Activists and Medical Professionals Claim Russia Is Covering up the Extent of the Pandemic." *The Washington Post (Online)*, June 27, 2020.

Drèze, Jean. "India Is in Denial About the COVID-19 Crisis." *Scientific American*, August 25, 2020, https://www.scientificamerican.com/article/india-is-in-denial-about-the-covid-19-crisis/.

Drezner, Daniel W. "The Death of the Democratic Advantage?" *International Studies Review* 24, no. 2 (2022): viac017.

Duncan, Ian, and Felicia Sonmez. "Trump Extends Distancing Guidelines." *The Washington Post*, March 30, 2020, A1.

Dungca, Nicole, Jenn Abelson, and John Sullivan. "'They Didn't Move Fast Enough'." *The Washington Post*, March 30, 2020, A1.

Dwoskin, Elizabeth, Abha Bhattarai, Juliet Eilperin, and Ashley Parker. "Promised Drive-through Testing Sites Haven't Materialized." *The Washington Post*, March 28, 2020, A17.

Economist. "And They Call It Peace." February 28, 2008, https://www.economist.com/europe/2008/02/28/and-they-call-it-peace.

———. "A Wave of Covid-19 Reveals Flaws in China's Health System." *The Economist*, December 19, 2022, https://www.economist.com/china/2022/12/19/a-wave-of-covid-19-reveals-flaws-in-chinas-health-system.

———. "Covid-19 Deaths in Wuhan Seem Far Higher Than the Official Count." *The Economist*, May 30, 2021, https://www.economist.com/graphic-detail/2021/05/30/covid-19-deaths-in-wuhan-seem-far-higher-than-the-official-count.

———. "Omicron Comes to Mexico, a Place That Never Really Shut Down." *The Economist*, January 22, 2022, https://www.economist.com/the-americas/2022/01/22/omicron-comes-to-mexico-a-place-that-never-really-shut-down.

Editorial. "China's New Covid Nightmare Could Become a Global Catastrophe." *The Washington Post (Online)*, December 20, 2022.

Eilperin, Juliet, Laurie McGinley, Steven Mufson, and Josh Dawsey. "In the Absence of a National Testing Strategy, States Are Going Their Own Way." *The Washington Post*, April 8, 2020, A9.

———. "What Did Xi Jinping Know About the Coronavirus, and When Did He Know It?" *The Washington Post (Online)*, February 19, 2020.

Eksi, Betul, and Elizabeth A. Wood. "Right-Wing Populism as Gendered Performance: Janus-Faced Masculinity in the Leadership of Vladimir Putin and Recep T. Erdoğan." *Theory and Society* 48 (2019): 733–51.

Elgsaas, Ingvill Moe. "The Arctic in Russia's Emergency Preparedness System." *Arctic Review on Law and Politics* 9 (2018): 287–311.

Elmer, Keegan. "China's Coronavirus Testing Rules for Frozen Meats Give Importers a Chill." *South China Morning Post*, December 5, 2020.

———. "Coronavirus: People Are Forging Tests to Return to China from Russia." *South China Morning Post*, June 23, 2020.

Elster, Jon. "Some Notes on 'Populism'." *Philosophy & Social Criticism* 46, no. 5 (2020): 591–600.

Erlanger, Steven. "China's Missteps and Aggressive Diplomacy Fuel a Global Backlash to Its Ambitions: [Foreign Desk]." *New York Times*, May 4, 2020, A6.

Esmerk. "Russia: Coronavirus Treatment Rules on Outpatient Basis Changed." *M-Brain Russia News*, November 9, 2020, LexisNexis.

———. "Russia: Health Ministers in Omsk and Samara Regions Step Down." *M-Brain Russia News*, April 1, 2020, LexisNexis.

———. "Russia: Ministry Constructing Medical Center for 160 Patients in Novosibirsk." *M-Brain Russia News*, April 10, 2020, LexisNexis.

———. "Russia: Ministry of Health Appoints Acting Minister of Astrakhan Region." *M-Brain Russia News*, April 8, 2020, LexisNexis.

———. "Russia: New Minister of Health in Komi Republic." *M-Brain Russia News*, April 24, 2020, LexisNexis.

Eunjung Cha, Ariana, Loveday Morris, and Michael Birnbaum. "Experts Not Sure Why COVID-19 Death Rates Have Dropped." *The Washington Post*, October 11, 2020, A18.

Fahrenthold, David A., Anne Gearan, and Lee Michelle Ye Hee. "Trump Is Still Shaking Hands, and He Hasn't Been Tested." *The Washington Post*, March 14, 2020, A8.

Farhi, Paul. "Western Journalists Are Pushed Out of China." *The Washington Post*, September 17, 2020, C1.

Federal. "On the Frontlines of COVID Response This Agency Makes Safety Paramount." *The Federal Times*, July 17, 2020, https://www.federaltimes.com/management/2020/07/17/on-the-front-lines-of-COVID-response-this-agency-makes-safety-paramount/.

Feng, Emily. "How China's Massive Corruption Crackdown Snares Entrepreneurs Across the Country." *National Public Radio*, March 4, 2021.

Fewsmith, Joseph. "Xi Jinping's Fast Start." *China Leadership Monitor* 41, no. 3 (2013): 4.

Fifield, Anna. "China Watches as Illness Circles Back." *The Washington Post*, March 5, 2020, A14.

———. "In China, Some Worry the Official Illness Count Is Too Low." *The Washington Post*, January 23, 2020, A15.

———. "In Wuhan, a Shortage of Doctors, Hospitals and Beds. But the Stress Is Plentiful." *The Washington Post*, January 25, 2020, A1.

———. "Quickly Spreading Virus Raises Fears across China." *The Washington Post*, January 21, 2020, A1.

Fifield, Anna, and Lyric Li. "China Curtails Cemetery Rituals." *The Washington Post*, April 4, 2020, A12.

Fifield, Anna, Lena H. Sun, and Lenny Bernstein. "China Tries to Contain Virus as First U.S. Case Confirmed." *The Washington Post*, January 22, 2020, A13.

Financial Times. "China Ends Four Decades of Growth; Historic Contraction ; GDP Plunges 6.8% in Starkest Economic Signal from Global Pandemic." *Financial Times*, April 18, 2020, 2020.

Firozi, Paulina, and Hannah Knowles. "States Impose Tougher Restrictions as U.S. Virus Cases Surpass 11 Million." *The Washington Post*, November 16, 2020, A7.

Fisher, Max. "An Iron Fist with Flaws a Virus Can Fit Through: [Foreign Desk]." *New York Times (Online)*, January 26, 2020.

Fisher, Marc, and Chris Dixon. "'Too Many': U.S. Toll Nears 150,000." *The Washington Post*, July 30, 2020, A1.

Fisher, Marc, Shayna Jacobs, and Poe Kelley. "As Toll Nears 250,000, We Remain Entrenched." *The Washington Post*, November 19, 2020, A1.

Fisher, Marc, Clarence Williams, and Lori Rozsa. "Across Nation, Masks Are the Latest Political, Cultural Divide." *The Washington Post*, April 20, 2020, A1.

Fomina, Joanna. "Poland: How Populists Have Exploited the Coronavirus." Carnegie Endowment for International Peace, April 28, 2020, https://carnegieendowment.org/2020/04/28/poland-how -populists-have-exploited-coronavirus-pub-81648.

Foster, Andrew D., and Mark R. Rosenzweig. "Democratization and the Distribution of Local Public Goods in a Poor Rural Economy." Brown University, 2004.

Fowler, Geoffrey A., Lenny Bernstein, and Laurie McGinley. "California Seeks out Patient's Contacts." *The Washington Post*, February 28, 2020, A1.

Frances Stead, Sellers. "Experts: Public Health Is Underfunded." *The Washington Post*, March 13, 2020, A14.

Frankel, Todd C. "Ind. County Health Leaders: Politics Hinders COVID-19 Fight." *The Washington Post*, October 30, 2020, A18.

———. "States' Different Definitions of a Fever Highlight Lack of a National Strategy." *The Washington Post*, May 16, 2020, A5.

Fraze, Taressa, Anne Elixhauser, Laurel Holmquist, and Jayne Johann. "Public Hospitals in the United States, 2008." Healthcare Cost and Utilization Project, September, 2020, https://www.hcup -us.ahrq.gov/reports/statbriefs/sb95.pdf.

Fred Weir Special, correspondent. "As Russia Reopens, Putin Takes a Back Seat to Local Leaders." *The Christian Science Monitor*, June 22, 2020.

Frey, Carl Benedikt, Chinchih Chen, and Giorgio Presidente. "Democracy, Culture, and Contagion: Political Regimes and Countries Responsiveness to Covid-19." In *Covid Economics* 18. University of Oxford, 2020.

Friedman, Uri. "COVID-19 Lays Bare the Price of Populism." *The Atlantic*, May 9, 2021.

Gagnon, Jean-Paul, Emily Beausoleil, Kyong-Min Son, Cleve Arguelles, Pierrick Chalaye, and Callum N. Johnston. "Editorial: What Is Populism? Who Is the Populist?" *Democratic Theory* 5, no. 2 (Winter 2018): vi–xxvi.

Gan, Nectar. "How Vietnam Managed to Keep Its Coronavirus Death Toll at Zero." CNN, May 30, 2020, https://www.cnn.com/2020/05/29/asia/coronavirus-vietnam-intl-hnk.

Gang, Chen. "Institutionalization in the Politics of China's Disaster Management." *The Copenhagen Journal of Asian Studies* 32, no. 1 (2014): 26–48.

Garner, Dwight. "An Angry, Eerie View from inside Quarantine in China: [Review]." *New York Times*, May 19, 2020, C5.

Garraty, John A. "The New Deal, National Socialism, and the Great Depression." *The American Historical Review* 78, no. 4 (October 1973): 907–44.

Gearan, Anne. "Trump Skips Mask in Plant Visit, Defying Ford's Request and Michigan Law." *The Washington Post*, May 22, 2020, A7.

———. "With Shifting Advice, Trump Sows Confusion on Opening." *The Washington Post*, April 24, 2020, A7.

Gearan, Anne, and Josh Dawsey. "President's Latest Indoor Rally Defies State Health Rules." *The Washington Post*, September 15, 2020, A6.

Gearan, Anne, Brady Dennis, Philip Rucker, and Josh Wagner. "As States Get Testing Funds, Trump Paints Rosy Picture." *The Washington Post*, May 12, 2020, A1.

Gearan, Anne, and Jacqueline Dupree. "Trump Hails Arizona - as It Grapples with a Huge Spike." *The Washington Post*, August 6, 2020, A6.

Gearan, Anne, Derek Hawkins, and Siobhán O'Grady. "States' Early Reopenings Fueled 50% Rise in Cases in June." *The Washington Post*, July 2, 2020, A6.

Gearan, Anne, Marisa Iati, and Jacqueline Dupree. "U.S. Passes 4 Million Cases; Pace of Infections Doubles." *The Washington Post*, July 24, 2020, A9.

Gearan, Anne, Seung Min Kim, and Erica Werner. "Trump: Rivals Hype Crisis for Political Gain." *The Washington Post*, February 29, 2020, A1.

Gearan, Anne, Laurie McGinley, Lenny Bernstein, and Ariana Eunjung Cha. "Trump Says He's Taking Unproven Medication." *The Washington Post*, May 19, 2020, A1.

Gearan, Anne, and Toluse Olorunnipa. "Economic Aid Deal Brokered Amid Expanding Nationwide Tumult Trump Declares a National Emergency." *The Washington Post*, March 14, 2020, A1.

Gearan, Anne, Brittany Shammas, and Lateshia Beachum. "White House Says Virus Is under Control Despite Surges." *The Washington Post*, June 30, 2020, A8.

Gearan, Anne, and Felicia Sonmez. "As U.S. Cases Top 1 Million, Testing Rate Is Below Average." *The Washington Post*, April 29, 2020, A4.

Gearan, Anne, Felicia Sonmez, and Erica Werner. "Administration Describes Dash for a Vaccine Usable by January." *The Washington Post*, May 1, 2020, A4.

Gearan, Anne, and John Wagner. "Trump Calls Michigan Protesters 'Very Good People'." *The Washington Post*, May 3, 2020, A4.

Gearan, Anne, Scott Wilson, and Annie Gowen. "As Limits Return, Fauci Raises Alarm." *The Washington Post*, July 1, 2020, A1.

Geddes, Barbara. "What Do We Know About Democratization after 20 Years?" *Annual Review of Political Science* 2 (June 1999): 115–44.

Genç, Kaya. "COVID-19 in Turkey: A Nation on Edge." 397, no. 10287 (May 13 2021): *The Lancet*, 1794–96.

Geppert, Cynthia. "All Hands on Deck: The Federal Health Care Response to the COVID-19 National Emergency." *Federal Practitioner* 37, no. 8 (2020): 346–47.

Ghobarah, Hazem Adam, Paul Huth, and Bruce Russett. "Comparative Public Health: The Political Economy of Human Misery and Well-Being." *International Studies Quarterly* 48 (2004): 73–94.

GHS. "Global Health Security Index: Building Collective Action and Accountability." Nuclear Threat Initiative (NTI), October 2019, https://www.ghsindex.org/wp-content/uploads/2020/04/2019 -Global-Health-Security-Index.pdf.

Gifford, R. "The Dragons of Inaction: Psychological Barriers That Limit Climate Change Mitigation and Adaptation." *American Psychologist* 66, no. 4 (2011): 290.

Goldstein, Amy. "Administration Pledges More Equipment but Still Puts Testing Onus on States." *The Washington Post*, May 25, 2020, A9.

———. "Federal Officials Organize Large-Scale Testing in 3 Cities in Hard-Hit Sun Belt." *The Washington Post*, July 8, 2020, A9.

———. "Health-Care Chain Sued by Hospital Workers." *The Washington Post*, August 21, 2020, A7.

———. "Most Insurers Will Waive Costs for Tests, but Not Sick Visits or Treatment." *The Washington Post*, March 14, 2020, A13.

———. "Stockpile of Emergency Medical Supplies Is Moving Back under HHS Control." *The Washington Post*, June 19, 2020, A10.

Goldstein, Amy, and H. Sun Lena. "Abrupt Change in U.S. Testing Guidelines Worries Public Health Experts." *The Washington Post*, August 27, 2020, A9.

Goldstein, Amy, H. Sun Lena, and Beth Reinhard. "States' Needs Overwhelm Unprepared Stockpile." *The Washington Post*, March 29, 2020, A1.

Goldstein, Amy, and Laurie McGinley. "Trump Calls FDA's Plan for Tougher Vaccine Standards a 'Political Move'." *The Washington Post*, September 24, 2020, A4.

Goldstein, Amy, Laurie McGinley, and Yasmeen Abutaleb. "Trump Says Drive-through Testing Sites Are in the Works." *The Washington Post*, March 14, 2020, A4.

Goldstein, Amy, and Sean Sullivan. "CDC Chief: Most Won't Get Vaccine Till Mid-'21." *The Washington Post*, September 17, 2020, A1.

Gorman, Lisa, and Christopher Stoney. "Missed Opportunities: Public Health Disaster Management in Canada." *Journal of Public Management & Social Policy* 22, no. 2 (2015): 1–16.

Goryushina, E.M. "Disaster Politics in the South of Russia." In *IOP Conference Series: Earth and Environmental Science* 459, no. 4: p. 0420202, IOP publishing, 2020.

Grodsky, Brian. *The Democratization Disconnect: How Recent Democratic Revolutions Threaten the Future of Democracy*. Boulder: Rowman & Littlefield, 2016.

Grove, Thomas, and Georgi Kantchev. "Russia's Economy Suffers Double Hit from Oil Slump and Coronavirus; as Infections Grow, Russia Finds a Shortfall in Oil Revenue Hurts Its Ability to Offer the Kind of Emergency Support Provided in the West." May 20, 2020, https://www.wsj.com/articles/russias-economy-suffers-double-hit-from-oil-slump-and-coronavirus-11589976001.

Grove, Thomas, and Ann M. Simmons. "Three Doctors in Russia Have Fallen out of Hospital Windows; the Incidents Occurred as More Medical Professionals Are Speaking out About the Stress of Treating Coronavirus." May 7, 2020, https://www.wsj.com/articles/three-doctors-in-russia-have-fallen-out-of-hospital-windows-11588887817.

Guan, Tianru, and Yilu Yang. "Rights-Oriented or Responsibility-Oriented? Two Subtypes of Populism in Contemporary China." *International Political Science Review* 42, no. 5 (2021): 672–89.

Guarino, Ben, Bailey Sarah Pulliam, Laura Meckler, and Katie Zezima. "Schools Close, National Guard Deployed to Help New York Suburb Stem Spread of Coronavirus." *The Washington Post*, March 11, 2020, A1.

Guarino, Ben, and Isaac Stanley-Becker. "New York Scrambles to Prepare for Crisis's Peak." *The Washington Post*, April 2, 2020, A4.

Guerin, Orla. "Coronavirus: How Turkey Took Control of Covid-19 Emergency." *BBC*, May 29, 2020.

Gurganus, Julia. "Putin's Populism Trap." Carnegie Endowment for International Peace, November 21, 2017, https://carnegieendowment.org/2017/11/21/putin-s-populism-trap-pub-74788.

Guzman, Joseph. "90 Percent of Americans Now Staying Home to Prevent Coronavirus Spread." *The Hill*, March 27, 2020, https://thehill.com/changing-america/well-being/prevention-cures/489813-majority-of-americans-staying-home-as-much-as.

Haggard, Stephan, and Robert Kaufman. "Revising Social Contracts: Social Spending in Latin America, East Asia, and the Former Socialist Countries, 1980–2000." *Revista de Ciencia Política* 24, no. 1 (2004): 3–37.

Hale, Henry E. "Eurasian Polities as Hybrid Regimes: The Case of Putin's Russia." *Journal of Eurasian Studies* 1, no. 1 (January 2010): 33–41.

———. "Regime Cycles: Democracy, Autocracy, and Revolution in Post-Soviet Eurasia." *World Politics* 58, no. 1 (2005): 133–65.

Hanson, Jonathan K. "Democracy and State Capacity: Complements or Substitutes?" *Studies in Comparative International Development* 50 (2015): 304–30.

Harding, Robin, and David Stasavage. "What Democracy Does (and Doesn't Do) for Basic Services: School Fees, School Inputs, and African Elections." *Journal of Politics* 76, no. 1 (January 2004): 229–945.

Harper, Jo. "High Corporate Debt Dampens Russia's Growth Prospects." Deutsche Welle, January 22, 2021, https://www.dw.com/en/high-corporate-debt-dampens-russias-growth-prospects/a-56312161.

Harris, Shane, Felicia Sonmez, and Mike DeBonis. "Governors from Both Parties Contradict Trump on Testing." *The Washington Post*, April 20, 2020, A4.

Hass, Ryan. "Assessing China's 'Common Prosperity' Campaign." Brookings Institution, September 9, 2021, https://www.brookings.edu/blog/order-from-chaos/2021/09/09/assessing-chinas-common-prosperity-campaign/.

Hauslohner, Abigail, and Haisten Willis. "Georgia Bars Municipalities from Mandating Masks as More States Now Require Them." *The Washington Post (Online)*, July 16, 2020.

Häussler, Thomas, Hannah Schmid-Petri, Silke Adam, Ueli Reber, and Dorothee Arlt. "The Climate of Debate: How Institutional Factors Shape Legislative Discourses on Climate Change: A Comparative Framing Perspective." *Studies in Communication Sciences* 16, no. 1 (2016): 94–102 .

Hawkins, Derek, and Marisa Iati. "Calif. Is Third State to Exceed 10,000 Deaths." *The Washington Post*, August 9, 2020, A3.

———. "CDC Warns of Risks to Children as Some Schools Attempt to Resume Classes." *The Washington Post*, August 17, 2020, A6.

Hawkins, Derek, Marisa Iati, and Jacqueline Dupree. "U.S. Case Count Soars Past 5 Million." *The Washington Post*, August 10, 2020, A2.

Hawkins, Derek, and Marissa Lati. "Birx Warns of 'New Phase' of Pandemic and Calls for Greater Precautions." *The Washington Post*, August 3, 2020, A9.

Hawkins, Derek, Felicia Sonmez, and Hannah Knowles. "Officials Sound Familiar Alarms as Cases Surge." *The Washington Post*, July 20, 2020, A3.

Healy, Andrew, and Neil Malhotra. "Myopic Voters and Natural Disaster Policy." *American Political Science Review* 103, no. 3 (August 2009): 387–406.

Heijmans, Annelies. "The Everyday Politics of Disaster Risk Reduction in Central Java, Indonesia." Chap. 13 In *Disaster, Conflict and Society in Crises: Everyday Politics of Crisis Response*, edited by Thea Hilhorst. New York: Routledge, 2013, 223 p.

Hernández, Arelis R., Stead S. Frances, and Ben Guarino. "Texas, Florida Walk Back Reopenings." *The Washington Post*, June 27, 2020, A1.

Hernández, Javier C. "As China Tries to Stifle Coverage, Defiant Journalists Do Exposés: [Foreign Desk]." *New York Times (Online)*, March 16, 2020.

———. "China Eyes Party Gadfly Who Bashed Xi over Virus: [Foreign Desk]." *New York Times*, April 8, 2020, A19.

———. "China Locks Down Xinjiang in West to Stop Covid, Angering Residents: [Foreign Desk]." *New York Times*, August 26, 2020, A5.

———. "China Peddles Falsehoods to Obscure Origin of COVID Pandemic." *New York Times (Online)*, December 6, 2020.

———. "China Reaches a Containment Milestone with No New Local Infections: [Foreign Desk]." *New York Times*, March 19, 2020, A6.

———. "China Revels as Unrest Spreads across U.S.: [Foreign Desk]." *New York Times*, June 3, 2020, A12.

———. "China Spins Coronavirus Crisis, Hailing Itself as a Global Leader." *New York Times (Online)*, March 3, 2020.

———. "Chinese Tycoon May Face Prosecution after Expulsion from Communist Party: [Foreign Desk]." *New York Times (Online)*, July 24, 2020.

———. "'We Couldn't Be Poorer': Pandemic Hinders China's Antipoverty Efforts: [Foreign Desk]." *New York Times*, October 26, 2020, A12.

HHS. "Strategic National Stockpile (Sns)." U.S. Department of Health and Human Services, September 5, 2023, https://chemm.hhs.gov/sns.htm.

Higgins, Andrew. "A Doctor Who Accused Russia of Underreporting Virus Totals Is Detained: [Foreign Desk]." *New York Times*, April 5, 2020, A6.

———. "After Months of Denial, Russia Admits the Virus Is Taking Hold." *New York Times (Online)*, April 10, 2020.

———. "As Russia Braces for Coronavirus, Putin Lets Underlings Take the Heat." *New York Times (Online)*, March 30, 2020.

———. "Hit Hard by Coronavirus, Russia Holds a Mostly Mask-Free Victory Parade." *New York Times (Online)*, June 24, 2020.

———. "New Data Triples Russia's COVID-19 Death Toll." *New York Times (Online)*, December 29, 2020.

———. "New Data Triples Russia's Death Toll." *New York Times (Online)*, December 29, 2020.

———. "Putin, Russia's Man of Action, Is Passive, Even Bored, in the Coronavirus Era." *New York Times (Online)*, April 30, 2020.

———. "Russia Voting Affirms a Foregone Conclusion: [Foreign Desk]." *New York Times*, July 2, 2020, A18.

Hindustan Times. "China Warns Coronavirus Transmission Ability Getting Stronger, Braces for More Cases." *Hindustan Times*, January 26, 2020.

Hofstede. "Compare Countries." Hofstede Insights, https://www.hofstede-insights.com/fi/product/compare-countries/.

Holliday, Shabnam J. "Populism, the International and Methodological Nationalism: Global Order and the Iran–Israel Nexus." *Political Studies* 68, no. 1 (2020): 3–19.

HRW. "Nicaragua: Doctors Fired for Covid-19 Comments." Human Rights Watch, June 23, 2020, https://www.hrw.org/news/2020/06/23/nicaragua-doctors-fired-covid-19-comments.

———. "Sri Lanka: Increasing Suppression of Dissent." Human Rights Watch, August 8, 2020, https://www.hrw.org/news/2020/08/08/sri-lanka-increasing-suppression-dissent.

Hsiang, Solomon, Daniel Allen, Sébastien Annan-Phan, Kendon Bell, Ian Bolliger, Trinetta Chong, Hannah Druckenmiller, et al. "The Effect of Large-Scale Anti-Contagion Policies on the COVID-19 Pandemic." *Nature* 584, no. 7820 (2020): 262–67.

Huang, Kristin. "China to Disinfect Frozen Food Imports to Curb Coronavirus Spread." *South China Morning Post*, November 10, 2020.

Huang, Yanzhong. "The SARS Epidemic and Its Aftermath in China: A Political Perspective." Chap. 2 In *Learning from SARS: Preparing for the Next Disease Outbreak: Workshop Summary*, edited by Katherine Oberholtzer, Laura Sivitz, Alison Mack, Stanley Lemon, Adel Mahmoud, and Stacey Knobler, 116–36. Washington, DC: The National Academies Press, 2004.

Huifeng, He, and Sidney Leng. "As China's Coronavirus Rebound Gathers Steam, Export-Oriented Manufacturers Struggle to Find Workers." *South China Morning Post*, December 25, 2020.

Huiyao, Wang. "China's Experience Shows Coronavirus Second Wave Need Not Be a Disaster." *South China Morning Post*, July 2, 2020.

Huynh, Luu Duc Toan. "What Vietnam's Localized Lockdown Policy Showed: It Did Not Work and Was Too Late." *Policy Debates* 57, no. 9 (November 29 2022): 1882–92.

IHME. "COVID-19 Results Briefing." Institute for Health Metrics and Evaluation, December 15, 2022, https://www.healthdata.org/sites/default/files/covid_briefs/62_briefing_Russian_Federation.pdf.

Imago. "People Watch a Victory Day Military Parade Marking the 75th Anniversary of the Victory over Nazi Germany in World War Ii." Imago, June 24, 2020, https://www.imago-images.com/st/0101806535.

Intellinews. "Putin Eases Russia's Coronavirus Lockdown Restrictions." *Intellinews - Russia This Week*, May 11, 2020, https://www.intellinews.com/putin-eases-russia-s-coronavirus-lockdown-restrictions-182927/.

International Churchill Society. "The Worst Form of Government." International Churchill Society, https://winstonchurchill.org/resources/quotes/the-worst-form-of-government/.

ITAR-TASS. "5–6 Misinformation Campaigns About Coronavirus Exposed Daily in Russia." March 20, 2020.

———. "All Medical Institutions in Russia Must Be Ready to Treat Coronavirus Patients - Minister." April 15, 2020.

———. "All of Russia's Organizations Concerned Worked Effectively During Pandemic - Peskov." December 27, 2020.

———. "Armed Forces Dispatched to Fight Coronavirus Outbreak at Russia's Largest Gold Mine." May 18, 2020.

———. "Battle against Coronavirus in Russia Continues, Putin Cautions." September 28, 2020.

———. "Bed Fund for COVID-19 Patients in Russia Is Almost 90% Full - Deputy Health Minister." October 13, 2020.

———. "Checkpoints at Russia's Border with China in Amur Region to Stay Closed Till February 1." January 26, 2020.

———. "Coronavirus Cases Double in Russia's Dagestan - Watchdog." April 4, 2020.

———. "Coronavirus Cases in Russia Rise to 438 over Past Day - Prime Minister." March 23, 2020.

———. "Coronavirus Death Rate in Russia Does Not Exceed 1% - Consumer Rights Watchdog Chief." April 28, 2020.

———. "Coronavirus Situation in Russia's Dagestan Stabilized - Minister." June 30, 2020.

———. "COVID-19 Situation in Russia to Improve Due to Introduced Measures - Putin." September 24, 2020.

———. "COVID-19 Situation in Russia under Control - Peskov." October 23, 2020.

———. "Daily Coronavirus Figures Vary across Russia, Says Chief Sanitary Doctor." November 23, 2020.

———. "Deputy PM Says Russia Did Not Impose New Lockdown Due to Readiness to Fight Pandemic." December 28, 2020.

———. "Diplomat Slams as Fake News Eu's Saying Russia Spreads False Information About Coronavirus." March 19, 2020.

———. "Economic Recession Due to Pandemic Not So Deep in Russia as in Other Countries, Says Putin." September 10, 2020.

———. "Emergencies Ministry Teams Disinfect About 1,000 Social Facilities across Russia." April 8, 2020.

———. "Four New Coronavirus Cases Confirmed in Russia over Past 24 Hours." March 7, 2020.

———. "Globalization Principles Fail to Work Amid Pandemic - Chairman of Russia's Ruling Party." July 14, 2020.

———. "Government Ready to Build Field Hospitals across Russia If Necessary, Says Official." March 17, 2020.

———. "Governor of Russia's Kaliningrad Region Announces Lockdown Starting on March 31." March 30, 2020.

———. "Ideas Promoted by Russia before Pandemic Become More Popular - Lavrov." April 25, 2020.

———. "Masks to Remain Mandatory in Russia for the Next Month or Two - Watchdog Chief." May 25, 2020.

———. "Medical Workers Can Be Redistributed between Russia's Regions to Fight Pandemic - Kremlin." October 12, 2020.

———. "Minister Says Russia's Infectious Diseases Service Was Not Fully Prepared for Pandemic." October 13, 2020.

———. "More Than 1.3 Million People Examined for Coronavirus in Russia - Watchdog." January 27, 2020.

———. "More Than 100 Medical Staff Test Positive for Coronavirus in Russia's St. Petersburg." April 17, 2020.

———. "More Than 450 Organizations Join Russia-Wide 'We Are Together' Help Campaign." March 23, 2020.

———. "More Than 50,000 Medical Students Help Doctors to Fight Pandemic in Russia - Minister." December 1, 2020.

———. "Mortality in Russia in January-April 2020 Down on 2019 - Deputy PM." May 29, 2020.

———. "Most Coronavirus Cases in Russia Local Transmissions - Deputy PM." April 4, 2020.

———. "Nearly 500 Doctors Die from Coronavirus in Russia - Healthcare Watchdog." June 18, 2020.

———. "No Direct Grounds to Impose Further Coronavirus Lockdowns in Russia - Sanitary Watchdog." September 28, 2020.

———. "No Plans to Impose Tough Quarantine in Russia, Crisis Center Says." March 22, 2020.

———. "No Plans to Introduce Strict Quarantine in Russia for Winter Holidays, Kremlin Says." December 14, 2020.

———. "No Reason to Panic Due to Coronavirus in Russia - Deputy PM." March 17, 2020.

———. "No Risk of Further Spread of Coronavirus in Russia - Rospotrebnadzor." January 31, 2020.

———. "No Sense in Imposing Face Mask Requirement across Entire Russia - Health Minister." November 27, 2020.

———. "No Wholesale Harsh Restrictions Amid COVID-19 Pandemic in Russia Are Due - Putin." October 21, 2020.

———. "Nothing Critical About Coronavirus in Russia, Fake News Come from Abroad - Putin." March 4, 2020.

———. "Number of Coronavirus Cases in Russia Rises from 34 to 45 - Officials." March 13, 2020.

———. "Number of People Willing to Return to Russia from US Increases Amid Unrest - Diplomat." June 6, 2020.

———. "Number of Severe COVID-19 Cases in Russia Decreases - Health Minister." September 24, 2020.

———. "'On Solid Ground': Russia's Fortitude Helped Weather COVID Storm of 2020, Kremlin Says." December 23, 2020.

———. "Over 15 Mln Tests for COVID-19 Held in Russia." June 15, 2020.

———. "Over 6 Mln Coronavirus Tests Conducted in Russia, Says Watchdog." May 14, 2020.

———. "Over One Million Coronavirus Tests Conducted in Russia - Watchdog." April 9, 2020.

———. "Pandemic Unmasks Negative Implications of New Western Values - Russia's Security Chief." June 17, 2020.

———. "Potential of Russia's Health Service System Grows - Putin." December 2, 2020.

———. "Public Order, Security in Russia to Be Safeguarded in Pandemic - Putin." April 3, 2020.

———. "Public Order, Security in Russia to Be Safeguarded in Pandemic - Putin." April 3, 2020.

———. "Putin Calls Efficient Russia's Battle against Coronavirus." September 15, 2020.

———. "Putin Did Everything for Russia to Cope with Pandemic from Day One, Russian PM Says." October 22, 2020.

———. "Putin Fully Informed About COVID-19 Situation in Russia - Kremlin." December 2, 2020.

———. "Putin Orders Permanent Monitoring of Russia's Economic Situation." March 29, 2020.

———. "Putin Says Coordination Was a Key Factor in the Fight against COVID-19 in Russia." September 5, 2020.

———. "Putin Says Coronavirus Situation in Russia Is Improving." June 4, 2020.

———. "Putin: Russia Contains Coronavirus Spread but Cannot Block Threat." March 25, 2020.

———. "Putin: Russia Managed to Avoid Critical Disruptions in Ppe Supplies for Healthcare Workers." June 3, 2020.

———. "Putin: Russia to Hold Victory Day Parade on Red Square and in Other Cities on June 24." May 26, 2020.

———. "Readiness as the New Reality: How COVID-19 Made Russia's Healthcare System Shift Gears." May 26, 2020.

———. "Risk of Chinese Coronavirus Spreading to Russia Is Low, Watchdog Assures." January 21, 2020.

———. "Roscomnadzor Says Ready to Block Websites Spreading Fake New on Coronavirus in Russia." March 18, 2020.

———. "Roskomnadzor Studies Articles in Western Media for Fakes About Coronavirus in Russia." May 14, 2020.

———. "Russia Allocates 4.5% of GDP to Mitigate Consequences of Pandemic - Putin." November 21, 2020.

———. "Russia Allocates Funds to Ensure All Regions Are Ready to Combat COVID-19 - Minister." April 20, 2020.

———. "Russia Conducts over 1.5 Mln Coronavirus Tests, Ranked Second in the World." April 15, 2020.

———. "Russia Does Not Have a Comprehensive COVID-19 Restrictions Plan - Kremlin." November 16, 2020.

———. "Russia Fully Halts International Flights Amid Coronavirus." March 27, 2020.

———. "Russia Has All Tools to Maintain Financial Stability - PM." March 12, 2020.

———. "Russia Has Means to Solve Problems in Any Coronavirus Scenario - Putin." April 8, 2020.

———. "Russia Has One of World's Lowest Coronavirus Mortality Rates - Health Minister." April 22, 2020.

———. "Russia Imposes Entry Ban for Foreigners from March 18 to May 1 over Coronavirus Risks." March 16, 2020.

———. "Russia in 'Peculiar' Position Due to Low Oil Prices and Coronavirus - First Deputy PM." March 16, 2020.

———. "Russia Introduces Large Fines for Spreading Fake News on Coronavirus." March 30, 2020.

———. "Russia Managed to Avoid Panic, Crime Situation Deterioration During Pandemic - Ex-Premier." June 9, 2020.

———. "Russia Managed to Slow Down Pace of Coronavirus Epidemiology Spread, Says Putin." April 28, 2020.

———. "Russia Not Planning New Coronavirus Restrictions - Crisis Center." November 23, 2020.

———. "Russia Opens Quarantine Points in Border Areas with China." February 2, 2020.

———. "Russia Passes Spain to Rank Second in Coronavirus Cases Globally." May 12, 2020.

———. "Russia Proposes Three-Stage Lockdown Exit Strategy." May 6, 2020.

———. "Russia Ranks About 50th in Cases of COVID-19 Per 100,000 Residents - Official." April 28, 2020.

———. "Russia Ranks Coronavirus among Dangerous Diseases Along with HIV and Plague." February 2, 2020.

———. "Russia Remains at 40th Place on COVID-19 Incidence Per 100,000 People - Watchdog." September 14, 2020.

———. "Russia Sets up Council Coordinating Anti-Coronavirus Efforts - PM." March 14, 2020.

———. "Russia Sets up Two-Week Stock of Medicines over Coronavirus." March 16, 2020.

———. "Russia Suspends Trains to and from Ukraine, Moldova, Latvia over Coronavirus." March 15, 2020.

———. "Russia Taking All Necessary Prophylactic Measures against Coronavirus - Official." February 3, 2020.

———. "Russia to Classify Deliberate Coronavirus Contamination as Terrorism or Sabotage." March 25, 2020.

———. "Russia to Prolong Existing Restrictions against Coronavirus until April 1 - Official." February 26, 2020.

———. "Russia to Spend 4.5% of GDP on Support for Economy, Households in 2020, Says Putin." October 29, 2020.

———. "Russia Was Better Prepared for COVID-19 Pandemic Than Majority - Security Council." July 13, 2020.

———. "Russia Will Step up Fight against Coronavirus, Pledges Putin." March 18, 2020.

———. "Russia's Central Election Commission Approves Results of Constitutional Vote." July 3, 2020.

———. "Russia's Chechnya Closes Administrative Borders Amid Coronavirus Outbreak." March 28, 2020.

———. "Russia's Coronavirus Cases Growth on the Decline for the Past Three Days." April 24, 2020.

———. "Russia's Coronavirus Cases Top 3,500 - Response Center." April 2, 2020.

———. "Russia's Coronavirus Death Rate Lower Than in Other States - Expert." April 20, 2020.

———. "Russia's Coronavirus Death Rate Lower Than in the World - Deputy Prime Minister." May 20, 2020.

———. "Russia's Coronavirus Infection Curve Going Down, but It's Not Time to Relax - Kremlin." July 17, 2020.

———. "Russia's Coronavirus Situation Is Stabilizing - Watchdog Chief." December 25, 2020.

———. "Russia's Coronavirus Situation Manageable, Although Difficult in Some Regions - Putin." November 18, 2020.

———. "Russia's Daily COVID-19 Rate Is 8 Per 100,000 People - Watchdog Chief." October 13, 2020.

———. "Russia's Emergencies Ministry Disinfects 20,900 Transport Buildings, 4,100 Km of Roads." May 17, 2020.

———. "Russia's Entry Ban Not to Be Applicable to CIS, Abkhazian, South Ossetian Nationals." March 23, 2020.

———. "Russia's Far Eastern Region Introduces Digital Passes to Curb Coronavirus." April 6, 2020.

———. "Russia's Government to Use $67.09 Mln to Purchase of 1,200 Ambulances." April 2, 2020.

———. "Russia's Health Ministry Sends Medics to Kamchatka to Help Combat Coronavirus Infection." June 5, 2020.

———. "Russia's Health Workers, Coronavirus Prevention Headquarter Working Very Well - Kremlin." March 31, 2020.

———. "Russia's Healthcare System Proved to Be Flexible and Ready to Mobilize - Putin." June 28, 2020.

———. "Russia's Human Rights Chief Dismisses Rumors on Coronavirus Spread in Moscow." March 2, 2020.

———. "Russia's Measures against COVID-19 Were Timely and Correct, Prime Minister Says." July 22, 2020.

———. "Russia's Measures Can Compensate for Negative Economic Processes - Kremlin." March 13, 2020.

———. "Russia's Medical Biological Agency Hopes to Have Anti-Coronavirus Vaccine in 11 Months." March 20, 2020.

———. "Russia's PM Orders to Prepare a Priority Actions Plan Due to Coronavirus." March 16, 2020.

———. "Russia's Sanitary Security Measures at Voting Stations Well Thought out - Who." June 30, 2020.

———. "Russia's Second Stage of Exiting Lockdown to Open Educational Facilities, Allow Walks." May 6, 2020.

———. "Russia's Watchdog Advises Russians against Visiting China Amidst Outbreak." January 24, 2020.

———. "Russia's Yamalo-Nenets Region Goes on Lockdown over Coronavirus - Authorities." March 31, 2020.

———. "Situation with Spread of Coronavirus in Russia Is under Control - President Putin." March 17, 2020.

———. "State of Emergency Declared in Two Districts in Russia's Far East." February 2, 2020.

———. "Task Force Requests Restrictions on Public Gatherings in Russia over Coronavirus." March 11, 2020.

———. "TASS: Kremlin Not Considering Possibility of Declaring Emergency Situation in Russia Amid Coronavirus Outbreak - Spokesman." April 1, 2020.

———. "Threat of Coronavirus Spread in Russia Minimized, Says PM." March 12, 2020.

———. "US' Allegations About Russia's Spreading Misinformation About Coronavirus Seen as Fake." February 22, 2020.

———. "Western Media Are Mouthpieces Spreading Coronavirus Falsehoods against Russia - Ryabkov." April 17, 2020.

———. "Western Media Spread Fake News of Russia's COVID Death Toll to Distract Public Attention." May 13, 2020.

Itkowitz, Colby, and Marissa J. Lang. "Death Toll Surges Past 2,000 in U.S." *The Washington Post*, March 29, 2020, A1.

Jackman, Robert W. *Power without Force : The Political Capacity of Nation-States.* Analytical Perspectives on Politics. Ann Arbor: University of Michigan Press, 1993.

Jacobs, Shayna, Ben Guarino, Jada Yuan, and Barrett Devlin. "Trump Approves Aid to N.Y. As State Braces for Shutdown." *The Washington Post*, March 23, 2020, A12.

Jakes, Lara, and Myers Steven Lee. "U.S. Designates China's Official Media as Operatives of the Communist State." *New York Times (Online)*, February 18, 2020.

Janes, C., Isaac Stanley-Becker, and Rachel Weiner. "In States across the U.S., Cases Still on Rise." *The Washington Post*, June 11, 2020, A1.

Janes, C., and William Wan. "Ailing Public Health Units Further Stifled Amid Pandemic." *The Washington Post*, September 1, 2020, A9.

Jansen, Robert S. "Populist Mobilization: A New Theoretical Approach to Populism." *Sociological Theory* 29, no. 2 (2011): 75–96.

Jarausch, Konrad H. *Broken Lives: How Ordinary Germans Experienced the 20th Century.* Princeton: Princeton University Press, 2018.

Jarquín, Mateo, and Salvador Martí i Puig. "Nicaragua: Denying the Health Crisis and the Political Crisis." Chap. 3 In *COVID-19's Political Challenges in Latin America*, edited by Michelle Fernandez and Carlos Machado, 35–45. Springer, 2021.

Jász, Márton. "Pandemic Started Exactly One Year Ago in Hungary." *Hungary Today*, April 3, 2021, https://hungarytoday.hu/pandemic-started-exactly-one-year-ago-in-hungary/.

Jędrzejczyk, Tadeusz, and Łukasz Balwicki. "Poland Country Snapshot: Public Health Agencies and Services in the Response to COVID-19." European Observatory on Health Systems and Policies, March 1, 2022, https://eurohealthobservatory.who.int/news-room/articles/item/poland-country -snapshot-public-health-agencies-and-services-in-the-response-to-covid-19.

Johnson, Carolyn Y., and Laurie McGinley. "Faulty Test and Community-Transmission Case Highlight Containment Concerns." *The Washington Post*, February 28, 2020, A13.

Johnson, Carolyn Y., Laurie McGinley, Josh Dawsey, and Christopher Rowland. "Trump's Vaccine Timeline Doubted." *The Washington Post*, May 16, 2020, A1.

Johnson, Carolyn Y., Laurie McGinley, Juliet Eilperin, and Emma Brown. "Labs Step up as Americans Clamor for More Testing." *The Washington Post*, November 5, 2022, A10.

Johnson, Carolyn Y., Laurie McGinley, and Lena H. Sun. "Faulty CDC Test Delays Ability to Monitor Disease's Spread in United States." *The Washington Post*, February 26, 2020.

Johnson, Jenna, Amy B. Wang, and Josh Dawsey. "Biden Calls for Shared Sacrifice to Conquer Virus." *The Washington Post*, November 26, 2020, A1.

Johnson, Jenna, Amy B. Wang, and C. Janes. "Biden Assails Trump's Efforts to Fight Pandemic." *The Washington Post*, December 30, 2020, A1.

Johnson, Miles. "Italian Applause Videos Fuel Suspicions of China Propaganda; Aid Supplies." *Financial Times*, May 4, 2020.

Jost, John T., and Brenda Major. "Emerging Perspectives on the Psychology of Legitimacy." Chap. 1 In *The Psychology of Legitimacy: Emerging Perspectives on Ideology, Justice, and Intergroup Relations*, edited by John T. Jost and Brenda Major, 3–32. New York: Cambridge University Press, 2001.

Kadirgamar, Ahilan. "Sri Lanka: Elections, Polarized Politics, and the Pandemic." Carnegie Endowment for International Peace, April 28, 2020, https://carnegieendowment.org/2020/04/28/sri-lanka -elections-polarized-politics-and-pandemic-pub-81649.

Kahn, Matthew E. "The Death Toll from Natural Disasters: The Role of Income, Geography, and Institutions." *The Review of Economics and Statistics* 87, no. 2 (May 2005): 271–84.

Kammas, Pantelis, and Vassilis Sarantides. "Do Dictatorships Redistribute More?" In *Sheffield Economic Research Paper Series*, edited by University of Sheffield, 1–36. Sheffield, 2016.

Kamrava, Mehran. "Non-Democratic States and Political Liberalisation in the Middle East: A Structural Analysis." *Third World Quarterly* 19, no. 1 (1998): 63–85.

Kane, John. *The Politics of Moral Capital.* Contemporary Political Theory. Cambridge; New York: Cambridge University Press, 2001.

Kane, Paul. "Businesses Seek Nationwide Rules to Face Pandemic." *The Washington Post*, July 5, 2020, A2.

Kang, Yi. *Disaster Management in China in a Changing Era.* Springer Briefs in Political Science. Berline: Springer-Verlag Berlin Heiderlberg, 2015.

Kaniasty, Krzysztof, and Fran H. Norris. "Mobilization and Deterioration of Social Support Following Natural Disasters." *Current Directions in Psychological Science* 4, no. 3 (June 1995): 94–98.

Kantchev, Georgi. "Russia Begins to Roll Out Its Sputnik V Coronavirus Vaccine; Doctors, Teachers and Social Workers in Moscow Are among the First to Receive the Shot." *Wall Street Journal (Online)*, December 5, 2020.

———. "Russia Cuts Interest Rates to Post-Soviet Low; Central Bank's Rate Cut Comes as Economic Pain Penetrates All Sectors of Russian Society." *Wall Street Journal (Online)*, June 19, 2020.

———. "Russia Cuts Interest Rate to Shore up Faltering Economy; the Central Bank Takes Action as the Country Lurches Towards a Recession." *Wall Street Journal (Online)*, April 24, 2020.

Kantchev, Georgi, and Drew Hinshaw. "Hit Hard by Coronavirus, Russia Joins Global Race for a Vaccine; Being First Would Provide Putin More Economic and Political Leverage as 'Vaccine Nationalism' Spreads." *Wall Street Journal (Online)*, June 11, 2020.

Karl, Schmitter. "What Democracy Is ... And Is Not." *Journal of Democracy* 2, no. 3 (1991): 75–88.

Kasparov, Garry. "Russia Claims It Has Covid-19 under Control. The Facade Is Cracking." *The Washington Post (Online)*, March 29, 2020, 2020.

Kavakli, Kerim Can. "Did Populist Leaders Respond to the COVID-19 Pandemic More Slowly? Evidence from a Global Sample." Bocconi University, 2020, https://covidcrisislab.unibocconi.eu/sites/default/files/media/attach/Kerim-Can-Kavakli.pdf.

Keefer, Philip, Eric Neumayer, and Thomas Plumper. "Earthquake Propensity and the Politics of Mortality Prevention." *World Development* 39, no. 9 (2011): 1530–41.

Kellenberg, Derek K., and Ahmed Mushfiq Mobarak. "Does Rising Income Increase or Decrease Damage Risk from Natural Disasters?" *Journal of Urban Economics* 63 (2008): 788–802.

Kessler, Glenn. "Tracking the President's False or Misleading Claims About Threat from the Virus." *The Washington Post*, March 22, 2020, A4.

KFF. "Global COVID-19 Tracker" KFF, January 20, 2023, https://www.kff.org/coronavirus-covid-19/issue-brief/global-covid-19-tracker/.

Khurshudyan, Isabelle. "Coronavirus Is Testing the Limits of Russia's Surveillance State: Moscow Held Back on Requiring Digital Bar Codes to Leave Home, but Other Regions Are Pushing Ahead with Mobile Tracking." *The Washington Post (Online)*, April 5, 2020.

———. "In Dagestan, a Covid Recount Adds to Questions on Russia's Overall Numbers: Russia Boasts of a Low Mortality Rate. But in Dagestan, Pneumonia and Other Causes Were Not Part of Pandemic Totals." *The Washington Post (Online)*, August 3, 2020.

———. "In Russia, Rising Concern for Health-Care Workers." *The Washington Post*, May 7, 2020, A14.

———. "Russia's Low Count Raises Skepticism, Even with Moscow's Mayor." *The Washington Post*, March 25, 2020, A14.

Kim, Seung M., and Toluse Olorunnipa. "Some Gop Senators Want Greater Federal Role in Testing." *The Washington Post*, April 22, 2020, A6.

Kim, Seung M., Maria Sacchetti, and Brady Dennis. "Every American Can Be Tested for Virus, Pence Promises." *The Washington Post*, March 4, 2020, A8.

Klinenberg, Eric. *Heat Wave: A Social Autopsy of Disaster in Chicago.* Chicago: University of Chicago Press, 2002.

Knowles, Hannah. "States Enacting New Virus Measures." *The Washington Post*, November 15, 2020, A3.

Knowles, Scott Gabriel. *The Disaster Experts Mastering Risk in Modern America.* Philadelphia: University of Pennsylvania Press, 2011.

Kolesnikov, Andrei. "Putin's War Has Moved Russia from Authoritarianism to Hybrid Totalitarianism." Carnegie Endowment for International Peace, April 29, 2022, https://carnegieendowment .org/2022/04/19/putin-s-war-has-moved-russia-from-authoritarianism-to-hybrid-totalitarianism -pub-86921.

Koon, Wee Kek. "China Has Been Plagued, and Shaped, by Epidemics - It Has Also Overcome Them." *South China Morning Post*, December 21, 2020.

Kramer, Andrew E. "Russia, Expecting Plaudits for Vaccine, Is Miffed by Its Cool Reception." *New York Times (Online)*, August 23, 2020.

———. "Russia Is Slow to Administer Virus Vaccine Despite Kremlin's Approval." *New York Times (Online)*, November 24, 2020.

Kugler, Maurice, and Shakti Sinha. "The Impact of COVID-19 and the Policy Response in India." Brookings Institution, July 13, 2020, https://www.brookings.edu/blog/future-development/2020 /07/13/the-impact-of-covid-19-and-the-policy-response-in-india/.

Kuo, Lily. "China Grapples with New Cases Ahead of the Lunar New Year." *The Washington Post*, December 30, 2020, A9.

Kupferschmidt, Kai, and Jon Cohen. "China's Aggressive Measures Have Slowed the Coronavirus: They May Not Work in Other Countries." *Science*, March 2, 2020, https://www.science.org/ content/article/china-s-aggressive-measures-have-slowed-coronavirus-they-may-not-work-other -countries?cookieSet=1.

Kurlantzick, Joshua. "How Jokowi Failed the Test of COVID-19 in Indonesia." *World Politics Review*, June 9, 2020, https://www.worldpoliticsreview.com/amid-lackluster-response-by-jokowi -indonesia-reels-from-covid-19/.

Kyle, Jordan, and Limor Gultchin. "Populists in Power around the World." Tony Blair Institute for Global Change, November 7, 2018, https://www.institute.global/insights/geopolitics-and-security /populists-power-around-world.

LaBrecque, Leon. "The Cares Act Has Passed: Here Are the Highlights." March 29, 2020, 2020.

Laclau, Ernest. *On Populist Reason.* London: Verso Books, 2002.

Lake, David A., and Matthew A. Baum. "The Invisible Hand of Democracy: Political Control and the Provision of Public Services." *Comparative Political Studies* 34, no. 6 (August 2001): 587–621.

Lam, Nadia. "How China Claimed Victory over the Coronavirus." *South China Morning Post*, November 12, https://www.scmp.com/news/china/article/3109393/how-china-claimed-victory -over-coronavirus.

Lamothe, Dan. "Pentagon Combats Conspiracy Theories as National Guard Assists in Response." *The Washington Post*, March 24, 2020, A4.

Lancet. "India's COVID-19 Emergency." *Lancet* (London: England) 397, no. 10286 (2021): 1683 .

Lau, Mimi. "Coronavirus: China Sets Trial Date for Citizen Journalist Zhang Zhan." *South China Morning Post*, December 18, 2020.

Lau, Mimi, and Phoebe Zhang. "Coronavirus: Students Protest against China University Lockdowns Citing Lack of Virus Cases, Lack of Consistency." *South China Morning Post*, September 24, 2020.

Lazarev, Egor, Anton Sobolev, Irina V. Soboleva, and Boris Sokolov. "Trial by Fire: A Natural Disaster's Impact on Support for the Authorities in Rural Russia." *World Politics* 66, no. 4 (October 2014): 641–48.

Lazo, Luz, and Katherine Shaver. "Checkpoints Targeting out-of-State Drivers Draw Scrutiny." *The Washington Post*, April 15, 2020, A8.

Lee, Amanda. "China Needs to Weigh Economic 'Consequences' of Coronavirus Stimulus, Top Beijing Researcher Says." *South China Morning Post*, July 27, 2020.

Lee, Michelle Y.H. "CDC Voting Safety Guidelines Endorse Mail, Early Balloting." *The Washington Post*, July 8, 2020, A9.

Leng, Sidney. "China's Plan for 2.5-Day Weekend to Aid Coronavirus-Hit Economy Met with Mixed Reactions." *South China Morning Post*, July 23, 2020.

Lerman, Rachel, Katie Shepherd, and Telford, T. "Twitter Penalizes Trump Jr., Citing Misinformation on Coronavirus." *The Washington Post*, July 29, 2020, A18.

Levitsky, Steven. "Populism and Competitive Authoritarianism." Paper presented at the Memo Prepared for "Global Populisms as a Threat to Democracy" conference, Stanford University, 2017.

Levitsky, Steven, and Lucan Way. *Competitive Authoritarianism: Hybrid Regimes after the Cold War*. Cambridge: Cambridge University Press, 2010.

Lew, Linda. "Coronavirus Pandemic Shows Global Consequences of China's Local Censorship Rules." *South China Morning Post*, June 7, 2020.

———. "Twitter Removes 23,750 China-Linked Accounts for Spreading Disinformation." *South China Morning Post*, June 12, 2020.

Lewis, James. "Corruption: The Hidden Perpetrator of under-Development and Vulnerability to Natural Hazards and Disasters." *JAMBA: Journal of Disaster Risk Studies* 3, no. 2 (May 2011): 464–75.

Lewis, Peter. "Growth without Prosperity in Africa." *Journal of Democracy* 19, no. 4 (October 2008): 95–109.

Li, Cheng, and Diana Liang. "Rule of the Rigid Compromiser." Brookings Institution, Spring 2019, https://www.brookings.edu/articles/rule-of-the-rigid-compromiser/.

Li, He. "Populism in China." In *The Routledge Handbook of Chinese Studies*, edited by Tan, Chee-Beng, 376–88: Routledge, 2021.

Li, Yuan. "Coronavirus Weakens China's Powerful Propaganda Machine: The New New World." *New York Times (Online)*, February 26, 2020.

———. "Emergency Measures Create Hurdles for Farmers and Small Businesses: [Foreign Desk]." *New York Times (Online)*, February 1, 2020.

———. "In China, Virus Spurred Rush of Blame Shifting: [Foreign Desk]." *New York Times*, February 5, 2020, A1.

———. "In Ousting U.S. Reporters, China Signals New Kind of Self-Confidence: [Foreign Desk]." *New York Times*, March 19, 2020, A19.

———. "Online Revolt in China as a Doctor Is Lionized: [Business/Financial Desk]." *New York Times*, February 8, 2020, B1.

———. "With Selective Coronavirus Coverage, China Builds a Culture of Hate [with Graphic(S)]." *New York Times (Online)*, April 22, 2020.

Lijphart, Arend. *Patterns of Democracy: Government Forms and Performance in Thirty-Six Countries*. New Haven: Yale University Press, 2012.

Lin, Thung-hong. "Governing Disaster: Political Institutions, Social Inequality and Human Vulnerability." In *2012 Annual Meeting of Taiwanese Sociological Association*, 1–55, 2012.

Linz, Juan. "The Perils of Presidentialism." *Journal of Democracy* 1, no. 1 (Winter 1990): 51–70.

Linz, Juan, and Alfred C. Stepan. "Toward Consolidated Democracy." *Journal of Democracy* 7, no. 2 (April 1996): 14–33.

Litvinova, Daria. "Putin Reveals He Was Vaccinated with Russia's Sputnik V." *Associated Press News*, June 30, 2021.

Liu, Yihong. "Crisis Rhetoric and Policy Change in China: Toward a Dynamic Process Model of Crisis Exploitation." edited by Ultrecht University. Ultrecht, Netherlands, 2019.

Lo, Kinling. "Coronavirus: Living Samples Found on Frozen Food Packaging in East China's Qingdao, CDC Says." *South China Morning Post*, October 18.

Long, Heather. "Details of Trump's Executive Actions Paint a Less Generous Picture of Aid." *The Washington Post*, August 10, 2020, A16.

Long, Heather, Jeff Stein, Lisa Rein, and Tony Romm. "Staffing, Antiquated Technology Slow the Delivery of Virus Relief." *The Washington Post*, April 18, 2020, A1.

Louwerse, Tom, and Simon Otjes. "How Populists Wage Opposition: Parliamentary Opposition Behaviour and Populism in Netherlands." *Political Studies* 67, no. 2 (2019): 479–95.

Luo, Renfu, Linxiu Zhang, Jikun Huang, and Scott Rozelle. "Village Elections, Public Goods Investments and Pork Barrel Politics, Chinese-Style." *Journal of Development Studies* 46, no. 4 (April 2010): 662–84.

Lynch, David J. "Raging Virus Triggers New Shutdown Orders and Economy Braces for Fresh Wave of Pain." *The Washington Post*, November 15, 2020, A1.

Ma, Josephine. "Can China Become a Leading Producer of Covid-19 Vaccines?" *South China Morning Post*, October 27, 2020.

Mackintosh, Thomas. "China Covid: Five Deaths under Country's New Counting Method." *BBC*, December 20, 2022.

Magnusson, Bruce. "Democratization and Domestic Insecurity: Navigating the Transition in Benin." *Comparative Politics* 33, no. 2 (January 2001): 211–30.

Makarenko, B. "Populism and Political Institutions: A Comparative Perspective." *Herald of Public Opinion. Data. Analysis. Discussion* 1, no. 124 (2017): 15–28.

Mamonova, Natalia. "Understanding the Silent Majority in Authoritarian Populism: What Can We Learn from Popular Support for Putin in Rural Russia?" *Critical Agrarian Studies* 46, no. 3 (2019): 201–26.

Mares, Isabela, and Matthew E. Carnes. "Social Policy in Developing Countries." *Annual Review of Political Science* 12 (2009): 93–113.

Maynes, Charles. "Belarus Leader Says He Survived Coronavirus." *VOA News*, July 29, 2020, https://www.voanews.com/a/covid-19-pandemic_belarus-leader-says-he-survived-coronavirus/6193613.html.

———. "With Record-High Deaths, Moscow and Other Parts of Russia Enter a Partial Lockdown." National Public Radio, October 28, 2021, https://www.npr.org/2021/10/28/1049976625/moscow-russia-covid-deaths-lockdown.

McCarthy, Simone. "Coronavirus: China Positions Itself for 'Vaccine Diplomacy' Push to Fight Covid-19." *South China Morning Post*, August 4, 2020.

———. "Coronavirus: People in China 'the Most Willing among 15 Countries to Take a Vaccine'." *South China Morning Post*, December 30, 2020.

McCarthy, Simone, and Zhuang Pinghui. "China's Sinopharm Reports Strong Interim Results for Its Covid-19 Vaccine." *South China Morning Post*, December 30, 2020.

McDonell, Stephen. "China Covid: Xi's Face-Saving Exit from His Signature Policy." *BBC*, December 5, 2022.

McGinley, Laurie. "FDA Suspends Most Inspections of Foreign Manufacturers." *The Washington Post*, March 11, 2020, A19.

McGinley, Laurie, and Yasmeen Abutaleb. "White House Effort to Undermine Fauci Criticized." *The Washington Post*, July 14, 2020, A5.

McGinley, Laurie, Yasmeen Abutaleb, and Josh Dawsey. "White House Challenges FDA Vaccine Standards." *The Washington Post*, September 26, 2020, A1.

McGinley, Laurie, Yasmeen Abutaleb, and Lena H. Sun. "Health Officials Ramp up Effort to Convince Public That Vaccine Decisions Will Be Based on Science, Not Politics." *The Washington Post*, August 9, 2020, A6.

McGinley, Laurie, and Carolyn Y. Johnson. "FDA Pulls Emergency Approval for Antimalarial Drugs Promoted by Trump." *The Washington Post*, June 16, 2020, A7.

McGinley, Laurie, and Carolyn Y. Johnson. "FDA Set to Back Higher Standard for Vaccine." *The Washington Post*, September 23, 2020, A1.

McGinley, Laurie, Carolyn Y. Johnson, and Josh Dawsey. "Trump Accuses 'Deep State' at FDA of Delaying Virus Vaccines, Treatments." *The Washington Post*, August 23, 2020, A8.

McGinley, Laurie, Lena H. Sun, Yasmeen Abutaleb, and Josh Dawsey. "Government Scientists Pushing Back against President." *The Washington Post*, November 2, 2020, A4.

McKee, Martin. "Learning from Success: How Has Hungary Responded to the COVID Pandemic?" *GeroScience* 42, no. 5 (July 27 2020): 1217–19.

McNie, E.C. "Reconciling the Supply of Scientific Information with User Demands: An Analysis of the Problem and Review of the Literature." *Environmental Science & Policy* 10 (2007): 17–38.

Meckler, Laura, and Moriah Balingit. "Should Schools Shut? Reactions Vary." *The Washington Post*, March 12, 2020, A20.

Meckler, Laura, and Rachel Weiner. "Delayed CDC Guidelines Offer Low-Key Guide to Reopening." *The Washington Post*, May 20, 2020, A8.

Mengo, Bedah. "Kenya's Most COVID-19 Cases Imported from Outside China: Analysis." *Xinhua General News Service*, May 12, 2020.

Meyer, Robert J. "Why We under-Prepare for Hazards." In *On Risk and Disaster: Lessons from Hurricane Katrina*, edited by Ronald Daniels, Donald F. Kettle, and Howard Kunreuther, 153–73. Philadelphia: University of Pennsylvania Press, 2006.

Miao, Ying. "Can China Be Populist? Grassroot Populist Narratives in the Chinese Cyberspace." *Contemporary Politics* 26, no. 3 (2020): 268–87.

Mietzner, Marcus. "Populist Anti-Scientism, Religious Polarisation, and Institutionalised Corruption: How Indonesia's Democratic Decline Shaped Its COVID-19 Response." *Journal of Current Southeast Asian Affairs* 39, no. 2 (2020): 227–49.

Miller, Greg, and Ellen Nakashima. "President's Intelligence Briefing Book Repeatedly Cited Virus Early in Year." *The Washington Post*, April 28, 2020, A8.

Minchin, Louise. "Breakfast - 9:20 Am Gmt." *BBC News 24*, January 18, 2020.

Miroff, Nick. "Fema Struggles with Sprawling Crisis as Season of Natural Disasters Lurks." *The Washington Post*, March 25, 2020, A17.

———. "In Survey, U.S. Mayors Cite Need for Supplies." *The Washington Post*, March 28, 2020, A3.

Miroff, Nick, Hannah Natanson, Kim Bellware, and Katherine Shaver. *The Washington Post*, March 16, 2020, A1.

Mitnick, Joshua. "Israel's Cautionary Coronavirus Tale." *Foreign Policy*, July 22, 2020, https://foreignpolicy.com/2020/07/22/israel-coronavirus-second-wave-netanyahu/.

Moffitt, Benjamin. "The Populism/Anti-Populism Divide in Western Europe." *Democratic Theory* 5, no. 2 (Winter 2018): 1–16.

Moon, Bruce E., and William J. Dixon. "Politics, the State, and Basic Human Needs: A Cross-National Study." *American Journal of Political Science* 29, no. 4 (November 1985): 661–94.

Mooney, Chris, Sarah Kaplan, and Juliet Eilperin. "States, Not Science, Get to Define 'Outbreak,' Hampering Efforts to Curb Virus." *The Washington Post*, October 8, 2020, A12.

Morello, Carol. "Health Experts Issue Urgent Call for Change of Course as U.S. Economy Tanks." *The Washington Post*, July 31, 2020, A6.

———. "Hearing Underscores U.S. Failure to Halt Virus." *The Washington Post*, August 1, 2020, A9.

———. "New Cases Rise in Midwest as They Plateau in Sun Belt." *The Washington Post*, July 29, 2020, A9.

Moritsugu, Ken. "Afraid of Needles? China Using Inhalable COVID-19 Vaccine." *Associate Press News*, October 26, 2022.

Morrison, J. Stephen, Scott Kennedy, and Yanzhong Huang. "China's Zero-Covid: What Should the West Do?" Center for Strategic and International Studies, June 27, 2022, https://www.csis.org/analysis/chinas-zero-covid-what-should-west-do.

Mozur, Paul. "China's Internet Police Crack Down on Outrage: [Business/Financial Desk]." *New York Times*, March 18, 2020, B6.

Mudde, Cas, and Cristóbal Rovira Kaltwasser. "Studying Populism in Comparative Perspective: Reflections on the Contemporary and Future Research Agenda." *Comparative Political Studies* 51, no. 13 (2018): 1667–93.

Mufson, Steven, Yasmeen Abutaleb, and Juliet Eilperin. "States Plead for Federal Testing Help Amid Push to Reopen." *The Washington Post*, April 18, 2020, A7.

Müller, Jan-Werner. *What Is Populism?* Philadelphia: University of Pennsylvania Press, 2016.

Mulligan, Casey B., Richard Gil, and Xavier Sala-i-Martin. "Do Democracies Have Different Public Policies Than Nondemocracies?" *Journal of Economic Perspectives* 18, no. 1 (Winter 2004): 51–74.

Myers, Steven Lee. "China Had a Fail-Safe Way to Track Contagions: Officials Failed to Use It: [Foreign Desk]." *New York Times*, March 30, 2020, A1.

———. "China Ousts 2 Party Officials Amid Outrage About Coronavirus Response." *New York Times (Online)*, February 13, 2020.

Myers, Steven Lee, and Chris Buckley. "Novel Virus Tests China's Authoritarian Bargain: [Foreign Desk]." *New York Times*, January 27, 2020, A1.

Myers, Steven Lee, and Giulia Marchi. "Virtual Shutdown Clears out China's Capital: [Foreign Desk]." *New York Times*, February 4, 2020, A7.

Nakamura, David. "Amid Pandemic, Trump Is Making Promises He Can't Keep." *The Washington Post*, March 20, 2020, A4.

———. "Competing Events Highlight Trump's, Biden's Different Approaches to Pandemic." *The Washington Post*, December 9, 2020, A22.

———. "On CDC Tour, Trump Plays Medical Expert by Second-Guessing the Professionals." *The Washington Post*, March 8, 2020, A5.

———. "Trump Overrides Virus Precautions Set up for His Own Events." *The Washington Post*, August 8, 2020, A7.

Nakamura, David, Yasmeen Abutaleb, and Josh Dawsey. "Pressure Mounts on Trump to Launch Coordinated Response to Epidemic." *The Washington Post*, January 31, 2020, A19.

Nakamura, David, Josh Dawsey, and Yasmeen Abutaleb. "As Infections Rise, Trump Again Attacks Fauci's Guidance." *The Washington Post*, October 14, 2020, A6.

Nakamura, David, Josh Dawsey, and David A. Fahrenthold. "After Downplaying Risks, Trump Pivots to Precautions." *The Washington Post*, March 15, 2020, A11.

Nakamura, David, and Ashley Parker. "'It Totally Belittled the Moment': Many Look Back in Dismay at Trump's Tossing of Paper Towels in Puerto Rico." *The Washington Post*, 13 September, 2018.

Nakashima, Ellen, Elizabeth Dwoskin, and Anna Fifield. "Twitter Suspends 23,000 Accounts, Alleges Ties to China's Communist Party." *The Washington Post*, June 12, 2020, A11.

Nakazawa, Katsujikoon. "China Portrays 'Xi the Great,' Tamer of Floods." *Nikkei Asia*, August 27, 2020.

Newswire. "All Necessary Measures to Fight New Coronavirus in Russia Taken - Popova." *Russia & CIS General Newswire*, January 22, 2020.

———. "Center to Identify Fake News Included in Council for Resisting Coronavirus in Russia." *Russia & CIS General Newswire*, March 30, 2020.

———. "Children's Hospital Chief Physician, Ambulance Paramedic Die of Covid-19 in Buinaksk in Russia's Dagestan." *Russia & CIS General Newswire*, May 27, 2020.

———. "Coronavirus Death Rates 7.4 Times Lower in Russia Than in World as a Whole - Deputy PM Golikova." *Russia & CIS General Newswire*, May 11, 2020.

———. "Coronavirus Morbidity on Decline in Russia - Health Ministry." *Russia & CIS General Newswire*, December 29, 2020.

———. "Coronavirus Problem Spreading into Russia's Provinces - Putin (Part 2)." *Russia & CIS General Newswire*, April 17, 2020.

———. "Coronavirus Situation Stabilizing in Russia, yet Differs from One Region to Another - Rospotrebnadzor Head Popova." *Russia & CIS General Newswire*, December 15, 2020.

———. "Covid-19 Growth Rates May Slow Down in Russia by May - Health Ministry's Chief Epidemiologist (Part 2)." *Russia & CIS General Newswire*, March 27, 2020.

———. "Covid-19 Situation in Russia Becoming More Complicated, Is Manageable - Peskov (Part 2)." *Russia & CIS General Newswire*, November 24, 2020.

———. "Despite Unfavorable Conditions, Russia to Fulfill All Social Commitments - Matviyenko." *Russia & CIS General Newswire*, March 14, 2020.

———. "Effective Healthcare System Allowed Russia to Deal with Coronavirus - Peskov." *Russia & CIS General Newswire*, June 10, 2020.

———. "Emergency Declared in 3rd District in Russia's Primorye Territory to Address Spread of Coronavirus." *Russia & CIS General Newswire*, February 3, 2020.

———. "Entry to Russia for Chinese Citizens to Be Suspended Starting Feb 20 (Part 2)." *Russia & CIS General Newswire*, February 18, 2020.

———. "Foreign Media May Lose Accreditation in Russia for Fakes - State Duma Commission." *Russia & CIS General Newswire*, May 28, 2020.

———. "Future of FT, NYT in Russia to Depend on Whether They Retract Russia Covid-19 Death Toll Articles - Foreign Ministry." *Russia & CIS General Newswire*, May 14, 2020.

———. "Government Allots About 2 Bln Rubles to Build Medical Centers in Russia's Dagestan - Mishustin." *Russia & CIS General Newswire*, May 28, 2020.

———. "Group of Military Medics, Engineers, Chemists Created in Russia's Novosibirsk, Kemerovo Regions." *Russia & CIS General Newswire*, March 26, 2020.

———. "Kremlin Admits Certain Shortage of Means of Individual Protection against Coronavirus in Russia." *Russia & CIS General Newswire*, March 20, 2020.

———. "Kremlin Views Coronavirus Situation in Russia as 'Quite Serious' (Part 2)." *Russia & CIS General Newswire*, October 26, 2020.

———. "Matviyenko: No Panic Should Be Caused over Coronavirus Spread, Russia Keeps Situation under Control." *Russia & CIS General Newswire*, January 30, 2020.

———. "Moscow City Hall Denies Open Russia Authorization of Opposition Rally." *Russia & CIS General Newswire*, March 13, 2020.

———. "No Regions in Russia Remain Unaffected by New Coronavirus as 1st Case Recorded in Republic of Altai." *Russia & CIS General Newswire*, April 16, 2020.

———. "Number of People in Self-Isolation Due to Coronavirus Situation Almost Doubles in Russia - Poll." *Russia & CIS General Newswire*, April 8, 2020.

———. "Over 5,000 Military Medics Might Be Engaged in Fighting Coronavirus Epidemic in Russia by Mid-May - Shoigu." *Russia & CIS General Newswire*, April 17, 2020.

———. "Peskov Denies Enhanced Quarantine Measures, Another Self-Isolation Period in Russia Being Discussed (Part 2)." *Russia & CIS General Newswire*, September 17, 2020.

———. "Putin Hopes Coronavirus in Russia Can Be Overcome Earlier Than in 3 Months." *Russia & CIS General Newswire*, March 26, 2020.

———. "Putin Hopes Improved Coronavirus Situation Will Allow Russia to Focus on Long-Term Agenda (Part 2)." *Russia & CIS General Newswire*, May 14, 2020.

———. "Putin Says Russia Exiting Coronavirus Situation with Confidence, in Contrast with U.S (Part 2)." *Russia & CIS General Newswire*, June 14, 2020.

———. "Putin Sees Russia's Strength in Its Multiethnic Nature." *Russia & CIS General Newswire*, June 14, 2020.

———. "Putin Signs Decree on Measures to Ensure Sanitary-Epidemiological Wellbeing of People on Territory of Russia Amid Coronavirus (Part 2)." *Russia & CIS General Newswire*, April 2, 2020.

———. "Putin: No Need to Issue General Order to All Businesses across Russia to Limit Operations (Part 2)." *Russia & CIS General Newswire*, April 3, 2020.

———. "Putin: Russia Still Hasn't Passed Peak of Coronavirus Epidemic, Should Avoid Mistakes Made by Others." *Russia & CIS General Newswire*, April 7, 2020.

———. "Quantities of Coronavirus Test Systems Sufficient in Russia, Rospotrebnadzor Set to Provide All Regions with Them - Golikova." *Russia & CIS General Newswire*, March 16, 2020.

———. "Rospotrebnadzor Chief: 366 Observation Facilities Prepared in Russia for Coronavirus Quarantine." *Russia & CIS General Newswire*, February 29, 2020.

———. "Rospotrebnadzor Epidemiologist Says Rise in New Covid-19 Cases in Russia Due to More Testing." *Russia & CIS General Newswire*, November 16, 2020.

———. "Rospotrebnadzor to Propose Stricter Liability for Violation of Quarantine Rules in Russia (Part 2)." *Russia & CIS General Newswire*, February 17, 2020.

———. "Russia Could Tighten Epidemiological Control on Domestic Flights - Source." *Russia & CIS General Newswire*, January 31, 2020.

———. "Russia Doing Everything Necessary to Stop Coronavirus but the Infection Has Negative Impact on Global Economy - Putin (Part 2)." *Russia & CIS General Newswire*, March 1, 2020.

———. "Russia Has All Necessary Tools to Develop Coronavirus Vaccine in near Future - Putin (Part 2)." *Russia & CIS General Newswire*, March 17, 2020.

———. "Russia Has Been Able to Protect Its Citizens from Coronavirus in General - Putin (Part 2)." *Russia & CIS General Newswire*, June 28, 2020.

———. "Russia May Begin Easing Coronavirus Restrictions after May 12 - Rospotrebnadzor Head (Part 2)." *Russia & CIS General Newswire*, April 27, 2020.

———. "Russia Mobilizes Its Medical Institutions for Coronavirus Fight - Golikova." *Russia & CIS General Newswire*, March 17, 2020.

———. "Russia Not Considering Coronavirus-Related Lockdown for Now - Peskov." *Russia & CIS General Newswire*, October 2, 2020.

———. "Russia Preparing Action Plan to Neutralize Coronavirus Effects on Economy - Econ Ministry." *Russia & CIS General Newswire*, February 18, 2020.

———. "Russia Ranks 105th in World in Covid-19 Fatality Rate - Rospotrebnadzor." *Russia & CIS General Newswire*, October 19, 2020.

———. "Russia Restricting Foreign Arrivals from S. Korea on March 1 (Part 2)." *Russia & CIS General Newswire*, February 28, 2020.

———. "Russia Restricts Transborder Traffic, Passenger Rail Service with China." *Russia & CIS General Newswire*, January 31, 2020.

———. "Russia Sees Overall Mortality Grow by over 150% Year-on-Year in Nov 2020 - Rosstat." *Russia & CIS General Newswire*, December 28, 2020.

———. "Russia Should Ensure Quickest Possible Economic Recovery after Coronavirus Epidemic - Putin." *Russia & CIS General Newswire*, April 7, 2020.

———. "Russia Suspends Visa-Free Tourism, Issuance of Business Visas for China." *Russia & CIS General Newswire*, February 1, 2020.

———. "Russia Taking Large-Scale, Systemic Efforts to Avert Coronavirus Risk, Develop Vaccine - Peskov." *Russia & CIS General Newswire*, February 5, 2020.

———. "Russia to Continue Covid-19 Testing - Mishustin." *Russia & CIS General Newswire*, June 15, 2020.

———. "Russia to Restrict Air Traffic with Italy, Germany, France, Spain from March 13 - Coronavirus HQ (Part 2)." *Russia & CIS General Newswire*, March 11, 2020.

———. "Russia to Soon Launch Phone Hotline, Online System to Inform Citizens of Covid-19 Situation - Mishustin." *Russia & CIS General Newswire*, March 16, 2020.

———. "Russia to Spend up to 300 Bln Rubles to Support Economy, People in Fight against Coronavirus - PM." *Russia & CIS General Newswire*, March 16, 2020.

———. "Russia Went through Hardships in 2020, Needs Unity - Putin." *Russia & CIS General Newswire*, December 31, 2020.

———. "Russia's Coronavirus Response System, Available Hospital Beds Make It Possible to Avoid Lockdown for Now - Kremlin (Part 2)." *Russia & CIS General Newswire*, October 12, 2020.

———. "Russia's Draft Budget Turns out to Be Tense Amid Covid-19 - Mishustin (Part 2)." *Russia & CIS General Newswire*, October 26, 2020.

———. "Russia's Southern Regions See Increase in Coronavirus Cases after Start of Tour Season." *Russia & CIS General Newswire*, August 5, 2020.

———. "Russia's Unemployment Situation Not 'Threatening' - Labor Minister." *Russia & CIS General Newswire*, May 13, 2020.

———. "Schools across Russia Advised to Temporarily Move Classes Online - Education Ministry." *Russia & CIS General Newswire*, March 14, 2020.

———. "Second Covid-19 Wave in Russia on Same Scale as First One Unlikely - Health Minister Murashko (Part 2)." *Russia & CIS General Newswire*, July 3, 2020.

———. "Situation Thus Far Not Developing in Best Way, Russia to See Budget Deficit in 2020 - Siluanov." *Russia & CIS General Newswire*, March 18, 2020.

———. "Six Coronavirus Cases Registered in Russia since Mid-Feb - Rospotrebnadzor." *Russia & CIS General Newswire*, March 3, 2020.

———. "Threat of Novel Coronavirus Importation to Russia Exists - Peskov." *Russia & CIS General Newswire*, January 31, 2020.

Nian, Yuan Yang, Nian Lui, Sue-Lin Wong, and Qianer Lui. "Seizing the Moment for Surveillance; FT Big Read. China; for All Its Monitoring Powers, China's Efforts to Track Coronavirus Cases Have Often Been Haphazard. Private Companies Have Been Reluctant to Hand over Data but Are Facing Heavy Government Pressure to Comply." *Financial Times*, April 3, 2020.

Nicole, Dungca, Jenn Abelson, and John Sullivan. "'They Didn't Move Fast Enough'." *The Washington Post*, March 30, 2020, A1.

Nojomi, Marzieh, Maziar Moradi-Lakeh, and Farshad Pourmalek. "COVID-19 in Iran: What Was Done and What Should Be Done." *Medical Journal of the Islamic Republic of Iran* 35, no. 97 (July 29 2021).

Normile, Dennis. "'An Undebatable Political Decision': Why China Refuses to End Its Harsh Lockdowns." *Science*, April 15, 2022, https://www.science.org/content/article/undebatable-political-decision-why-china-refuses-end-its-harsh-lockdowns.

Norris, Pippa, and Ronald Inglehart. *Cultural Backlash: Trump, Brexit, and Authoritarian Populism.* Cambridge: Cambridge University Press, 2019.

NYT. "As U.S. Schools Move to Reopen Despite Covid-19, Teachers Threaten to Strike." *The New York Times*, August 21, 2020, https://www.nytimes.com/2020/08/19/world/covid-19-coronavirus.html.

———. "New Cases in China Appear to Be Slowing." *New York Times*, February 18, 2020, https://www.nytimes.com/2020/02/18/world/asia/china-coronavirus.html.

Ober, Josiah. "Thucydides on Athens' Democratic Advantage in the Archidamian War." Social Science Research Network, 2009.

Obradović, Sandra, Séamus A. Power, and Jennifer Sheehy-Skeffington. "Understanding the Psychological Appeal of Populism." *Current Opinion in Psychology* 35 (2020): 125–31.

O'Brien, Thomas. "Populism, Protest and Democracy in the Twenty-First Century." *Contemporary Social Science* 10, no. 4 (2015): 337–48.

O'Grady, Siobhán, Lenny Bernstein, Anna Fifield, and William Wan. "'They've Been through a Lot': More Americans Flee Wuhan." *The Washington Post*, February 6, 2020, A1.

O'Reilly, Kevin. "Why CDC Was Right to Revise Coronavirus Testing Guidelines." American Medical Association, September 23, 2020, https://www.ama-assn.org/delivering-care/public-health/why-cdc-was-right-revise-coronavirus-testing-guidelines.

Olorunnipa, Toluse. "In About-Face, Trump Dons Mask at Walter Reed." *The Washington Post*, July 13, 2020, A2.

———. "To Trump, Economy Determines Discourse." *The Washington Post*, May 8, 2020, A1.

———. "Trump Messaging Sows Confusion in Outbreak Response." *The Washington Post*, July 14, 2020, A5.

———. "Virus Briefing Returns with New Approach." *The Washington Post*, July 22, 2020, A1.

Olorunnipa, Toluse, Yasmeen Abutaleb, and Josh Dawsey. "Trump Shifts Focus from Virus to Jobs and Law and Order." *The Washington Post*, June 6, 2020, A4.

Olorunnipa, Toluse, Shawn Boburg, and Arelis R. Hernández. "Rallies against Governors' Stay-at-Home Orders Grow." *The Washington Post*, April 18, 2020, A4.

Olorunnipa, Toluse, and Josh Dawsey. "Bad Numbers Push Trump to Bring Back Virus Briefing." *The Washington Post*, July 21, 2020, A1.

Olorunnipa, Toluse, Josh Dawsey, and Yasmeen Abutaleb. "Major Surge in Infections Exposes U.S. Failures." *The Washington Post*, June 28, 2020, A1.

———. "Trump Taps Pence to Lead Emerging Coronavirus Effort." *The Washington Post*, February 27, 2020, A1.

Olorunnipa, Toluse, Ariana Eunjung Cha, and Laurie McGinley. "Drug Promoted by Trump as 'Game Changer' Increasingly Linked to Deaths." *The Washington Post*, May 16, 2020, A7.

Olorunnipa, Toluse, and Anne Gearan. "Facing a Global Crisis, Trump Doubles Down on His Go-It-Alone Approach." *The Washington Post*, March 13, 2020, A19.

Olorunnipa, Toluse, Seung Min Kim, and Scott Wilson. "Trump Voices New U.S. Containment Guidelines." *The Washington Post*, March 17, 2020, 2020, A1.

Olorunnipa, Toluse, Nick Miroff, and Dan Lamothe. "Trump Invokes Wartime Powers to Bolster U.S. Response." *The Washington Post*, March 19, 2020, A6.

Olorunnipa, Toluse, and Erica Werner. "Partisan Gridlock Hardens Amid Surging Pandemic and Stalling Economy." *The Washington Post*, October 18, 2020, A14.

Olorunnipa, Toluse, Griff Witte, and Lenny Bernstein. "Trump Applauds States Reopening Ahead of Guidance." *The Washington Post*, May 5, 2020, A1.

Olson, Richard Stuart. "Toward a Politics of Disaster: Losses, Values, Agenda, and Blame." *International Journal of Mass Emergencies and Disasters* 18, no. 2 (August 2000): 265–87.

Otrachshenko, Vladimir, Olga Popova, and Pavel Solomin. "Misfortunes Never Come Singly: Consecutive Weather Shocks and Mortality in Russia." *Economics and Human Biology* 31 (2018): 249–58.

Owen, Catherine, and Eleanor Bindman. "Civic Participation in a Hybrid Regime: Limited Pluralism in Policymaking and Delivery in Contemporary Russia." *Government and Opposition* 54, no. 1 (2019): 98–120.

Panizza, Francisco. "Trump: Once a Populist Always a Populist." London School of Economics and Political Science, November 13, 2020, https://blogs.lse.ac.uk/government/2020/11/13/trump-once-a-populist-always-a-populist/.

Pariseault, Amanda B. "Current Status of COVID-19 Vaccines Rollout Nationwide: July 2021 Update for the Attorney General Community." National Association of Attorneys General, August 10, 2021, https://www.naag.org/attorney-general-journal/current-status-of-covid-19-vaccines-rollout-nationwide-july-2021-update-for-the-attorney-general-community/.

Parker, Ashley. "White House Looks to Move Trump Away from Spotlight." *The Washington Post*, April 28, 2020, A7.

Parker, Ashley, Yasmeen Abutaleb, and Josh Dawsey. "Lots of Players, but No Consensus on a Game Plan." *The Washington Post*, April 12, 2020, A1.

Parker, Ashley, Yasmeen Abutaleb, and Lena H. Sun. "How the Trump Administration Squandered Its Response Time." *The Washington Post*, March 8, 2020, A1.

Parker, Ashley, Josh Dawsey, and Yasmeen Abutaleb. "10 Days of Distraction for Trump after Virus Warning." *The Washington Post*, September 17, 2020, A1.

———. "For Trump, This Pandemic Is All About the Numbers - and They Aren't Good." *The Washington Post*, March 13, 2020.

———. "Top Virus Official Is New Target for Trump." *The Washington Post*, August 4, 2020, A1.

Parker, Ashley, Josh Dawsey, Yasmeen Abutaleb, and Philip Rucker. "Amid Election Fight, Trump Tunes out Spike in Cases." *The Washington Post*, November 15, 2020, A1.

Parker, Ashley, Josh Dawsey, Yasmeen Abutaleb, and Lena H. Sun. "Scientists at Trump's Side Have to Toe a Difficult Line." *The Washington Post*, April 23, 2020, A1.

Parker, Ashley, Josh Dawsey, Annie Linskey, and Dan Diamond. "Trump Tested Positive for Coronavirus before First Debate with Biden, Three Former Aides Say." *The Washington Post*, December 1, 2021.

Parker, Ashley, and Philip Rucker. "Trump Seems Poised to Let Others Lead on Reopening." *The Washington Post*, May 18, 2020, A1.

Parker, Ashley, Philip Rucker, and Rucker Ashley Parker, and Philip. "The President Turns to the Experts He's Long Maligned." *The Washington Post*, February 28, 2020, A12.

Pelling, Mark, and Kathleen Dill. "Disaster Politics: From Social Control to Human Security." In *Environment, Politics and Development Working Paper Series*, edited by King's College Department of Geography, 1–24. London, 2008.

Perry, Elizabeth J. "The Populist Dream of Chinese Democracy." *The Journal of Asian Studies* 74, no. 4 (2015): 903–15.

Perry, Ronald W. "What Is a Disaster?" Chap. 1 In *Handbook of Disaster Research*, edited by Rodríguez Havidán, Enrico L. Quarantelli, and Russell R. Dynes, 1–15. Springer, 2007.

Peters, B. Guy, and Jon Pierre. "A Typology of Populism: Understanding the Different Forms of Populism and Their Implications." *Democratization* 27, no. 6 (2020): 928–46.

Pinghui, Zhuang. "China Admits Coronavirus Exposed 'Weak Links' in Health System as Government Promises to Strengthen Disease Response." *South China Morning Post*, May 23, 2020.

———. "China Approves Sinopharm's Covid-19 Vaccine, Promises the Public Free Jabs." *South China Morning Post*, December 31, 2020.

———. "China's Public Health Insurance Agency Says It Can't Afford to Provide Covid-19 Vaccine for Free." *South China Morning Post*, October 13, 2020.

———. "Coronavirus: China CDC Chief Becomes Vaccine 'Mouse' in Shot in Arm to Research." *South China Morning Post*, July 31, 2020.

———. "Coronavirus: Frozen Food Firms as Culprit in Two Outbreaks in China, Sparking Warning over Cold Imports." *South China Morning Post*, October 28, 2020.

———. "On China's Coronavirus Front Line, Not Everyone Wants a Vaccine - Just Yet." *South China Morning Post*, December 23, 2020.

Presidential Bulletin. "Russia - April 8." *Russia & CIS Presidential Bulletin*, April 8, 2020.

———. "Russia - April 8." *Russia & CIS Presidential Bulletin*, April 8, 2020.

———. "Russia - April 13." *Russia & CIS Presidential Bulletin*, April 13, 2020.

———. "Russia - April 17." *Russia & CIS Presidential Bulletin*, April 17, 2020.

———. "Russia - April 22." *Russia & CIS Presidential Bulletin*, April 22, 2020.

———. "Russia - April 27." *Russia & CIS Presidential Bulletin*, April 27, 2020.

———. "Russia - April 28." *Russia & CIS Presidential Bulletin*, April 28, 2020.

———. "Russia - May 6." *Russia & CIS Presidential Bulletin*, May 6, 2020.

———. "Russia - May 12." *Russia & CIS Presidential Bulletin*, May 12, 2020.

———. "Russia - May 18." *Russia & CIS Presidential Bulletin*, May 18, 2020.

———. "Russia - May 22." *Russia & CIS Presidential Bulletin*, May 22, 2020.

———. "Russia - May 27." *Russia & CIS Presidential Bulletin*, May 27, 2020.

———. "Russia - June 1." *Russia & CIS Presidential Bulletin*, June 1, 2020.

———. "Russia - June 3." *Russia & CIS Presidential Bulletin*, June 3, 2020.

———. "Russia - June 9." *Russia & CIS Presidential Bulletin*, June 9, 2020.

———. "Russia - June 15." *Russia & CIS Presidential Bulletin*, June 15, 2020.

———. "Russia - July 13." *Russia & CIS Presidential Bulletin*, July 13, 2020.

———. "Russia - July 22." *Russia & CIS Presidential Bulletin*, July 22, 2020.

———. "Russia - July 29." *Russia & CIS Presidential Bulletin*, July 29, 2020.

———. "Russia - September 24." *Russia & CIS Presidential Bulletin*, September 24, 2020.

———. "Russia - September 29." *Russia & CIS Presidential Bulletin*, September 29, 2020.

———. "Russia - October 19." *Russia & CIS Presidential Bulletin*, October 19, 2020.

———. "Russia - October 23." *Russia & CIS Presidential Bulletin*, October 23, 2020.

———. "Russia - October 27." *Russia & CIS Presidential Bulletin*, October 27, 2020.

———. "Russia - October 28." *Russia & CIS Presidential Bulletin*, October 28, 2020.

———. "Russia - November 13." *Russia & CIS Presidential Bulletin*, November 13, 2020.

———. "Russia - November 19." *Russia & CIS Presidential Bulletin*, November 19, 2020.

———. "Russia - December 2." *Russia & CIS Presidential Bulletin*, December 2, 2020.

———. "Russia - December 9." *Russia & CIS Presidential Bulletin*, December 9, 2020.

———. "Russia - December 10." *Russia & CIS Presidential Bulletin*, December 10, 2020.

———. "Russia - December 17." *Russia & CIS Presidential Bulletin*, December 17, 2020.
———. "Russia - December 28." *Russia & CIS Presidential Bulletin*, December 28, 2020.
Qiang, Zhang, Qibin Lu, Deping Zhong, and Xuanting Ye. "The Pattern of Policy Change on Disaster Management in China: A Bibliometric Analysis of Policy Documents, 1949–2016." *International Journal of Disaster Risk Science* 9 (2018): 55–73.
Qin, Amy. "A Fever of 104, Hours to Wait, and No Relief." *New York Times*, February 3, 2020, A1.
———. "China Expands Chaotic Dragnet in Coronavirus Crackdown." *New York Times (Online)*, February 13, 2020.
———. "China's Leader, under Fire, Says He Led Coronavirus Fight Early On." *New York Times (Online)*, February 15, 2020.
Qin, Amy, and Li Cao. "Survivors Fume as China Insists on Quiet Burials: [Foreign Desk]." *New York Times*, April 4, 2020, A1.
Qin, Amy, and Javier C. Hernández. "China Reports First Fatality from New Virus." *New York Times*, January 11, 2020.
Qin, Amy, Myers Steven Lee, and Elaine Yu. "Beijing Imposes Extreme Limits on Ill in Wuhan: [Foreign Desk]." *New York Times*, February 7, 2020, A1.
Quinn, Dennis P., and John T. Woolley. "Democracy and National Economic Performance: The Preference for Stability." *American Journal of Political Science* 45, no. 3 (July 2001): 634–57.
Raschky, P.A. "Institutions and the Losses from Natural Disasters." *Natural Hazards Earth Systems Science* 8 (2008): 627–34.
Rattner, Nate, and Robert Towey. "After Weeks of Declines, U.S. Covid Cases Have Stalled at a High Level: 'The Ers Are Packed'." *CNBC*, November 11, 2021.
Reinhard, Beth, and Emma Brown. "Face Masks in National Stockpile Have Not Been Substantially Replenished since 2009." *The Washington Post*, March 10, 2020.
Reinhard, Beth, Emma Brown, Reis Thebault, and Sun H. Lena. "Many States Aren't Giving Their 'Probables' Data to CDC." *The Washington Post*, June 9, 2020, A14.
Reuters. "New Zealand Says No Word from China on Coronavirus in Frozen Meat." *South China Morning Post*, November 16, 2020.
———. "Russia Reports 50,000 COVID-19 Cases for Second Day Running." *Reuters*, September 3, 2022.
———. "Russia Scraps Remaining COVID Restrictions." *Reuters*, July 1, 2022.
Ripley, Amanda. *The Unthinkable: Who Survives When Disaster Strikes – and Why.* New York: Three Rivers Press, 2008.
Rivera, Fernando I., and Marc R. Settembrino. "Sociological Insights on the Role of Social Capital in Disaster Resilience." *Disaster Resiliency: Interdisciplinary Perspectives* 5, no. 2 (2013): 48–60.
Robinson, Neil, and Sarah Milne. "Populism and Political Development in Hybrid Regimes: Russia and the Development of Official Populism." *International Political Science Review* 38, no. 4 (2017): 412–25.
Rodriguez, H., W. Diaz, J.M. Santos, and B.E. Aguirre. "Communicating Risk and Uncertainty: Science, Technology, and Disasters at the Crossroads." Chap. 29 In *Handbook of Disaster Research*, edited by Rodríguez Havidán, Enrico L. Quarantelli, and Russell R. Dynes. Springer, 2007: 476–88.
Roffey, Roger. "Russia's Emercom: Managing Emergencies and Political Credibility." edited by Lars Höstbeck. Stockholm: Swedish Ministry of Defense, 2016.
Roll, Richard, and John R. Talbott. "Political Freedom, Economic Liberty, and Prosperity." *Journal of Democracy* 14, no. 3 (2003): 75–89.
Romm, Tony. "Return to Work or Risk Jobless Aid, States Warn." *The Washington Post*, May 5, 2020.
———. "State Department Blames 'Swarms of Online, False Personas' from Russia for Wave of Coronavirus Misinformation Online." *The Washington Post (Online)*, March 5, 2020.
Romm, Tony, Erica Werner, and Jeff Stein. "Trump's Orders Deemed 'Paltry'." *The Washington Post*, August 10, 2020, A1.

RosCongress. "Russian National Helpline." RosCongress, March 19, 2021, https://roscongress.org/en/blog/hotline/.

Rosenberg, Eli, and Heather Long. "Unemployed Americans Feel Sting of Abandonment." *The Washington Post*, August 28, 2020, A1.

Roth, Brad R. *Governmental Illegitimacy in International Law*. Oxford: Clarendon Press; Oxford University Press, 1999.

Rousseau, Jean-Jacques. "On Philosophy, Morality, and Religion." Chapter 5: Letter From J.J. Rousseau to M. de Voltaire. In *On Philosophy, Morality, and Religion*, edited by Christopher Kelly, 51. University Press of New England, 2007.

Rowland, Christopher. "Hospitals, Doctors Wiping out Supplies of Unproven Coronavirus Treatment." *The Washington Post*, March 21, 2020, A5.

———. "More Lifesaving Ventilators Are Available, but Hospitals Can't Afford Them." *The Washington Post*, March 19, 2020, A8.

———. "Vaccine Politics, Skewed by Trump's Polarizing Approach, Will Complicate Biden's Path to a Unified Pandemic Response." *The Washington Post*, December 13, 2020, A7.

Rowland, Christopher, Debbie Cenziper, and Lisa Rein. "White House Efforts to Sidestep FDA Revealed." *The Washington Post*, November 2, 2020, A19.

Rowland, Christopher, and Ariana Eunjung Cha. "Expected Patient Surge Threatens to Flood U.S. Hospitals." *The Washington Post*, March 16, 2020, A10.

Rowland, Christopher, Isaac Stanley-Becker, Jacob Bogage, Abha Bhattarai, and Laura Reiley. "Major Firms Lobbying for Workers' Spot on Vaccine List." *The Washington Post*, December 21, 2020, A1.

Rowland, Christopher, Lena H. Sun, Isaac Stanley-Becker, and Carolyn Y. Johnson. "Vaccine Rollout Smaller Than Pledged." *The Washington Post*, December 6, 2020, A1.

Rowland, Christopher, Jon Swaine, and Josh Dawsey. "Spurred by Trump, Unproven Drug Regimen Is Fast-Tracked." *The Washington Post*, March 27, 2020, A1.

Rucker, Philip. "As Dark Reality Sets in, President Beats a Retreat on Reopening U.S." *The Washington Post*, March 30, 2020, A1.

———. "Governors Led as President Minimized Pandemic." *The Washington Post*, March 17, 2020, A1.

———. "Trump Takes Spotlight but Leaves Key Calls Largely to States, Cities." *The Washington Post*, March 25, 2020, A11.

Rucker, Philip, Yasmeen Abutaleb, Josh Dawsey, and Robert Costa. "A Lost Summer: How Trump Fell Short in Confronting the Virus." *The Washington Post*, August 9, 2020, A1.

Rucker, Philip, Yasmeen Abutaleb, and Ashley Parker. "Messaging Undermines U.S. Efforts on Virus." *The Washington Post*, March 4, 2020, A1.

Rucker, Philip, and Robert Costa. "Trump's Crisis Response Short on Consistency, Long on Blame." *The Washington Post*, April 3, 2020.

Rucker, Philip, Josh Dawsey, and Yasmeen Abutaleb. "In Trump Plan, Governors Take on Burdens of Testing, Reopening." *The Washington Post*, April 17, 2020, A1.

Rucker, Philip, Josh Dawsey, Yasmeen Abutaleb, Robert Costa, and Lena H. Sun. "As Deaths Mounted, Trump Fixated on Stalled Economy." *The Washington Post*, May 3, 2020, A1.

Rucker, Philip, Josh Dawsey, Yasmeen Abutaleb, and Sun H Lena. "Outcry, Warnings over Trump's New Cure Idea." *The Washington Post*, April 25, 2020, A1.

Rucker, Philip, and Anne Gearan. "Trump Announces 30-Day Ban on All Travel from Europe Amid Pandemic." *The Washington Post*, March 12, 2020, A14.

Rucker, Philip, and Seung M. Kim. "Gop Leaders Break with Trump on Masks as Cases Climb." *The Washington Post*, July 1, 2020, A7.

Rucker, Philip, and Ashley Parker. "Uneven Performance by Trump in 'Wartime President' Role." *The Washington Post*, March 21, 2020, A5.

Rucker, Philip, Jeff Stein, Josh Dawsey, and Ashley Parker. "Trump May Ditch Safety Guidelines to Jolt Economy." *The Washington Post*, March 24, 2020, A1.

Rui, Guo. "China Jails Citizen Journalist Zhang Zhan for Four Years over Wuhan Coronavirus Reports." *South China Morning Post*, December 28, 2020.

———. "China to Make up to 50 Million Flu Vaccine Doses Available Amid Covid-19 Pandemic, Official Says." *South China Morning Post*, September 5, 2020.

———. "President Xi Stands Besides Covid-19 Heroes and Hails China's 'Decisive Action' in Containing Coronavirus." *South China Morning Post*, September 8, 2020.

Russia. "Direct Line with Vladimir Putin." The Russian Government, June 15, 2017, http://www.en .kremlin.ru/events/president/news/54790.

———. "First Meeting of the Government Coordination Council to Control the Incidence of Coronavirus Infection in Russia." The Russian Government, March 16, 2020, http://government.ru/en /news/39164/.

Ryabovolova, Alina, and Julie Hemment. "'Je Suis Satisfaction:' Russian Politics in the Age of Hybrid Media." *East European Politics* 36, no. 1 (January 2 2020): 9–26.

Ryan, Missy. "Russia Spent Millions on Secret Global Political Campaign, U.S. Intelligence Finds." *The Washington Post*, September 13, 2022.

Sachs, Wolfgang. "Climate Change and Human Rights." *Development* 51 (2008): 332–7.

Saha, Sarani. "Democratic Institutions and Provision of a Public Good." University of California, Santa Barbara Departmental Working Papers, 2007, http://escholarship.org/uc/item/55f3c17g.

Samuels, David J., and Matthew Soberg Shugart. "Presidentialism, Elections and Representation." *Journal of Theoretical Politics* 15, no. 1 (2003): 33–60.

Samuels, Richard J. *3.11: Disaster and Change in Japan.* Ithaca: Cornell University Press, 2013.

Scherer, Michael, and Josh Dawsey. "Trump Claims Coronavirus Is 'Ending' as Infections Spike." *The Washington Post*, October 27, 2020, A6.

———. "Trump: People Tired of 'Fauci and All These Idiots'." *The Washington Post*, October 20, 2020, A1.

Scherer, Michael, and Ashley Parker. "As Trump Pushes Reopening, Democrats Embrace Caution." *The Washington Post*, May 23, 2020, A6.

Schnirring, Lisa. "China Releases Genetic Data on New Coronavirus, Now Deadly." University of Minnesota Center for Infectious Disease Research and Policy, https://www.cidrap.umn.edu/covid -19/china-releases-genetic-data-new-coronavirus-now-deadly.

Schultz, Kenneth A, and Barry R. Weingast. "The Democratic Advantage: Institutional Foundations of Financial Power in International Competition." *International organization* 57, no. 1 (2003): 3–42.

———. "The Democratic Advantage: Institutional Foundations of Financial Power in International Competition." *International Organization* 57, no. 1 (Winter 2003): 3–42.

Sebők, Miklós, Ágnes M. Balázs, and Csaba Molnár. "Punctuated Equilibrium and Progressive Friction in Socialist Autocracy, Democracy and Hybrid Regimes." *Journal of Public Policy* 42, no. 2 (2022): 247–69.

Shammas, Brittany, Ariana Eunjung Cha, Ben Guarino, and Jacqueline Dupree. "Mounting Cases Push Hospitals to Brink." *The Washington Post*, December 17, 2020, A1.

Shammas, Brittany, and Reis Thebault. "Fauci Warns of 'Surge Upon a Surge' as Air Travel Hits Highs During Holidays." *The Washington Post*, December 29, 2020.

Sharkov, Damien. "Putin Backs Down on Controversial Pension Reform after Huge Popularity Drop." *Newsweek*, 29 August, 2018.

Shartova, Natalia, Vladimir Tikunov, and Olga Chereshnya. "Health Disparities in Russia at the Regional and Global Scales." *International Journal for Equity in Health* 20 (2021): 1–16.

Shen, Xinmei. "Facial Recognition Data Leaks Are Rampant in China as Covid-19 Pushes Wider Use of the Technology." *South China Morning Post*, October 8, 2020.

Shen, Xiaoxiao, and Jiehan Liu. "Measuring Populism: Evidence from China." In *Social Science Research Network*. Social Science Research Network, 2022.

Shepherd, Christian. "Fresh Outbreak in China's North-East Threatens to Stall Coronavirus Recovery." *Financial Times*, April 20, 2020.

———. "Wuhan Revises up Death Toll Amid Claims of Cover-up; China." *Financial Times*, April 18, 2020.

———. "Wuhan Diary Stirs Tussle for Control of Virus Response Narrative; China." *Financial Times*, May 16, 2020.

Shepherd, Christian, and Emma Zhou Beijing. "China Strict Travel Ban Leaves Nationals Stranded Abroad; Second Wave Fears." *Financial Times*, May 9, 2020.

Sherman, Justin. "Russia's Fight against the Coronavirus May Give Putin Even More Power." *The Washington Post (Online)*, June 2, 2020.

Shih, Gerry. "China Detains a Leading Critic of Xi." *The Washington Post*, July 7, 2020, A11.

———. "China Rushes to Limit Political Risk from Health Crisis." *The Washington Post*, January 30, 2020, A15.

Shih, Gerry, and Lena H. Sun. "Outbreak of Possible New Virus in Central China Raises Alarms across Asia." *The Washington Post*, January 9, 2020, A14.

Shih, Gerry, Lena H. Sun, Simon Denyer, and Joel Achenbach. "U.S. Steps up Efforts to Contain Coronavirus." *The Washington Post*, January 28, 2020, A1.

Shirk, Susan L. "China in Xi's New Era the Return to Personalistic Rule." *Journal of Democracy* 29, no. 2 (November 12 2018): 22–36.

Siddiqui, Faiz, and Heather Kelly. "Bay Area's Remote-Work Expansion May Show What's to Come Elsewhere." *The Washington Post*, March 12, 2020, A11.

Simmons, Ann M. "Coronavirus Forces Putin to Delay Vote That Could Keep Him in Power; Referendum Originally Planned for April Is Final Hurdle to Allowing Russia's President to Potentially Stay in Office until 2036." *Wall Street Journal (Online)*, March 25, 2020.

———. "In Russia, Putin Wrestles with Economic Impact of Coronavirus; What Was Tipped to Be Marquee Year for Kremlin Leader Has Turned into One of Toughest Challenges of His 20-Year Reign." *Wall Street Journal (Online)*, May 5, 2020.

———. "Moscow, Center of Russia's Coronavirus Crisis, Emerges from Lockdown; Infections Remain High as City Authorities Begin Reopening and Putin Prepares for Parade, Referendum." *Wall Street Journal (Online)*, June 9, 2020.

———. "Russia's Covid Surge Exacts a Heavy Toll on Its Emergency Responders; a Shortage of Paramedics Pushes Wait Times for Ambulances to 24 Hours as the Virus Continues to Reach New Highs." *Wall Street Journal (Online)*, November 7, 2020.

———. "Russia Sets July 1 Vote on Constitutional Changes Allowing Putin to Extend His Rule; Outcome Could Allow President Potentially to Stay in Office until 2036, Surpassing Soviet Dictator Josef Stalin's Nearly Three Decades in Power." *Wall Street Journal (Online)*, June 1, 2020.

Simmons, Ann M., and Georgi Kantchev. "Putin Extends Stay-at-Home Order through April in Russia; Despite Measures Taken by Federal and City Authorities, Leader Says It Wasn't Possible 'to Turn the Tide' of the Spread of Coronavirus." *Wall Street Journal (Online)*, April 2, 2020.

Simmons-Duffin, Selena, and Pien Huang. "A Year in, Experts Assess Biden's Hits and Misses on Handling the Pandemic." National Public Radio, January 18, 2022, https://www.npr.org/sections/health-shots/2022/01/18/1073292913/a-year-in-experts-assess-bidens-hits-and-misses-on-handling-the-pandemic.

Singh, Karan Deep. "As India's Lethal Covid Wave Neared, Politics Overrode Science." *New York Times*, September 14, 2021.

Siow, Maria. "Cambodia's Caution over China's Covid-19 Vaccine a Signal to US: Analysts." *South China Morning Post*, December 20, 2020.

Sonmez, Felicia, Paige W. Cunningham, and Meryl Kornfield. "Mixed Signals on Virus Orders." *The Washington Post*, April 27, 2020, A1.

Sonmez, Felicia, and Darryl Fears. "Trump Aide Raises Tensions with CDC." *The Washington Post*, May 18, 2020, A1.

Sonne, Paul, and Missy Ryan. "As Beds Go Unfilled, States Scale Back Army Corps Makeshift Hospitals." *The Washington Post*, April 25, 2020.

Stanley-Becker, Isaac. "Promises of Fast Vaccine Risk Warping Views Further." *The Washington Post*, May 21, 2020, A1.

———. "Vaccination Totals Lag Amid Snags, Confusion." *The Washington Post*, December 31, 2020, A1.

Stanley-Becker, Isaac, and C. Janes. "Pockets of U.S. Still Resisting Urgent Mantra to Stay at Home." *The Washington Post*, April 3, 2020, A1.

Stanley-Becker, Isaac, Toluse Olorunnipa, and Seung M. Kim. "Trump Fomenting Defiance of Strictures." April 18, 2022, A1.

Stanley-Becker, Isaac, William Wan, and Ben Guarino. "States Reopening Lack Benchmarks for Reimposing Rules." *The Washington Post*, May 16, 2020, A7.

Stanley-Becker, Isaac, and Rachel Weiner. "In Deciding to Reopen, Some Governors Reject Counsel of Their Medical Experts." *The Washington Post*, April 24, 2020, A7.

Stasavage, David. "Democracy, Autocracy, and Emergency Threats: Lessons for COVID-19 from the Last Thousand Years." *International Organization* 74, no. S1 (2020): E1–E17.

Stead Sellers, Frances, and Ben Guarino. "Many States Falling Short on Efforts to Trace Contacts." *The Washington Post*, June 15, 2020, A1.

Stead-Sellers, Frances, and Abigail Hauslohner. "Growing Shortages of Health-Care Workers Strain Hospitals." *The Washington Post*, July 27, 2020, A10.

Stein, Jeff, and Tony Romm. "President Trump's Attempt to Bypass Congress on Stimulus Is Offering Only Limited Economic Relief." *The Washington Post*, August 23, 2020, A1.

Steinberg, Ted. *Acts of God: The Unnatural History of Natural Disaster in America.* New York: Oxford University Press, 2006.

Steinhardt, H. Christoph. "Loosening Controls in Times of an Impatient Society: Chinese State-Society Relations During Xi Jinping's Honeymoon Period." *International Affairs at LSE* (April 10 2013).

Stevenson, Alexandra. "China Expels 3 Wall Street Journal Reporters as Media Relations Sour." [In English]. *New York Times (Online)* (February 19 2020).

Stevenson, Alexandra, and Li Cao. "China's Coronavirus Back-to-Work Lessons: Masks and Vigilance." *New York Times*, May 12, 2020.

Strauss, Valerie. "Fla. Judge Blocks School Reopening Order; State Appeals Case." *The Washington Post*, August 25, 2020, A3.

Stronski, Paul. "Russia's Response to Its Spiraling COVID-19 Crisis Is Too Little, Too Late." Carnegie Endowment for International Peace, October 28, 2021, https://carnegieendowment.org/2021/10/28/russia-s-response-to-its-spiraling-covid-19-crisis-is-too-little-too-late-pub-85677.

Sui-Lee, Wee. "Activists Say China Uses Quarantines to Stifle Dissent." *New York Times*, July 31, 2020, A12.

———. "As Deaths Mount, a Race to Screen Ever More Patients to Slow an Epidemic: [Foreign Desk]." *New York Times*, February 10, 2020, A8.

———. "China Hustles for Vaccine, Despite Patchy Reputation: [Business/Financial Desk]." *New York Times*, May 5, 2020, B1.

———. "China, in Vaccine Wager, Gives Unproven Shots to Thousands: [Foreign Desk]." *New York Times*, September 27, 2020, A1.

———. "Chinese Goal: Quick Vaccine for 50 Million." *New York Times*, December 30, 2020, A1.

Sui-Lee, Wee, and Elsie Chen. "China's Rush to Vaccinate Poses Risks." *New York Times*, November 18, 2020.

Sui-Lee, Wee, and Mariana Simões. "China Skirts Convention for Vaccines." *New York Times*, July 17, 2020, B1.

Sun, Lena H. "Leading U.S. Public Health Agency - the CDC - Is Sidelined During Pandemic." *The Washington Post*, March 20, 2020, A9.

Sun, Lena H. "Administration Officials Seek Greater Control over CDC Coronavirus Reports." *The Washington Post*, September 13, 2020, A16.

Sun, Lena H. "CDC Reverses Itself after New Advice on Testing Draws Sharp Criticism." *The Washington Post*, September 19, 2020, A7.

———. "Political Jabs, Errors Erode Trust in CDC at Key Time." *The Washington Post*, September 29, 2020, A1.

———. "States Say They Lack Funds to Dispense a Virus Vaccine." *The Washington Post*, October 30, 2020, A3.

Sun, Lena H., and Joel Achenbach. "CDC: Coronavirus May Have Infected 24 Million in U.S." *The Washington Post*, June 26, 2020, A1.

Sun, Lena H., Lori Aratani, William Wan, and Antonio Olivo. "A Scramble to Execute U.S. Order on Travel." *The Washington Post*, February 4, 2020, A1.

Sun, Lena H., and Josh Dawsey. "Church Choir Warning Removed from CDC Reopening Guidance." *The Washington Post*, May 29, 2020, A2.

———. "CDC Walks a Tightrope as Pandemic Meets Politics." *The Washington Post*, July 10, 2020, A6.

———. "White House Reviews Expanded Guidance on Reopening Society in Phases." *The Washington Post*, April 8, 2020, A4.

Sun, Lena H., and Amy Goldstein. "Disappearance of Virus Data from CDC Website Spurs Outcry." *The Washington Post*, July 17, 2020, A11.

Sun, Lena H., William Wan, and Yasmeen Abutaleb. "Plans to Contain Virus Emerge in Bottom-up Effort." *The Washington Post*, April 11, 2020, A1.

Swaine, Jon, Robert O'Harrow, and Aaron C. Davis. "HHS Official Shifted Stockpile's Focus." *The Washington Post*, May 5, 2020, A1.

Tan, Yvette, Tessa Wong, and Stephen McDonell. "China Congress: Xi Jinping Doubles Down on Zero-Covid as Meeting Opens." *BBC*, October 16, 2022.

Tang, Frank. "China Warned to Prepare for 'Big Rise' in Bad Loans as Financial System Braces against Coronavirus, Rising Global Tensions." *South China Morning Post*, July 24, 2020.

Tang, Wenfang. *Populist Authoritarianism: Chinese Political Culture and Regime Sustainability.* Oxford: Oxford University Press, 2016.

Taplin, Oliver. *A Dictionary of Classical Greek Quotations.* New York: I.B. Tauris, 2016.

Taylor, Adam. "As Pandemic Rages, Democracy and Human Rights Are Backsliding Worldwide." *The Washington Post*, October 4, 2020, A28.

———. "Chinese Journalists Offer a Glimpse Behind State's Propaganda on Covid-19." *The Washington Post*, April 10, 2020, A16.

Taylor, Luke. "The Venezuelan Health-Care Workers Secretly Collecting COVID Stats." *Nature*, August 25, 2021, https://www.nature.com/articles/d41586-021-02276-1.

Tepe, Sultan, and Ajar Chekirova. "Faith in Nations: The Populist Discourse of Erdoğan, Modi, and Putin." *Religions* 13, no. 5 (2022): 445.

Teslova, Elena. "Moscow Mayor Imposes Home Quarantine for People over 65." Andalou Agency, March 23, 2020, https://www.aa.com.tr/en/asia-pacific/moscow-mayor-imposes-home-quarantine -for-people-over-65/1775599.

Thebault, Reis, Lenny Bernstein, Andrew B. Tran, and Annys Shin. "Spike in Non-Virus Deaths Suggests Delay in Seeking Care." *The Washington Post*, July 3, 2020, A10.

Thompson, Steve. "In Contact Tracing Race, Few States Reveal Speed." *The Washington Post*, July 5, 2020, A1.

Thompson, Steve, Juliet Eilperin, and Brady Dennis. "A Boost in Tests, but Lack of Takers." *The Washington Post*, May 18, 2020, A1.

Thu, Huong Le. "Delta Variant Outbreak Challenges Vietnam's COVID-19 Response Strategy." Brookings Institution, August 11, 2021, https://www.brookings.edu/blog/order-from-chaos/2021 /08/11/delta-variant-outbreak-challenges-vietnams-covid-19-response-strategy/.

Timberg, Craig, Elizabeth Dwoskin, and Moriah Balingit. "Protests Spread, Fueled by Economic Woes and Internet Subcultures." *The Washington Post*, May 3, 2020, A1.

Tran, Andrew B, Leslie Shapiro, and Emma Brown. "Pandemic's Overall Death Toll in U.S. Likely Surpassed 100,000 Weeks Ago." *The Washington Post*, June 3, 2020, A25.

Trofimov, Yaroslav, and Thomas Grove. "Putin's Global Ambitions Are Upended by Coronavirus's Heavy Toll in Russia; Russian President's Efforts to Showcase the Country's Strength Abroad Backfired Amid Virus Troubles at Home." *Wall Street Journal (Online)*, June 6, 2020.

Troianovski, Anton. "As Coronavirus Overruns Russia, Doctors Are Dying on the Front Lines." *New York Times (Online)*, May 14, 2020.

———. "As Virus Spreads in Russia's Caucasus, Rumors Swirl over Strongman's Health." *New York Times (Online)*, May 22, 2020.

———. "In Russia, the Lockdown Is Over. But Putin Stays in His Bubble." *New York Times*, October 2, 2020, A1.

Trudolyubov, Maxim. "Late in the Game, Russia Steps up to Covid-19." *New York Times (Online)*, April 7, 2020.

Truex, Rory. "Consultative Authoritarianism and Its Limits." *Comparative Political Studies* 50, no. 3 (2017): 329–61.

UN. "Bachelet Dismayed at Restrictions on Human Rights NGOs and Arrests of Activists in India." United Nations Office of High Commissioner for Human Rights, October 20, 2020, https://www.ohchr.org/en/press-releases/2020/10/bachelet-dismayed-restrictions-human-rights-ngos-and -arrests-activists-india?LangID=E&NewsID=26398.

UNDP. "Human Development Insights." Human Development Reports, https://hdr.undp.org/data -center/country-insights#/ranks.

UNDRR. "Disaster." United Nations Office for Disaster Risk Reduction, https://www.undrr.org /terminology/disaster#:~:text=A%20serious%20disruption%20of%20the,and%20environmental %20losses%20and%20impacts.

Urinboyev, Rustamjon. *Migration and Hybrid Political Regimes: Navigating the Legal Landscape in Russia.* Oakland: University of California Press, 2020.

Viser, Matt, and Sean Sullivan. "Virus Again Front and Center in Campaigns." *The Washington Post*, October 7, 2020, A1.

Volkov, Denis. "Marc Plattner: "If Russia Had Become Democratic, the World Would Look Very Different Now." Institute of Modern Russia, April 2, 2015, https://imrussia.org/en/politics/2220 -marc-plattner-if-russia-had-become-democratic-the-world-would-look-very-different-now.

Von Soest, Christian, and Julia Grauvogel. "How Do Non-Democratic Regimes Claim Legitimacy? Comparative Insights from Post-Soviet Countries." *German Institute of Global and Area Studies*, no. 277 (2015).

Wan, William, Reed Albergotti, and Joel Achenbach. "Amid Restrictions, a Debate Arises: Save Lives or Save the Economy?" *The Washington Post*, March 25, 2020, A1.

Wan, William, and Philip Bump. "Decrees Influenced Choices to Stay Home, Study Suggests." *The Washington Post*, April 14, 2020, A11.

Wan, William, and Jacqueline Dupree. "U.S. Breaks Record for Daily Cases." *The Washington Post*, October 24, 2020, A1.

Wan, William, and Mark Guarino. "Officials Weigh New Restrictions, but Face Angry Backlash, as Cases Surge." *The Washington Post*, November 14, 2020, A9.

Wan, William, Katie Mettler, Miriam Berger, and Carolyn Y. Johnson. "Spreading Coronavirus Kills First U.S. Patient." *The Washington Post*, March 01, 2020, A1.

Wang, Vivian. "China, Citing Fewer Cases, Tries to Rewrite Its Role in Crisis." *New York Times*, April 9, 2020, A6.

———. "Chinese Citizen Journalist Receives 4 Years in Prison for Virus Reports: [Foreign Desk]." *New York Times*, December 29, 2020, A9.

———. "Coronavirus Epidemic Keeps Growing, but Spread in China Slows." *New York Times (Online)*, February 18, 2020.

———. "With Propaganda Push in China, Wuhan Emerges as a Star." *New York Times*, November 7, 2020, A7.

———. "U.S. Escalates Media War with New Restrictions on Chinese Journalists [with Graphic(S)]." *New York Times*, May 9, 2020.

Wang, Yaqiu. "China's Covid Success Story Is Also a Human Rights Tragedy." Human Rights Watch, January 26, 2021, https://www.hrw.org/news/2021/01/26/chinas-covid-success-story-also -human-rights-tragedy.

Wang, Yi-ting, Valeriya Mechkova, and Frida Andersson. "Does Democracy or Good Governance Enhance Health? New Empirical Evidence 1900–2012." In *The Varieties of Democracy Institute*, edited by University of Gothenberg, 1–40. Gothenberg, 2015.

Wang, Zhengxu, and Ern Ser Tan. "The Conundrum of Authoritarian Resiliency: Hybrid and Non-democratic Regimes in East Asia." *Taiwan Journal of Democracy* 9, no. 1 (July 2013): 199–219.

Warburton, Eve. "Indonesia: Polarization, Democratic Distress, and the Coronavirus." Carnegie Endowment for International Peace, April 28, 2020, https://carnegieendowment.org/2020/04/28/ indonesia-polarization-democratic-distress-and-coronavirus-pub-81641.

Ward, Artemus. "Potter Stewart." The Free Speech Center, https://www.mtsu.edu/first-amendment/ article/1359/potter-stewart.

Warner, Jeroen. "The Politics of 'Catastrophization'." Chap. 5 In *Disaster, Conflict and Society in Crises: Everyday Politics of Crisis Response*, edited by Thea Hilhorst. New York: Routledge, 2013: 92–110.

Weiner, Rachel. "Demand Strains Testing Capacity as Infections Soar." *The Washington Post*, July 2, 2020, A1.

———. "Republican Governors Begin to Soften on Mask Mandates." *The Washington Post*, July 11, 2020, A5.

Weiner, Rachel, and Ariana Eunjung Cha. "Amid Threats and Political Pushback, Public Health Officials Are Leaving Posts." *The Washington Post*, June 23, 2020, A5.

Weiner, Rachel, and Rosalind S. Helderman. "States Are 'on Their Own' as They Try to Expand Testing." *The Washington Post*, June 12, 2020, A9.

Weiner, Rachel, and William Wan. "Backlogs in Test Results Hobble Virus Response." *The Washington Post*, July 13, 2020, A1.

Weir, Fred. "Coronavirus Shortages Give Russia's Charity Sector a New Spark." *The Christian Science Monitor*, June 9, 2020.

Weiss, Sandra. "Mexico 'Flying Blind' in Pandemic Response." Deutsche Welle, August 18, 2020, https://www.dw.com/en/mexico-coronavirus-cases-update/a-54615046.

Weitzman, Martin L. "Fat-Tailed Uncertainty in the Economics of Catastrophic Climate Change." *Review of Environmental Economics and Policy* 5, no. 2 (Summer 2011): 275–92.

Werner, Erica, Yasmeen Abutaleb, Lenny Bernstein, and Lena H. Sun. "Administration Elevates Response to Coronavirus." *The Washington Post*, February 1, 2020, A1.

Werner, Erica, and Rachael Bade. "In Move That May Revive Talks, Trump Calls for Major Relief Bill." *The Washington Post*, September 17, 2020, A18.

Werner, Erica, Mike DeBonis, Paul Kane, and Jeff Stein. "House Moves toward Passing Virus Relief Package." *The Washington Post*, March 14, 2020, A12.

Werner, Erica, Jeff Stein, and Rachael Bade. "McConnell Details Stance on Relief Bill." *The Washington Post*, July 7, 2020, A13.

Werner, Erica, Jeff Stein, and Mike DeBonis. "White House Seeks $1 Trillion Stimulus." *The Washington Post*, March 19, 2020, A1.

Werner, Erica, Jeff Stein, and Lena H. Sun. "White House Seeks $1.8 Billion in Emergency Funding for Virus Response." *The Washington Post*, February 25, 2020, A16.

Whalen, Jeanne, Tony Romm, Aaron Gregg, and Tom Hamburger. "States and Hospitals Compete for Scarce Medical Supplies." *The Washington Post*, March 25, 2020, A18.

White House. "President Donald J. Trump Is Beginning the Next Phase in Our Fight against Coronavirus: Guidelines for Opening up America Again." White House Archives, April 16, 2020, https://trumpwhitehouse.archives.gov/briefings-statements/president-donald-j-trump-beginning-next-phase-fight-coronavirus-guidelines-opening-america/.

———. "Press Briefing by Press Secretary Kayleigh McEnany." White House Archives, May 12, 2020, https://trumpwhitehouse.archives.gov/briefings-statements/press-briefing-press-secretary-kayleigh-mcenany-051220/.

———. "Remarks by President Trump and Vice President Pence at a Meeting with Governor Reynolds of Iowa." White House Archives, May 6, 2020, https://trumpwhitehouse.archives.gov/briefings-statements/remarks-president-trump-vice-president-pence-meeting-governor-reynolds-iowa/.

———. "Remarks by President Trump and Vice President Pence in a Video Teleconference with Governors on COVID-19." White House Archives, March 19, 2020, https://trumpwhitehouse.archives.gov/briefings-statements/remarks-president-trump-vice-president-pence-video-teleconference-governors-COVID-19/.

———. "Remarks by President Trump at Naval Station Norfolk Send-Off for U.S.Ns Comfort | Norfolk, Va." White House Archives, March 28, 2020, https://trumpwhitehouse.archives.gov/briefings-statements/remarks-president-trump-naval-station-norfolk-send-off-usns-comfort-norfolk-va/.

———. "Remarks by President Trump at Signing of a Proclamation in Honor of National Nurses Day." White House Archives, May 6, 2020, https://trumpwhitehouse.archives.gov/briefings-statements/remarks-president-trump-signing-proclamation-honor-national-nurses-day/.

———. "Remarks by President Trump at the Operation Warp Speed Vaccine Summit." White House Archives, December 8, 2020, https://trumpwhitehouse.archives.gov/briefings-statements/remarks-president-trump-operation-warp-speed-vaccine-summit/.

———. "Remarks by President Trump in a Press Briefing on COVID-19 Testing." White House Archives, May 11, 2020, https://trumpwhitehouse.archives.gov/briefings-statements/remarks-president-trump-press-briefing-COVID-19-testing/.

———. "Remarks by President Trump in Meeting with Republican Members of Congress." White House Archives, May 8, 2020, https://trumpwhitehouse.archives.gov/briefings-statements/remarks-president-trump-meeting-republican-members-congress/.

———. "Remarks by President Trump in Press Briefing | September 16, 2020." White House Archives, September 16, 2020, https://trumpwhitehouse.archives.gov/briefings-statements/remarks-president-trump-press-briefing-september-16-2020/.

———. "Remarks by President Trump in Press Briefing." White House Archives, April 14, 2020, https://trumpwhitehouse.archives.gov/briefings-statements/remarks-president-trump-press-briefing/.

———. "Remarks by President Trump in Roundtable Discussion on Supporting Native Americans | Phoenix, Az." White House Archives, May 5, 2020, https://trumpwhitehouse.archives.gov/briefings-statements/remarks-president-trump-roundtable-discussion-supporting-native-americans-phoenix-az/.

———. "Remarks by President Trump on Protecting Seniors with Diabetes." White House Archives, May 26, 2020, https://trumpwhitehouse.archives.gov/briefings-statements/remarks-president-trump-protecting-seniors-diabetes/.

———. "Remarks by President Trump, Vice President Pence, and Members of the Coronavirus Task Force in Press Briefing." White House Archives, March 24, 2020, https://trumpwhitehouse.archives.gov/briefings-statements/remarks-president-trump-vice-president-pence-members-coronavirus-task-force-press-briefing-9/.

———. "Remarks by President Trump, Vice President Pence, and Members of the Coronavirus Task Force in Press Conference." White House Archives, March 13, 2020, https://trumpwhitehouse.archives.gov/briefings-statements/remarks-president-trump-vice-president-pence-members-coronavirus-task-force-press-conference-3/.

———. "Remarks by President Trump, Vice President Pence, and Members of the Coronavirus Task Force in Press Briefing." White House Archives, March 24, 2020, https://trumpwhitehouse

.archives.gov/briefings-statements/remarks-president-trump-vice-president-pence-members-coro-navirus-task-force-press-briefing-9/.

———. "Remarks by President Trump, Vice President Pence, and Members of the Coronavirus Task Force in Press Briefing." White House Archives, April 17, 2020, https://trumpwhitehouse.archives.gov/briefings-statements/remarks-president-trump-vice-president-pence-members-coronavirus-task-force-press-briefing-april-17-2020/.

———. "Remarks by President Trump, Vice President Pence, and Members of the Coronavirus Task Force in Press Briefing." White House Archives, April 27, 2020, https://trumpwhitehouse.archives.gov/briefings-statements/remarks-president-trump-vice-president-pence-members-coronavirus-task-force-press-briefing-33/.

———. "Remarks by President Trump, Vice President Pence, and Members of the Coronavirus Task Force in Press Conference." White House Archives, March 13, 2020, https://trumpwhitehouse.archives.gov/briefings-statements/remarks-president-trump-vice-president-pence-members-coro-navirus-task-force-press-conference-3/.

———. "Remarks by President Trump, Vice President Pence, and Members of the Coronavirus Task Force in Press Briefing." White House Archives, April 7, 2020, https://trumpwhitehouse.archives.gov/briefings-statements/remarks-president-trump-vice-president-pence-members-coronavirus-task-force-press-briefing-21/.

———. "Remarks by President Trump, Vice President Pence, and Members of the Coronavirus Task Force in Press Briefing." White House Archives, March 22, 2020, https://trumpwhitehouse.archives.gov/briefings-statements/remarks-president-trump-vice-president-pence-members-coro-navirus-task-force-press-briefing-8/.

———. "Remarks by President Trump, Vice President Pence, and Members of the Coronavirus Task Force in Press Briefing." White House Archives, March 16, 2020, https://trumpwhitehouse.archives.gov/briefings-statements/remarks-president-trump-vice-president-pence-members-coro-navirus-task-force-press-briefing-3/.

———. "Remarks by President Trump, Vice President Pence, and Members of the Coronavirus Task Force in Press Briefing." White House Archives, April 3, 2020, https://trumpwhitehouse.archives.gov/briefings-statements/remarks-president-trump-vice-president-pence-members-coronavirus-task-force-press-briefing-18/.

———. "Remarks by President Trump, Vice President Pence, and Members of the Coronavirus Task Force in Press Briefing." White House Archives, March 24, 2020, https://trumpwhitehouse.archives.gov/briefings-statements/remarks-president-trump-vice-president-pence-members-coro-navirus-task-force-press-briefing-9/.

———. "Remarks by President Trump, Vice President Pence, and Members of the Coronavirus Task Force in a Fox News Virtual Town Hall." White House Archives, March 24, 2020, https://trump-whitehouse.archives.gov/briefings-statements/remarks-president-trump-vice-president-pence-members-coronavirus-task-force-fox-news-virtual-town-hall/.

———. "Remarks by President Trump, Vice President Pence, and Members of the Coronavirus Task Force in Press Briefing." White House Archives, March 28, 2020, https://trumpwhitehouse.archives.gov/briefings-statements/remarks-president-trump-vice-president-pence-members-coro-navirus-task-force-press-briefing-13/.

———. "Remarks by President Trump, Vice President Pence, and Members of the Coronavirus Task Force in Press Briefing." White House Archives, April 14, 2020, https://trumpwhitehouse.archives.gov/briefings-statements/remarks-president-trump-vice-president-pence-members-coronavirus-task-force-press-briefing-25/.

WHO. "SARS: How a Global Epidemic Was Stopped." World Health Organization Regional Office for the Western Pacific, 2006, https://iris.who.int/handle/10665/207501.

———. "Summary of Probable SARS Cases with Onset of Illness from 1 November 2002 to 31 July 2003." World Health Organization, July 24, 2015, https://www.who.int/publications/m/item/summary-of-probable-sars-cases-with-onset-of-illness-from-1-november-2002-to-31-july-2003.

Wilkie, Christina. "Joe Biden Calls for a Nationwide Mask Mandate as He Pushes His Plan to Combat Coronavirus." *CNBC*, August 13, 2020.

William, David. "How CDC Stumbled in Race for a Virus Test." *The Washington Post*, December 28, 2020, A1.

Williams, Stewart. "Rethinking the Nature of Disaster: From Failed Instruments of Learning to a Post-Social Understanding." *Social Forces* 87, no. 2 (2008): 1115–38.

Willoughby, Emma. "An Ideal Public Health Model? Vietnam's State-Led, Preventative, Low-Cost Response to COVID-19." Brookings Institution, June 29, 2021, https://www.brookings .edu/blog/order-from-chaos/2021/06/29/an-ideal-public-health-model-vietnams-state-led-pre-ventative-low-cost-response-to-covid-19/#:~:text=The%20world%20noticed%20Vietnam's%20 success,effort%20to%20stop%20the%20virus.

Wisner, Ben, Piers Blaikie, Terry Cannon, and Ian Davis. *At Risk: Natural Hazards, People's Vulnerability and Disasters.* New York: Routledge, 2004.

Wisner, Ben, and Henry R. Luce. "Disaster Vulnerability: Scale, Power and Daily Life." *GeoJournal* 30, no. 2 (June 1993): 127–40.

Witte, Griff. "A New Hot Spot, but No Statewide Stay-Home Call." *The Washington Post*, April 14, 2020, A1.

———. "Growing Chorus Pushes for Renewed Shutdown Orders." *The Washington Post*, July 10, 2020, A1.

———. "N.M. Activates 'Crisis Care' to Free up ICU Beds." *The Washington Post*, December 11, 2020, A9.

———. "States Are Reopening: Cities Aren't." *The Washington Post*, May 2, 2020, A1.

Witte, Griff, Ariana Eunjung Cha, and Josh Dawsey. "In Resisting Masks, U.S. Lost Early Virus Weapon." *The Washington Post*, July 29, 2020, A1.

Witte, Griff, Meryl Kornfield, and Hannah Denham. "Calif. Pulls 'Emergency Brake' as States Race against Virus." *The Washington Post*, November 7, 2020.

Witte, Griff, M.B. Sheridan, Joanna Slater, and Liz Sly. "Surge in Caseload Driven by Poorer Nations - and U.S." *The Washington Post*, July 15, 2020, A1.

Witte, Griff, Isaac Stanley-Becker, Cleve R. Wootson Jr., and Andrea Eger. "Warily, U.S. Cracks Doors Open." *The Washington Post*, April 26, 2020, A1.

Witte, Griff, Katie Zezima, Ariana Eunjung Cha, and Tim Craig. "Across the Nation, Disparity in Containment Policy Is Vast." *The Washington Post*, March 18, 2020, A12.

Wong, Edward, Matthew Rosenberg, and Julian E. Barnes. "Chinese Operatives Helped Sow Panic in U.S., Officials Say." *New York Times*, April 23, 2020, A13.

Wong, Tessa, and Nathan Williams. "China Covid: Protests Continue in Major Cities across the Country." *BBC*, November 27, 2022.

Woodruff, Emily, and Staff Writer. "Mardi Gras 2020 Spawned up to 50k Coronavirus Cases, Likely from a Single Source, Study Says." Nola, February 9, 2021, https://www.nola.com/news/corona-virus/article_e4095910-6af1-11eb-a3bc-336456794a5b.html.

World Bank. "From Recovery to Rebalancing." December 2020, https://thedocs.worldbank.org/en/ doc/264421608625565168-0070022020/original/ceuDecember2020Final.pdf.

WorldOMeter. "Coronavirus Cases." WorldOMeter, https://www.worldometers.info/coronavirus/ #countries.

———. "COVID-19 Coronavirus Pandemic." WorldOMeter, January 21, https://www.worldometers .info/coronavirus/.

Xie, Echo. "China Plans to Overhaul Health System, but Better Communication with Public Is Off the Radar." *South China Morning Post*, June 8, 2020.

Xin, Zhou. "China's Coronavirus Success Boosts Confidence That Its System Is the Best Answer to the Country's Challenges." *South China Morning Post*, December 28, 2020.

Xing, Guoxin. "Hu Jintao's Political Thinking and Legitimacy Building: A Post-Marxist Perspective." *Asian Affairs: An American Review* 36, no. 4 (2009): 213–26.

Xinhua. "11 under Investigation over Prison Coronavirus Outbreak in East China." *Xinhua General News Service*, March 4, 2020.
———. "1st Ld: China Releases Investigation Report on Issues Concerning Dr. Li Wenliang." *Xinhua General News Service*, March 19, 2020.
———. "1st Ld-Writethru: China Focus: Wuhan Sends 34,000 Gov't Workers, Party Members to Fight Coronavirus in Communities." *Xinhua General News Service*, February 11, 2020.
———. "1st Ld-Writethru: China Resumes Construction of Major Civil Aviation Projects." *Xinhua General News Service*, March 6, 2020.
———. "1st Ld-Writethru: China Sends over 30,000 Medics to Aid in Battle against COVID-19 in Wuhan." *Xinhua General News Service*, February 17, 2020.
———. "1st Ld-Writethru: China Tightens Crackdown on Violence against Medical Workers." *Xinhua General News Service*, February 21, 2020.
———. "1st Ld-Writethru: COVID-19 Cases Confirmed in East China Prison, Concerned Officials Removed." *Xinhua General News Service*, February 21, 2020.
———. "1st Ld-Writethru: Health Official Suspended in China's Qingdao after Fresh COVID-19 Cases." *Xinhua General News Service*, October 15, 2020.
———. "1st Ld-Writethru: Offenses Concerning Imported COVID-19 Cases in China Made Public." *Xinhua General News Service*, April 3, 2020.
———. "1st Ld-Writethru-Xinhua Headlines: China's Unprecedented Measures Effectively Contain Epidemic." *Xinhua General News Service*, January 31, 2020.
———. "2nd Ld Writethru-Xinhua Headlines: China Penalizes Derelict Officials in Coronavirus Fight." *Xinhua General News Service*, February 5, 2020.
———. "Across China: China's Villages, Communities Mobilized in Fight against Epidemic." *Xinhua General News Service*, February 6, 2020.
———. "Across China: China's Villages, Communities Mobilized in Fight against Epidemic." *Xinhua General News Service*, February 6, 2020.
———. "Across China: China's Young Medics Show Responsibility, Perseverance in Fighting Epidemic." *Xinhua General News Service*, March 9, 2020.
———. "Across China: Deep in Chinese Mountains, Folk Songs Spread Anti-Virus Messages." *Xinhua General News Service*, February 11, 2020.
———. "Across China: Epidemic Prevention in Grassland." *Xinhua General News Service*, March 11, 2020.
———. "Across China: Internet Court Handles Cases Despite Coronavirus Epidemic." *Xinhua General News Service*, March 10, 2020.
———. "Ai Tech Aids Anti-Epidemic Fight." *Xinhua General News Service*, June 28, 2020.
———. "Battle-Hardened Medics to Support China's Border City." *Xinhua General News Service*, April 11, 2020.
———. "Biz China Weekly: Pmi, Forex Reserves, Foreign Trade, Anti-Epidemic Credit Support." *Xinhua General News Service*, March 7, 2020.
———. "Calling Novel Coronavirus "China Virus" Extremely Irresponsible: Fm Spokesperson." *Xinhua General News Service*, March 4, 2020.
———. "Central China Province Issues E-Coupons to Boost Consumption Amid Epidemic." *Xinhua General News Service*, March 28, 2020.
———. "Central China Province to Offer 1 Bln Yuan of Loans to Virus-Hit Cultural, Tourism Sectors." *Xinhua General News Service*, March 27, 2020.
———. "China Boosts Employment with Major Cut in Social Insurance Contributions." *Xinhua General News Service*, July 22, 2020.
———. "China Calls for Global Crackdown on COVID-19 Disinformation." *Xinhua General News Service*, June 10, 2020.
———. "China Calls for Higher Capability, Wider Range of COVID-19 Testing." *Xinhua General News Service*, April 22, 2020.

———. "China Capable of Ensuring Daily Necessities Supply Amid Epidemic, Official." *Xinhua General News Service*, February 1, 2020.

———. "China City Hands out 238-Mln-USD E-Vouchers to Spur Virus-Hit Consumption." *Xinhua General News Service*, March 26, 2020.

———. "China Cracks Down on Illegal Acts of Refusing Isolation Treatment, Deliberately Spreading Coronavirus." *Xinhua General News Service*, February 7, 2020.

———. "China Deploys Medical Experts, Resources to Border Regions to Battle COVID-19." *Xinhua General News Service*, April 13, 2020.

———. "China Distributes 1.9 Bln Yuan of Price Subsidies Amid COVID-19 Impact." *Xinhua General News Service*, April 10, 2020.

———. "China Faces Increasing Risks of Imported COVID-19 Cases: NHC." *Xinhua General News Service*, November 13, 2020.

———. "China Faces Rising Risk of Imported COVID-19 Cases: Official." *Xinhua General News Service*, March 6, 2020.

———. "China Ferries 332,000 Workers Back to Work with Special Trains." *Xinhua General News Service*, March 16, 2020.

———. "China Focus: Bring COVID-19 under Control with Joint Efforts." *Xinhua General News Service*, May 18, 2020.

———. "China Focus: Bring COVID-19 under Control with Joint Efforts." *Xinhua General News Service*, May 18, 2020.

———. "China Focus: China at "Crucial Stage" to Control Novel Coronavirus, Experts Say." *Xinhua General News Service*, January 22, 2020.

———. "China Focus: China Beefs up Novel Coronavirus Tracking and Prevention with Big Data." *Xinhua General News Service*, February 2, 2020.

———. "China Focus: China Hands out Vouchers to Spur Virus-Hit Consumption." *Xinhua General News Service*, March 19, 2020.

———. "China Focus: China Has Taken Strictest Measures to Curb Epidemic: NHC." *Xinhua General News Service*, February 1, 2020.

———. "China Focus: China Has Taken Strictest Measures to Curb Epidemic: NHC." *Xinhua General News Service*, February 1, 2020.

———. "China Focus: China Lifts 76-Day Lockdown on Virus-Hit Wuhan." *Xinhua General News Service*, April 8, 2020.

———. "China Focus: China Lifts 76-Day Lockdown on Virus-Hit Wuhan." *Xinhua General News Service*, April 8, 2020.

———. "China Focus: China Says Its COVID-19 Peak Is Over." *Xinhua General News Service*, March 12, 2020.

———. "China Focus: China Scales up Land Border Control in Epidemic Response." *Xinhua General News Service*, April 13, 2020.

———. "China Focus: China Values Privacy by Using Encrypted Data in Battle against Epidemic." *Xinhua General News Service*, March 9, 2020.

———. "China Focus: Chinese Cities Launch Voucher Campaigns to Boost Epidemic-Hit Consumption." *Xinhua General News Service*, March 25, 2020.

———. "China Focus: Emergency Use of COVID-19 Vaccines Expands to Larger Scale." *Xinhua General News Service*, December 30, 2020.

———. "China Focus: Free Online Medical Services Help Curb Coronavirus Outbreak." *Xinhua General News Service*, February 2, 2020.

———. "China Focus: Internet Helps in China's Fight against Novel Coronavirus." *Xinhua General News Service*, February 3, 2020.

———. "China Focus: Internet Helps in China's Fight against Novel Coronavirus." *Xinhua General News Service*, February 3, 2020.

———. "China Focus: Internet Helps in China's Fight against Novel Coronavirus." *Xinhua General News Service*, February 3, 2020.

———. "China Focus: Modern Technology Aids Spring Farming Amid Epidemic." *Xinhua General News Service*, March 9, 2020.

———. "China Focus: Nation Tightens Epidemic Control Amid New Local Cases." *Xinhua General News Service*, December 28, 2020.

———. "China Focus: Online Services Lend a Hand to Everyday Life Amid Epidemic." *Xinhua General News Service*, February 25, 2020.

———. "China Focus: Unmanned Aerial Vehicles Assist Fight against Novel Coronavirus." *Xinhua General News Service*, February 10, 2020.

———. "China Focus: Wuhan Buses Hit the Road after Two-Month Lockdown." *Xinhua General News Service*, March 25, 2020.

———. "China Helps Stranded Individuals Tide over Epidemic." *Xinhua General News Service*, March 14, 2020.

———. "China Honors Late Female Role Models Battling COVID-19." *Xinhua General News Service*, March 13, 2020.

———. "China Informs Public Right after COVID-19 Human-to-Human Spread Determined: White Paper." *Xinhua General News Service*, June 7, 2020.

———. "China Intensifies Screening of Asymptomatic COVID-19 Infections." *Xinhua General News Service*, April 9, 2020.

———. "China Issues 6.6 Bln Yuan in Subsidies to Offset Price Hike Amid COVID-19." *Xinhua General News Service*, April 10, 2020.

———. "China Issues Measures to Support Hubei Free-Trade Zone." *Xinhua General News Service*, June 4, 2020.

———. "China Launches Large Online Job Vacancy Market." *Xinhua General News Service*, March 20, 2020.

———. "China Offers Allowances to over 400,000 Children in Need Amid Epidemic: Official." *Xinhua General News Service*, April 10, 2020.

———. "China Opposes U.S. Stigmatization by Calling Coronavirus 'Chinese Virus'." *Xinhua General News Service*, March 17, 2020.

———. "China Orders Prison Overhaul after COVID-19 Outbreak." *Xinhua General News Service*, March 4, 2020.

———. "China Prosecutes 1,144 Suspects Involved in Epidemic-Related Crimes." *Xinhua General News Service*, March 4, 2020.

———. "China Prosecutes 1,919 Suspects Involved in Epidemic-Related Crimes." *Xinhua General News Service*, March 27, 2020.

———. "China Readies 20,000 Tonnes of Pork for COVID-19-Affected Areas." *Xinhua General News Service*, March 19, 2020.

———. "China Reopens Reception Venues for Public Complaints." *Xinhua General News Service*, April 10, 2020.

———. "China Reports 291 Confirmed Cases of New Coronavirus-Related Pneumonia." *Xinhua General News Service*, January 21, 2020.

———. "China Sees No Major Movement of Industrial and Supply Chains to Other Countries Due to Epidemic: Fm Spokesperson." *Xinhua General News Service*, March 11, 2020.

———. "China Sends 25,633 Medics to Battle COVID-19 in Hubei." *Xinhua General News Service*, February 15, 2020.

———. "China Sends 25,633 Medics to Battle COVID-19 in Hubei." *Xinhua General News Service*, February 15, 2020.

———. "China Sends over 11,000 Medics to Wuhan Amid Epidemic." *Xinhua General News Service*, February 7, 2020.

———. "China Sets up "Three Defense Lines" to Prevent Imported Virus Outbreak: Expert." *Xinhua General News Service*, March 24, 2020.

———. "China Steps up Inactivated COVID-19 Vaccine Development." *Xinhua General News Service*, June 1, 2020.

———. "China Strengthens Personnel Movement Control in Medium- and High-Risk Regions." *Xinhua General News Service*, June 25, 2020.

———. "China Strengthens Personnel Movement Control in Medium- and High-Risk Regions." *Xinhua General News Service*, June 25, 2020.

———. "China Stresses Harsh Punishment on Epidemic-Related Crimes." *Xinhua General News Service*, February 11, 2020.

———. "China Tightens COVID-19 Control Policies for Inbound Flights." *Xinhua General News Service*, December 16, 2020.

———. "China Tightens Crackdown on Violence against Medical Workers." *Xinhua General News Service*, February 21, 2020.

———. "China to Air Documentary on COVID-19 Fight." *Xinhua General News Service*, August 31, 2020.

———. "China to Emerge from COVID-19 in Better Shape Than U.S.: Media." *Xinhua General News Service*, June 29, 2020.

———. "China to Step up Financial Support for SMEs." *Xinhua General News Service*, March 31, 2020.

———. "China to Strengthen Epidemic Control Along Land Border." *Xinhua General News Service*, April 2, 2020.

———. "China to Strengthen Epidemic Control Along Land Border." *Xinhua General News Service*, April 2, 2020.

———. "China to Strengthen Prevention, Control of Asymptomatic COVID-19 Infections." *Xinhua General News Service*, March 30, 2020.

———. "China to Take More Steps to Stabilize Economic, Social Development." *Xinhua General News Service*, March 3, 2020.

———. "China Transports 84,000 Workers by Train for Resumption of Production." *Xinhua General News Service*, February 27, 2020.

———. "China Turns to Tech Tools in Precise Control of Epidemic." *Xinhua General News Service*, February 19, 2020.

———. "China Underscores Allocation of CPC Members' Donation for COVID-19 Fight." *Xinhua General News Service*, March 28, 2020.

———. "China Unveils New Measures to Keep Foreign Trade, Investment Stable." *Xinhua General News Service*, March 11, 2020.

———. "China Urges U.S. To Respond to Concerns of Its People, World on Epidemic." *Xinhua General News Service*, April 27, 2020.

———. "China Urges U.S. To Stop COVID-19 Stigmatizing." *Xinhua General News Service*, July 6, 2020.

———. "China Wants U.S. Bio-Labs Open to Media Scrutiny: Fm Spokesperson." *Xinhua General News Service*, August 12, 2020.

———. "China's Border Town to Build Temporary Hospital as Imported COVID-19 Cases Rise." *Xinhua General News Service*, April 9, 2020.

———. "China's Border Town to Build Temporary Hospital as Imported COVID-19 Cases Rise." *Xinhua General News Service*, April 9, 2020.

———. "China's Central Bank Further Cuts Rate for Medium-Term Loans." *Xinhua General News Service*, April 15, 2020.

———. "China's Central SOEs Mobilize to Fight against Coronavirus." *Xinhua General News Service*, February 18, 2020.

———. "China's Chengdu to Test All Residents in Virus-Hit District." *Xinhua General News Service*, December 11, 2020.

———. "China's Coronavirus-Stricken Province Races to Tackle Shortage of Protective Gear." *Xinhua General News Service*, January 28, 2020.

———. "China's Daily Nucleic Acid Testing Capacity Tops 3 Mln: Official." *Xinhua General News Service*, June 24, 2020.

———. "China's Dalian Conducts Citywide COVID-19 Tests." *Xinhua General News Service*, December 22, 2020.

———. "China's Dalian Samples over 4.75 Mln People for COVID-19 Tests." *Xinhua General News Service*, December 25, 2020.

———. "China's Determination to Achieve Goal of Poverty Elimination Unwavering: Official." *Xinhua General News Service*, March 12, 2020.

———. "China's Economic Fundamentals Not Affected by COVID-19: Xi." *Xinhua General News Service*, March 10, 2020.

———. "China's Fight against COVID-19 Stands the Test of Time: Foreign Ministry." *Xinhua General News Service*, June 3, 2020.

———. "China's Fight against COVID-19 Stands the Test of Time: Foreign Ministry." *Xinhua General News Service*, June 3, 2020.

———. "China's First Patent Granted for COVID-19 Vaccine." *Xinhua General News Service*, August 17, 2020.

———. "China's Fiscal Revenue Down 9.9 Pct in First Two Months." *Xinhua General News Service*, March 24, 2020.

———. "China's Guizhou Cleared of COVID-19 Cases." *Xinhua General News Service*, March 16, 2020.

———. "China's Hubei Punishes Officials for Misdeeds in Anti-Virus Fight." *Xinhua General News Service*, February 12, 2020.

———. "China's Hubei to Comb for Patients with Fever." *Xinhua General News Service*, February 18, 2020.

———. "China's Industrial Output Falls 13.5 Pct as Virus Hurts Activities." *Xinhua General News Service*, March 16, 2020.

———. "China's Local Gov't Bond Issuance Hits 442.9 Bln Yuan in October." *Xinhua General News Service*, November 17, 2020.

———. "China's Poverty Relief Fund Tops 139 Bln Yuan in 2020." *Xinhua General News Service*, March 31, 2020.

———. "China's Public Transportation Services Resumed from Epidemic Standstill." *Xinhua General News Service*, April 4, 2020.

———. "China's Public Transportation Services Resumed from Epidemic Standstill." *Xinhua General News Service*, April 4, 2020.

———. "China's Qingdao Completes City-Wide COVID-19 Sampling." *Xinhua General News Service*, October 16, 2020.

———. "China's Resort-Rich Province Moves to Resume Tourism Sector." *Xinhua General News Service*, March 12, 2020.

———. "China's Tax, Fee Cuts Approximate 2.4 Trillion Yuan." *Xinhua General News Service*, January 1, 2021.

———. "China's Tianjin Completes COVID-19 Testing in Two Medium-Risk Areas." *Xinhua General News Service*, November 11, 2020.

———. "China's Tianjin Discharges Last COVID-19 Patient." *Xinhua General News Service*, March 15, 2020.

———. "China's Urumqi Conducts Citywide COVID-19 Tests." *Xinhua General News Service*, July 21, 2020.

————. "Chinese City Announces Policy Support for Epidemic-Affected Companies." *Xinhua General News Service*, February 3, 2020.

————. "Chinese City Sacks 6 Officials over Poor Performance in Anti-Coronavirus Effort." *Xinhua General News Service*, February 2, 2020.

————. "Chinese Embassy Refutes Media Reports About China Concealing COVID-19 Situation." *Xinhua General News Service*, April 4, 2020.

————. "Chinese People Show Patriotism in Coronavirus Fight: Spokesperson." *Xinhua General News Service*, February 6, 2020.

————. "Chinese Premier in Wuhan, Demands All-out Efforts in Epidemic Prevention, Control." *Xinhua General News Service*, January 27, 2020.

————. "Chinese Vice Premier Stresses Community-Level Prevention in Fight against Epidemic." *Xinhua General News Service*, February 17, 2020.

————. "Chinese Vice Premier Visits Hospital, Communities Amid Coronavirus Outbreak." *Xinhua General News Service*, January 31, 2020.

————. "Commentary: Bashing China over Pandemic Despicable, Futile." *Xinhua General News Service*, April 29, 2020.

————. "Commentary: Blood and Sweat in China's Anti-Virus War to Be Glorified in World Cause." *Xinhua General News Service*, March 10, 2020.

————. "Commentary: China Acts Responsibly in Global Fight against Coronavirus." *Xinhua General News Service*, March 6, 2020.

————. "Commentary: China Boosts National Pride in Coronavirus Fight, but Not to Export 'Chinese Model'." *Xinhua General News Service*, May 9, 2020.

————. "Commentary: China's Countermeasures against U.S. Press Bullying Legitimate." *Xinhua General News Service*, March 18, 2020.

————. "Commentary: China's Human Rights Progress Deserves Applause Instead of Smearing." *Xinhua General News Service*, July 18, 2020.

————. "Commentary: China's Transparency in Epidemic Control Should Not Be Doubted." *Xinhua General News Service*, February 14, 2020.

————. "Commentary: China-Bashing Syndrome Makes Coronavirus Pandemic Deadlier." *Xinhua General News Service*, April 6, 2020.

————. "Commentary: Collectivism Plays Indispensable Role in China's COVID-19 Fight." *Xinhua General News Service*, March 17, 2020.

————. "Commentary: Facts Speak Loud for China's Openness, Transparency in COVID-19 Fight." *Xinhua General News Service*, April 6, 2020.

————. "Commentary: Facts Speak Loud for China's Openness, Transparency in COVID-19 Fight." *Xinhua General News Service*, April 6, 2020.

————. "Commentary: Honoring Anti-Virus Heroes Will Boost China's March Ahead." *Xinhua General News Service*, September 7, 2020.

————. "Commentary: In COVID-19 Response, China Deserves Credit in Human Rights Protection." *Xinhua General News Service*, May 26, 2020.

————. "Commentary: Institutional Strength: China's Key to Beating Novel Coronavirus." *Xinhua General News Service*, March 10, 2020.

————. "Commentary: Smearing China's Goodwill to Europe Hurts Fight against COVID-19." *Xinhua General News Service*, April 16, 2020.

————. "Commentary: Washington's China Media Cap Exposes Fake Press Freedom." *Xinhua General News Service*, March 5, 2020.

————. "COVID-19 Tests Conducted in China Three Times Higher Than in U.S. Since Coronavirus Outbreak: Media." *Xinhua General News Service*, June 29, 2020.

————. "East China City Finds Coronavirus in Imported Pork." *Xinhua General News Service*, December 3, 2020.

———. "East China City Fires 2 Officials over Dereliction of Duty in Anti-Epidemic Effort." *Xinhua General News Service*, February 3, 2020.

———. "East China City Starts Trial of 2.5-Day Weekend." *Xinhua General News Service*, July 13, 2020.

———. "East China Province Lifts Lockdown on Residential Communities." *Xinhua General News Service*, March 19, 2020.

———. "East China Province Offers Vouchers to Stimulate Consumption." *Xinhua General News Service*, May 19, 2020.

———. "East China's Qingdao Conducts City-Wide COVID-19 Testing after New Cases Emerge." *Xinhua General News Service*, October 12, 2020.

———. "Economic Watch: A Tale of Two Fronts: Resilient China Cranks up Economy Amid COVID-19 Fight." *Xinhua General News Service*, March 26, 2020.

———. "Economic Watch: A Tale of Two Fronts: Resilient China Cranks up Economy Amid COVID-19 Fight." *Xinhua General News Service*, March 26, 2020.

———. "Economic Watch: China Accelerates Reform to Empower Private Sector Amid COVID-19." *Xinhua General News Service*, September 9, 2020.

———. "Economic Watch: China Readies Stronger Policies to Revive Economy as Virus Disrupts Activities." *Xinhua General News Service*, March 16, 2020.

———. "Economic Watch: Long-Awaited Holiday Ignites Spending Revival in China." *Xinhua General News Service*, May 6, 2020.

———. "Factbox: China's Fight against Novel Coronavirus Outbreak." *Xinhua General News Service*, April 15, 2020.

———. "Factbox: China's Fight against Novel Coronavirus Outbreak." *Xinhua General News Service*, April 15, 2020.

———. "Factbox: China's Fight against Novel Coronavirus Outbreak." *Xinhua General News Service*, March 2, 2020.

———. "Factbox: China's Fight against Novel Coronavirus Outbreak." *Xinhua General News Service*, April 17, 2020.

———. "Factbox: China's Fight against Novel Coronavirus Outbreak." *Xinhua General News Service*, March 10, 2020.

———. "Factbox: China's Fight against Novel Coronavirus Outbreak." *Xinhua General News Service*, April 5, 2020.

———. "Factbox: China's Progress in Economic Resumption." *Xinhua General News Service*, August 10, 2020.

———. "Factbox: China's Progress in Economic Resumption." *Xinhua General News Service*, September 21, 2020.

———. "Factbox: China's Targeted Support for SMEs During Epidemic." *Xinhua General News Service*, March 3, 2020.

———. "Feature: Faces in China's Anti-Epidemic Fight." *Xinhua General News Service*, February 17, 2020.

———. "Imported Package Sample Tests Positive for COVID-19 in Ne China City." *Xinhua General News Service*, September 20, 2020.

———. "Lending Support for Anti-Virus Fight Reaches over 200 Bln USD in China." *Xinhua General News Service*, March 13, 2020.

———. "Live COVID-19 Updates: China Reports 16 New Imported Cases, Cuba Makes Progress in Vaccine Development." *Xinhua General News Service*, October 4, 2020.

———. "Live COVID-19 Updates: Over 4.2 Mln Undergo COVID-19 Testing in East China City." *Xinhua General News Service*, October 13, 2020.

———. "Most Regions of China at Low-Risk of COVID-19: Official." *Xinhua General News Service*, March 22, 2020.

———. "Ne China City Tests 1.25 Mln in a Day after New COVID-19 Cases Reported." *Xinhua General News Service*, July 27, 2020.

———. "Nearly 140,000 Test Negative after New COVID-19 Cases in East China." *Xinhua General News Service*, September 26, 2020.

———. "Northeast China's Dalian Adds 4 Medium-Risk COVID-19 Areas." *Xinhua General News Service*, December 30, 2020.

———. "Over 1,700 Prosecuted for Epidemic-Related Crimes in China." *Xinhua General News Service*, March 20, 2020.

———. "Over 100 Chinese Cities Adopt Qr Codes for Coronavirus Control, Work Resumption." *Xinhua General News Service*, February 20, 2020.

———. "Profile: Zhong Nanshan: Outspoken Doctor Awarded China's Top Honor." *Xinhua General News Service*, August 15, 2020.

———. "Rumor Buster: Facts Prove COVID-19 Cases in China Are Really Going Down." *Xinhua General News Service*, March 17, 2020.

———. "S. China Province Raises Tax Rebate Rates to Shore up Foreign Trade Firms Amid Epidemic." *Xinhua General News Service*, March 25, 2020.

———. "Shifting Blame to China Won't Help U.S. Curb Epidemic: Spokesperson." *Xinhua General News Service*, March 12, 2020.

———. "Spotlight: New Research Shows COVID-19 May Have Been in L.A. Before China Announces Its Outbreak." *Xinhua General News Service*, September 11, 2020.

———. "State Council Unveils New Measures to Mitigate Coronavirus Impact on Chinese Economy." *Xinhua General News Service*, February 26, 2020.

———. "Streets in N. China City Classified as COVID-19 Medium-Risk Zones." *Xinhua General News Service*, November 22, 2020.

———. "SW China's Chongqing Lowers Coronavirus Response Level." *Xinhua General News Service*, March 11, 2020.

———. "Thousands Prosecuted for Epidemic-Related Crimes in China." *Xinhua General News Service*, August 28, 2020.

———. "Two Cities in Northeast China Launch Citywide Nucleic Acid Testing." *Xinhua General News Service*, December 11, 2020.

———. "Understanding the Two Sessions: Why Must China Hold the Two Sessions?" *Xinhua General News Service*, March 22, 2020.

———. "Wuhan Remains China's Main Battlefield against Epidemic: Official." *Xinhua General News Service*, February 25, 2020.

———. "Xi Focus: Amid Hardships, Xi Leads China's Sprint to Milestone." *Xinhua General News Service*, May 28, 2020.

———. "Xi Focus: Chronicle of Xi's Leadership in China's War against Coronavirus (1)." *Xinhua General News Service*, September 7, 2020.

———. "Xi Focus: Chronicle of Xi's Leadership in China's War against Coronavirus (3)." *Xinhua General News Service*, September 7, 2020.

———. "Xi Focus: Chronicle of Xi's Leadership in China's War against Coronavirus (1)." *Xinhua General News Service*, September 7, 2020.

———. "Xi Focus: Chronicle of Xi's Leadership in China's War against Coronavirus (3)." *Xinhua General News Service*, September 7, 2020.

———. "Xi Focus: Chronicle of Xi's Leadership in China's War against Coronavirus (5)." *Xinhua General News Service*, September 7, 2020.

———. "Xi Focus: Commanding China's Fight against Novel Coronavirus Outbreak." *Xinhua General News Service*, February 2, 2020.

———. "Xi Focus: Commanding China's Fight against Novel Coronavirus Outbreak." *Xinhua General News Service*, February 2, 2020.

———. "Xi Focus: Xi Leads China's Economic Reopening on Sustainable Track." *Xinhua General News Service*, May 15, 2020.

———. "Xi Focus: Xi Leads China's Search for Safest Path to Growth Amid COVID-19 Control." *Xinhua General News Service*, April 24, 2020.

———. "Xi Focus-Timeline: Xi Leads China to Fight COVID-19 with Sci-Tech." *Xinhua General News Service*, March 4, 2020.

———. "Xi Orders Resolute Efforts to Curb Virus Spread." *Xinhua Financial News*, January 20, 2020.

———. "Xi Says Positive Trend of China's Epidemic Control Is Expanding." *Xinhua General News Service*, February 23, 2020.

———. "Xi Stresses Prioritizing People's Safety, Property in Flood Prevention, Control." *Xinhua General News Service*, 21 July, 2021.

———. "Xi Takes Charge of China's COVID-19 Response: White Paper." *Xinhua General News Service*, June 7, 2020.

———. "Xi to Attend Meeting Commending Role Models in China's Fight against COVID-19 Epidemic." *Xinhua General News Service*, September 6, 2020.

———. "Xi: Rely on People to Win Battle against Epidemic." *Xinhua General News Service*, January 27, 2020.

———. "Xinhua Commentary: China Confident in Minimizing Impact of Sporadic COVID-19 Outbreaks." *Xinhua General News Service*, December 29, 2020.

———. "Xinhua Headlines: China Beefs up Action against Novel Coronavirus as Cases Increases." *Xinhua General News Service*, January 26, 2020.

———. "Xinhua Headlines: China Builds New Hospital in 10 Days to Combat Coronavirus." *Xinhua General News Service*, February 2, 2020.

———. "Xinhua Headlines: China Determined to Win Battle against Poverty Despite Epidemic." *Xinhua General News Service*, March 18, 2020.

———. "Xinhua Headlines: China Endeavors to Ensure Supply of Masks, Necessities Amid Epidemic." *Xinhua General News Service*, February 3, 2020.

———. "Xinhua Headlines: China Goes All out to Contain Novel Coronavirus Amid Travel Rush." *Xinhua General News Service*, January 22, 2020.

———. "Xinhua Headlines: China Mobilizes Medical Teams to Fight New Coronavirus." *Xinhua General News Service*, January 24, 2020.

———. "Xinhua Headlines: China, Europe Willing to Promote Multilateralism, Oppose Cold War Rhetoric." *Xinhua General News Service*, September 2, 2020.

———. "Xinhua Headlines: China's Dalian Going All out to Stem New COVID-19 Infections." *Xinhua General News Service*, July 29, 2020.

———. "Xinhua Headlines: China's Wuhan Closes All 16 Temporary Hospitals." *Xinhua General News Service*, March 10, 2020.

———. "Xinhua Headlines: In Tough Year, China Makes Decisive Progress in Ending Absolute Poverty." *Xinhua General News Service*, December 31, 2020.

———. "Xinhua Headlines: Qingdao Safeguards China's COVID-19 Control with Swift Response." *Xinhua General News Service*, October 21, 2020.

———. "Xinhua Headlines: Rumor Buster: Six Facts About China's Fight against COVID-19." *Xinhua General News Service*, April 9, 2020.

———. "Xinhua Headlines-Xi Focus: How China Fights War against COVID-19 under Xi's Command." *Xinhua General News Service*, February 25, 2020.

Xu, Bin. "Durkheim in Sichuan: The Earthquake, National Solidarity, and the Politics of Small Things." *Social Psychology Quarterly* 72 (2009): 5–8.

Xu Klein, Jodi. "US Increasingly Excludes China from Coronavirus Research Projects." *South China Morning Post*, July 7, 2020.

Yan, Alice. "Coronavirus: Second Wave over Winter 'Inevitable' in China, Infectious Disease Expert Says." *South China Morning Post*, September 21, 2020.

————. "Coronavirus: Two Health Officials in China Removed after Cluster of 12 Cases Found at East Coast Hospital." *South China Morning Post*, October 15, 2020.

Yang, William. "COVID: Why Is Discontent Growing over Shanghai's Lockdown?" Deutsche Welle, April 18, 2022, https://www.dw.com/en/china-why-is-public-discontent-growing-over-shanghais -covid-lockdown/a-61504275.

————. "No Way out in Sight for China's Zero-COVID Strategy." Deutsche Welle, October 19, 2022, https://www.dw.com/en/no-way-out-in-sight-for-chinas-zero-covid-strategy/a-63489794.

Yang, Yuan, Nian Liu, Qianer Liu, and Robin Yu. "China Medics Query 'Zero New Cases' Claim; National Health Commission; Official Figures Suggest Breakthrough but Experts Cast Doubt on Data." *Financial Times*, March 28, 2020.

Yongnian, Zheng, and Lance L.P. Gore. *China Entering the Xi Jinping Era.* New York: Routledge, 2014.

Yuan, Jada, and Ben Guarino. "The Military's Medical 'Relief Valves' Remain Mostly Empty in New York." *The Washington Post*, April 12, 2020, A7.

Zakaria, Fareed. *The Future of Freedom: Illiberal Democracy at Home and Abroad.* 1st ed. New York: W.W. Norton, 2003.

Zalewski, Tomasz. "Poland Divided over Elections and COVID Restrictions." Atlantic Council, May 13, 2020, https://www.atlanticcouncil.org/blogs/new-atlanticist/poland-divided-over-elections-and -covid-restrictions/.

Zapotosky, Matt. "Applying Terrorism Statutes Is Explored." *The Washington Post*, March 26, 2020, 2020, A6.

————. "Barr Warns against Hoarding Masks, Drugs That Trump Touted." *The Washington Post*, March 26, 2020, A6.

————. "Justice Department Seeks New Emergency Judicial Powers." *The Washington Post*, March 24, 2020, A12.

————. "Justice Dept. Seems to Side with Church in Lawsuit over Drive-in Services." *The Washington Post*, April 15, 2020, A4.

Zapotosky, Matt, Kim Bellware, and Jacqueline Dupree. "U.S. Deaths Pass 3,700; Officials Say Worst Is yet to Come." *The Washington Post*, April 1, 2020, A4.

Zapotosky, Matt, Barrett Devlin, and Abagail Hauslohner. "13 Charged in Plot to Seize Mich. Governor." *The Washington Post*, October 9, 2020, A1.

Zapotosky, Matt, Marisa Iati, and Josh Wagner. "With Fewer Restrictions, States Tiptoe toward Reopening." *The Washington Post*, May 5, 2020, A4.

Zapotosky, Matt, Isaac Stanley-Becker, and John Wagner. "Single-Day Death Toll in U.S. Tops 1,000 as Trump Insists Country Will Recover." *The Washington Post*, April 3, 2020, A3.

Zapotosky, Matt, and John Wagner. "Trump Reverses, Says Task Force to Convene 'Indefinitely'." *The Washington Post*, May 7, 2020, A6.

Zapotosky, Matt, John Wagner, and Amanda Coletta. "Trump Announces CDC Guidance That All Americans Wear Cloth Masks." *The Washington Post*, April 4, 2020, A3.

Zapotosky, Matt, William Wan, Dan Balz, and Emily Guskin. "Poll: Americans Deeply Wary of Opening Economy." *The Washington Post*, May 6, 2020, A1.

Zezima, Katie, Joel Achenbach, Tim Craig, and Lena H. Sun. "Pandemic Takes a Dramatic Toll as Institutions, Routines Shut Down." *The Washington Post*, March 14, 2020, A1.

Zezima, Katie, Tim Craig, William Wan, and Felicia Sonmez. "Who Declares Virus a Global Pandemic." *The Washington Post*, March 12, 2020, A1.

Zezima, Katie, John Hudson, Colby Itkowitz, and Nick Miroff. "Restrictions Rise, Along with Number of Cases." *The Washington Post*, March 20, 2020, A1.

Zezima, Katie, Scott Wilson, Dan Lamothe, and Katie Mettler. "One in Five Americans Told to Stay Home as Authorities Brace for More Cases." *The Washington Post*, March 21, 2020, 2020, A6.

Zhang, Lijia. "How Will China's 'Zero-Covid' Policy Affect Public Support for the Government? It's Complicated." *South China Morning Post*, October 29, 2022.

Zhang, Phoebe. "Coronavirus Found in China on Frozen Chicken Wings from Brazil." *South China Morning Post*, August 13, 2020.

Zhao, Kiki. "The Coronavirus Story Is Too Big for China to Spin." *New York Times (Online)*, February 14, 2020.

Zhen, Liu. "Coronavirus: China Reports More Positive Tests on Imported Frozen Food." *South China Morning Post*, November 15, 2020.

Zheng, Linzi, Lu Zhang, Ke Chen, and Qingsong He. "Unmasking Unexpected Health Care Inequalities in China Using Urban Big Data: Service-Rich and Service-Poor Communities." *Plos One* 17, no. 2 (2022): e0263577.

Zheng, William. "Chinese Rate Government 'More Capable Than Ever before', Long-Term Harvard Study Finds." *South China Morning Post*, July 21, 2020.

———. "Dozens of Chinese Officials Punished over Latest Wave of Covid-19 Cases." *South China Morning Post*, March 22, 2022.

Zhong, Raymond. "Beijing Tightens Its Grip on News Coverage as Cases Continue to Surge: [Foreign Desk]." *New York Times*, February 6, 2020.

———. "$9 Cabbages and Emergency Pork: Health Crisis Tests Food Supply Chain: [Foreign Desk]." *New York Times*, February 5, 2020.

———. "China's Virus Apps May Outlast the Outbreak, Stirring Privacy Fears." *New York Times*, May 26, 2020.

Zhong, Raymond, and Paul Mozur. "To Tame Coronavirus, Mao-Style Social Control Blankets China." *New York Times (Online)*, February 15, 2020.

Zhong, Raymond, Paul Mozur, Jeff Kao, and Aaron Krolik. "'Be Sleek and Silent': How China Censored Bad News About Covid: [Foreign Desk]." *New York Times*, December 20, 2020.

Zhou, Cissy. "Coronavirus: China's Pandemic Lifeline for Small Firms Draws Lukewarm Response from Business Owners." *South China Morning Post*, May 22, 2020.

Zhou, Laura. "Coronavirus: China Offers US $4,500 Reward for Information About Illegal Foreigners." *South China Morning Post*, October 30, 2020.

Zhu, Melissa. "Inside China Tech: Privacy Vs Urgency in Covid-19 Contact Tracing." *South China Morning Post*, June 6, 2020.

Index

accountability, 19, 127, 134–35; electoral, 19, 20; hybrid regime, 54; non-democrat, 20; non-democratic populist, 7–8; political, 4

agency, 18

Alliance of Doctors, 117

American Civil Liberties Union, 172

anti-corruption campaign, Xi J. 86

anti-establishment, 32

anti-malarial, 160, 166

anti-pluralism, 33

anxiety, vaccine, 53

apps, tracking, 101–2, 120

Aristophanes, 195

asymptomatic carriers, 50, 158

Atlas, S., 166–67

authoritarian/ism, 26, 28, 30, 46, 47, 86–87, 105, 118, 202, 216; clientelism, 54; competitive, 9; consultative, 23; delegation, 68; disaster management, 19, 210; leadership, 3, 6–7; legitimacy, 23; political autonomy, 88; populism, 7–8, 24–25, 126, 203–5; scapegoating, 68. *See also* China; Russia

autonomy, 128; political, 88

BBC Monitoring, 35

Belarus, 211

Biden, J., 202

Birx, D., 167

Bolsonaro, J., 212

border control: Russia, 126; Russia-China, 54, 118–19; United States, 61–62, 162

Brazil, 51, 212

Bueno de Mesquita, B., 15

bureaucracy, 5, 7, 22, 32

Cambodia, 105

camera surveillance, 102

cell phone: contact tracing, 64, 91, 101; tracking apps, 101–2, 120

censorship, 47, 93; internet, 94–96

Centers for Disease Control and Prevention (CDC), 60–61, 66, 158–59; COVID-19 test, 156, 165–66

centralized decentralization, 58

Chechnya, 126

Chen W., 53

China, 8–10, 29, 32, 45, 67, 213; Academy of Military Medical Sciences, 53; Communist Party meetings, 89; COVID-19 case count, 51, 95; disaster management, 196, 214; dissent, 95; epidemic briefings, 48–49; fiscal stimulus spending, 52, 88–89; forced quarantine, 95; information control, 89–90, 93–94, 199; internet, 94–95; lockdowns, 48,

development, 212; expert policy guidance, 201; Russia, 29–31. *See also* Russia
hydroxychloroquine, 162

identity, 31; Chinese, 32; politics, 21
ideology, 213
image projection, 68
immunity, herd, 45
impact, 17–18
India: COVID-19 mortality rate, 208; COVID-19 response, 208–9
individualism, 212–13
Indonesia, 212
inequality, 18, 21
information control, 68, 89–90, 104; China, 199; digital information, 93–94; fact-checking, 98; propaganda, 95–96, 103; Russia, 133, 199; United States, 198
inspections, 89, 92
Institute of Bioengineering, 52–53
internet, 102; censorship, 94–95; monitoring, 96
Iran, 212
Israel, 214
ITAR-TASS, 35

Japan, 52
Johnson, B., 30
"just-in-time" model, 160

Lancet, The, 209
large-N quantitative study, 207–8
leadership, 22, 34, 66–67, 159, 197; authoritarian, 3, 6–7; D. Trump, 162; decentralized, 55–56; devolutionary delegation, 25–26; hybrid, 27–28, 201, 210; image projection, 68; Xi J., 89–91; populist, 6; top-down delegation, 25–26
legitimacy, 54, 86, 100; authoritarian leader, 23; Communist Party, 101; non-democratic regime, 7, 22; populist, 5

Li K., 90, 93
Li W., 85, 94
liberal democracy, 21
liberalism, 21–22
lockdown, 8, 45, 49–50, 52, 86, 104–5; China, 88, 93; Hubei Province, 48; Hungary, 209; India, 208; Russia, 58–59, 128; United States, 155, 170; Wuhan, 47–48
Lukashenko, A., 211

Maduro, N., 207–8, 211
mask mandates, 45; Russia, 122; Trump's disregard for, 162; United States, 173–74, 178
media, 2, 4, 7, 11, 19, 170; BBC Monitoring, 35; epidemic briefings, 48–49; expulsion of American journalists in China, 95–96; fake news, 118, 133–34, 164; ITAR-TASS, 35; public relations, 57; Russia, 9; state, 49, 51, 87–88, 92; Xinhua news agency, 35. *See also* state media
medical equipment: price gouging, 100, 172; shortages, 48, 56–57, 117–18, 137, 171, 172
messaging, 24, 25, 86, 103, 133, 178–79; COVID-19, 55; responsibility for the COVID-19, pandemic, 103–4; Trump's downplaying of COVID-19, 160–61; US's COVID-19 response, 160. *See also* information control
Mexico, COVID-19 response, 213
military: role in China's COVID-19 response, 87, 89; role in Russia's COVID-19 response, 120; role in US's COVID-19 response, 171
Mishustin, M., 118, 119, 124, 125, 131, 137–38
mitigation: disaster, 3–4; US COVID policy, 160
Modi, N., 208–9
morbidity/mortality rate, 33–34; China, 51–52; Russia, 57–58, 123, 136;

About the Author

Brian K. Grodsky is a former U.S. diplomat and reporter and current professor of comparative and international politics at the University of Maryland, Baltimore County. He is also a practitioner in the disaster sphere, having worked for more than two decades on local and national fire/rescue/emergency medical teams. This book sits at a crossroads between his longtime research agenda and his disaster response experience. His three most recent books all explore challenges in democratizing states (*The Democratization Disconnect*, 2016; *Social Movements and the New State*, 2012; and *The Costs of Justice*, 2010).

www.ingramcontent.com/pod-product-compliance
Lightning Source LLC
Chambersburg PA
CBHW022303280326
41932CB00010B/960